UNHOLY ALLIANCES

*Working the Tawana
Brawley Story*

UNHOLY ALLIANCES

Working the Tawana Brawley Story

Mike Taibbi &
Anna Sims-Phillips

Harcourt Brace Jovanovich, Publishers

SAN DIEGO   NEW YORK   LONDON

"Jive at Five: How Big Al and the Bully Boys bogarted the movement," © 1988 by Playthell Benjamin, first published in *The Village Voice*, July 1988

© Jesse Walker, "Tawana's Case Stalls," *Amsterdam News*, April 1988

© Eric Lincoln, foreword to Gayraud S. Wilmore's *Black Religion and Black Radicalism*, Doubleday, 1973

WCBS-TV transcripts on pages 15, 18–20: © CBS Inc. 1987. All rights reserved.

WCBS-TV transcripts on pages 53–54, 88, 122–123, 171–172, 201, 246, 300–310, 340, 341: © CBS Inc. 1988. All rights reserved.

Library of Congress Cataloging-in-Publication Data
Taibbi, Mike.
Unholy alliances: working the Tawana Brawley story/by Mike
Taibbi and Anna Sims-Phillips.—1st ed.
p. cm.
ISBN 0-15-188050-6
1. Rape—New York (State)—Investigation—Case studies.
2. Brawley, Tawana. 3. Police—New York (State)—Complaints
against. 4. Wappingers Falls (N.Y.)—Race relations—Case studies.
I. Phillips, Anna Sims- II. Title.
HV8079.R35T35 1989
364.1'532'0974733—dc19 89-31093

Design by Camilla Filancia
Printed in the United States of America

First edition

A B C D E

For our families
Beverly, Lionel, Matthew, Lionel II, and Eric

All active mass movements strive . . . to impose a fact-proof screen between the faithful and the realities of the world. To rely on the evidence of the senses and of reason is heresy and treason. It is startling to realize how much unbelief is necessary to make belief possible.

ERIC HOFFER, The True Believer

ACKNOWLEDGMENTS

WE HAD A GOOD DEAL of help in the preparation of this book, all of it essential. Our families (to whom *Unholy Alliances* is dedicated) provided unwavering support—encouragement on the bad days, and isolation and protection on the good days.

Michael Heard, a colleague and friend, gathered and organized much of our research materials and cheerfully did whatever had to be done to move the project along.

Chris Borgen, our senior and better, gave us the benefit of his wisdom and knowledge.

Other broadcast colleagues were helpful in a variety of crucial ways. Roger Colloff, Paul Sagan, Jean Harper, and Steve Paulus managed to both keep us on the job and keep us going on the book. Jim Fleischmann, John Premack, and Jeff Morgan provided technical assistance in our research and in the preparation of the manuscript.

Because the events and issues at hand were so complex, we relied often on the wise counsel of Peter Matson and on the logistical help of his assistant, Adrian Weiss. And though lawyers are viewed by many writers with alarm at worst and resignation at best, we received invaluable guidance and assistance during our reporting of the story and the writing of this book from CBS lawyers Rick Altabef, Jonathan Sternberg, Susanna Lowy, and Douglas Jacobs.

Friends—some of whom are also colleagues—stood ready to help: Cheryl Williams, Willie Mae Young, Eric Ober, Donna Ziede, Paul Toomey, Neil Brown, Gene Lothery, Davison Paull, Roseanne Colletti, Lesky Crosson, and Gregory Nowell were among those who shared our personal struggles and aided our search for understanding.

And finally, though they must remain anonymous, there are the people we conveniently label "sources," who are at the root of any reporters' comprehension of agonizing events. At times, certain sources were troubled to their core by their relationships with us, and we did our best to assure them we would minimize the risk to them and maximize the fair use of the information they provided. We hope, in this book, to have done no less than that.

M.G.T.
A.S.P.

PREFACE

THEY COULD HAVE been heroes.

The minister and the two lawyers from New York City could have seized upon the case developing some 70 miles to the north and hammered home an important lesson about the stubborn inequities in our overwhelmingly white criminal justice system. The press, even the predominantly white mainstream press, would have helped convey the lesson, because it mattered and because it made good copy.

Imagine if the first story about the alleged gang rape of Tawana Brawley had been different in a few crucial details. What if she was a talented and pretty *white* teenager from a modest middle-class family in Dutchess County, a girl who loved to read, a cheerleader? What if *that* teenager was found wrapped in a large plastic garbage bag, shivering and nearly unconscious, covered in excrement, missing one shoe, wearing ripped and burned jeans—and so clearly traumatized that she could not speak and did not respond to painful stimuli administered by emergency medical technicians? What if anti-white racial epithets had been written on her clothing and torso; and if in the hospital, in answer to the question "Were you raped?" she'd scribbled the words "a lot," and in answer to the question "Who did it?" she'd scrawled "black cop."

If those had been the circumstances, would it have been considered reasonable that some early witnesses described the young girl as "probably a homeless person"? Would the search for her missing shoe and for the source of the burn marks on her jeans have been so cursory as to have taken only minutes? And when it was confirmed within hours that she was actually found yards from her old apartment, would that apartment have been ignored so completely that the sliding back door was left unsecured, allowing a stranger to sneak in and spend the night? Would law-enforcement officials have declined to act swiftly upon the startling if sketchy allegations suggesting multiple rape by a black cop? Would the young girl, so apparently traumatized that she could not or would not speak to her own family, have been released from the hospital only hours after being admitted?

These provocative questions could fairly have been raised about the actual incident by the Reverend Al Sharpton and lawyers C. Vernon Mason and Alton Maddox, all three men having assumed public roles in the aftermath of earlier racial incidents in New York City. Instead, they announced their answers, and claimed that each was confirmed and could be documented. Tawana Brawley, a black teenager, had been raped and sodomized by a gang of white men and left to die, they said they knew; one of her assailants had urinated in her mouth and medical tests had detected "five types of semen" on her body, they said they knew. They described Tawana's assailants first as a "pack of Ku Klux Klansmen"; then as a "racist cult inside the Dutchess County sheriff's office" that was connected to the Irish Republican Army; and finally as a group of white men, including a part-time cop, an assistant prosecutor, and a state trooper, all of whom they named.

In 1987, the year of the alleged attack on Tawana Brawley, there were 1,672 murders in New York City. There were tens of thousands of assaults, thousands of rapes. There were confirmed—even admitted—racial attacks, several resulting in death for the victims. But the Brawley family advisers made their stand on a case north of the city which, based on past and current history, *could* have happened, but the evidence, even in the beginning, suggested it had not.

Yet every time the minister and the two lawyers called a press conference, what they said they knew about what had happened to Tawana Brawley was reported.

WE WERE AMONG the pack of reporters assigned to the Tawana Brawley case. To us, coming into the story two and a half months after it broke, it seemed at first like a relatively straightforward problem made more complicated by some distinctly fiery rhetoric. If there was a crime (and we believed, as many did, that *something* had happened to Tawana Brawley), then there was evidence and there were people who knew of that evidence yet for some reason or reasons had not communicated its existence in any persuasive way through any of the normal channels.

We had no special qualifications for the assignment. Other reporters were experienced, as we were, in the relatively mundane tasks of obtaining records and developing sources. Others were also skeptical of bombastic declarations, demanding of proof, mindful of the methodology of crime reporting.

But we were given the time, free of daily deadlines, to work on the case. And we work for television. Those two factors meant that what we saw and learned, and what we reported, inexorably became part of the story itself. Because very quickly, as media critic Edwin Diamond pointed out, the Tawana Brawley story ceased being the chronicle of what had happened to a young black girl over four days in November 1987 and became instead an unseemly engagement between three champions of racially charged rhetoric and those in law enforcement and government—and in the New York press— who served alternately as their foils or their unwitting allies.

That engagement cost the state hundreds of thousands of dollars. It forced many people with a public voice and responsibility into a terrible and maddening silence. It heightened racial tension in a city already traumatized by a series of "race-based conflicts."

Before the Brawley story was over we found ourselves tested in ways we never thought possible. There was a lot of support; still, we found our reporters' notions about fairness and ethics held up to the harshest light, and were made to examine our own motives in ways few stories ever encourage—or perhaps even allow. Toward the end, the Brawley story was a festering sore that had fouled the air, and it seemed that still more rhetoric and that terrible silence would be its only by-products.

But, in the end, something changed. Pieces of the truth were forced into the open air; not the whole truth: that's still hidden. But enough of it emerged, through the efforts of forensic scientists and investigators and, yes, the press, so that there was room and time at last, away from the noise of the headlines and the six o'clock news, for people to measure those bits of truth and privately choose what was worthy of belief. The rhetoric has been silenced. The silence, though, remains.

WHILE WE SHARE many views and our perspectives and judgments are often similar, we are not one voice. We are black and white, a woman and a man, from Harlem and Hawaii, and different in small ways too numerous to list. That presented a problem to be solved in writing about our shared work as journalists covering the Tawana Brawley story.

We chose a device used by other co-authors: we refer to

ourselves in the third person. Since the device relies on an unidentified narrator's voice, it requires that the reader accept Mike Taibbi and Anna Phillips as characters in the story. Protected by the anonymous narrator, they might be coddled or imbued with uncommon abilities. It is hoped, however, that we've forced our narrator to tell it straight: sometimes Taibbi and Phillips do well, and sometimes, as the narrator insists the reader understand, they don't do well at all.

SOME LAST WORDS about the form of the book.

Obviously, we did not question our colleagues and sources on their state of mind or their thoughts as the story was evolving. In many instances, we interviewed or reinterviewed crucial characters and folded their recollections into the narrative.

Where possible, all quotes are transcribed directly from video or audio tapes, and recollected exchanges are corroborated to the extent we were able to do so. We've changed the names of some individuals, noted in each instance by a last initial and an asterisk.*

AUTHOR'S NOTE

FINALLY, IT SHOULD BE noted that the individual stories that make up the book are presented chronologically for the purpose of illustrating both the case and what we believed to be true at the time we reported those stories. The best reporting is still an exercise in an imprecise craft. A given day's deadline, and the limitations in skill and evidence, leave every account open to improvement, refinement, or correction. This should be clear in the pages that follow; it may be clearer yet if new information comes to light following the publication of this book.

We can say that every one of the more than 100 reports we filed on the Tawana Brawley case was our best and truest account of the best information we had at the time.

We say that too about this book.

UNHOLY ALLIANCES

Working the Tawana
Brawley Story

1

"Her name is Tawana Brawley. . . . The girl."

ANNA PHILLIPS LET LOOSE one of her distinctive laughs, her patented let-it-fly cackle, and the three people in her audience roared along with her. Howie Schlechtman, one of the videotape librarians, poked a finger in Phillips's direction and she slapped it away playfully while firing off another one-liner. Schlechtman scowled in apparent anger, but another spasm of guffaws seized Phillips, Jersey assignment manager Donna Ziede, and consumer reporter Roseanne Colletti. It was late morning in the third week of November 1987, in the newsroom of WCBS-TV, Channel 2, in New York City. Everybody's deadline was hours away. Schlechtman's desk, in the pinched far corner of the chaotic assignment station, was a regular schmoozing pit. The small group around Phillips chatted amiably, exchanging jokes or stories or raw gossip. They seemed, in their animated familiarity, to be old friends and close colleagues, and they were.

On the other side of the room Steve Paulus, then the newsroom's assignment manager, stood talking to reporter Mike Taibbi, who'd joined the staff at the beginning of the month.

"What about her? Try Anna," Paulus suggested, nodding toward Phillips. Taibbi was looking for someone to work with on a crudely fascinating but somewhat disturbing story he'd decided to check out. A resident of the south side of Newark, New Jersey, had told him the week before that a new mortician had opened shop in the neighborhood and ought to be investigated. The tipster and his wife had sought the mortician's services when a relative had died, and what they'd seen and learned firsthand had horrified them. The "preparation room" had rough wooden floors and exposed plywood walls; there were bloodstains everywhere. When the tipster's wife complained that stitches were showing around her deceased aunt's mouth, the mortician's son had impatiently yanked the stitches free and resewn the small crease right in front of her. The final bill was thousands over the original estimate. And, worst of all, neighborhood children claimed they'd found teeth and gristle and other human body parts in the vacant lot beside the mortuary. Other people had told the tipster when he began to ask questions on his own that they'd seen the mortician and his staff dump buckets of what appeared to be blood and human viscera in the open sewer drain at the curb.

"I want to work the neighborhood," Taibbi told Paulus. "Careful. Eyeball the guy's operation. Maybe pull some paper in Newark, is he doing any morgue business, a little phone work. That kind of thing." He cocked his head but couldn't tell what the latest spasm of laughter was about on the other side of the assignment station. "She up to it? What's her name, Anne?"

"Anna," Paulus corrected. "Anna Phillips. Just try her, she's damn good. She's working with Roseanne now, consumer stuff. See if Anna's clear. I'll talk to Roseanne if she is. What, couple hours? The afternoon?"

" 'Bout that."

TAIBBI, THOUGH THE STATION'S newest hire, was at age thirty-eight a twenty-year veteran of the reporting wars. From his earliest days in newspapering he'd specialized in breaking stories. He liked the front page, liked thinking his byline stood for something distinctive. In the business of news gathering they called it investigative reporting, a term he disdained. *All* reporters are supposed to investigate, he lectured at every opportunity; it's part of the definition of the job. At base level, reporters do what everybody else does: they see things happen, hear what people say, pick up something in the wind, and then tell someone else about it. But you're a reporter, you're a *craftsman*, because you do it better. You ask more questions, better questions. You demand better answers. You do, in fact, investigate. The term Taibbi preferred to describe what he did for a living was *enterprise* reporting.

"SO, ANNA. HOW LONG you been here?"

"Eight years. Yeah, about that, now."

They were rolling west through the Lincoln Tunnel in Taibbi's truck, Chet Baker and Gerry Mulligan on the stereo. Phillips had been at the station eight years, but she'd only been in News the past three. She didn't tell Taibbi that, though. When the word had filtered down back in September that Taibbi had been signed away from rival WNBC, Channel 4, Phillips and her colleagues in the Channel 2 newsroom quickly worked the grapevine: good reporter, intense, but a potential problem. Can be a demanding pain in the ass, and downright cold when he wants to be. "Difficult to work with," was one frequent assessment. Gets good stuff, though. A pro. Broke the story about former Miss America Bess Myerson stiffing a federal grand jury, and Myerson was suspended the next day. Cost Rupert Murdoch $6 million when he reported that Murdoch's *New York Post* had ignored signed contracts with Canadian paper mills so he could buy cheap South African newsprint.

Taibbi had broken from the gate in a hurry at Channel 2, scoring early scoops on an AIDS victim who had sexually abused two children for a full year after his diagnosis and yet through a technicality was beyond the reach of the law, and on a Long Island lawyer who was a key player in some black market adoptions that had gone sour, with tragic results. Phillips was curious when Taibbi asked her to work with him on the Newark story, curious in part because she'd already met him and he obviously didn't remember.

It was more than a year ago, she recalled. The latest Tylenol Killer scare was sweeping the metropolitan area, and Phillips had been assigned to produce a sidebar to the lead story on just how easy it was to reseal an opened Tylenol bottle, even in an era of supposedly tamper-proof seals. She had puzzled over the assignment for a few minutes when a childhood memory came to her: the Polk Hobby Shop on Fifth Avenue. All those Saturday afternoons of her Harlem childhood waiting for her brothers to finish yapping with the ever-talkative salesmen about trains or models or whatever. Polk had everything! She was out the door in minutes, an unopened bottle of Tylenol capsules in hand, and joined a waiting camera crew.

It was an easy shoot, and just the right call. She was wrapping up when a Channel 4 camera crew marched into the store, trailed by a slouching, bearded, cap-wearing fellow who obviously had the same idea she'd had. Only he hadn't brought along his own bottle of Tylenol to open and reseal. "Hey, Mike Taibbi from Channel 4," he'd announced by way of introduction to both the salesman and Phillips. Then, to Phillips alone, "Yeah. I remember this place. Only way to go. Listen, could you maybe leave your lights up for a few minutes. And, oh yeah. Could we use your Tylenol bottle? Didn't get our own yet." Phillips didn't know who the hell

Mike Taibbi was, but he seemed to know what he wanted
and didn't leave much room for the niceties or for anyone's
objections. She was put off, definitely irritated, but she left
the lights up and handed over the bottle. He was done in less
than ten minutes. The salesman was amused, and his performance with the hot plastic sealer was better the second
time around.

A CITY BOY, she thought, remembering that day. Has to be.
Who else would know about Polk? He might be another white-
boy reporter who needs a black producer to help him get over
in the ghetto, but then again, maybe he'd get over on his
own. So she was curious, and not inclined to discourage any
curiosity he had about her. Eight years sounded better than
three, she thought; and besides, she was determined to let
him know quickly enough that she'd done damn good work
of her own in the news business, however limited her résumé. She'd won awards for three projects in which she'd
had key roles. In two of the stories, a census scam in New
York and a discriminatory housing ring in New Jersey, she'd
been an undercover operative. She stole a glance at Taibbi:
jeans, leather jacket, and sneakers. Chain-smoking Camels.
Thick black beard, that same worn cap, pulled down low.
She considered her own appearance: classic suit, dress pumps,
makeup and hair just right as always. Who is this guy, she
thought, smiling for no apparent reason.

She'd loved stories, had been captivated by storytellers, for
as long as she could remember. Her late father had owned a
grocery store in Harlem, and had started each day in furious
debate with his regular customers over the stories of the day.
As soon as Phillips had learned to read, which was earlier
than for most children, he had assigned her the daily task of
reading him the headlines in the morning papers—the *Daily
News*, the *Mirror*, the *Tribune*, the *Times*. It was only after
a couple of years of the ritual that she'd realized a terrible
truth: her father was illiterate. And then, a wonderful truth:

the stories that followed the headlines were rich in detail, the stuff of wonder. Her father was an energetic and colorful debater, she came to recognize, but he relied very little if at all on the facts. She read the stories through and through, and read them again. When *she* told stories, she knew early on, she wanted to have the facts.

THE HOUSE OF Robinson Funeral Home was exactly as the tipster had described it. Robin's-egg blue frame building dominating an exposed corner of Springfield and Bergen avenues, in one of the struggling neighborhoods of Newark's south side. Taibbi and Phillips parked the truck up the street and out of sight and agreed to split up to work the neighborhood.

"Careful, now," Taibbi warned. "Don't give anything away. It's just, you know, 'We've done some reporting on the neighborhood . . .' Mention the big fire on South Seventh last week, and we heard some things about the new funeral home, and if there's nothing to it it's no big deal and we're outta here. Okay? You don't want to—"

'I know. Jesus," Phillips interrupted. "I know Newark and you don't. I've got people here, and I know my way around the streets! Don't worry about it. I'll see you at the truck, about a half hour."

Phillips, half black and half Puerto Rican and until four years ago a lifelong native of Harlem, shook her head as Taibbi walked away. He came off like a streetwise tough, and maybe he was, she thought, but he was still an outsider poking around a neighborhood just like the neighborhoods she'd known all her life. She turned on her heel and went to work.

An hour later the two of them were sitting in the fourth-floor walk-up apartment of the woman whose two older children had seen "the teeth, and guts and stuff." Taibbi looked out the window, to the spot in the vacant lot where the children had made their grisly discovery. Phillips bounced the baby of the house on her lap. The baby took to her like she was her mother, smiling and laughing, and while Phillips

cooed at the infant she fired questions at the two older children and their mother. Taibbi looked back from the window
to the scene in the small kitchen. A cramped, dirty, too-cold
place with newspapers for window shades and the grime of
poverty everywhere. There were rat droppings along the
baseboards, and rats themselves made occasional appearances.

Yes, it's horrible, the mother was agreeing with Phillips.
Children shouldn't have to see stuff like that. In the woman's eyes there was another view, though: in the world and
the circumstances in which she and her children were compelled to live, so much was horrible that the grisly discovery
in the lot next door was not something to go crazy about.
Taibbi remained silent as Phillips worked the room, having
given way when she'd taken over. In twenty minutes she had
it all; names and addresses of the other witnesses and what
they'd seen, agreements to "keep it quiet" and to do camera
interviews the next day, offers by the children to show the
reporters exactly where the bodies came in and "where they
used gasoline or something to wash the maggots out of the
body bag one day, right outside," even the name of the mortician's landlady, who, it turned out, had been one of the
targets of a Phillips investigation the year before on Newark's failed revitalization.

"A real opportunist," Phillips said of the landlady when
she and Taibbi were back on the street. "When we're done
here, I'll show you where her shop is. Just a few minutes
from here."

They knew the story was there and spent another hour
casing the neighborhood and settling on surveillance locations. They waited in the car at one point and, slouching low
over the dashboard, got a good look at their man.

"We call him the Buzzard," one neighbor had said disgustedly. They went out to busy Bergen Avenue and flagged down
a passing city morgue wagon, questioning the driver about
John Doe assignments to city funeral homes. The House of
Robinson had gotten a few, he said. Some had been AIDS
victims.

Back in the office, Taibbi told Paulus and news director Paul Sagan that it looked like they had a story, and then grabbed his notes and prepared a detailed memo. Depending on what the records search and a camera surveillance turned up, it could be a long story or even two reports by next week, he wrote. He looked for Phillips and found her at her desk in the Annex down the hall from the main newsroom. There was strategy to discuss, lists to make out. It was, in many ways, the stage of a story that Taibbi liked best: to know for the first time it's a story, and to figure out how to get from here to there. Phillips, though, was on the phone.

". . . well, no. I don't know what we're going to do yet. She just died. But I mean, you're in the neighborhood, you know, and I thought if it could work out it might be more convenient. . . ."

Taibbi listened as she finished her conversation. A broad smile on her face, she turned to the reporter excitedly. "That was—"

"I know. The Buzzard."

Phillips's smile sagged a little.

"Well, listen! He gave me prices, told me how many bodies he's handled, who works there, and I talked to a source in the AG's office—"

"Yeah, okay." He leaned against a file cabinet and looked away for a few seconds. "Listen," he said. "You do that, you don't work with me. Period. You don't misrepresent yourself, ever. No tricks. Ever. The kind of reporting I do is difficult and dangerous . . . not physically, I'm not talking about that. But I mean in how it affects people's lives, careers. There's a lot of rules, and if you're going to work with me you're going to have to learn them. It's the only way I know how to do it. Okay?"

Phillips wanted to argue, to lash back at this self-important "veteran." Hell, she was thirty-five, a wife and a mother; she was no kid either. And she'd done what she'd done, taken risks and even worked undercover, before she even knew who

Mike Taibbi was. But there was something in his expression, a weariness and an almost withering intensity, that kept her from shouting back. She finally just nodded her head and said, "Okay," barely audibly. She'd taught herself the business, had come in nights and weekends when she got her chance so she could learn her way around the editing room and arm herself with the technical and editorial knowledge no one would have taken the time to teach her; but it didn't matter now, she guessed. Taibbi wasn't interested in her past, only in her present if the present included working with him. They sat down with their lists, divided up the calls and public records each would attend to, then went their separate ways.

THE FIRST TAIBBI-PHILLIPS report on the House of Robinson led the six o'clock news on Monday, November 30. It had the predictable effect, disgusting many viewers but also holding them spellbound. It was a story and a horror that could only have occurred in a certain kind of neighborhood encapsulated by both neglect and an institutional cynicism. Taibbi's script made that point, and Phillips, who put the piece together with editor Harry Cannon, wrung the most out of the interior shots of the Reverend Mr. Robinson's tawdry "preparation room." She and Taibbi had interviewed the Buzzard himself there, and he'd made a number of damaging admissions on camera. The simple fact that the story was broadcast led officials in two state agencies to vow immediately that the House of Robinson would be investigated. Cause and effect, story and consequence: it was powerful stuff.

When the story ended and Taibbi had returned from the set and the on-camera tag with which he'd concluded his piece, he and Phillips met in the newsroom and accepted compliments on their first collaboration. Paulus said, "Not bad . . ." and, to Taibbi alone, "I told you, right? She's got it." Taibbi nodded.

Taibbi stared at one of the monitors as the six o'clock

broadcast continued. He wasn't really listening or watching at first, just thinking. Then the stentorian tones of one of the station's veteran reporters, Chris Borgen, pierced his reverie.

"What's this one?" Taibbi said, turning to Paulus and Phillips. The three of them watched the rest of Borgen's story. Something about a black teenager in a town upstate. There was the teenager. Pretty, teary, and not talking, clutching a teddy bear, eyes unfocused. They listened to Borgen's narration.

". . . says she was raped repeatedly by a gang of white men, one of them wearing a policelike badge, over a period of four days. . . . She remains like this . . . dazed . . . incoherent . . . on the verge of collapse . . . able to say only that she'd been kidnapped."

"Jesus," Phillips said.

"Where is this?" Taibbi asked.

Paulus had turned to walk away, having been summoned by someone on the assignment desk. He looked back at his new reporting team.

"Place called Wappingers Falls," he said. "Her name is Tawana Brawley. Tawana. The girl."

2

"I'd love a piece of that story. . . ."

IT STARTED ON A SLOW SUNDAY, the last day of the long Thanksgiving break. Tom Farkas, Channel 2's weekend assignment editor, nursed a cup of coffee and scanned the morning papers and the early wires. Not much. Madonna had filed for divorce from Sean Penn, but neither of the two young lovelies was in town. There were riots in Cuba, a prison uprising in Georgia, a fatal train wreck down south, and a typhoon that had killed 1,600 in the Philippines, but they were all day-old stories at least and had already been mined for local pegs or judged to have none. A cab driver had been murdered out in Queens overnight, but even the free-lance stringers had ignored it. Too far out of Manhattan, too commonplace, Farkas thought. Ditto the two mob rubout victims dug up in the backyard of the Acme American Repair

Company in Brooklyn. *Newsday* had a solid advance on the transit police phony arrest scandal, and the *Daily News* an exclusive on a phony nurse scandal that had burned several prominent hospitals. But it was Sunday of the Thanksgiving weekend: no chance of any official response, and no way to chase either story, really. When the phone rang, Farkas was mildly startled to see it was the Viewer Hotline. He checked his watch as he reached for the receiver: 8:15, an odd time and an odd day for that phone to be ringing.

"Channel 2."

"Uh, hello. This is the number you call if you spot news?"

"That's right, ma'am. Can I have your name?"

The caller paused for a second. "Uhm, my name is Juanita Brawley. You see, I'm the aunt of the young lady . . . the victim? I just think the story should get out. She was kidnapped by this gang of men. White men. They were cops."

Farkas grabbed for a pen and started writing. Ordinarily, he knew, anyone who screened the Hotline calls found only the smallest percentage to be of any value. But there was something about the woman's voice.

". . . she'd gone to visit a friend in Newburgh after school last week, and then she disappeared. It was a couple of days," the caller continued evenly. "When they found her yesterday, she was . . . they said she was covered in, like, excrement. You know. And there was 'nigger' and 'KKK' written on her."

"There was . . . what?" Farkas pressed the receiver to his ear.

"That's right. They wrote 'nigger' and 'KKK' on her, scratched onto her chest and stomach, and the FBI is on it now."

Another phone was ringing persistently, an inside number only a colleague would know. Farkas asked if she minded being put on hold. She said she was at her office and would call him back in a few minutes.

"What's the young lady's name? I mean, your niece?" he asked before hanging up.

"Yes, Brawley," Juanita said. "B-R-A-W-L-E-Y. She's Ta-wana, my sister's daughter. My sister has a job and a baby, so I've been taking care of most of this."

Juanita Brawley called back in a few minutes and finally—almost reluctantly, Farkas thought, for someone who thought "the story should get out"—gave him her home number and her sister Glenda's number in Wappingers Falls. When Farkas explained that he might be interested in sending up a reporter and a camera crew, Juanita raised objections at first; she didn't think Tawana was up to talking about her ordeal. Finally, though, she relented. Farkas said he'd call her back one more time to confirm.

He was all alone in a newsroom that at the peak of a weekday was the working venue for nearly a hundred people. Minus the chaos of the deadline and any other human beings, it was a soiled and hard-used slab of a room, its cluttered work stations abandoned for the weekend, a room lined with edit suites and anchors' and managers' offices locked tight. The silence of a weekend morning was an odd and special silence: no early calls from the early managers embarking on their commute from Jersey or Connecticut, no network over-night talk/news shows to pierce the void. Only the first editions of the day's papers, delivered the night before; the computer stations where the assignment editor could consult the wire services; and the phones.

At thirty-two, Farkas was relatively new in the news business and had only been on the assignment desk for a few months. His prior experience in broadcasting was on the network side, handling satellite logistics and booking bulletin interruptions in network programming. He walked over to the maps hanging on the wall to his right. Wappingers Falls, Juanita had explained, was in Dutchess County in the Hudson River Valley. The metropolitan area map ended in Westchester. At the top someone had drawn two arrows pointing north, with the legend "Call an Affiliate!" written in bold lettering. Farkas laughed to himself, then went to the desk drawer where the additional maps were filed. He found a screw-on map for upstate regions and matched it to the one on the wall. There it was, Wappingers Falls. About sixty or seventy miles north, he estimated. Maybe a little less. The Taconic Parkway or the Thruway, he mused, tracing each route with his finger. Either way, it would be a rolling, winding drive. Hour and a half each way, easy. Call it four hours round trip, add a couple of hours on the ground for interviews at the house, the hospital, the cops, the location where the girl was found; now it's a six- or seven-hour shoot. Farkas knew CBS had an NFL doubleheader scheduled that would blow out the early newscast at 6:30, leaving the Eleven as the only cast of the day. He checked his watch again. Almost 9:00. Fourteen hours was a lot of time, enough even for a six- or seven-hour possible story in a place called Wappingers Falls. It's doable, he thought, as he sat at his desk again and reached for the phone, dialing seven familiar digits.

"Federal Bureau of Investigation," a male voice answered.

"Yeah, this is Tom Farkas at Channel 2. We got a call from a woman upstate who says her niece was abducted and raped by a gang of men, and—"

"This is the duty officer. There's no one else here," the voice cut in.

"Uh, I know. The thing is this woman says her niece was found yesterday and that the FBI is already investigating, and I just wanted to—"

"What's the subject's name?"

"Uh, Brawley. Tawana Brawley. She's fifteen. From Wappingers Falls."

There was a pause on the line. Farkas drummed his fingers nervously.

"We are investigating," the duty officer said.

Farkas waited.

"That's all I can say. We're investigating. You'll have to call back tomorrow."

Farkas tried a few more questions, to no avail. Turning to his typewriter, he hammered out the first memo on the Tawana Brawley case.

Kidnap/Racial incident:

The incident concerns a 15-yr-old black girl, Tawana Brawley, who was kidnapped Wednesday afternoon on her way home from a friend's house in Newburgh, N.Y. According to the girl's aunt, Juanita Brawley, Tawana was found dazed and confused Saturday afternoon in a neighborhood where her family once had a residence. Passersby noticed her incoherent state and brought her to St. Francis Hospital in Poughkeepsie. Upon examining the young girl, doctors observed that her hair had been chopped off, her body smeared with feces, and the word KKK written in Magic Marker across her chest. On her stomach, "nigger nigger" was written. She had been raped; her face bruised, body scratched. She was treated for her injuries as well as shock and released to her mother and aunt early this morning. The popular, attractive cheerleader from Ketchum H.S. in Wappingers Falls is so shaken she is unable to speak. Police from the Poughkeepsie sheriff's office came to the girl's bedside to question her. According to her aunt she recoiled in fear and, had she the strength, she would have fled; the officers were white. The family implored the department to find a black officer. Sometime later an Officer Young came to the hospital. Through notes on a pad and the blinking of eyes, police were told that she was raped and that the assailants, as many as three or four, were wearing uniforms. The Dutchess County sheriff's dep't is handling the investigation. I confirmed that the FBI has been contacted on the case.

Lisa Sharkey Gleicher, the weekend producer, called Farkas at 9:30, later than usual because of the preemption of the early newscast. He explained the story in Wappingers Falls, referring to his memo for details.

"The Bureau is investigating," he said. "That's confirmed. I figure they only investigate because it's a kidnapping or be-

cause there's a civil rights violation, right? I'm getting nothing from local PD up there, or from the county sheriff's office.
Some guy named Skoralick is the sheriff. I left a message at
his office, and called his home number and no one answered.
Nothing from the hospital where they brought her, St. Francis. But we've got the family, maybe the girl herself will talk,
and the confirmation from the Bureau."

"Well," Gleicher said, thinking, "sounds wild. Let's see . . .
I've got a Dennis Cunningham film review and another piece
in the can. Randall's coming in as the late reporter. Mary?"

"Yeah," Farkas answered. He'd already figured it was a
natural for Mary Murphy, a young and scrappy reporter who
specialized in police beat stories. "I've got a memo prepared
for her, based on what the aunt says, and directions up there.
I don't know exactly what she'll get, but whatever's there,
she'll come back with it.

"It's a gamble, I know," Farkas continued. "But hey, if half
the story's true, it's still a helluva story. It has all the ingredients."

"Well, it's certainly worth checking out," Gleicher said.
"Geez . . ."

"You know, Lisa, Juanita's facts are consistent, each time
I've talked to her. Lucid, nothing hysterical. I mean, she's got
a really sordid tale, a kind of *To Kill a Mockingbird* story,
and she just figures that by telling us it'll get out. That's it.
She says she didn't talk to anybody else, no other press."

"Exclusive!"

"Yah," Farkas answered. "So far. I told her it's really ironic
something like this should happen just when the Howard
Beach trial was winding down, you know, another vicious
racial attack on somebody. And this is . . . I mean, it sounds
like a really sinister kind of thing that can happen in a
small town."

FARKAS CALLED JUANITA BRAWLEY to confirm the appointment and then, for his own peace of mind, made one more

call. Steve Paulus, whose family had a home in Dutchess County, had a one-word response: "Wow!" The station's assignment manager spent three words instructing Farkas.

"Go for it."

MARY MURPHY WAS HOPING for an easy day and a good story to get her through it. Only twenty-eight, she was a recent hire at Channel 2, but a popular one. She'd worked as a street reporter at independent station WPIX, and anybody who knew her knew she was relentless. If not the absolutely most polished performer, she was, all agreed, the hardest worker. She was the student who did all the reading, and then did extra reading, and got not only an A but a comment from the teacher lauding her for her industriousness. But she was still a rookie at Channel 2 and thus assigned to weekends. Since she was also covering the Howard Beach trial of three white youths from Queens who'd been among a gang that chased a black youth onto the Belt Parkway, where he'd been struck by a car and killed, that meant she was working six- and seven-day weeks. Even tireless Mary Murphy could hope for an easy day.

"Here you go, Mary," Farkas said when she walked into the newsroom. He handed her his memo on Juanita Brawley's call.

"Interesting story," she said when she finished reading it. "You think Tawana will talk, though?"

"Juanita doesn't know. But you're set up to go to the house, anyway."

Murphy hooked up with her crew, Frank Pivalo and Dan Smyksy, and they poked northward up the Taconic Parkway. There was a prior arrangement that when they got to Wappingers Falls they'd call Glenda Brawley from the 7-Eleven on Route 9 and her boyfriend, Ralph King, would meet them and lead them to the apartment. King was gracious when he arrived, and he drove his smoke-gray Lincoln Continental

Mark VII slowly, mindful at each traffic light that the Channel 2 crew was still with him.

They entered the living room of a modest, neat apartment. The white walls and the plants gave it a modern look, but there wasn't much that suggested the clutter of a settled home. Two women were seated at a table in the rear of the big room.

"This is Glenda," Ralph said, "and her sister, Juanita." A small boy squealed in greeting, hopping up to Murphy and tugging for attention. "And this is Tyice," Ralph explained. "Our son."

Juanita rose and stepped forward, issuing instructions to the crew about where to set up their camera and lights. She was clearly in charge. But Murphy's attention was riveted on the young girl lying on the couch beneath a burgundy comforter, clutching a teddy bear and appearing not to notice the commotion around her. Tawana, Murphy knew immediately. She was pretty, but her short hair was disheveled and seemed to be roughly cut; her eyes drifted, unfocused.

"I know Tawana's a young girl," Murphy heard herself saying, "but if you're going to do a story for television and you want the best account you want to talk to the person affected directly by the whole thing. I mean, if you want to advance the story and get some action, as you say."

Juanita was nodding, and then saying, "Yes, yes." Murphy hid her surprise; she'd expected resistance, at least. There was something very wrong with Tawana Brawley, she guessed, looking at the young girl.

AT 11:00 P.M. ON SUNDAY, November 29, the viewers of 1.2 million television sets in metropolitan New York were tuned to Channel 2 and saw and heard the first report on the assault and rape of Tawana Brawley. It was the lead to the broadcast. Producer Lisa Sharkey Gleicher played it up big.

MURPHY NARRATION:
The Christmas lights had just been strung in Wappingers Falls, New York, population six thousand. But in-

side one apartment, fifteen-year-old Tawana Brawley now clutches a teddy bear for support, struggling to tell us about an ordeal of terror that began Tuesday when, she says, a white man dressed as a police officer forced her into his car near a local gas station.

TAWANA: *He told me to shut up.*
MURPHY: *He told you to shut up?*
TAWANA: *He was a cop.*
MURPHY: *He was a police officer?*
TAWANA: *Showed me a badge.*

MURPHY NARRATION:
Tawana choked back tears remembering how another man drove them to the woods where, she says, she was surrounded by a group, and raped and sodomized. Medical evidence shows her vaginal area was bruised. Lab tests will confirm the degree of sexual assault.

MURPHY: *Were there two men there?*
TAWANA: *A lot of men.*
MURPHY: *A lot of men?*
TAWANA: *. . . called me a nigger.*
MURPHY: *They called you a nigger?*

MURPHY NARRATION:
Tawana's mother and aunt told us for five days they tried to track her down, starting with the Newburgh police ten miles away, because that's where the teenager had been visiting a girlfriend.

When Tawana Brawley finally did turn up, police found she had collapsed near this condominium where her family used to live. The Brawleys had only moved a week and a half ago. Tawana did not remember how she got here. But Tawana's Aunt Juanita, who raised her for ten years, remembers too well how she looked.

JUANITA: *She had feces smeared all over her, in her hair. Her pants were burned. Um, she was incoherent. I saw*

"KKK" scrawled on her, written on her chest, right over her breasts. Further down there was "nigger nigger" written on her stomach.

MURPHY NARRATION:
Juanita Brawley told us her niece recoiled with fear when white detectives tried to question her. They finally tracked down a black police officer. But the Dutchess County sheriff is claiming the family is not helping with the investigation.

SHERIFF FRED SKORALICK: It's my understanding she didn't speak to the black officer, she wrote something on a piece of paper stating it was something, possibly white people with a badge. Uh, he couldn't make out head or tails . . .

MURPHY NARRATION:
The sheriff told us the FBI has been notified. But the nagging questions persist about why no Missing Persons teletype had been printed up when Tawana Brawley disappeared. We asked one local cop about the dark un-marked car Tawana says she was pushed into.

WAPPINGERS FALLS POLICE OFFICER MARK LIEBERMANN: There's old police vehicles that have, you know, been sold to private individuals at auctions, which still have the appearance of a police vehicle.

MURPHY NARRATION:
Tawana's mother did call us with an update, reporting the girl now remembers seeing a shoulder holster on the man who abducted her. Right now she only hopes the teenager returns to her outgoing self, an English honors student who told us she wants to enter the service so she can pay her way through college. I'm Mary Murphy, Channel 2 News.

Watching her story as it aired that night, Murphy pon-dered the questions and contradictions that were already apparent. A hardened New York street reporter imbued with the requisite cynicism, she'd come to trust her instincts, which had proven to be sound and dependable over the years. Tawana appeared believable. She could barely talk, and had seemed to be fighting for saliva to lubricate each word she did get out; the reporter had had to lead her through the interview, repeating the answers she thought she'd heard. The girl appeared fragile and damaged, pressing her teddy bear to her chest in convulsive movements. She'd broken out in tears several times. Her eyes were filled with fear.

But Murphy, who within days would be shut off by the family for no clear reason, had found Glenda Brawley's demeanor curious, to say the least. She had not expressed outrage in her interview, and in fact didn't appear to be angry. She'd seemed disconnected from her daughter in some way, never offering the gestures of comfort and reassurance one might have expected to see. Twenty-four hours after her daughter had been discovered in a horribly degraded condition, and listening as the terrible narrative of abduction and gang rape was repeated for the camera, Glenda Brawley had appeared . . . uninterested.

And, too, Murphy had had to struggle to find something in her interview with Fred Skoralick that would not sound plainly inflammatory in a story that demanded a high degree of sensitivity. The lanky and otherwise taciturn sheriff had launched without prodding into a diatribe on the whole Brawley household. He was skeptical of the story, period, he said. Juanita thought she was some kind of civil rights activist, he added, and she and Glenda and Ralph had all had their run-ins with the law. He wouldn't say what those run-ins were about, but the tone of his voice and the apparent depth of his skepticism nagged Murphy then and, as she watched her piece, still did. As Skoralick spoke on the air, the reporter listened for something that few if any of her viewers were likely to pick up. When Skoralick's interview cut ended and Murphy resumed her narration, his continuing comments were faded but not eliminated. The reporter listened carefully, ignoring

her own voice, and heard the sheriff's last words clear as
a bell:

"We don't know whether someone put her in the garbage
bag she was found in, or whether she got into the bag
herself."

NEITHER TAIBBI NOR PHILLIPS saw Murphy's original story and
the papers hadn't picked it up in the ensuing days, and though
they'd watched Chris Borgen's follow-up report with keen interest they were concentrating instead on finding a new story
to keep their partnership going. Phillips was still assigned to
Roseanne Colletti's consumer unit and she both admired
Colletti and considered her a close friend, and she'd also been
added to the team covering the end stage of the raucous
Howard Beach trial. But her first effort with Taibbi on the
House of Robinson "Body Parts" reports had excited her in a
way that nothing she'd done in television ever had. It wasn't
lost on Phillips that in the mostly white, mostly male, mostly
ego-driven world of television news reporting, Taibbi's atti-
tude toward her from the start was curiously egalitarian. Although he obviously had an enormous ego, and carried himself
with an aloof and sometimes irritating self-assurance, he had
treated her, a black woman, not as "his" producer or assistant but as a partner with a mandate to truly share the work.
Throughout the "Body Parts" project, they had divided the
records research, the phone call list, the surveillance assignments; he solicited her knowledge and analysis constantly,
sought her approval and editing on his scripts before submit-
ting them to management. He did the writing and appeared
on air; she called the shots in the editing room and turned
all the raw materials into television. When "Body Parts" was
over, Phillips was eager to try it again.

For his part, Taibbi saw in Anna Phillips a reason to return
to his favored practice of collaborative reporting. From his
earliest days in newspapering, in New Jersey and Boston and
throughout his career in television, he'd done his best work

in formal or informal collaboration with someone else. For a while, at WCVB-TV Boston, his "partner" was John Premack, who was as good a reporter as he was a cameraman, which was very good indeed. Later, at WNEV-TV, Taibbi teamed with a producer named Paul Toomey, an indefatigable researcher whose personal need to know was boundless.

Taibbi and Toomey ran a five-person investigative reporting team called the Newsbreakers, which in Taibbi's mind advanced collaborative reporting to a level he'd thought unattainable in local television. Toomey's obsession with methodology resulted in written protocols for every phase of the job; maintaining source relationships, running down fresh leads, utilizing the Freedom of Information Law to obtain public records, conducting stakeouts, selecting field techniques that violated no laws and maximized the chances for success, identifying the proper chronology in the pursuit of a story and then obeying that chronology absolutely, confirming and fact-checking, scheduling preproduction and postproduction in the most efficient manner to optimize the quality of the report when broadcast, involving management at the appropriate junctures. And, perhaps most important, Taibbi had decided with Toomey that the standard procedures for legal review would have to be changed drastically to conform to their more ambitious agenda.

Investigative reporting on television had copied the model established in print journalism; that is, journalists researched their subject, submitted a draft of their story to the lawyers, and then sat back and waited for the inevitable changes the lawyers would insist were necessary. It was enormously time-consuming, creating an equation that called for blockbuster successes in order to justify the time and resources spent in preparation of each report. In the city room of a great newspaper the so-called investigative reporters could work in isolation from the dozens or even scores of other reporters. But in television, even in the biggest markets, the news desk had only about a dozen reporters a day to cover the same quantity of news. If you were going to do investi-

gative reporting for television, Taibbi assumed, you were just
going to have to do it faster. Thus the Newsbreakers system
of legal review was radically different: Taibbi and Toomey
retained a team of four lawyers from an outside firm who
were involved from the moment a commitment was made to
pursue a story. If a search of similar cases showed that even
if the reporters were successful their targets would likely escape any meaningful censure, let alone prosecution, then the
investigation—the story—was simply spiked. In the schedule of productivity Taibbi and Toomey envisioned, there was
no time to waste. The lawyers, on retainer, advised them on
each aspect of their investigations: which field techniques
were legal in which jurisdictions (one-party taped phone conversations, for example, were allowed in some states but were
felony violations of local wiretap statutes in other states);
what conclusions could be fairly drawn given the evidence
in hand; what language had been identified in prior case citations as being troublesome, and therefore barred.

In one year, Taibbi and Toomey broadcast more than a
hundred reports; many were follow-ups of their previous
stories, but perhaps a third were original reports that the rest
of the press corps had to follow. Their targets came to know
that if Taibbi and Toomey were on their case, the resulting
report would be factual, dispassionate, and careful. The two
were often threatened with litigation but were rarely actually sued and never sued successfully. And they had no
agenda, political or intellectual or otherwise. On one occasion, they worked three months on an investigation of a state-
level commissioner, only to discover the week before air that
several of the key allegations they'd been probing simply didn't
add up. They dropped the story, and moved on. They even
reduced their personal motto to an axiom that hung on the
wall for a time: THE STORY'S THE BOSS. All that mattered were
the facts as they were discovered, not the amount of time
and resources invested, not anybody's preconceptions, not
February Sweeps or management's needs, not even the align-
ment of a reporter's legitimate passions. It was an unforgiv-

ing code, as flinty in its own way as the old Chicago City News Service credo: IF YOUR MOTHER SAYS SHE LOVES YOU, CHECK IT OUT. Finally, the task of fighting with management to keep the Newsbreakers alive wore Taibbi down. He took a fellowship at the University of Chicago Law School and then a job as a general assignment reporter at WNBC in New York for three years, during which time he did occasional investigative reports but mostly just covered the daily business of New York.

The road to the front lines of New York television was different for Anna Phillips. After high school, she worked for an airline so she could see a bit of the world. When she finally accepted the notion that a college education was a necessity, she sprinted through to a City College degree in two and a half years. Her entrée to WCBS was through a minority internship program, her first paying job as a secretary in Station Services. But the stories that had fascinated her in her youth were happening on the news side of the building; she was determined to get to News, and when the station's new New Jersey Bureau was opened, she found her own opening. She progressed from there in steady increments, propelled not so much by ambition as by curiosity. She'd done well in occasional undercover assignments for investigative reporters John Stossel and then Arnie Diaz, and had enjoyed working with Colletti on the Troubleshooter consumer unit, primarily as a producer. She might have stayed there, happily, for years if not for Taibbi and "Body Parts."

PHILLIPS WAS SICK with the flu when the idea for their next project occurred to her. It was a story she'd been carrying around in her back pocket for three or four months; she'd been unable to interest other reporters in it. She called Taibbi from home.

"Mike, that story about the transit police making those phony arrests? Listen, I've got a story about a Port Authority cop who did the same thing, but it's worse than that."

She went on to describe her story. A white Port Authority cop named Billy Gray had developed a habit of assaulting minorities. He'd been disciplined internally a couple of times, and once the Port Authority Police Department had been forced to settle out of court when Gray allegedly beat a sixteen-year-old black youth, after catching him crossing the tracks, and sent him to the hospital for three days. In another instance, Gray had wildly fired a nine-millimeter automatic pistol in the direction of a car in which three blacks were riding. Finally, Phillips told Taibbi, Gray had assaulted an eighteen-year-old Puerto Rican in a locked emergency room at Hoboken station because he had been "playing his radio too loud," and the youth had struck back.

"The kid was six-three. He took the cop's gun and radio," Phillips explained, "and tossed the radio on the tracks and ditched the gun in a vacant lot. He turned himself in the next day, but because he'd taken the gun he was looking at a mandatory sentence. This kid's in jail. He doesn't even speak English. He'd just come to this country and gotten his first job, in construction. He was going to give his first paycheck to his mother, but now he's in jail. He's innocent—"

"The jails are full of innocent people," Taibbi answered, unimpressed. "That's all that's in there. Doesn't make my dick hard."

Phillips was annoyed. And determined. "Listen, Mike. There's a story here. What's the matter with it?"

"Show me. Get me a source. Show me some evidence. On the surface, I'm just not interested in another guy in jail who says he didn't do it."

Phillips did a slow burn, convinced that her would-be partner wasn't taking her seriously. She called her original source. Yes, he said reluctantly, he'd meet with her and Taibbi and decide afterward whether he was going to go all the way.

The source, a cop himself, went all the way. He described everything he knew about Billy Gray's record, providing dates, times, details in abundance. Taibbi took Phillips to the clerk's office where the records were maintained on the adjudication and sentencing of the Puerto Rican youth who'd gone to jail.

"You get the docket number, and it opens you up for everything there is on the case, and sometimes more. Watch."

Phillips had had plenty of experience researching records in her work for Colletti's consumer unit, but pulling criminal case records was new to her. She stood silent at the reception desk as Taibbi schmoozed the clerk, asking for the original indictment, accompanying affidavits, anything from the Miscellaneous Business Docket, the sentencing decision, and any pre-sentence memoranda. At one point the clerk, a middle-aged woman who was clearly delighted to be talking to a New York television personality, took Taibbi into the back room of the records office. He emerged with a small smile. When he and Phillips were back in the car, he whipped out his booty: a confidential memorandum that was not part of the public record, conceding that the defendant, Edguardo Aguilar Lopez, was only pleading guilty "with an explanation." The explanation was that he'd struck back at Billy Gray in self-defense, that he believed he was about to be killed by the cop.

"You can't put the document on the air," Taibbi said. "But it's good to know it's there. You've got to know that."

They went to a coffee shop and examined the rest of the records they'd collected. The original defense attorney from the public defender's office, it turned out, had since set up a private practice. They went to visit her first, to check out the other public defender who ultimately handled the case and was listed in the sentencing report as attorney of record. The lawyer, who had entered the guilty plea for an indigent client who went to jail proclaiming his innocence, was nervous and defensive, especially when he learned later that the two reporters had run a check on him; but he came across. No, he'd not been informed by the prosecutor of Gray's previous disciplinary record or of Gray's documented practice of assaulting minorities. With Taibbi and Phillips pressing him

from both sides, he heard himself agreeing he would later sit
for an on-camera interview. He handed over the entire record
of the case, including the original police reports and statements by a half-dozen witnesses.

It was Phillips who came up with the coup de grace. The
next day she drove Taibbi to Hoboken and told him to wait
in the car. A half hour later she returned with a packet of
twenty "crime scene" photographs taken after the incident.
The photographs directly contradicted forty-seven points in
the statement made by Gray and tended to prove that Lopez
had been telling the truth. For example, Gray had claimed
Lopez attacked him without warning outside the emergency
room. But the photographs showed the only bloodstains were
in the *middle* of the emergency room, Gray's hat placed carefully on a shelf. And the photographs had never been provided to Lopez's attorney.

"*Brady* versus *Maryland*," Taibbi said, recalling a lesson
from his days with Toomey. "The prosecution can't withhold evidence that tends to exculpate a defendant. There's
the pictures, there's Gray's record. They're gonna have to let
the kid out!" Suddenly, he liked Phillips's story a whole lot.

They dubbed the reports "Good Cop–Bad Cop," two seven-
minute stories that made the case for Edguardo Lopez and
against Billy Gray, against the prosecutor, and against the
head of the Port Authority Police Department. Phillips, who
spoke fluent Spanish, had interviewed Lopez in prison and
translated, on camera. Each report won a newsroom ovation.
Two weeks later, Taibbi and Phillips revisited the prosecutor
and Lopez's defense attorney; Taibbi informed each man that
the reporters would simply continue to do stories on the case
until and unless a clear injustice was redressed. Within weeks,
Lopez was released from prison.

I've found my voice, Phillips thought, when "Good Cop–
Bad Cop" hit home.

I'm in business again, Taibbi thought. She's not Toomey.
She's different. But just as good.

PAUL SAGAN knew he had something going. Only twenty-eight, he was news director for the flagship station of the CBS network. Serious in mien, the scion of a Chicago family of newspapermen, academics, and intellectuals—including his second cousin, the astronomer Carl Sagan—and given to power suspenders and sober discussions about journalism and ethics, he'd given Taibbi virtually unrestricted freedom right from the start, because that freedom was the essential component of the agreement to hire the reporter in the first place. He knew about Taibbi's history with Toomey and the News-breakers; in fact, the only tapes he had asked to review before hiring him were the Newbreakers reports from Boston.

Those reports struck a chord with Sagan. Broadcast news at the network level had never captured his interest. His father, who'd owned a string of weekly newspapers in the Chicago area, had indoctrinated him early on in a specific kind of relationship between journalism and the community. "The famous 'three men shaking hands photo,' " Sagan had said of his training. "One guy giving the check, two other guys receiving it. Civic affairs stuff. Dad's papers had the Stars and Stripes column, who smashed his car, who got picked up DWI—all the mundane stuff that really affects people's lives." Sagan stuffed inserts in the mailroom, fell into an intern program at KNXT in Los Angeles, worked with Bill Kurtis at WBBM in Chicago when Kurtis was making his bones on the Agent Orange story, and then began his rise at WCBS in New York as a "three-piece desk assistant," becoming the youngest newswriter, the youngest producer, the youngest executive producer, and, finally, the youngest news director. It was always the "three men shaking hands" and the DWI stories that impressed him as being important, as opposed to the grand overviews of the world at large. Taibbi's Newsbreakers reports were what he believed was meaningful in broadcast reporting.

Still, he had felt that Taibbi's first collaboration with Anna Phillips on the "Body Parts" story was a one-time thing; but "Good Cop—Bad Cop" had knocked him out, and he knew it was Phillips's story. Phillips had then gone back to the consumer unit—neither she nor Taibbi had lobbied even once to keep the partnership going—but when Taibbi got to work on follow-up reports on a lawyer who'd brokered several illegal adoptions that had turned sour with tragic results, Sagan noticed that Phillips was always there, providing research or offering suggestions. The case of Joel Steinberg and Hedda Nussbaum dominated the headlines for a few weeks, as it would again a year later: the unmarried Greenwich Village couple had illegally adopted two children, one of whom, a beautiful blond and blue-eyed six-year-old girl named Lisa, had died after a terrible beating. Taibbi, with Phillips prominently in the background, had obtained the records of the city's Fatality Review Committee, which showed that while Lisa's death was indeed a tragedy, there were more than a hundred similar tragedies a year in New York, most of them in the neglected minority ghettos. And the doctor who'd placed the second child with Steinberg and Nussbaum had had a questionable role in several other controversial adoptions Taibbi had identified.

"JUST AN IDEA," Sagan said, having called Taibbi into his office. "A few weeks ago, there was that story about the United Nations War Crimes Commission Files, the files where they got the documents connecting Kurt Waldheim to Nazi atrocities. The story was there, and then it sank without a trace. You and Anna want to see about the files? I mean, has anybody read them, does anyone know what's in them?"

If Taibbi was skeptical and worried about embracing a project simply for its potential appeal as a February Sweeps special, Phillips was plainly distressed. She knew little about the Nazi era, beyond what she could remember from college, and had never viewed the Holocaust as a subject of overpowering personal interest. But the two reporters agreed to check it out.

The story, they soon learned, was a giant. The files of the War Crimes Commission had been buried for forty years; they contained what amounted to indictments against more than 30,000 war criminals, most of them Nazis, with eyewitness statements punctuating the most graphic narratives imaginable of one atrocity after another. Taibbi and Phillips were the first broadcasters granted access to the files, and they reviewed thousands of the so-called indictments. Almost none had resulted in prosecutions in the seventeen nations that had made up the War Crimes Commission. That meant that in the United States, as in other countries, there were likely to be found war criminals who'd escaped detection entirely.

The reporters concentrated on the case of one man, a retired auto worker named Peter Quintus who lived in Washington, Michigan, north of Detroit. There were seventeen witnesses in the files who identified him as one of the Tottenkopf "Death's Head Battalion" guards at the Maidanek concentration camp in Poland, a guard who was on duty on a November day in 1943 when, in twelve hours, 20,000 Jews were shot to death and shoved into predug ditches while the killers feasted on venison and brandy, and waltzes blared over loudspeakers. Taibbi and Phillips went to Michigan and found their man after a day-long stakeout; Phillips then located a Maidanek survivor, who said, passionately and on camera, "I don't care if they put him in jail. I don't care even if they deport him. But I want people to know about it. I want people to know that he . . . was . . . there!"

It was powerful stuff, a ratings grabber. When their "Nazi Files" series ran in the first week of February 1988, Taibbi and Phillips were clearly if unofficially a team. Phillips was convinced she was being allowed to travel to places she never thought would be within her reach as a journalist. If she wanted to read a half-dozen books on her subject, or call for a computer run of everything CBS had ever broadcast on the Holocaust and the Nazi era, and then wanted to screen more than 250 videotapes, taking days to do so, she suddenly had the freedom to do it. Taibbi had found a colleague whose energy and curiosity were a match for his, whose organizational skills were unparalleled in his experience; a partner who had the confidence to force him to perform better. Phillips had reviewed his first script for "Nazi Files" and pronounced it inadequate. "It just doesn't have it." So he'd rewritten the script—four times—until she was satisfied. And, in the end, she took control of the editing room entirely, expelling Taibbi when it became apparent to her that he was just getting in the way.

THE DAY AFTER the last "Nazi Files" report, Sagan called Phillips into his office. The station's coverage on the Tawana Brawley story was stalled, he explained; he wanted her to work with reporter Chris Borgen. Without saying so, he was also suggesting that because she was black, and because she'd coordinated the final reports on the Howard Beach case, she might have the best chance to move the story off the dime.

An elegant man whose family was predominantly of French and Guadeloupe extraction, Borgen was a former New York City cop who for a quarter-century had enjoyed an unparalleled reputation in the world of New York television. Rightly regarded as the premier crime reporter in a city where crime reporting was what mattered most, he had kept the Brawley story alive through the months of December and January. But Borgen was old school, a lone wolf, too: he graciously acknowledged the phone calls and contacts Phillips was making on his behalf and, each morning, went his own way without consulting her. The story was still stuck.

Taibbi, meanwhile, was scuffling to regain his footing after the high of the "Nazi Files" series. He was poking around on a questionable story about the rumored abandonment of Port Newark for points south by a number of foreign car makers, because of rampant theft. Maybe the story was there, maybe it wasn't; he didn't like or wholly trust his sources. But it wasn't coming together quickly and, in a word, it was hardly sexy.

One afternoon, after another desultory and inconclusive shoot in Newark, Taibbi stood over the shoulder of managing editor Jean Harper and watched the top of the five o'clock broadcast. Borgen was running still another follow-up on the Brawley story; attorneys Alton Maddox and C. Vernon Mason, the family's lawyers, and self-proclaimed civil rights activist Rev. Al Sharpton were loudly denouncing the governor, the attorney general, and all the investigators in the case as participants in a massive cover-up. Sharpton, eyes boring into the lens and the words flowing passionately from a face framed in a James Brown coif, was a mesmerizing figure in an electric-blue suit, with a huge medallion lying against his chest. He spoke in the cadence of television; he was perfect, Taibbi thought. He's got it down.

And in the middle of the bombast, there appeared a familiar face with its impossibly small voice expressing shock at the attack on Tawana Brawley.

"Me and Don King came together," said heavyweight champion Mike Tyson, "and we was thinking we could do something useful for her. I was talking to my new wife about this; sometimes things happen and nothing can be done."

Tyson said he would write a check for $50,000 and that Tawana would be the first to benefit from his new fund, "a kind of Hands-Across-America thing," he explained, smiling. Boxing promoter King said he'd match the champ's donation.

"I visited this girl two days ago," Tyson continued, "and spent seven hours with her. I expected her to be in bad shape, much worse. Maybe in bed. But she really came around. She was happy."

Anna Phillips, at that very hour, was trying to tune in a fuzzy broadcast on CNN in her hotel room in Rio de Janeiro. She and her husband, Lionel, and a half-dozen friends had flown south for Carnivale; but she was worried and thought often about the story she'd left behind. She strained to hear Tyson and got most of it, wondering what it meant to the story and wondering too whether her once and future partner was clued in at all.

"Whaddya think?" Harper asked Taibbi in New York. "Something, huh?"

"Jesus," he muttered.

"And you know about Cosby and Ed Lewis [the publisher of *Essence* magazine] . . . they're in for twenty-five grand, I think. Reward money."

Taibbi shook his head imperceptibly, concentrating hard on the images on the screen.

"I'd love a piece of that story," he said quietly. "I surely would."

Harper, a former news director herself and the one person in the entire newsroom who knew precisely what everyone else was doing or should be doing at all times, reached into the bottom drawer of her desk and extracted a thick file.

"Here," she said evenly, handing it to Taibbi. "I've been clipping on this thing myself, pretty much since the beginning. Knock yourself out."

3

---

*"We come to you with
hate in our hearts. . . ."*

"COME ON IN, GUYS, sit down," Paul Sagan said amiably.
"Mike, you want to close the door?" The regular morning
staff meeting had just ended, and the news director had summoned Phillips, Taibbi, Borgen, and Harper to his office.

"I think the thing to do," Sagan began, a bit tentatively,
"is to talk about how we're going to divide this thing up.
There's the day-of-air stuff everybody's got to cover, and that's
hard enough to keep up with. The grand jury's seated next
week, and we'll be able to go live from Poughkeepsie and
stay with that part of it. But obviously there's more than
that, too."

Borgen, who'd carried the story virtually on his own for
more than two months, studied the face of the twelfth boss
he'd worked for in his years at Channel 2. It was the face of

a man less than half his own age who looked even younger than that.

"Well," Borgen answered firmly. "I've briefed Mike on where the story is now. Anna of course has been working on it already. I think, since I have something of a rapport with the family and have been following the business with the special prosecutor and so on, that I can stay on that side of it. You know, where the case is officially, and the family's positions, the charges back and forth, et cetera."

"And Mike and Anna just root around," Harper cut in. "See what they can come up with, like witnesses and evidence?"

"Precisely," Borgen answered amiably. If he was offended by the assignment of Taibbi and Phillips, he didn't let on.

It was just what Sagan wished to hear. Taibbi and Phillips sat impassively, but they too were slightly unnerved. They respected Borgen enormously and didn't want him or any of their colleagues to think they were cutting in on the veteran's story. But they wanted in: Phillips, energized by her new role in the newsroom, wished simply to solve the case, find out what had happened to the girl, and identify the culprits. Taibbi was simply juiced up by any story that seemed to be hot, and this one was as hot as any he'd seen in years.

"So," Sagan said, "what happens now, besides what we already know, and where do we go from here?"

Borgen ran through a concise review of the latest developments in the story and listed several aspects where some Taibbi/Phillips gumshoeing might be fruitful.

"We're gonna take a road trip this afternoon," Taibbi said. "Chris thinks, and we agree, that so much has gone on already, in Wappingers Falls and Poughkeepsie, not to mention here and in Albany, that we'd have a better chance of hitting the ground running if he gave us a tour through the story."

"He knows all the players," Phillips added. "A few introductions wouldn't hurt. Plus, we can get the lay of the land."

"You guys up to speed on what's been written so far?" Sagan asked.

"I've got my own file," Phillips said, "and I've copied stuff out of Chris's. Mike read the file Jean gave him."

Sagan nodded distractedly and looked down at the pad on which he'd been scribbling notes. He'd been quoted in a *Washington Post* story about the case as saying he believed news organizations in New York and across the country had an obligation to be especially sensitive to stories with racial overtones, and that the news organization he ran had demonstrated that needed sensitivity in its coverage of the Tawana Brawley story. In Mike Taibbi and Anna Phillips he had a team that could be fairly described as a hired gun; now, four months into his first job as news director, he was aiming that gun at a story so rhetorically charged as to carry the unmistakable hint of danger. Sagan, something of a health nut despite his pale and gaunt appearance, felt the acids spin in the pit of his stomach.

It would become a familiar sensation.

IF IT HAD BEEN five degrees colder on February 23, 1988, the driving rain would have been a crippling snowstorm, and the trip north in Taibbi's truck would have taken four hours at least instead of two. While Taibbi drove, Borgen and Phillips pulled clips from their files and dissected the details of the case, and of the stories about the case.

Since Mary Murphy's first report nearly three months earlier, not much had changed in the central allegations about what happened to Tawana Brawley. The claim on the teenager's behalf was that she had been abducted at around 8:30 P.M. on Tuesday, November 24, after returning home to Wappingers Falls from the city of Newburgh, some ten miles away. When she stepped off her bus a white male emerged from the passenger seat of a dark sedan and hustled her into the backseat. She'd screamed, for her mother, for the police. But the man, flashing a "policelike" badge and a shoulder holster, had shouted at her, "Shut up, stupid—I am the police!" He struck her in the head, and before she lapsed into unconsciousness she noticed there was another person in the car—a white man in the driver's seat. When the teenager awoke, she found herself in "a wooded area," the first news accounts said, "surrounded by white men . . . six white men in all." They proceeded to rape and sodomize her, continually, for the next ninety hours, until Saturday, November 28. At 1:45 that afternoon Tawana Brawley was found lying in a fetal position behind her family's old apartment. A plastic garbage bag was pulled up to her neck, a sweater wrapped crudely around her matted, roughly-cut short hair and secured by a purse strap whose loose end was held tight in her clenched teeth. When paramedics pulled the bag away a terrible stench arose: Tawana's body was covered with feces. And someone had written across her pink shirt, and on her torso, the letters "KKK," and the words "nigger nigger" and "nigger ete." Her pants had been scorched in the crotch area, she was missing one of her red shoes. Her pulse was weak; she seemed to be slipping in and out of consciousness.

In the weeks following the discovery of Tawana Brawley in the garbage bag, virtually every news organization in the New York area reported extensively on the case, and though the treatment was hardly uniform and had become progressively more skeptical, the collective effect was essentially to validate Tawana Brawley's story. On December 6 Richard Pienciak of the *Daily News* wrote that the normally peaceful Hudson Valley was "shaken by racial strife" and by charges that the Ku Klux Klan was involved in two incidents, one of them the alleged kidnap and gang rape of Tawana Brawley. The other incident was a "small riot" at the Orange County jail involving black and Hispanic inmates who'd "been hosed down, shackled and beaten by guards who shouted racial slurs." Several inmates had told reporters, Pienciak wrote, that three of the guards had worn white sheets over their heads during the attack (though a subsequent investigation determined that had never happened). The *News* quoted Alton Maddox, one of Tawana's attorneys, who described the area as a "hotbed of Klan activity." And Tawana's Aunt Juanita said of her, "She can hardly talk. And she still can't walk."

On December 14, in the first piece on the case in the *New York Times*, Esther Iverem wrote, "Miss Brawley, who is black, had been beaten," and repeated the basic story of her sexual assault—repeated sodomy but not rape in the *Times* version—by six white men, "one of whom wore a police badge." Iverem added that "local law enforcement officials have questioned the truthfulness of the girl's statements," and that those statements, all agreed, had not been made in any substantive way to any of the local, state, or federal investigators assigned immediately to the case.

Newsday weighed in next, with a story headlined, "Race-Sex Attack Enrages a Town." "She hasn't walked, and has barely smiled . . . since November 28th," reporter Michael Cottman wrote. Her hair had been "pulled out and cut off," and the teenager had told her family and the police that "six white men had attacked and sexually assaulted her." Juanita Brawley was quoted: "We just want Tawana to get back that twinkle in her eye."

The *Washington Post*, the newspaper credited with breaking the Watergate scandal, latched onto the Brawley case with some original reporting on what appeared to be another burgeoning scandal. Tawana had been found "lying on a dirt road," wrote *Post* reporter Marianne Yen on January 27, and even when sleeping these days shows "a lot of anxiety and tension." She still walked with a limp. "I can't dance anymore," Tawana told Yen. "I used to be a good dancer." Her two-year-old brother, Tyice, the article concluded, "is just beginning to talk but has already learned to say 'KKK.'"

The most pointed and incautious coverage was in the *Amsterdam News*, the black New York weekly. Tawana was "assaulted in the woods for four days by a wolfpack of Ku Klux Klansmen," the paper reported without qualification a week after the incident. Maddox was quoted as saying the cop Tawana "identified" was in trouble: "His superiors claim he's lying, and he has been threatened with the loss of his job. It's a real mess." Two weeks later, beneath the front-page headline "Klans Planning Big Queens Cross-Burning Rally," the paper quoted Hank Erich Schmidt, identified as the "Exalted Cyclops of the National Klan." He vowed to lead the New York White Knights in the lighting of a seventy-foot-high electrical cross in front of a black housing project in Astoria. "We're going to show the dark people a thing or two," Schmidt said. There never was a cross lighting. The Exalted Cyclops wasn't heard from again.

Every local news station in New York City, and local news stations based in Poughkeepsie and Albany, had settled into a pattern of coverage of the story based for the most part on new revelations that appeared in print or on developments in the case generated by either the Brawley advisers or the government and law-enforcement officials who had become the advisers' foils and adversaries.

None of the local television stations, with the exception of Channel 2's Mary Murphy and Chris Borgen, had made headway with either the family or the story. And while print reporters did better, none of the television or news reporters had spoken to Tawana Brawley about her assault. All relied on press conferences or interviews with the Brawley family advisers, Rev. Al Sharpton and attorneys Alton Maddox and C. Vernon Mason, for the story of what had happened to Tawana.

BEFORE THE BRAWLEY story became a regular component of the nightly broadcasts, neither Taibbi nor Phillips had known a great deal about Maddox and Mason. Phillips knew a bit more, having covered the end of the Howard Beach trial, in which they'd played a part, but had never met either man.

Maddox, forty-one, was born in Newnan, Georgia, the son of a schoolteacher mother and preacher father. Gentlemanly and almost courtly in carriage, halting and plainly uncomfortable as a public speaker, he was capable nonetheless of hurling the rhetorical dagger, often at the most unexpected moment. He was viewed by many in the black community, even those who sympathized with his positions, as a myopic nationalist—a black separatist—who identified with the early Malcolm X and sought not to change but to replace the existing power structures in law and government. He'd prepared for his career as an activist lawyer by working in his early New York years at Harlem Legal Services and as the head of the National Conference of Black Lawyers Juvenile Justice Project. During the Howard Beach trial even Charles "Joe" Hynes, the special prosecutor assigned by Gov. Mario Cuomo to handle the investigation and the trial, credited Maddox with an "impressive legal strategy" that helped shape the case as a national symbol of racial problems.

Vernon Mason was much more the politician. Where Maddox was intractable and made no attempt to disguise his contempt—hatred might be the more accurate word—for whites behind his courtly facade, the forty-one-year-old Mason, even in the early stages of the Brawley case, seemed reasonable, even accessible. An attractive man and a contrived if occasionally effective orator who spoke often and with undeniable passion of his Arkansas childhood, Mason had run for Manhattan district attorney in 1986 against the incumbent, Robert Morgenthau, and had collected one-third of the primary vote.

Al Sharpton was a known quantity to everyone in Taibbi's truck, although much of what was known about him was contradictory, unbelievable, unexplainable, or nearly apocryphal. Of his life as an activist, Sharpton had once told the *New York Times*, "I've been screaming ever since the doctor slapped me at birth," and indeed the public record of his life seemed to bear that out. He claimed to have given his first sermon, "Let Not Your Heart Be Troubled," at the age of four, and at ten was licensed as a Pentecostal minister. At sixteen, appearing in Detroit with gospel singer Mahalia Jackson, Sharpton was hailed as the "Wonder Boy Preacher."

In the two or three years before the Brawley case, the rotund Sharpton had become a ubiquitous figure—although often one who arrived late and from the fringe—at any New York news event or story involving race issues that had headline potential. It was tempting to reporters to dismiss Sharpton as a hot-air balloon whose threats and promises were essentially weightless; but sometimes they came true. There *would* be a demonstration or a disruption that affected some corner of city life. Or he *would* have at his side a victim or a witness or a key figure in a legitimate story that the press corps as a whole was pursuing. Besides, Sharpton was a dependably dramatic figure and a truly gifted speaker who had mastered the language of the soundbite, the pithy, concise, rhetorically compelling statement that was the essential component of local television news reporting.

There were television executives, producers, and reporters throughout the city who had urged in recent years that coverage of Al Sharpton—like coverage of other apparent self-promoters—ought to be confined to those stories in which he had an authenticated role, or ought to be eliminated altogether. Phillips herself had pressed that argument two years before the Brawley case, telling then news director Frank Gardner that Sharpton's posturing and speechmaking during the trial of subway gunman Bernhard Goetz had nothing to do with the story. "Black folks choose their leaders just like white folks do," Phillips had lectured during a morning discussion of whether or not to cover the latest Sharpton "event" on the list of scheduled events called the daybook. "We vote for them, or we respond when they exhibit meaningful leadership. Nobody ever voted for Sharpton, and as far as I can tell the only people he's been leading around are the media. We're giving this guy credibility," she had insisted, "and he has none in the black community."

But the truth was that Sharpton had *something*, and kept getting media coverage. The list of blacks who had mentored him or stood with him or simply allowed him into their inner circle—no matter for how short a time—was impressive, and couldn't be ignored. It stretched across two decades, from the late congressman Adam Clayton Powell, Jr., the mythic Harlem politician who counseled Sharpton on how to create his own myth, to the Reverend Jesse Jackson, who appointed the Wonder Boy Preacher (who was then a high school sophomore) the New York Youth Leader of the Southern Christian Leadership Conference's "Operation Breadbasket"; from James Brown, the "godfather of soul," whose hairstyle Sharpton adopted as his own trademark, to Don King, who allowed Sharpton entrée into the worlds of boxing and music promotion, and, finally, to C. Vernon Mason and Alton Maddox. They were lawyers—serious lawyers with a political mission—but when Sharpton joined them he expanded the team by more than one loud mouth. He all but ensured that they—and whatever issue or case they attached themselves to—would get on television, and stay there. Television in New York, starting with its lurid tabloid coverage of the Goetz case, had provided the guarantee.

BUT ON FEBRUARY 23, poking north in a driving rainstorm, Taibbi and Phillips were not interested in joining the editorial writer's debate about the roles played by the three Brawley advisers. The fuel for the debate was the growing list of charges—increasingly ugly charges—emanating from the Brawley team; and with the factual case of what happened to Tawana Brawley in a kind of stasis, the charges, mere words, were what filled the papers and the nightly newscasts. Taibbi and Phillips wanted instead to get to the story, to the players and places in its genesis. The first stop was the tiny village of Wappingers Falls.

"Here's the thing," Borgen explained, as they pulled off at the first exit after crossing the Hudson River over the Newburgh-Beacon Bridge. "There's the town of Wappinger, and the village of Wappingers Falls. Two different entities. That's what created some jurisdictional problems in the beginning, why when she was found, actually in Wappinger, it was the Dutchess County sheriff's office—Skoralick's office—who responded. Okay, slow down here."

Borgen's tour was typical Borgen; that is, logical, comprehensive, and filled too with idiosyncratic detail. He showed them the gas station on Route 9D whose proprietor, Phil, seemed always to be aware of both the developments in the case and the local gossip. Phil kept copies of the local papers for a day or two after publication and always found time to chat with the few out-of-town reporters who made his station a regular stop. Borgen pointed out restaurants to avoid or to patronize eagerly, the Full Belli Deli (a gathering spot for teenagers Tawana's age), the bars reputed to be redneck hangouts, even the homes for sale (including a small but lovely porched house just north of the Garner Fire Station that Borgen thought was priced attractively at $79,000).

"Now, turn left here," Borgen instructed. "Go slow. There, that's it."

The Brawley family apartment was near the end of a curved dead-end street named Carmine Drive in a modest complex called Leewood Arms. Taibbi and Phillips recognized the two-story structure from Borgen's reports.

"Let me see who's home," Borgen said. "You should meet the family."

But Glenda Brawley's companion, Ralph King, who opened the front door, wasn't interested in meeting any more reporters. He kept Borgen standing in the rain for long minutes, shaking his head emphatically and trying several times to close the door. Borgen kept King talking, gesturing once back toward the truck, but finally shrugged his shoulders and spread his hands in resignation.

"Not interested," he said, sliding into the backseat and shuddering against the cold. "Oh well, c'mon. There's plenty more to do."

Even in the gray of a wet winter day, Wappingers Falls exhibited the charm of a small village. There were pretty churches, Bethel Baptist and Zion Episcopal, Goring Hall and other graceful old buildings leading down to the falls over Wappinger Creek, and an antiquated two-story home that had been converted to the village library. Keepsake Realty advertised a "three bedroom, new, $134,000." Drivers honked in greeting or flashed their headlights when they paused at intersections or slowed in heavy traffic. The homes were neat and well-kept on small manicured lots, and East Main Street with its packed-in shops sloped away down a winding road from the village centerpiece, the Mesier Homestead. East Main was lined with old family business, Sal's Music Center and the Wagon Wheel Pizza among them. In the Wagon Wheel, two generations of the same family owners had collected scores of axioms and country bromides and tacked them to the walls: IF YOU WERE ON TRIAL AS A CHRISTIAN, posed one, WOULD THERE BE ENOUGH EVIDENCE TO CONVICT YOU? GOD SO LOVED THE WORLD, proclaimed another, THAT HE DIDN'T SEND A COMMITTEE. There were two versions of one saying that seemed particularly apt during the Tawana Brawley case: IF YOU CAN KEEP A COOL HEAD IN THESE TIMES, PERHAPS YOU JUST DON'T UNDERSTAND THE SITUATION.

The village police department and the village water department occupied the pre–Revolutionary War Mesier residence, which had been deeded to the town after the turn of the century. The police chief, Lt. William McCord, displayed an easy country friendliness despite the flood of press attention that had descended upon Wappingers Falls. Short and appearing even stockier than he was because of the bulletproof vest he wore incongruously under his police-issue shirt, he leaned casually against the wall of the waiting room in his matchbox-sized "department," made sure Taibbi and Phillips had said hello to his assistant, Heidi, and seemed ready to settle in for another long discussion about the case that had put his village on the map. Borgen cut him off politely at the first available juncture, explaining that his mission was to get his colleagues oriented on the story as quickly as possible.

"All right," McCord said genially. "I'm sure I'll get to talk to them again."

––––––

FROM MESIER PARK, Borgen guided Taibbi and Phillips past the house on South Remsen Street where Harry Crist, an IBM technician and a part-time cop in neighboring East Fishkill, had committed suicide on December 2, four days after Tawana had been discovered. Crist's rented attic apartment was only four blocks from the new Brawley family apartment on Carmine Drive, and his blond hair and pale mustache roughly matched the description of one of the assailants the Brawley advisers claimed Tawana had given. With the suicide coming so soon after Tawana's reappearance, the advisers had quickly established Crist as a "suspect," stating as "fact" that the teenager had known him "for years" and had often run into him on her way to school. Borgen, the ex-cop, emphasized that as far as he knew, there wasn't *any* evidence linking Crist to Tawana, but the possibility of a link had not been eliminated yet. Crist's parents lived only a few hundred yards from their son, in a home with the family name imprinted on the sidewalk out front. Harry, only twenty-nine at his death, had been waked at a funeral home down the street.

THEY STOPPED FOR COFFEE at the Dunkin Donuts on Route 9, a reputed gathering place for local police buffs, and then parked across the street from Paino's Mobil Station at Meyers Corner, a mile south. Tawana's bus from Newburgh had supposedly stopped to let her off in front of Paino's on November 24, and a Paino's mechanic named Tommy Masch had found his name in print as another possible "suspect." Masch, twenty years old and admittedly "scared" by the unwanted attention, was a would-be race driver and a police and fire buff, and was part of the crowd at the Dunk, the stories went. A friend of Harry Crist's, he too had blond hair and a mustache, and supposedly was fond of flashing a police auxiliary badge when he showed up at the scenes of fires and accidents. He drove a recycled state police cruiser and was a volunteer fireman.

An insightful column that morning by *Daily News* columnist Bob Herbert had placed the anguish of the Tawana Brawley case into up-to-date perspective through an examination of the suspicions concerning Tommy Masch: Masch, Herbert wrote, had had his life turned upside down and inside out because of inferences based on the flimsiest circumstantial suggestions that he could have been involved. "I know my name keeps coming up," Masch told the black columnist, sitting tensely in the passenger seat of the writer's car. "I'm watching the case." He'd offered to take a polygraph test but the logistics had been screwed up, twice: now he was clearly on the defensive, was tired of the press hanging around, was thinking of moving. The three reporters peered through the rain and the flapping wipers but couldn't see anyone at Paino's who matched the description of Tommy Masch. Clearly, Taibbi and Phillips agreed, they'd have to learn more about Masch, and Crist, and the crowd at the Dunk.

The next stop was Roy C. Ketchum High School, where Tawana was a student. The principal, Gordon Hirt, had weeks ago stopped responding to press inquiries and had gotten tougher on reporters who sought to interview Tawana's classmates. Borgen shook his head as Taibbi wheeled the truck through a U-turn at the school entrance. "Long shot getting anything there. It's been tried."

It was also a long shot, Taibbi and Phillips knew, that they'd get anything new by working the Pavillion Apartments a mile and a half east of Meyers Corner. The Brawleys had lived there in apartment 9D until they were evicted for nonpayment of rent a week and a half before Tawana's disappearance, and Tawana had been found behind the building on November 28. But the number of reporters on the story had swelled to nearly a hundred, and many had completed the drill of knocking on doors and slogging across the sodden common that separated the two banks of apartment blocks that made up the Pavillion complex.

"We'll take our turn at some point," Taibbi observed, as he pulled away from the Pavillion and headed back in the direction of Route 9. "But that's certainly not gonna be the first step. Anybody check this other apartment complex, what is this, the White Gates?" Borgen shook his head. Everybody in the truck watched as a group of young children stepped down from their school bus and trudged through the puddles to their apartments in the complex only a few hundred yards from the Pavillion Apartments. There were tennis courts and a basketball hoop, and a pool that was covered over for the winter. It was three in the afternoon and they'd been in the truck a long time. Taibbi looked across at Phillips, sitting glumly in her suit and high heels, and then back at Borgen, still damp and wrinkled from his failed front-stoop encounter with Ralph King. "Gimme a few minutes," he said. "I'm just gonna try a few doors. The kids are coming home. Their parents have gotta be around."

A half hour later he returned to the truck and pulled his notebook from the pocket of his rumpled trenchcoat.

"Got a guy whose brother works at Paino's," he explained, mildly animated for the first time in hours. "Only took four doors. Says the suspicion about Tommy Masch is all bullshit, and that his brother can talk about everyone else they've looked at as possible suspects, including Harry Crist, and explain *why* it's bullshit. Everybody's pissed as hell, and he thinks his brother will talk to us. Hasn't talked to anyone else yet," he added, waving his notepad. "Home numbers, the guy and his brother. It's a start. A way in, anyway. . . . Where to, Mr. Borgen?"

"Pough-keep-sie," Borgen sang in his best basso profundo, consulting his wristwatch. "Let's see. Three-thirty now . . . it's six miles but we'll hit the Route 9 traffic and the day-shift IBM-ers letting out. But you must see Poughkeepsie. That's where the story will play out. And you must meet Bill Grady."

BY THE LAST WEEK of February a key unanswered question about the Tawana Brawley case—and the question frequently at the center of the daily denunciations by the Brawley advisers—was why Bill Grady, the second-term Dutchess County district attorney, had abruptly quit the case. He'd seated his own county grand jury on December 19, and his office had interviewed "hundreds of witnesses" and presented approximately thirty of those witnesses to the grand jury. But on January 21 he suddenly dropped out, appealing to supervising Justice Judith Hillery that he was forced to recuse himself because of a potential conflict of interest. Hillery, assessing Grady's "potential conflict" in a private hearing whose minutes she then ordered sealed, agreed that Grady had sufficient reason to quit and promptly appointed two local defense attorneys, David Sall and William Burke, to serve as joint special prosecutors. But within twenty-four hours, Sall and Burke backed out as well, suggesting in private correspondence that their own investigation would likely be plagued by problems related to the same conflict. Hillery agreed again, and again said nothing for the public record. On January 26 Gov. Mario Cuomo appointed Attorney General Robert Abrams special prosecutor in the Tawana Brawley case, and after spending several weeks putting his team together and organizing his investigation, Abrams was poised to seat his own special grand jury.

BILL GRADY MADE IT PLAIN he was in a hurry. A small, spare man in a trenchcoat, with the pinched, thin-skinned face of someone fighting middle age through regular exercise, he explained without holding eye contact that he didn't have time to chat; he had to pick up his kids and then make a racquetball game. Borgen, Taibbi, and Phillips had literally bumped into the district attorney when the elevator in the Dutchess County Courthouse had opened at the third floor, Grady's floor, and when the man himself stepped inside, the three reporters simply rode back down with him. The elevator moved very slowly.

"How's your game?" Taibbi asked, after Borgen had made the introductions.

"Oh. Oh, pretty good, actually. Why, do you play?" Grady closed his eyes as though recognizing he'd made a mistake by inviting an actual conversation.

"I can play," Taibbi answered evenly. "Actually I used to play a lot." That was the truth. "I like to play for money." That was untrue. "Anna and I are gonna be on this story from this point on, and maybe we can get together and talk about the case so far. Off the record, not for attribution. No cameras. What's your calendar look like the next couple days?"

The elevator opened on the ground floor; Grady wanted to walk away but couldn't. He tried to extend his hand to say good-bye, but Taibbi had already turned to Phillips and was fast-talking about their own flexible schedules.

"You know," he said, "I understand they've still got the records sealed, about you recusing yourself. But if Crist is an open lead and there's a reason you couldn't pursue that lead, maybe that makes sense—"

"I can't talk about that. I *won't* talk about that."

"Yeah, I know, I know that. What I'm saying is that they're making an issue of it, in terms of the cover-up they're alleging is going on, and if there's a reason that makes sense we'd like to be able to report it. Like I said, strictly a backgrounder."

"We're really coming in late," Phillips offered. "And we've got all the time we need to check things out, to make sense of things about the case itself, about what actually happened. It's been crazy, all the other aspects about Abrams's appointment, and why won't Tawana talk and what's the latest outrageous statement by Sharpton and the lawyers. We're kind of going back to the beginning."

Grady looked at Borgen, whose face was fixed in its famous smile, but he offered no help.

"Well, I'm not really talking about it; I mean, doing interviews anymore—"

"I'm not asking for anything new," Taibbi interjected. "Nor anything necessarily on camera or on the record. But as Anna said, we're coming in late; we just want to get up to speed.

Background. Period. You know as well as anyone—maybe more than anyone else—this isn't a case where you can afford to be wrong. We just don't want to make any mistakes." He stared at the smaller man, and lit a cigarette deliberately.

"Well. Well, really, the only time I've got tomorrow is about eight in the morning. I've got meetings after that." Grady had been fending off the New York City press for months. He knew that only a dozen or so of the out-of-town reporters had committed to the story to the extent that they were staying in Dutchess County full-time, most of them at the Wyndham Hotel across the street from his office, and knew that, logistically, an interview at eight in the morning would likely be impossible for someone coming up from the city and would likely buy him time.

"I'll be there," Taibbi said quickly. "No problem. Anna may or may not be up with me, since we're not staying up here tonight and she lives out in Jersey, or she might be working another aspect of it. But as we've been telling you, we've got a lot of catching up to do. Listen," he said, shaking Grady's hand, "have a good game tonight. And think about playing me sometime. I'll throw a racquet in my truck. I'm a killer." Taibbi laughed.

Grady offered the smallest smile and a vague nod.

Borgen whipped through the end of the tour, pointing out the office of the Dutchess County sheriff; Alex's Restaurant on Market Street (where, he insisted, the best rice pudding in the Hudson Valley could be had for a song); the Wyndham Hotel, where the visiting press corps was ensconced; the Cannon Street office of lawyer David Sall, the one-day special prosecutor; and the armory of Battery A, First Battalion Artillery of the New York Army National Guard, where Bob Abrams's grand jury would consider the evidence and attempt to learn what happened to Tawana Brawley during four days in November 1987.

They were silent during the ride south on Route 9 toward Wappingers Falls. Taibbi and Phillips had had a useful tour; and they had the home number of one of Paino's mechanics and an appointment in the morning with Bill Grady. Borgen knew his own schedule would take him to the next day's already scheduled press conference by the Brawley advisers. Except for coffee and doughnuts at the Dunk, they hadn't eaten all day; but no one suggested stopping. They were heading back to the city.

Except for one more stop.

"Yeah, here's the place," Taibbi said apropos of nothing at all, pulling awkwardly into a broad parking lot. "Saw it in the rear-view mirror on the way up." The place was called ARAX Photo, and the banner advertisements in the front bay windows boasted of wedding photos and high school yearbooks. "Everybody's pretty young in this thing. I haven't seen a picture of Harry Crist. Maybe he and Masch are in some yearbook they've got on file, and Tawana from a prior year. Who knows. And besides, I want to pick up a local phone book. Give me some numbers to call when I get home tonight."

ARAX Photo didn't do the yearbooks for Ketchum High School, as it turned out. But the manager, with some amusement at the request, did give Taibbi a local phone book on the promise that he'd return it. Which he never did.

Three hours later, sitting in bed in his New York apartment, Taibbi leafed casually through the Dutchess County telephone directory, writing down the phone numbers of names familiar from the clip files, and then started making calls. As a Rutgers College freshman working the graveyard shift at the *New Brunswick Home News*, he'd been advised by his first managing editor that there was nothing like a phone call at home, at night, to loosen up a potential source. During business hours that same source would likely toe the company line or kick a reporter up to public relations, especially if he had no personal relationship with the reporter. But at night, dinner and a few drinks down, he or she would take a beat, safe and at home, and if the approach was right would often talk a blue streak, off the record and not for attribution, of course. In his newspaper days and in his early

television years, Taibbi had tried to maintain a habit of soliciting or finding home numbers and making an hour or two
of calls every night. As his reporting became more specialized the practice had itself been refined; fewer blind calls,
more calls by prior arrangement, more of what he'd labeled
"home visits." But the fundamental principle was still the
same: move your fingers, make the calls; go easy, don't pan-
der, have something to offer, listen well.

The Paino's employee helped a bit; he offered a general
denial that anybody in the Dunkin Donuts crowd had anything to do with Tawana Brawley or even knew her, and then
launched into a broadside assault against the press for ha-
rassing anyone and everyone who worked at the station. It
was the anger in his voice, from the very beginning of the
phone call, that was impressive. And, the reporter thought,
convincing.

The next few calls were strikeouts. Tom Young, the black
Poughkeepsie police officer who spoke to Tawana at St. Francis Hospital after she'd been discovered, refused to come to
the phone; the night nursing supervisor at St. Francis would
not be drawn into a conversation about the case; and Sheriff
Fred Skoralick had nothing to say on or off the record. But
Judith Hillery, the judge at the center of the story about who
quit the Brawley case, and why, stayed on the phone for a
long time, finally agreeing to a camera interview the next
day. The initial piece on the case by Taibbi and Phillips
featured the first on-camera interview with Judge Hillery,
and the first substantial explanation of why Bill Grady,
and then David Sall and William Burke, had abandoned the
case.

TAIBBI NARRATION:
*On the streets of Poughkeepsie, the Dutchess County
seat, they're nearly boiling over these days at the now
constant inferences . . . that this is a pocket of racism
where an old boy network will do anything to protect
itself, where a barbaric assault on a fifteen-year-old girl*

could never be properly or fairly investigated or prosecuted.

JUDGE HILLERY: *My feeling in talking with members of the community is that this is a matter that ought to be brought to trial. . . . It's a community that's upset about being perceived as racist.*

TAIBBI NARRATION:
Justice Judith Hillery is defensive and frustrated . . . both for herself and for her colleagues in the county legal system. It was Judge Hillery who made two key decisions, which on the surface could be seen to encourage an outsider's view of Dutchess County as a place incapable of policing itself.

First, District Attorney William Grady was allowed to remove himself from the Brawley case . . . a potential unspecified conflict of interest was the stated reason.

And then local attorney David Sall and his aide were excused from a special prosecutor's role for the same reason. Judge Hillery accepted their explanation; that the circumstances and the facts revealed "preclude us . . . and for that matter any other local attorney in this county . . . from proceeding with all possible aspects of this investigation."

JUDGE HILLERY: *There were valid legal reasons why the prosecutor couldn't proceed with the case, and there were valid legal reasons why the assigned prosecutors could not proceed with the case.*

TAIBBI NARRATION:
But we have learned that the "revealed fact" is that any local prosecutor would have been certain to have called as an alibi witness an assistant district attorney connected to one of the possible suspects in the case. . . .

Taibbi had kept his 8:00 A.M. meeting with Bill Grady, while Phillips, who'd set her alarm for 4:00 so she could make the trip with him, worked with cameraman Jim Quodomine, shooting generic cover shots along Market Street. The D.A. gave the reporter a good hour, describing his investigation in considerable detail and insisting that if he hadn't been "forced" to quit the case, he'd have brought before his grand jury "every resident of the Pavillion Apartments," if that's what it would have taken to prove or disprove Tawana Brawley's story. He would not talk about the testimony of the thirty or so witnesses who had appeared before the grand jury but, he said without animation, none had provided any evidence of an assault or rape. Taibbi stopped writing and looked up from his notebook. No, the D.A. said in answer to the unspoken question. He would not say that for the record or on camera. Was Harry Crist a suspect? the reporter asked, lighting his third cigarette of the hour. Grady paused. "I would not characterize him as a suspect. An open lead, that's all," he answered. The night before, the Paino's mechanic had said that one of Crist's friends was an assistant district attorney named Stephen Pagones and had added, angrily, that neither man even knew Tawana Brawley. Taibbi knew driving up that morning that his last question to Grady would be about Pagones and Pagones's relationship with Crist.

"About your conflict of interest, Mr. Grady," he said carefully. "If Crist is an 'open lead,' as you say, and if you have an assistant, and I'm talking about Steve Pagones, who was a friend of Crist's and a potential alibi witness, I mean, is that the conflict?"

Grady examined the fingernails of his right hand before peering steadily at the reporter sitting back casually in his chair on the other side of his desk.

"You said it, I didn't," Grady said quietly, adding immediately that he was out of time.

JUDGE JUDITH HILLERY was a pleasant middle-aged woman in a comfortable red print dress, a favorite-aunt sort for whom a role in a controversy seemed incongruous. Reluctant though she was to be interviewed on camera, she had agreed to it in her phone conversation with Taibbi. And the nonconfrontational and informed tone of both the preinterview and the recorded interview had set her at ease. There wasn't much on her calendar, she said, and the morning court session wasn't due to start for a half hour at least. It was useful, she agreed, directing her comment to Anna Phillips, for someone with standing in the community to have said what she'd said about the unfair characterizations of racism in her county. "My feeling," she said emotionally, leaning toward Phillips, "is that the people in this county who I know really want this matter resolved. If Tawana chooses not to cooperate, it will always be up in the air. It's so frustrating, hearing in the local media and now even in the national media that this is a racist area. But I *know* the KKK is not active in this area, not anymore. A long time ago there was some activity. I remember reading about it when I was in law school, and then again when there were riots in the sixties. But that was twenty years ago; there's been nothing since then, nothing. If something happened to Tawana Brawley, she has to talk, she has to. If she doesn't, the case could die; but it would never go away. . . ." The judge seemed genuinely overwrought at her own words. Phillips shook her head sympathetically. Taibbi chose the moment to stand up, reaching for his hat.

"Excuse me. Anna, I'll see you downstairs in a bit. There's someone else I want to see, and he's got an appointment at ten." He extended his hand to the judge, who shook it warmly. "Your Honor. Thanks for talking with us. We really appreciate it."

As he left he heard his partner continue the conversation with Judge Hillery. People just like Anna, he thought to himself. They just do.

"So why did Sall quit?" he heard Phillips asking, her voice so pleasant and unthreatening. "That part I don't understand. I mean we know something about Grady's conflict, that's why we didn't press you on it in the interview. . . ."

IT WAS ONLY three blocks to David Sall's office. Taibbi had called after his talk with Grady, and Sall's secretary had indeed told him that Sall had a 10:00 A.M. appointment. The lawyer was still seated at his desk when Taibbi was ushered in. He was free in the afternoon, Sall said, mild suspicion in his voice. One o'clock would be fine. No camera, of course.

Back on Market Street, Taibbi rejoined cameraman Jim Quodomine and did several versions of a stand-up bridge, the on-camera segment of his report. It was only when he finished his last take that he noticed he was without his shoulder bag, the all-purpose satchel he used to carry notebooks and files, maps and receipts, a tape recorder, an earpiece, a beeper and spare batteries, and all the other flotsam of a television reporter's life. Absent-minded to an impressive degree, Taibbi was always misplacing a notebook, his wallet, or the bag itself, and Phillips had learned that part of the job was to pick up after him. It was not, she pointed out frequently, an endearing quality. Quodomine told him Phillips was still up in the judge's chambers.

In fact, Phillips and Judge Hillery had been joined by a court stenographer, who'd been summoned by the judge and who, as Taibbi entered the room, was reading from her own notes. The reading stopped while Phillips introduced Taibbi to the stenographer and then explained what was going on.

"Judge Hillery doesn't have a copy of David Sall's letter, but it was entered into the record and she agreed to have it read to us."

Taibbi wanted to smile, but did not. "Forgot my bag," he said instead.

"I know," Phillips answered sarcastically. "I was going to bring it down. What else is new. . . ?"

THEIR FIRST STORY put Taibbi and Phillips on the board in the way they wanted, an incremental advance in the story with some new material, off-camera entrées to Bill Grady and David Sall, and the unexpected interview with Judge Hillery. But their first effort was obscured by explosive developments away from the center of the case and an intensification right to the flashpoint of the rhetoric flying from the Brawley team. That same day, February 28, the lead story by Chris Borgen and by every other news organization was the arrest of Samuel Evans, a printing machine operator in the New York office of Attorney General Bob Abrams, for the theft of a copy of 200 pages of testimony from the now-defunct Dutchess County grand jury that had been investigating the Brawley case. Evans, a forty-nine-year-old black man, had stolen several documents, including the copy of the grand jury transcript, out of "curiosity," according to Manhattan District Attorney Robert Morgenthau. Abrams admitted his embarrassment and responsibility, emphasized that Evans had made no effort to sell or distribute the transcript, and insisted the arrest would not affect his own investigation in any way whatsoever since he was impaneling his own grand jury the following Monday. According to some news accounts Evans, who'd resigned his printer's job two weeks before the arrest, was turned in by a homosexual lover to whom he'd shown the documents.

"A disturbing and unfortunate development," Abrams said of the whole episode. "But it won't compromise our probe at all." He added that the stolen material contained very few details not already disclosed in the press.

To the Brawley advisers, however, the arrest of "the Special Prosecutor's printer" added fuel to their already fiery rhetoric. Calling again for the resignation of Bob Abrams as special prosecutor, a constant theme in the last week of February, Sharpton fairly shouted at the inevitable news conference: "This underscores the ineptness and incompetence that we've been talking about. It's a sad commentary that this is the third prosecutor and they only seem able to prosecute themselves or a member of their staffs."

On Sunday, February 27, the Brawley trio pushed even harder. After leading a thousand bused-in New Yorkers through the streets of Poughkeepsie in a "Day of Outrage" demonstration, Sharpton grabbed the bullhorn and addressed the crowd pressing close in front of the Dutchess County sheriff's office. Claiming that the advisers "and everybody else" knew the identity of "all six of Tawana's attackers," Sharpton issued a challenge to Gov. Mario Cuomo.

"Deputize Maddox," he shouted as wet snow began to fall. "Name him special prosecutor. Give Maddox the power and we'll lock up all six men by six o'clock tomorrow. You say you'll do anything, Cuomo? Well, do that!"

The crowd began shouting, "Maddox! Maddox! Maddox!" Clenched fists were raised high, in the thickening snowstorm, and the chorus built to an ear-splitting pitch. "No Justice, No Peace! No Justice, No Peace!" Maddox took the bullhorn. He said it was a fact that "the governor of this state does not believe in equal protection under the law," and then he too addressed the governor.

"When we come to you, Governor Cuomo, we come to you with hate in our eyes. We come to you with hate in our hearts. We come to you with hate in our minds. We come to you with hate for all of the wicked things your people have done to us. We are not a happy people. You are not dealing with foot-shufflers when you deal with us."

It was an extraordinary statement, even by the standards already established by the Brawley team. But the statement, and the huge rally itself, had little if anything to do with the question of what had happened to Tawana Brawley. In terms of apparent news value, the claim by the advisers that they knew the identity of all *six* of the teenager's attackers stood out; prior to that day they'd said only that Tawana had described in detail *one* of her attackers, and in their series of news conferences they'd implied that certain individuals or groups were "connected" to the attack. Until the rally in Poughkeepsie, they had never claimed to know the whole story. Still, they offered nothing in the way of proof or evidence, or even the suggestion of either, to the scores of reporters and photographers who trudged along with the marchers and then stood in the snow for an hour of impassioned declamation.

TAIBBI AND PHILLIPS CHOSE not to cover the rally, though each flipped the channels and scoured the print accounts and was duly impressed by the tone of the advisers' assault and the evidently powerful support of their followers. Committed to working away from the story's center, the reporters stayed away. They followed their initial report on the abandoning of the case by Bill Grady and David Sall with a status report on the investigation and then a sidebar to Chris Borgen's lead story on the February 28 seating of Bob Abrams's special grand jury.

Then, on the first day of March, David Sall tossed an answering machine cassette tape across his desk, Taibbi caught it and pocketed it, and the story—and Channel 2's role in the story—changed irrevocably.

4

"Don't shoot your dog, Mike. . . ."

MOST OF THE NEW YORK REPORTERS in the mainstream press, particularly in local television, waded into the Tawana Brawley story knowing next to nothing about the true leaders at the grass roots of the troubled minority communities of the city. That lack of knowledge was surprising in some ways, because race issues and incendiary, headline-generating stories with racial overtones had proliferated in the mid-1980s to the point where a contextual grounding in New York's racial dynamics should have been a résumé requirement for every working reporter in town.

Starting with the 1983 case of Michael Stewart, the black photographer and graffiti artist who died of multiple trauma after an alleged beating by New York City transit cops, there was hardly a day when a story or follow-up story on some controversial incident of race-based violence against a minority victim was not lurking in some editor's mind, aching for the front page. Stewart's death was followed by the shooting of Eleanor Bumpurs, a Bronx grandmother who allegedly brandished a knife and a jar of lye in the direction of a squad of Emergency Service cops who then loosed not one but two shotgun blasts, killing her instantly. Bumpurs's death was followed by the shooting of four black youths by Bernhard Goetz, the so-called "Subway Gunman," who whipped out an unregistered pistol and fired away when he perceived the youths were about to rob him. The emblem of the Goetz case was the moment when Goetz, scanning his already shot and bleeding victims, said to one of them, in a burst of pent-up hatred and fear, ". . . You don't look so bad. Have another."

Then Edmund Perry, who escaped Harlem for an interlude at Phillips Exeter Academy and was headed for Stamford University, was gunned down in self-defense by a cop who knew only he'd caught and then restrained an armed robber. Michael Griffith was chased onto the Belt Parkway in Brooklyn and killed when he was struck by a car; Griffith and three friends had been attacked and routed by a pack of white youths who objected to the presence of blacks at a Howard Beach pizza stand. Yvonne Smallwood, a black woman from the Bronx, died mysteriously while in police custody. Those incidents, just a partial list, all became part of a "running story": in the 1980s the withering away or outright elimination of the entitlement programs that had supported an uneasy racial peace for more than a decade awakened the slumbering beast of racial antagonism, and the beast was hungry again.

But the New York version of the running story was itself part of the problem. Despite the constriction of the radio news industry (only the two all-news AM stations, WCBS-News Radio 88 and WINS, maintained what could be called fully staffed working newsrooms) and the shrinking number of newspaper editions, New York was a ruthlessly competitive news town. With four major metropolitan dailies, six local television stations, dozens of special-interest publications and broadcast outlets, two domestic and several foreign wire services and their broadcast operations—and more than 3,200 people at a given moment carrying official NYPD press cards— the battle to stay on top, particularly with an ongoing story, was waged in small advances often framed in garish or overstated promotions and headlines. The *Post's* "Headless Body in Topless Bar" front page established the competitive imperative: bring 'em into the tent, we'll find something to say. Yes, the question of racial violence, of escalating violence directed toward minorities with racism as the fuel, was a legitimate running story. But a press corps whose engine was the tabloid mentality or the world view of local television news had time and patience only for the headline, for the pitchman's wail that would get 'em into the tent.

And the pitchman who wailed the loudest, and who came to own more of the tabloid headlines and more of the precious minutes of exposure on local TV newscasts, was the Wonder Boy Preacher himself, by way of Brooklyn and Tilden High School, Alfred C. Sharpton.

In a brilliant analytical piece in the *Village Voice* in March, Playthell Benjamin, an activist himself, asserted that Sharpton had "bogarted" the civil rights movement in New York from the moment it became clear that key elements in the news media were more than willing to provide air time and column inches. Swooping in from the margins of events and demonstrations orchestrated by authentic activists, Benjamin wrote, Sharpton was hip to the red tally light that meant the camera was on, and knew precisely that when the huddled reporters, mostly white reporters, stopped talking to each other and tossed away their empty coffee cups and began scanning the scene for the story peg, it was time to smooth his pompadour, grab the nearest bullhorn, and start orating. And, as an orator, especially when he knew the mainstream media and their cameras and tape recorders were in attendance, Sharpton could be . . . well, scintillating. His speech-making style was a calculated pastiche of the verbal iconography of the black church and the buzzwords of the established movement, the cadences and inevitable cre-scendo in each performance crafted, often masterfully, toward a denouement and final exclamation that seemed pure rage: the rage of the victim, of the truly afflicted.

"The danger," Benjamin wrote, "resides in his ability to excite the emotions of his black audiences and the irrespon-sible ends to which he uses this gift. His hyperbolic tech-nique works like pouring salt into open wounds—it is unrestrained preachment that produces a gut response unin-formed by reflection. But like all charismatic leaders, Sharp-ton's appeal lies in the perception that he embodies his audience's pain and aspirations and that he is unafraid to speak the truth to powerful enemies."

So Al Sharpton, or "Rev'rnd Al," a nearly comic figure in his implausible sweatsuits or some other electric ensemble, ended up being portrayed as *the* spokesman for the civil rights movement in New York City. Most of the white reporters who gathered round him knew he was not taken seriously by movement veterans, who lacked his oratorical gift and, in fact, granted him his point-man status by the plain absence of public challenge. Were they approving, or merely timo-rous, or in cynical private agreement that whatever his ex-cesses, the Wonder Boy's hyperbolic personality served the greater good? Wrong question, not the story for the headline writers. They wanted "events" and "incidents," and a spokesman who made for good copy. The minister with the Martin Luther King, Jr., medallion flapping against his breastplate was a glove fit for the role of spokesman. After all, Sharpton knew about reporters' deadlines, knew what got over, spoke the modern language of soundbite. He was, and this was important, an engaging and terrifically funny guy away from the cameras. He was an easier hit for a rushed reporter than those activists who quietly organized tenant associations in places you couldn't get to or didn't want to get to, who put together citizen patrols, or who battled to stem the onrushing tide of the drug plague and the outgoing tide of supportive entitlement programs: activists who disdained the cheap celebrity and free "publicity" offered by the white-controlled press, who couldn't—or wouldn't—be reached with a simple phone call. No, everything about Al Sharpton was . . . *easy.* Convenient. And starting with the Goetz case, he was everywhere, it seemed. A viewer of local TV news or a reader of the city's newspapers could not have been unaware of him. In the aftermath of the killing of Michael Griffith and through the months of the Brawley case, Sharpton became, undeniably, one of the most widely recognizable figures in New York City.

And, astoundingly, he confounded his most virulent critics by surviving the ultimate scandal: *Newsday* and the *Village Voice* had revealed in late January 1988 that Al Sharpton was an informant for the FBI and the federal government. His confederates included known mob figures, and his targets (politicians and individuals from the worlds of entertainment and boxing, including promoter Don King) were *other blacks.* An informant with a tapped phone and a briefcase bug, Sharpton, it would later be learned, wore a body wire on more than a dozen occasions when he met or sat at lunches with his targets, the G-men standing by, earpieces in place. When the revelations of Sharpton's secret life as an informant hit home, Benjamin wrote, the rotund minister was "virtually banned by serious activists at a mass meeting held at the Harriet Tubman School in Harlem. The theme of the Tubman meeting was, 'Can a black leader serve the community and be an agent of the state?' The consensus was that it was not possible, and 'the police never wire you up once,' and, therefore, 'once a snitch always a snitch.' We left the meeting chanting, 'I'm wired up and can't tape no more' [a sardonic takeoff on the popular movement chant 'I'm fired up and won't take no more'], a slogan aimed right at Sharpton."

But Sharpton survived because attorneys Maddox and Mason stood with him as the advisers to Tawana Brawley. And the same press corps that had incubated, then nurtured, then been nurtured and manipulated by a figure of pure self-invention stood by Sharpton still; the reporters wanted the Brawley story, and to get it they'd have to go through Reverend Al.

ON MARCH 1, 1988, Mike Taibbi and Anna Phillips were keenly aware that the allegations spewing almost daily from Al Sharpton and attorneys Maddox and Mason were often reckless, sometimes laughable, and never substantiated. Nonetheless, except for a single, careful statement two days earlier by Brooklyn Assemblyman Roger Green protesting an especially egregious verbal torching by Sharpton—a statement pounced upon for its poor timing and intemperate insinuation not only by the advisers but by others in the leadership of the black community—no one challenged the Brawley team directly. The Tawana Brawley story already had its own niche in the folklore and mythology of the civil rights movement; and, as a story, it was simply too explosive, too horrible, and yet too believable for anyone of prominence in the black community to question.

A week earlier, Governor Cuomo had issued a press release stating it was time for Tawana to talk. "I understand the Attorney General has full and complete control of this investigation," Cuomo's statement read. "Nonetheless I believe [he] should ask the Grand Jury to require all those likely to have relevant evidence—including Tawana and her family—to cooperate fully with the investigation. The best thing for Tawana Brawley and the people of this state is to get to the truth of this matter. Unless we change our present course, I am afraid that we will not achieve this objective." The governor added, ominously, that unless the Brawley advisers responded positively to "obligations to the system which they cannot escape," including cooperating with Abrams, there were "remedies" available to the prosecuting attorney.

Sharpton, in Albany pushing his campaign to oust Abrams as special prosecutor, shouted for the cameras and reporters who had followed him north that there was "no way" Tawana Brawley would cooperate with an investigation headed by Bob Abrams.

"That's like asking someone who watched someone killed in the gas chamber to sit down with Mr. Hitler," he added, knowing the quote would lead every news account of his otherwise futile trip to the state capital.

Roger Green's sin was not to shake his head in disgust and embarrassment at the latest Sharpton outburst, as so many other prominent blacks had taken to doing habitually, but to do so in public, however carefully and only after some hard personal lobbying by Cuomo himself. It was "intellectually dishonest" to make such a statement about Abrams, Green said. He criticized Sharpton's "cavalier use of words like 'racism' and 'fascism,' " and warned against the use of "tactics that encourage race war" rather than needed coalition. Having shot his wad, Green declined to say whether *he* thought Tawana should cooperate with Abrams, and did not criticize Maddox or Mason at all. But he'd placed himself in the line of fire nonetheless, and Sharpton didn't even have to summon the obedient press corps to begin firing away. Everybody had called him.

Branding him another "Uncle Tom, a state pawn," Sharpton claimed, implausibly, that Green was "afraid the minister would challenge him for his Assembly seat." Sharpton's lethal blow drove Green from the news for the duration of the Brawley case: "He's obviously doing bidding for his sponsors. When you have a 16-year-old girl raped and maimed and sodomized, for Roger to attack the defenders of the girl and not attack those who attacked the girl, that shows where Roger's heart lies as an apologist for the system."

Not a single black leader in New York rose to Roger Green's

defense. In fact, Green almost lost his position as head of the Black and Hispanic Legislative Caucus. Sharpton's word, his unedited, unsubstantiated, and mass-communicated word, was the last word. Again.

DRIVING UP TO POUGHKEEPSIE that brisk and sunny March 1, Taibbi and Phillips had no idea that within forty-eight hours they would become Sharpton's next target. Their general plan for the day was to try and turn a 1:00 P.M. appointment with Lorraine Jackson-Ordia into an on-camera interview that would once again advance the story, even minimally. Jackson-Ordia, chairperson of the Dutchess County Committee Against Racism, had been the source of a potentially explosive story by reporter Billy House in the *Poughkeepsie Journal* on February 19. Tawana, according to Jackson-Ordia (who was unnamed in the original story), had scribbled a cryptic note while waiting in the lobby of a doctor's office at the Westchester Medical Center in Valhalla three days after she'd been discovered. "I want him dead. I want Skoralick," the teenager had supposedly written, an apparent reference to the Dutchess County sheriff. Four days later, with Taibbi and Phillips among those attending a press conference by the Brawley advisers at the Baptist Temple church in Newburgh, Jackson-Ordia had nudged her account a tantalizing step further.

"I was with Tawana when she wrote the note," she said. "I was the only one who saw her write it." She said no more, took no questions, willingly surrendered the podium to the three advisers. When the press conference ended and the dozens of reporters present crowded Sharpton, Mason, and Maddox, Phillips went directly to Jackson-Ordia, a black woman approximately her age. They traded phone numbers, spoke later by phone in three separate conversations, and agreed on an early afternoon appointment for the next day. Jackson-Ordia's morning was already booked: she was to be one of the first witnesses to be formally interviewed by the newly formed Brawley Task Force, the team of eight prosecutors and twelve investigators put together by Bob Abrams. Arriving in Poughkeepsie before 9:00 A.M., Taibbi and Phillips first linked up with Chris Borgen and his cameraman, Don Janney, who had their own tentative appointment with Todd McGue, the Short Lines bus driver who had supposedly dropped Tawana off in front of Paino's Mobil Station the night of her disappearance. Everybody would meet at the Wyndham for a noon lunch and compare notes, it was agreed.

"What are you two going to go for this morning?" Borgen asked amiably, shedding his topcoat in the surprisingly mild air.

"We thought we'd try Sall," Phillips answered. "We met him last week, actually Mike went back for a second meeting, and though he had a lot of complaints about a number of other reporters, he seemed to like us well enough. Must have been Taibbi's jokes; he had him falling out of his chair."

"Good, good," Borgen said. "Sall's all right. And he won't have disliked your story on why he quit the case."

David Sall did not stand to greet the Channel 2 reporters when they were ushered into his office. He accepted their handshakes and motioned them to the chairs on the other side of his desk. Taibbi tried his latest lawyer joke (though he was not a funny man, he had collected jokes for years and serviced his repertoire with a workable memory; he had jokes in every conceivable category and in a range of colors, and he'd even developed a nearly dependable sense of timing and propriety). Sall laughed politely. Head pinched down on his neck and the smoke from his ever-present Marlboro curling upward from his dense mustache, he seemed to be a man in a quiet rage who hadn't yet decided whether to vent any of that rage on two relative strangers. Taibbi launched another joke, better and sharper than the first; Phillips cackled aloud— even she hadn't heard that one. Sall laughed heartily this time, and the conversation turned quickly to the Brawley case and flowed easily. Whenever Sall seemed to be directing a comment or an answer to her partner, Phillips took advantage of the break and studied the office in quick focused glances, looking for clues that would reveal something about the man in front of her. She studied the military citations and plaques and medals on the walls and on several shelves—to "the Prosecutor," Capt. David B. Sall, Nürnberg District, 1980, read one army citation; another saluted his marine service as Lance Corporal David Sall, 1970. The marines *and* the army, she noted—and then she studied Sall himself.

He was tense or *intense;* she couldn't tell which. Stocky and with his necktie pulled up tight, Sall spoke in clipped, measured sentences. No casual asides. Not a comfortable man. He had held on to a fair amount of his military bearing; Phillips was not surprised when he started talking about his years as an assistant district attorney in Brooklyn. If David Sall was going to be a lawyer, she thought, he'd be a prosecutor. She looked around the office again, with its dark, nondescript paneling and modest, well-used furniture. He hadn't been in Poughkeepsie long, he said. Started out in the public defender's office, and a year earlier had joined another local attorney in private practice. A public defender? Phillips thought. And now defending small-time clients in sleepy Dutchess County, working out of an office that was hardly an advertisement for a brilliant career? Well, she thought: he's a man's man, that's for sure. Maybe someone who, like herself, had simply decided to leave the city and its urban mess for a quieter life-style. But I'm not sure he could have handled the Brawley case as special prosecutor, she thought, listening as Taibbi worked the ex-marine; he'd slipped comfortably into lawyers' jargon, a device that often excluded her but one she'd come to recognize as a sign that her partner was coming close. Phillips asked one more question of Sall—why, she wanted to know, were there military mementos from both the marines and the army?

Sall laughed. "Because I served in both," he said. "Really.

I reenlisted in the army after I'd left the marines. Went to Germany. I was a military prosecutor."

Phillips shook her head in genuine surprise and then, too obviously she thought to herself, glanced at her watch.

"Mike, gotta go. I've got that ten o'clock."

Taibbi nodded. Phillips turned to Sall and made her apologies. She'd sensed, as her partner had, that if Sall had anything at all, he was ready to give it up. In a synergism that had been surprising in its swift development, she knew and knew Taibbi knew when one of them was going to be the designated receiver. The week before, he'd left her with Judge Hillery, who'd summoned the court stenographer and quoted from Sall's resignation letter. She'd worked Jackson-Ordia. He had Sall. It was just as Taibbi had said from the beginning of their relationship: a partnership works when the whole is bigger than the sum of its parts. Only then. Theirs was working, she thought, heading toward Market Street and the Armory, where the Task Force was bent to its task and her afternoon appointment was being grilled, for the record.

SALL HAD MENTIONED a case he'd taken on involving a Vietnam veteran, and lumbered over to a shelf to retrieve a small leather box containing some medals and combat ribbons. He described them in detail.

"He's got the fucking Navy Cross," he said. "You know how many Navy Cross winners there are? Not much more than the fucking Congressional Medal of Honor," he said, not waiting for an answer.

"If he's got post-traumatic stress from Vietnam, you've got a defense against the original complaint," Taibbi offered, locked into his man. "There's ample precedent—"

"Sure, sure," Sall answered, lovingly replacing the medals and ribbons in their box. "But he failed to answer on a fucking DWI, and they picked him up on a fugitive warrant. I'm telling you this guy's a basket case. He's been extradited here and I've talked to him, I've talked to them, they're playing hardball."

"So what're you gonna do?"

Sall tapped the ash from his Marlboro, and kept tapping it well after the last ash had dropped.

"Watch."

He dialed the number for the assistant D.A. on the other side of Market Street who was prosecuting the case, and simply whiplashed him. Toward the end of the short conversation, which was heavy on the war hero angle and the combat stress problem, every charge against his client had been dropped except for the original complaint for DWI. Sall worked for a deal.

"You plead the fucking thing down, you give him time served, you're a hero," Sall said into the phone, an air of performance in his voice. Taibbi wondered if that was just Sall's style, the hard way honed in Brooklyn. "This guy's no criminal, and you know the original case is a piece of shit anyway. C'mon, you got better things to do, I got better things to do." He listened for a few seconds. "All right. All right. The guy can go for that, he'll take the plea and walk. I've talked to his mother, too. You're a fucking hero."

The phone in its cradle, Sall turned to his audience and spread his hands.

"See?"

Taibbi nodded with what he hoped was an expression of approval and respect.

"So what's got you so pissed off about the Brawley thing?" the reporter asked after a discreet interval. "You're out of it, and except for our story last week you haven't even been in the press that much lately. It's Grady they're after, mostly. But you looked like you were ready to blow when we came in."

Sall blinked deliberately and pressed his lips together in stern concentration. When his lips parted, the teeth behind them were clenched. It seemed forever before he finally spoke, and when he did his voice was a rasp of suppressed rage.

"Fucking Maddox," he hissed. "These guys . . . he and Mason. They're fucking lawyers. Lawyers! I'm a lawyer! They come up here over the weekend . . . I came in to see them. Hear what they had to say. And they lie! They just fucking lie! Yeah, Maddox is going to be the special prosecutor, that's what Sharpton says. The special prosecutor? And he's a vicious liar?"

"What was the lie?" Taibbi asked, leaning back deliberately.

Sall shook his head. "How many do you want to hear about? There's the stuff about the case itself. The *incident*," he said sarcastically. "Listen, they say she was raped and maimed and beaten? Forced to give oral sex to six men in the woods, for four days. In the woods! You think they're gonna lay her down gently, on a mattress or something? Uh uh. It's gonna be, 'Down, bitch!' "

Sall thrust his right hand in a violent downward motion, pantomiming the act. He leaned over his desk, and Taibbi bent forward to listen. Sall's voice was almost a whisper.

"There was nothing on her pants, her clothes, her skin. No dirt, grass, stains, twigs, you name it."

He paused to let it sink in. Taibbi wondered whether Sall was talking from hearsay—what he'd heard in courthouse scuttlebutt—or from his direct knowledge of the evidence. He decided against asking Sall about the source of his knowledge. Keep him talking, was the rule.

"That's lie number one," Sall said, sitting back. "Then, six white men, including cops. They know who the cops are, they can arrest everybody by sundown. You think six guys wouldn't be missed for four days over the Thanksgiving holiday? Or that someone wouldn't break? C'mon . . ."

That last bit of speculation was common enough, Taibbi pointed out. It had even appeared in the recent chronology accounts in the *New York Times* and the *Poughkeepsie Journal*, accounts that explored the questions and contradictions in the evolving version of the Tawana Brawley story.

"What else?" Taibbi prodded. "Why are you spitting about Maddox in particular?"

"I felt like . . ." Sall started, then collected himself to start again. "If I'd have come face to face with him, I would have decked him. I was that furious. Here he is, a lawyer, and he's talking about me quitting because I'm part of his fucking cover-up. One lawyer about another? Where the fuck does he come off? This guy shouldn't even be a lawyer, he's such a fucking liar! He's telling this big crowd, with all the cameras there, about how I did this and did that, part of the fucking cover-up—"

"So say it," Taibbi injected quickly. "Get on camera. I've got a crew down at the Wyndham. Say these guys are lying. Say there's no evidence, if you know that to be true, that she was forced to give oral sex to six guys in the woods. Use the camera. Fight fire with fire."

Sall worked his jaw, then slowly shook his head from side to side. Suddenly, he stood up. "C'mon. You wanna prove they're lying? C'mon."

He grabbed his topcoat and led Taibbi out of his office. He said nothing as he walked, with the reporter at his side, down Cannon Street to Market, where he turned right. Fifty yards up Market he turned without comment into one of the three banks on the block, greeted an assistant manager by name, and asked for the key to his safe deposit box. Taibbi stayed behind on the main floor and waited for Sall to return. They walked back to the office, still in silence, sat again, not talking. Sall reached into his inside lapel pocket and extracted an envelope. He showed the face of the envelope to Taibbi. It said, "Glenda Brawley message, January 21st." He pulled a microcassette from the envelope and placed it in his answering machine. Finally, he spoke.

"You know how they've always said it's the family that

decided not to cooperate with any investigation, the *family* never wanted to talk? The papers have quoted 'em, it's been on TV?"

Taibbi nodded. It had been a consistent position of the Brawley advisers that they were only following the wishes of the family, that it was the *family*—Tawana and her mother, Glenda, particularly—who chose at all points to decline to be interviewed by a prosecutor.

"I was prosecutor for a day," Sall said. "Remember? First thing I did, I called the house. I get Glenda. Sure, she and Tawana would be happy to come in. Very pleasant. No problem, none of this 'I've got to check with my lawyer' stuff. I come in early the next morning, and I get this. Listen." He pushed the play button on the answering machine.

David . . . this is Glenda Brawley, Tawana's mother. Uh, I'd like to cancel our appointment for in the morning. We're advised by our lawyers to hold off on doing anything as of right now. Ah . . . if you have any questions feel free to call me at home tonight or first thing in the morning. Thank you.

"Could you play it again?" Taibbi asked. He took out his notebook and tried to get it word for word in his own awkward shorthand. "Again," he said when it was over. "I want to listen to her tone of voice."

Glenda Brawley sounded friendly, sounded as if she was truly sorry that she and Tawana would not be coming in and that they had fully intended to meet with David Sall.

"Pretty interesting," Taibbi said lamely. He was trying to remember which articles from Jean Harper's clip file had included quotes from the advisers asserting that the family had chosen at all points not to cooperate. He remembered one piece from the *Times*. A few weeks ago, he thought.

Sall had taken the tape from the machine and replaced it in its envelope, which he smoothed deliberately in his large hands. He studied the reporter, seemed to be thinking hard. Taibbi said nothing; to ask outright would have gotten him nowhere, he gauged. It would have to be Sall's decision. Taibbi lit a cigarette. So did Sall.

"You'd really like to have this, wouldn't you?" Sall said after a small eternity. Taibbi just stared at him, intently. "What would you do with it, if I gave it to you?"

"I'd put it on television," the reporter answered quickly. "I would *not* say where I got it, though that doesn't matter. You'd have broken no law, and we wouldn't have either. It's a one-party taped conversation, legal in New York, and besides, she knows she's talking to an answering machine. She's not your client, there's no privilege. I didn't steal it. I couldn't be compelled to disclose its source."

Taibbi paused, dragged deeply on his cigarette before tamping it out in the stand ashtray beside him. He looked at Sall, whose eyes were wide open, unblinking.

"And you'd have made your point. If they lie, but you don't want to climb on camera and point the finger, let the tape show it. It's irrefutable; we have their quotes, we'd have Glenda on tape."

Sall's jaw was working again. He took the cassette out of the envelope, held it up to his eyes as though the tape itself would provide his answer. Then he tossed it across the desk. Taibbi caught it, slipped it in his blazer's inside pocket, and continued to stare at Sall.

"Return it," the one-day special prosecutor said simply.

"No problem," the reporter answered. He did not say thanks.

HALFWAY THROUGH LUNCH, Phillips looked up from her desultory plate of cheese fajitas and saw her partner striding toward the table. He was wearing his catbird grin as he pulled out a chair, waved a hello to Borgen and Janney, and then placed the cassette beside her.

"It's Glenda calling to cancel an appointment she and Tawana had made with Sall," he explained. "They were gonna meet with him, but her attorneys advised her to cancel."

"So what's the big deal?" Janney interrupted. Intellectually finicky and contentious by nature, Janney had been working the story with Borgen from the second day, and believed that Tawana had been assaulted. He'd been surprised that on his second visit to the Brawley apartment with Borgen, Tawana had asked the reporter, "Did you bring me anything?" and had also asked pointblank, "How much money [Borgen made] and how much money Borgen [had with him]." But Janney had written it off to the uniqueness of the circumstance, to a child's natural curiosity in the material age. He looked at Taibbi. "It's splitting hairs," he said.

But Phillips needed no further explanation. She surmised instantly that she and Taibbi had in their possession the first material evidence that it was the attorneys who were advising the family against cooperating, and that the family—Glenda and Tawana if the tape Taibbi had backed it up—wanted at least at one key point to cooperate but had been pulled back. Phillips knew that she and Taibbi would be putting a story on the air that would directly contradict a key claim by the Brawley advisers. Except for the advisers' counterattack on Roger Green, she had no frame of reference for what their response would be. A lot of people had doubts about Tawana Brawley's story, and certainly about the advisers' handling of the case: but no reporter had yet said directly that the Brawley advisers lied.

THEY RACED THROUGH the rest of the afternoon, grateful at the end of it that they'd obtained nothing else of consequence. Lorraine Jackson-Ordia seemed to be unduly taken with the importance of her own role in the case, but offered nothing new about Tawana's "I want Skoralick" note. She spent a great deal of time talking about other, unrelated racial incidents in the county, concentrating on the series of

complaints filed by an elderly black Wappingers Falls woman
named Elaine Disnuke. Disnuke, Jackson-Ordia asserted
emotionally, had been the target of a campaign of racial harassment that included incidents in which her windows had
been shot through, her house fire-bombed, and even a ma-
chete rigged diabolically over her front door to descend, le-
thally, the first time she left her own home. But in the middle
of her recitation Jackson-Ordia paused; she was horrified, she
said suddenly, that Phillips had brought Taibbi to the meeting and had a camera crew waiting outside. Her reaction puzzled Phillips, who had said clearly the night before that she'd
be bringing her partner along—you know, she'd said, that
tall guy with the beard who was at the press conference?—
and was hoping to find an aspect of the case that Jackson-
Ordia would be comfortable discussing on camera. There was
nothing, the woman said now, that she could even conceive
of discussing on camera. It would later turn out that investigators never confirmed the existence of the note and came
to doubt its existence.

As it happened, Jackson-Ordia lived directly across the street
from the headquarters of the Dutchess County sheriff. Taibbi
decided to try Skoralick, on his own. He'd done thousands of
police beat stories in his twenty-one years as a reporter, and
if he didn't automatically like cops, he got along all right
with them and certainly knew the lingo. Skoralick would not
let Taibbi beyond the secure waiting area, but he leaned
against the wall and talked for a half hour. He had his doubts
about Tawana's story; had 'em from the beginning, the gangly
sheriff said. Taibbi probed around the edges of the case, asked
specifically about the suggestion that there was no physical
evidence that Tawana had been sexually assaulted in the
woods, and got nowhere; Skoralick was out of it, he was tired
of talking about it and even more tired of hearing about it.
In fact, with his lined face and slumping carriage, he looked
plain tired. The reporter tried another gambit, a slightly risky
one; he told Skoralick he and his partner were going to put a

story on the air in the next day or so that would portray the advisers as liars, at least on one key point. "Well," the sheriff said, in something like a drawl. "I'll be watching, I'm sure."

IT WAS NIGHTFALL by the time Phillips and Taibbi got back to the Broadcast Center on West Fifty-seventh Street. They headed immediately into Paul Sagan's office to brief the news director on the story they were prepared to air. Taibbi lingered, talking about Sall and reviewing the potential problems that Legal would have to pass on. Phillips headed to the planning desk, grabbed a set-up sheet, rolled it into a typewriter carriage, and began to type.

"Paul," she said, getting the attention of the planning editor, Paul Fleuranges. "You got anything daybooked for tomorrow for C. Vernon Mason, or Maddox?"

Fleuranges pulled out the green oak-tag file he used to track the schedules of every known newsmaker in the tristate area, flipped to the page for March 2, and ran his finger down the list.

"Bronx Supreme, Mason. Nine A.M.," he said. "The Theodore Carelock case. Black educator from the Bronx who was beaten by cops, he says, on the way home at four A.M."

"I'm booking a crew for Taibbi, to be there *before* nine," she said without looking up from her typing.

"What've you got?" Fleuranges asked. A young veteran in the newsroom who often chafed at his inside role, he always wanted to know the details of every story.

"Good one," Phillips answered. "I think we'll score with it."

PRETRIAL MOTIONS in the Carelock case were being heard in a basement courtroom at Bronx Supreme. Taibbi scrambled when the courthouse opened to get permission to bring his cameraman, Boris Grgurovic, inside the building. The reporter sat in the front row and tried to get Vernon Mason's attention during the early breaks in the arguments. But Mason ignored him steadfastly, not even acknowledging his presence. The morning wore on; at one point, during a ten-minute recess, Taibbi commiserated in the hallway with Howard Manley, the young *Newsday* reporter who'd been covering the Carelock case and who shared Taibbi's passion for pro basketball. They talked hoop a bit, Manley fired off a few digs at Taibbi's enthusiasm for the aging Boston Celtics, and shared a laugh when Taibbi related the characterization of the Celtics as "South Africa's Team" by a friend, *Boston Globe* basketball beat writer Bob Ryan.

"What've they got now?" Manley asked. "Seven white guys?" Manley, a player himself once and even taller than Taibbi's six-three, happened to be black.

"No, Fred Roberts makes eight." Taibbi lit a cigarette, offered one to Manley. "Howard, you know I'm not covering this case. But tell me about Mason. From his arguments inside, he sounds like a pretty good attorney. I've heard him before, just stopping in on cases I wasn't covering. He knows his cites, he's concise enough when he wants to be. The judge seems to respect him as a lawyer. I like to hear how lawyers work—"

"Yeah, Mason's good," Manley said. "He does know his stuff, and he's got a good case here. But if you're talking about Brawley . . ."

"I'm talking about Brawley. But about Mason, too."

"Well." Manley dragged on his cigarette, then dropped it to the floor and stamped it out. "I don't know. I haven't been covering the Brawley case. But it seems like it's crazy, out of control."

A court officer opened the courtroom doors. The judge had returned to the bench.

"It's gonna get crazier," Taibbi said.

Mason never spoke to Taibbi inside the courtroom, ignoring the reporter's questions and the request for a few minutes after the hearing. When the judge called suddenly for an adjournment of the day's arguments, Taibbi left the court-room ahead of everyone else, alerting Grgurovic to fire up his camera. He sprinted through the corridor that led to the judge's chambers at the front of the courtroom and was told by a court officer that attorneys only exited through the public doors in the back. Taibbi returned to the public doors and waited. No Mason. He waited several minutes more and then tried the doors.

Locked!

"Boris, c'mon!"

They raced to the escalator and Taibbi took the moving stairs two steps at a time.

"The sidewalk!" he hollered back at Grgurovic. "Look for me in either direction, I'll hold him up!"

Sure enough, C. Vernon Mason had gotten permission to exit the courtroom through the judge's door and was striding quickly in the direction of the Grand Concourse.

"Mr. Mason!" Taibbi shouted, huffing badly as he walked alongside and thinking once again that it was time to quit smoking. "Mr. Mason . . . whew! I'm Mike Taibbi, as I said in the courtroom. I don't know why exactly you're trying to avoid me, but I need to ask you a couple of questions."

"Well, I'm really in a hurry," Mason said. "I've got to—"

"Listen. You're ducking me, though. Excuse me, could you stop for one second . . ."

Mason stopped suddenly and fixed a baleful glare on the reporter. Taibbi saw Grgurovic padding up the sidewalk, in a near trot, and grabbed the microphone as soon as the camera-man was in position.

"Mr. Mason, we're interested in the repeated contention by you and Mr. Maddox and Reverend Sharpton that it's been the Brawley family's decision alone to not cooperate with any special prosecutor."

"This is a case, Mike, where a family of a brutalized girl simply can't get justice," Mason began, quickly stepping into his press conference voice. "Nobody's asking why Grady left the case or about his conflict of interest, or why Cuomo, who wants to be president—"

"No, Mr. Mason, that's not what I'm asking about," Taibbi interrupted, his breath returning. "I'm asking specifically whether it was the family or the family advisers who decided there would be no cooperation."

Mason raised his voice a notch, pounding away again at the familiar themes of Governor Cuomo's political aspirations and the cover-up by officials in Dutchess County. A small crowd had formed, mostly blacks, and began punctuating Mason's more pointed statements with spasms of cheering or applause. Taibbi pressed again.

"Mr. Mason, was it the attorneys or the family who decided—"

"The family," Mason said impatiently. "*They* made a determination after it became apparent that the interest that Grady had was not in arresting any suspects or investigating the case."

"The family, right?"

"I don't know what you're getting at, Mike—"

"Mr. Mason, we're gonna run a story that includes a taped message from Glenda Brawley in which she says essentially that though she and Tawana had agreed to meet with David Sall she had to cancel the appointment because her *attorneys* had advised her to cancel."

Mason pushed his translucent glasses up the bridge of his nose and, angry, shouted at the reporter.

"If you got ahold of a tape, then David Sall ought to go before the disciplinary committee, that's my response to it! If David Sall released such a tape—talking to the mother of Tawana Brawley—'cause one of our concerns has been continually that we're concerned for these folks' safety, if he released such a tape he should go before the disciplinary committee. I certainly think Bob Abrams should be interested in that and Governor Cuomo, too."

"But Mr. Mason, the question is this: Is Glenda Brawley lying when she says she and Tawana were willing to meet with Sall but her advisers told her to cancel, or are the advisers lying? It's a simple question."

The crowd booed the question.

"Listen," Mason said. "We're very, very clear on this. For me to be saying Reverend Sharpton is lying or Glenda Brawley is lying, Mike, I won't dignify that question with an answer!"

Vernon Mason pushed his way through the crowd, and was gone.

PHILLIPS SPENT THE MORNING getting ready to put the piece together. Unlike print reporters, the effectiveness of whose work depended solely on the facts in hand and the writer's ability on the page, television reporters who sought to hit for power had dozens of individual technical processes at their disposal and needed to know when and in which combination to use them. Phillips, much more than her partner, had the knowledge and the patience to wade through the choices and make the right decisions. She played Glenda Brawley's tape several times on her own microcassette recorder, transcribing not only the words but the inflection in the message; when Glenda's words were superimposed on the screen in whatever effect Phillips chose, she wanted a concordance, a precise replication of the words and meaning, with italicizations if justified. She talked to Jean Harper and to Darby Smith, who would direct the afternoon coord session (in which special effects are built and tailored to specific stories). She called Graphics and ordered an ADDA animation effect, a tape recorder with its reels spinning, beneath which would appear the text of Glenda's message. By the time Taibbi returned from the Bronx and joined her in the editing room, she knew exactly how their report would look and sound. Screening the tape from the Bronx, Phillips knew they had it. Mason had said it again, on camera: the family had decided. Glenda's tape made it clear; someone was lying.

The piece ran at the top of the Six, and again at eleven. The advisers did not make themselves available for an immediate response, but Sharpton had his aide, Perry McKinnon, call every news organization and advise them to daybook a news conference for the following day, time TBA—to be announced.

THE NEWS CONFERENCE was scheduled for 4:30 in the afternoon in the basement of Bronx Supreme Court. Mason was still arguing motions in the Carelock case. It was raining again . . . the weather was an unpredictable mess in the winter of '87–'88. Because of the late hour, and because Taibbi was expected to lead both the Five and the Six with possible update reports as needed, the assignment desk had booked a live crew and a videotape crew, and sent along a young desk assistant named Michael Heard to help Taibbi and the crews by running tapes to the live truck so they could be fed or by simply monitoring the press conference if and when Taibbi had to be in front of the camera.

It was a mob scene. Every station sent camera crews; some, like Channel 2, dispatched both a live and a tape crew. Print and radio reporters and two dozen still photographers jockeyed for position behind a restraining cordon as Mason, Maddox, Sharpton, and Glenda Brawley and Ralph King took seats along a back wall.

Taibbi sought out David Diaz, a terrific reporter, an old friend, and a former colleague at Channel 4. "Jesus, David. They're loaded for bear, looks like. Whaddya think?"

Diaz laughed and shook his head. He'd gone up to Wappingers Falls at the very beginning and was immediately skeptical, and at a number of subsequent press conferences had aggressively challenged the advisers to stop making wild allegations and insulting everybody in sight and start talking about the evidence, if they had any.

"Thanks to you, Mike, we're up here in the Bronx on this lovely shitty day."

"Well," Taibbi said, unsure of how to take Diaz's comment. "I mean, Glenda's tape is what it is. Somebody's lying—"

"I know, I know," Diaz cut in. "I mean, it was a good story. But you know these guys are gonna try and tear you up."

That they did. Sharpton, as always, opened the program. Dressed in a black and red sweatsuit, he issued a general attack on the racist media for once again questioning the story of a young girl who was *raped* and *maimed* and *sodomized*, and tore off a few verbal blasts in the direction of Governor Cuomo and Bob Abrams, Bill Grady and David Sall, before handing the podium over to C. Vernon Mason.

Back at the Broadcast Center, the tension in the Channel 2 newsroom was high. The story—and the certainty that at any moment Channel 2 itself would be taking heavy incoming fire—was part of the reason. But there was also the normal time pressure that had the place needled out whenever there was significant uncertainty about the status of the lead story in the upcoming broadcast. At quarter to five, fifteen minutes to go, the live signal from the microwave live truck in the Bronx had not been locked in; no tape had been fed. Jean Harper and executive producer Terry Wood hadn't heard from Taibbi or the truck—a sore point with Wood and a bad habit of Taibbi's—and debated several contingency plans, slashing copies of the show format with broad pencil lines and arrows. Other reporters and editors and writers crisscrossed the claustrophobic newsroom, some tripping in their distraction on the soiled and dog-eared carpet squares that management had been promising for years would be replaced.

Phillips, meanwhile, sat tensely on a stool in Microwave

Control, the small room at the end of the editing corridor where a technician coordinated and helped lock in all
the incoming feeds from the live trucks in the field. The
technician, Andy Funk, was working on the feed from the
Bronx.

"Start panning, Mini-four," he instructed the truck crew.
In the rain, in the Bronx, technician Don Silverman nudged
the pin switch on his panning box, and looked up through
the raindrops as the four-foot dish atop his fully extended
forty-foot mast panned slowly.

"Okay, I've got something," Funk said. "Let me try and
bring you in on my end." He watched the Automatic Gain
Control and Azimuth readouts on the panel to his right, and
panned the receiving dish atop the Empire State Building.

"Okay, Mini-four, Empire's got it but I'm not happy yet.
Lock down your pan and give me some tilt. I've got your
carrier, but it's not there yet. Okay, okay, a little more. Okay,
lock it down. Hold it right there."

Funk made his own adjustments in Vertical and watched
the AGC readouts. "Twenty-two, twenty-five, twenty-six,
thirty," he said into his mike. "Okay, Mini-four, okay, you're
in."

Phillips skipped briskly out of Microwave Control and when
she got to the corner of the newsroom hollered across the
din to Harper and Wood.

"Jean! Terry! We're in. Our signal's locked in!"

It was two minutes to five. Obviously there'd be no time
for Taibbi or the truck to feed any tape or narration. Phillips
looked at the first scene that came on once Mini-4's color
bars had been taken down. Taibbi was standing self-con-
sciously in front of the live camera fiddling with the molded
earpiece that would allow him to hear both Program—what
was on the air—and any instructions from Control Room 46
back at the Broadcast Center. The rest of the press corps and
the press conference itself were arrayed behind him. Phillips
heard Mason's voice. Mason was screaming.

". . . and here David Sall, who says no local prosecutor can investigate this case, gives a tape to Mike Taibbi and no one's gonna do anything about that. . . ."

Phillips studied her partner on the incoming feed. He was plainly flustered, and not, she knew, just because of his long-standing aversion to live shots. She wondered how many minutes he'd been standing there, waiting for the live camera to lock in, while he was being attacked by name a few feet away. Control Room 46 asked Taibbi for an audio check.

"Okay, okay, I hear you," Taibbi said, his voice a little shaky. "I'll give you a slow ten. Nine-eight-seven-six—"

"Okay, Mike," a voice from Room 46 said. "You're okay, picture and sound. About a minute."

Mike Taibbi's live shot was painful to watch. Not a great ad-libber in the best of circumstances and still uncomfortable on camera, despite seventeen years of television experience, he struggled through a three-minute eternity during which he tried without notable success to reprise his story of the day before and paraphrase the responses from the Brawley team. Phillips watched in her own pain, writers John Lancellotti and Andrea Davis standing behind her in Microwave waiting to screen the tape that would soon be fed and to then help Phillips turn it around for later reports in the Five and Six.

Throughout his live report, Taibbi kept looking behind him, distracted when his name was shouted out again, and losing his train of thought. After still another false start he'd try again, the discomfort in his face mixed now and again with a flash of anger. Phillips knew her partner well; knew he had a deserved reputation for a hair-trigger temper and knew too how awful it must be for him standing there, trying for a measured professional voice while his integrity and reporting skills were being assaulted. She turned to Davis and Lancellotti, whose faces betrayed how awkward they too felt, witnessing the scene. Phillips sprinted to the control room, hovering over Darby Smith's shoulder. "He's losing it," Phillips said softly. "Come on, Mike. C'mon, Darby," she said under her breath, hoping the director would pull the plug soon.

He did, thankfully, Terry Wood having told Taibbi in his earpiece to wrap it up. And the rest of the reports, in the Five and the Six, allowed the reporter time to recover. He was able to feed several narrations, which Phillips, Lancellotti, and Davis covered quickly with video from the scene, and with his next reports merely live wraps around interior tape pieces, Taibbi had only to get in and out of the reports cleanly, fifteen seconds on either end, and he did. He talked about the trio's attacks against his own story, reiterating the details of the story and emphasizing that there would be no retraction, and was relieved to hear the Mason soundbite Phillips had selected to end the piece. It was general, the same old stuff:

> *As we sit here on March 3, 1988, sitting here in Bronx County, we are going to say that the litmus test for justice in the state and in the nation is going to be the case of Tawana Brawley.*

"Not too good," said Taibbi, who sat in the passenger seat of Mini-4, smoking another cigarette. "Christ, what a zoo. I hate those fucking things, going live with everybody behind you. . . ."

"It's all right, Mike." Michael Heard, a bright young man from a black middle-class background, had very little experience in the field but admired the work Taibbi and Phillips had done at the station and was glad to have been assigned to the Bronx live shot. "The rest of 'em were fine, just fine. And there's a lot of stuff to work with from the press conference, when you were doing the live shot. Here . . ."

He offered Taibbi his own notes on the press conference. Taibbi shook his head.

"Later, Michael. I'll go over it with you for the piece we cut for the Eleven. Is it still going on, downstairs?"

"Last I looked, a few minutes ago, yeah. Some reporters have left."

There were still three cameras, including the one manned by Channel 2's John Haygood, when Taibbi returned to the basement. The advisers were going through what the press corps had come to dub the Four Hundred Years of Oppression rap. And, true to form in the end stage of each performance, the reporters still in attendance were chipping away, trying to get something specific, anything, that could be a peg for their next-day stories.

Taibbi listened for a few minutes and, the live camera broken down and the pressure off, felt his anger rising again. Sharpton was speaking; Taibbi interrupted him.

"Listen, Mr. Sharpton. Mr. Sharpton!"

The rotund minister was surprised at the impertinence of the interruption, but stopped talking.

"Mr. Sharpton, you people have been here for over an hour and haven't said one new thing about this case. I mean, you're talking to a roomful of reporters who'd each shoot their dog if they could get to the bottom of what happened to Tawana Brawley. Why don't you just cut the horseshit and tell us what you know, give us something to work with!"

Sharpton, taken aback slightly, allowed his face to embrace a small smile. "Ooooh, don't shoot your dog, Mike. It's a nice dog. . . ."

And then he continued with the Four Hundred Years of Oppression.

The last reporters and cameramen filed out eventually, muttering under their breaths. Mike Taibbi and Anna Phillips would break away from the pack after that night, spending a great deal of time in Poughkeepsie, where the print reporting teams had set up camp, and in Wappingers Falls, Newburgh, and Monticello, where Tawana had been raised by her aunt and uncle. They began developing their own leads,

collected every available public record on the case, interviewed and reinterviewed the known witnesses who would
talk and some potential witnesses their own detective work
led them to seek out. Taibbi dusted off and trotted out every
investigative device he used to employ routinely in Boston—
Freedom of Information Law letters to officials who tried to
withhold records, cross-checks on facts and allegations in
contradiction with one another, maintenance calls to potentially important sources, and nighttime calls and home visits
when necessary—and the sum total of his efforts with Phillips increased their knowledge of the case while leaving their
frustrations intact.

To Taibbi, the Tawana Brawley story was still just another
complicated story, albeit one that seemed peculiarly resis-
tant to his established investigative methodology. He was
wrong in that view, and Phillips knew it. He thought he'd
simply had a bad night in the Bronx; he'd had others, on other
stories. But Phillips knew differently. She knew that to the
other side, to the Brawley team if not to the Brawley family
members themselves, it was war. And she guessed, uncomfortably, that it would remain a war as long as there was still
a chance that Tawana Brawley had been telling the truth.

Phillips believed that chance still existed.

5

"We can take care of ourselves. . . ."

THREE MONTHS INTO THE BRAWLEY CASE, every news organization in New York City had committed enormous resources to covering it. Part of that commitment had to do with the nature of the compelling scenario at the story's center: that an innocent, fifteen-year-old black girl could have been set upon by a gang of white men, and raped and brutalized for four whole days in a small town like Wappingers Falls.

But mostly the press held the Brawley story in full embrace because the champions of the story, the family advisers, had accomplished a seduction of unprecedented proportions. If *they* represented Tawana Brawley, if *they* alone knew her story and had access to it, then when *they* called a press conference the press, *all* the press, had to attend. And, cameras and tape recorders whirring, pencils flying, and the competitive imperative hard at work, stories were filed and broadcast. Privately, there wasn't a newspaper or television reporter on the story who didn't harbor doubts about some details of the original account; even more privately, many reporters knew that by the very act of pursuing their craft they were nourishing an unholy alliance with the advisers. If an individual reporter learned a new fact about the investigation, or merely obtained a provocative quote from an important enough figure, or even posed a question to the advisers based on a hunch or a totally uncorroborated lead, that new fact, provocative quote, or innocent question would unfailingly result in new charges or claims by the advisers and, increasingly, in "action" by the team that would of course attract saturation coverage.

For example, there was the famous "Rev. Al Grabs Tawana" front page in the *New York Post.* The *Poughkeepsie Journal* had run a story quoting Matthew Strong, the Monticello policeman who was Tawana's uncle and had raised her for the first twelve years of her life, as saying he was so tired of the case he was thinking of grabbing Tawana by the hand and "marching her down to Abrams and the Grand Jury" himself.

The quote was important because Strong, who resisted being interviewed and was humiliated at the publicity the case had thrust upon his family and extended family, was reputed to be the one person in the world whose word and counsel Tawana would heed. The pressure and press attention in Wappingers Falls had driven her back to Monticello in late February. She was living in Strong's home and attending Monticello High School. Strong was Tawana's father-figure; his daughter, Kenya, a bright and serious girl, was Tawana's age and was closer to her than any of the teenager's friends in Wappingers Falls, Newburgh, or Poughkeepsie.

According to an aide to Sharpton, when the minister read

Strong's quote, he called for his cream-colored Cadillac and raced up to Monticello, knowing that some reporters and photographers might still be there, even at night and a long way from home, trying to follow up on the *Journal* story. Sharpton was truly concerned, the aide later explained; he knew that Strong, a no-nonsense cop, was critical of the law-yers' tactics—in the *Journal* account he said "they'd be fired" if it was up to him—and specifically did not buy Sharpton's act. But Tawana did, or at least did to the extent that on the night of March 1 she followed Sharpton's lead. Holding the minister's hand, she walked slowly past a still photographer, Frank Leonardo of the *Post*, even pausing on Sharpton's com-mand so Leonardo could, as the minister put it, "take one picture."

"Where we're taking her, ain't nobody gonna find her," Sharpton shouted to Leonardo. The quote made the front page too, and gave the *Post* a print exclusive; any other newspaper with a photographer on the scene might have played the story the same way. Even though, as it turned out, there was no story. Months later Sharpton's aide would explain that he'd simply driven around the block, waited until Leonardo had left, and watched with Sharpton as Tawana skipped through familiar backyards and returned to Matthew Strong's home.

More sinister, though, were the stories or implications of stories that the Brawley advisers would then turn into dra-matic new "allegations" at still another press conference, which new allegations would then be broadly mass-commu-nicated. The "I want him dead. I want Skoralick" note that Tawana had allegedly written, a note no reporter ever saw, established the sheriff as a "suspect" in dozens of subsequent press conferences and statements by the advisers. Published reports that an elderly mailman with poor eyesight, Dominic Losee, had seen a "troop car" near the Pavillion Apartments, a car with as many as six white males in it, around the time of Tawana's disappearance, were repeated by the advisers time

after time as "proof" of Tawana's story, even though the
mailman's story was eventually discredited when he acknowledged that he wasn't certain of any details whatsoever,
not even his original claim that the men in the car were white.
A young boy, who later admitted he made the whole tale up,
had said at one point that he'd seen Tawana "dumped" from
a car on the day she was found; but his original story made
it to print, to the front page, and the advisers embraced it as
true, claiming later they'd learned the boy had been threatened into changing his tune. One of Alton Maddox's clients,
Willie James Bosket, said in a story printed in *Big Red News*,
a left-wing Brooklyn weekly, that while incarcerated in the
Shawangunk Correctional Facility in Wallkill he'd eaves-
dropped on a conversation among several white prison guards
who were planning what turned out to be the abduction and
sexual assault of Tawana Brawley; so, for a while, the advisers let it be known that prison guards from Shawangunk may
have been among Tawana's attackers, and that charge was
widely reported.

On March 7 the symbiotic, improbable, yet irresistible relationship between the Brawley advisers and the press reached
a new level, and perhaps a new low. Sharpton charged that a
"racist cult" with links to the Irish Republican Army, a cult
operating within the Dutchess County sheriff's department,
was responsible for the attack on Tawana Brawley. Local
television stations and every paper, including the *New York
Times*, quoted Sharpton's claim that an "inside source" within
the sheriff's department had revealed the existence of the cult.
According to the *Daily News*, Sharpton told a crowd of 350
worshipers in Poughkeepsie's Beulah Baptist Church that the
cult was run by former sheriff Lawrence Quinlan, who had
been "convicted of gun-running for the IRA." His "inside
source" could prove it all, Sharpton told the crowd. "We feel
this cult could strike again." As additional "proof," Sharpton
said at a later press conference, his "source" had described
several IRA "rituals" that were present in the Brawley case,

including the "spreading of excrement on the body as a protest" and the stuffing of cotton in the nose and ears as a way of preventing infection. Tawana had been found with dog feces smeared over her body and in her hair, and a "cottonlike" substance had been wadded in her nostrils and in one ear—among the few unchallenged facts in the case.

Quinlan, seventy, called the charges preposterous, and offered that Sharpton was nothing but a "rabble rouser and a liar." In 1978 Quinlan had been acquitted of charges that he had illegally sold three handguns impounded by the sheriff's department. There was no mention at the trial or in the trial record of the Irish Republican Army.

No reporters could find any evidence of IRA "rituals" involving feces-smearing and cotton-stuffing.

Said Martin Galvin, a spokesman for the Irish Northern Aid Committee, "Sharpton has outdone even the British in the slandering of the IRA."

Yet the story made headlines and was reported in great detail by every newspaper and most television stations that had been covering the story.

Weeks later one reporter who was on the case full-time said sheepishly, in the presence of other reporters at the Wyndham Hotel, including Taibbi and Phillips, that he'd unwittingly been Sharpton's "source." "We were sitting around bullshitting with Sharpton," he confessed, laughing at the memory, "talking about the Quinlan case. One thing led to another, and I raised the question—it was a question, not a statement of fact—of whether the IRA had these rituals. Next thing I know he's having another Poughkeepsie press conference, and he's got an 'inside source' who can prove the whole thing. Unbelievable."

Perhaps just as unbelievable was the fact that that same reporter wrote the Sharpton "racist cult" story straight, as though he'd had no role in its genesis.

Such was the state of reporting in the Tawana Brawley case in March 1988. The Brawley advisers and many in the press played pinball with rumors, unfounded allegations, and pre-posterous suppositions, and the product of the game too often ended up being broadcast or published.

Reporters who made real headway away from the circus orchestrated by the Brawley advisers saw their initiatives ig-nored or blithely dismissed. *Newsday*, for example, broke the story that Tawana's former boyfriend, Todd Buxton, had called her from prison back in December, and that two of those phone calls were taped; the reporters hadn't heard the tape, but the paper's source said that in the first call Tawana had giggled and said, ". . . the only thing the newspapers got right is my name and address." The advisers ignored the story.

In mid-March, during still another Poughkeepsie demon-stration, covered live by local radio station WKIP, a woman called the station and, unsolicited, told an astonishing story: her own daughter, who knew Tawana and had for a short time been a classmate when both girls lived in Poughkeep-sie, had told a similar story of abduction and rape "by a group of white men in a dark green car who took her to a wooded area" fully a year before. Her daughter had later admitted she made the whole story up. The Poughkeepsie police depart-ment confirmed that the story was a concoction, adding that the girl had attempted to cover up the fact that she had been sexually abused and had simply run away for a few days to escape the abuse. Her assailant was actually a black neigh-bor. Sharpton's curt and curious response: "I thought it was ridiculous to take a story that no one acknowledged Tawana even had knowledge of and try to imply that she tried to use it." Period.

The *New York Times* team, which by March had swelled to seven reporters, including veteran stars Robert McFadden, E. R. Shipp, Fox Butterfield, M. A. Faber, and Ralph Blumen-thal, stayed as far away as possible from unqualified coverage of the Brawley advisers' performances, concentrating instead on developing its typically encyclopedic examinations of the evidence in the case (with an occasional analytical piece thrown in on the strategies of the lawyers or the motives of Al Sharpton). Early on, the advisers ignored the *Times* completely; television and the tabloids were their arena.

And television, because of its historic disinclination to mount open-ended investigations of running stories, failed to intrude on the running story even when some of its best reporters dug up jarring evidence that called Tawana's story into question. For example, both David Diaz of Channel 4 and Tim Minton of Channel 7 combed the Pavillion Apartments (as had a number of print reporters) and came away with anonymous (and silhouetted) interviews that challenged one of the basic contentions of the Brawley team: that Tawana had been stuffed in the garbage bag and left to die. Both Diaz and Minton found the woman who said (and later testified) she'd seen Tawana actually *crawl into* the bag on the morning of November 28. But both reporters were also covering the advisers' almost-daily press conferences, and when Sharpton and the lawyers simply ignored their stories, the stories failed to insinuate themselves into the public dialogue about the case, and the advisers' campaign, buttressed by the engine of local television and the tabloids, rolled on.

As a team, Taibbi and Phillips had a number of built-in advantages unavailable to the reporters who'd been on the case from the beginning. For one thing, they'd come in late and had therefore not been drawn into the "relationship" with the Brawley advisers that had ensnared so many others; Channel 2's daily coverage of the advisers continued to be handled by other reporters, as needed. Taibbi and Phillips had no interest in the quick hit; their record as a team and Taibbi's entire career as an investigative reporter were built on carefully researched revelations that virtually ignored unsupported charges or theories. And, by the definition of their role as mandated by news director Paul Sagan, they were free of the deadline pressure that pushed other reporters to settle for the convenient quote generated by the latest statements from the advisers. "Develop your leads, wherever they take you," Sagan had instructed. "Phone home when you've got something. You're on the air when you've got a story."

Some of their early stories were of minimal value in moving the case forward. On March 8, in a piece they privately dubbed "Ralph's Rough Week," Taibbi and Phillips reported on the recent travails of Tawana's mother's live-in companion, Ralph King. In 1970 King had been convicted in the shooting death of his former wife, Wanda; trial records showed that he'd shot her four times in the head, at point-blank range, his infant son in the bedroom next door, after having failed to kill her in a prior attack in which he'd stabbed her sixteen times. Released from the Albion Correctional Facility in 1977, King had steered clear of the law since then and at the time of Tawana's disappearance was employed as a part-time driver for the Short Lines Bus Company. But rumor painted him as a regular pot smoker and possible dabbler in harder drugs— though he had never been convicted of any drug-related crime—and his violent temper was a matter of record.

Acting on a tip from a source, the Channel 2 reporters obtained the records of a minor traffic accident in which King had recently been involved in Hyde Park, New York. The accident summaries showed that King, when questioned by the white police officer who was first to respond, not only swore and threatened violence unless a black cop was sent to the scene, but also returned to police headquarters the next day and inexplicably resumed his enraged and threatening tirade. Hyde Park Police Chief James Dunegan, on camera, stated that King shouted repeatedly that he was "Tawana Brawley's stepfather" and could raise all kinds of hell, and that the decision was made to let King off easily. The reporters also learned that a few days after the accident King's Lincoln had been repossessed for nonpayment. "Took us six attempts," the repo-man told Taibbi. "But we weren't gonna give up."

The day the report aired, Phillips had accidentally run into King and Glenda Brawley two blocks from the Broadcast Center in Manhattan. They'd been walking across Eleventh Avenue with their son, Tyice, when Tyice, in Glenda's arms, was lightly struck by a New York Sanitation Department truck. Tyice was rushed to St. Luke's – Roosevelt Hospital, where it was determined he'd suffered no real injuries.

Although "Ralph's Rough Week" did not advance the Tawana Brawley story one iota, it caused two questions to stand out on the reporters' growing list: What was the money situation in the Brawley household that allowed Ralph and Glenda, a part-time driver and a factory-line assembler, to drive a new Lincoln among their three vehicles? And what was the relationship, if any, between Ralph's hair-trigger temper and Tawana's disappearance?

For the answer to the second question the reporters turned their attention to the city of Newburgh. Tawana had stopped in Newburgh the morning of her disappearance on her way to visit her jailed former boyfriend, Todd Buxton. It was in Newburgh that Tawana was last seen by any corroborated witnesses; Todd McGue, the bus driver who said he'd dropped Tawana off in Wappingers Falls, was alone with his story. None of the several other passengers supposedly on the bus ever came forward and confirmed McGue's story that Tawana had been along for the ride.

Buxton's family lived in an apartment tower on the east end of town, hard by the Hudson River. His mother, Geneva, had traveled with Tawana to the Orange County Jail to visit Todd and had returned with her to Newburgh.

In early January, Chris Borgen had interviewed Geneva Buxton and Saundra Buxton, Todd's sister. Because of deadline pressure only a single cut from those interviews had been broadcast, but the rest of the long, discursive conversation was revealing.

"Tawana just wasn't herself, all day," Geneva Buxton told Borgen. "She didn't eat nothing, not even any juice, which she always loved. All she had on was an acid-washed jeans jacket, and it was cold outside. When I heard later she never made it home I just figured she went someplace else and that something had happened to her. She didn't want to leave here, she let two buses go by. I said, 'You're gonna get in trouble,' but she said she was already in big trouble because she'd went to a party the week before and stayed out till five in the morning. Her mother had gave her permission, but she said her stepfather was very upset. 'He just keeps goin' on and on,' Tawana tells me."

Saundra Buxton told Borgen that "everybody in Newburgh thought the stepfather had 'done it,' " but Geneva shook her head. "I don't know nothing about that," she said. "But Tawana was real scared to go home. I offered her my couch, if she wanted to stay, but then I thought I didn't want him [King] coming down on me too." Her guess was that Tawana had stayed "somewhere in Newburgh," but she didn't know anything for certain.

Phillips and Taibbi had been to Newburgh only once before, filing a thin day-of-air story on an appearance in town by the Brawley advisers at the Baptist Temple Church. Phillips had made contact with Lorraine Jackson-Ordia that day and had also done some interviewing along Broadway, the main thoroughfare through the city. On the east end of Broadway, the dividing line between the black and Hispanic sections of town, many of the storefronts were boarded up and the businesses that were open spoke of hard times. The youngsters Phillips approached were giddy at the attention paid them by a New York reporter and her cameraman; most knew little or nothing about the Tawana Brawley saga, but a few claimed to know the Wappingers Falls teen personally. When one girl said she was convinced Tawana was lying, a middle-aged white man shouted at Phillips, not stopping to be interviewed on camera, "Why don't you just let [her] tell her story, leave us alone!"

But an elderly black women did stop, fixing Phillips in the

sternest glare. "Too many people aroun' here talkin' about Tawana Brawley," she said.

"But isn't this community outraged," Phillips cut in, "that a crime like this could even happen in this area?"

The woman started to walk away in disgust, then turned and stared at Phillips again, her jaw working. Finally she spoke, the voice of a weary teacher addressing the ignorant.

"I been living here all my eighty years, and I ain't never had no problem with the Ku Klux Klan. My problem is with the drug pushers. The KKK ain't never robbed my purse, but them damned junkies right over there on the corner done robbed me three times just this year. Do a story on them!"

Borgen had told Taibbi and Phillips that before venturing onto the rough streets of Newburgh they'd best check in with Deputy Police Chief Bill Bloom, who'd helped him in his earlier stories. But Bloom was off duty on their return visit. The duty sergeant on the night desk gave the reporters a street map and some pointers on the hot spots in the section of town known derisively as Crack Alley. But don't try it at night, he advised. "*I* wouldn't go there alone and unarmed." "We're from the city," Taibbi said haughtily. "We can take care of ourselves." The sergeant shook his head.

Crack Alley was a smaller version of the drug market-places that had turned so many New York City neighbor-hoods into war zones. At street corners along Lander, South, and Liberty streets small groups of young black males pressed together, eyes on anything that moved on foot or in cars. Dealers. A single pass through the neighborhood told the reporters all they needed to know about it. They found a dark-ened slab of curb beneath a shot-out street lamp and parked, engine running. Business was brisk enough, even on a cold night, customers leaning out of car windows or striding up to one group or another and being led to a door front for the quick pass. After watching for several minutes, they saw that the group of dealers nearest them had thinned to only three youths.

"Got your ID?" Taibbi asked Phillips, pulling out his own press card. "Let's go chat 'em up."

Though they waved their press cards, one youth stepped away quickly, breaking into a casual trot, snapping his head back several times to see what was going on. A tall white male and a well-dressed black woman had to mean trouble. There were two youths remaining; Phillips headed for one, Taibbi the other. Identifying themselves as reporters from New York pursuing the Tawana Brawley story, television reporters who obviously didn't have a camera with them and just wanted to talk—"off the record"—each managed to get a conversation going. Yes, a few people in the neighborhood knew Tawana, and there were stories going around about her and Todd, and about Todd's good friend Randy "D-Day" Davis, a jailed crack dealer. And Todd, by the way, had just gotten out of jail himself. Nervous, the two youths began looking past the reporters; sure enough, there were people approaching from further down South Street. Taibbi called to Phillips to start heading back with him to the car. It was dark, they were on alien turf. No need for a bad scene. Surprisingly, the youth he'd been talking to, Ronald R.,* walked with him, and leaned in once Taibbi was behind the wheel.

"You can't miss Todd," Ronald said. "He's driving one of them brand-new Suzuki jeeps. It's silver, the only one around."

"Where's he keep it?" Taibbi asked quickly. The group had re-formed back on the corner, a half-dozen pairs of eyes were staring at the intruders.

"Around," Ronald said. "In the neighborhood. Hey, I gotta—"

"Listen. Ronald, thanks. Look, you got a number where I can reach you, you know, just to check things out?" Phillips reached automatically for a pen, and flipped her dashboard press visor for something to write on. Ronald spat out his number, fast, and sauntered back to the group.

Taibbi and Phillips returned to Newburgh the next morning and were sitting in Bill Bloom's office at nine o'clock.

Bright and affable and slightly overweight, with amused close-set eyes of the deepest blue, Bloom said right away that he wasn't all that impressed with most of the press corps from the Big City. All they want is a handout. But he raised an eyebrow when the reporters described what they'd learned about D-Day Davis and Todd Buxton and a few other people during their brief foray to Crack Alley.

"Yeah, he's out of jail," Bloom said of Buxton. "And now you want to talk to him, right?"

"Well, there're those calls he supposedly made to Tawana," Phillips said, "the ones that were taped. And if he's out, does he know anything about what happened to her? Has he talked to her again? He's supposed to be the boyfriend, after all. . . ."

"I don't know," Bloom said. "I'm still trying to figure out how he gets out after a few months when his original charge is attempted manslaughter. I mean, he shot at a guy, someone he thought was ratting him out, I think it was. He got a deal somehow, for something."

Bloom was in a mood to talk, and without a deadline pressing down on them the reporters were happy to listen. They heard everything—from a history of the city to the recent history of Crack Alley. And then they heard what would be the lead to their next story.

"The thing is, and nobody's paid any attention to this," Bloom said, a smile of incredulity on his face, "Tawana's aunt and her mother both told us she was seen here, in Newburgh. It's in the Missing Persons reports each of them filed. Here . . ."

He flipped through the papers in a bin on his desk and handed over the two "6K" Missing Persons reports filed about Tawana Brawley. The first was dated November 24, the night the teenager had disappeared. Juanita Brawley had told the desk officer that her "niece had run away from Wappingers Falls and was staying in Newburgh off Liberty Street." Juanita explained that she'd raised Tawana in Monticello but that the girl "had been staying with her natural mother when she ran away."

The second 6K report was taken at 1620—4:20 in the afternoon—on November 28, the day Tawana had been discovered. Glenda Brawley had apparently driven to Newburgh to file the report two and a half hours *after* Tawana had been discovered!

"She stated her daughter was missing from her residence in Wappingers Falls," the duty officer wrote. "She came to Newburgh because she believes her daughter was seen by a friend in the area of Liberty and South Street."

Liberty and South were the heart of Crack Alley. The reporters knew immediately they would put the two Missing Persons reports on the air, but they needed to know more about Tawana's relationship to Crack Alley and its regulars, including Todd Buxton.

They hit the streets again, this time in the light of a sun-filled day. Working together and then singly, they knocked on doors and spoke to anyone who'd listen, collecting names and dates and anything else that might help later, talking to people in the basements and trade rooms of one crack house after another, and finally circling back to the Fish 'N Chips restaurant on Liberty Street, which served as their checkpoint. They gleaned information about Buxton and D-Day in small nuggets, and from one street type they learned the name of an out-of-town dealer who'd been claiming he knew something about Tawana's disappearance. A check with Bloom provided the dealer's hometown and surname. They were meandering back to their car, Phillips's Volvo this time, when one of the youths they'd spoken to earlier gave them the eye and tipped his head to his left. It was Buxton's silver Suzuki, heading south on Liberty.

It didn't take the driver of the Suzuki long to pick up the blue Volvo on his tail.

"Two in the jeep," Taibbi said. "Let's just stay on 'em, huh?"

"I'm good to go," Phillips said, snapping her seat belt in place on the passenger side. "I think Todd's the one in the passenger seat. Ooh, they gave him up in a hurry, huh?"

It was a wild ride that only sometimes paused for red lights and stop signs and took them all over the east end of Newburgh. Finally the Suzuki led the way into the parking lot of Buxton's apartment tower. On the north end of the main lot there was an outer lot, which the reporters knew from their morning survey was fenced off and led nowhere. If they followed Buxton all the way, his smaller vehicle, with its tighter turning circle, would likely escape. The Suzuki pulled into the outer lot and slowed to make its U-turn; instead of following, Taibbi wheeled hard to his left, blocking the passageway between the two lots. Stepping quickly from their car, Phillips and Taibbi waved their press cards above their heads, shouting, "We're reporters . . . press!" Buxton, who was in fact in the passenger seat and whom they recognized from photographs, moved his glare from one to the other. Leaning low and looking in from the driver's-side window, Taibbi identified himself and Phillips and tried a couple of questions. Phillips, standing just ahead of the driver's windshield post, tried to quickly memorize the details on the temporary registration pasted on the windshield. Buxton, surly but plainly frightened himself, took a couple of studied glances at the Volvo's license plate, an official press plate whose three-letter designation was the standard NYP. Buxton said several times that he didn't want to talk, had nothing to say, hadn't talked to Tawana since he got out of prison. "They won't let me talk to her, they just won't," he said angrily. "That's it. That's all I'm sayin'." Phillips pressed closer to her partner and bent to get a look at Buxton and perhaps fire off a question of her own. And then, in the same moment, both reporters saw it.

The driver, gripping the steering wheel with his right hand and leaning back rigidly into the seat, had with his left hand pulled away the bottom folds of his loose-fitting shirt. The barrel of a sawed-off shotgun was pointing upward, at an angle, the burnished metal gleaming dully in the sunlight. It was aimed directly at them.

They backed away deliberately, Taibbi saying in what he hoped was an offhand manner that they'd be back, that it was important, that they just wanted to get to the bottom of the Brawley story, and that if Buxton had anything to say he was going to have to say it at some point anyway.

Back in the car, they watched as the Suzuki burned rubber, pulling out and away. Taibbi turned to Phillips. "Jesus, didn't expect that."

"He must have . . . must have thought we were the police," Phillips answered, her voice wavering. "I saw him looking at my plates. Damn that NYP. They must have thought it stood for New York Police, everybody always does. Damn."

"Sorry," Taibbi said quietly, reaching for a cigarette.

THAT NIGHT, back in New York, Phillips dialed the number for Hermano L.,* the out-of-town drug dealer they'd heard was telling a story about Tawana Brawley. He lived in a small town in Sullivan County and spoke almost no English. Taibbi sat beside Phillips as she spoke in Spanish, drawing Hermano into conversation.

"Soy Anna Phillips del Canal Dos," she said in her normally pleasant, unthreatening voice. "Las noticias, en Nueva York?" She learned quickly that Hermano was from Puerto Rico, as was her family on her mother's side. Soon she had a steady conversation going "después somos compadres!" They had something in common; Hermano laughed. The ice was broken.

Ten minutes later Phillips hung up, studied her notes, and faced her partner. "He's jumpy, good at not answering direct questions," she explained. "And he's a snitch. I think for the feds too, but certainly for local PD in Newburgh. It'll make him very tough to use, but on the other hand he's used to collecting information and handing it over."

"So what'd he hand over?" Taibbi pressed.

"I don't know, really. I don't think anything, directly. But he said something about a party Tawana might have been at, during her disappearance; and he was more definite on this." She studied her notes some more, translating into English. "He said the word on the street . . . Okay, here it is. The word on the street is that Tawana might have been involved—no, caught in the cross fire, is what he meant—in a drug deal that went bad. Not that she was using or dealing, just that she was friends with certain people. Here it is exactly: some white guys from 'the other side of the river,' that is, Wappingers Falls, had bought some drugs from some Newburgh dealers, and they stiffed them on the money or the deal went sour, somehow. There was some kind of dispute, and Tawana, on the Newburgh end of it, got stuck in the middle. Could have been black or white that squeezed her. But," Phillips emphasized, "he says everybody knows the story isn't what Tawana says it is."

They went over the translation of Hermano's comments several times, settling on one version. At dawn the next morning they headed up to Newburgh again, this time with cameraman Jim Duggan. Bill Bloom spoke on camera, discussing the two Missing Persons reports. And this time, after loudly announcing their names, they talked their way into the Buxton apartment. At one point during the interview, Geneva called angrily to Todd, ordering him out of bed. Sleepy, incredulous that the two reporters he'd confronted the day before were now in his apartment, he stood still on his mother's command and answered a few questions.

In their first substantial report from Newburgh, Taibbi and Phillips discussed the two Missing Persons reports and questioned why, two and a half hours after Tawana had been discovered in Wappingers Falls, Glenda Brawley had driven to

Newburgh to report for the first time that her daughter was missing. They conveyed the "word on the street" from Hermano L., raising the possibility for the first time that Tawana's disappearance might have had something to do with her Newburgh acquaintances. And, with Duggan shooting liberally, they provided a videotape tour of Crack Alley, pods of dealers on a dozen corners, teenaged lookouts and runners and customers laden with gaudy gold and filling the mean streets in the middle of a school day. They'd spotted Todd Buxton's Suzuki after their initial encounter with him and followed him on his rounds. Late in the day, serendipity at work, they ran into Buxton again, standing beside the Suzuki and unhappily answering questions for the patrol cops who'd stopped him.

"They're gonna stay on you," Geneva Buxton had told her son on camera. "And sure enough," Taibbi's script concluded, "a couple of hours later, Todd and the jeep were stopped on Broadway. Just a couple of motor vehicle violations—but the picture was clear. He may be out of jail, but Todd Buxton is hardly out from under the microscope."

The Newburgh report had broken new ground and had changed the direction of Channel 2's Brawley coverage. Taibbi and Phillips wanted to spend time in Newburgh, visit Hermano L., keep working Buxton and his associates. Their story had drawn to them several important new sources, including a federal investigator who called to say it was about time someone picked up on the Missing Persons reports and on the rumors—which he was tracking on his own—that Tawana's disappearance might be linked somehow to Newburgh's drug activity and to some of the characters the reporters had come to know, at least by name.

The federal source also filled in the blanks for Taibbi and Phillips on many of the early elements of the case, offering, for example, that Tawana had not told "her story" in either of the two "formal" interviews she gave to investigators before the advisers slammed the door.

"I was notified immediately," the source explained. "I mean as soon as [the sheriff's office] got involved. That day. The FBI was pursuing a civil rights complaint, right away. I'm there, the Monday after the Saturday she's discovered, and I know everything that was said, everything that transpired."

The source had been one of five officials present during the second and last "interview" with Tawana Brawley—five officials including Otto Williams from the Dutchess County district attorney's office (the only black assistant prosecutor), Carl Amburgey, a detective from the sheriff's office, and Margaret Smith from the D.A.'s office because she handled sex crimes. It had been a chaotic scene, Juanita Brawley trying to run the show and Tawana saying very little while her head was cradled by Kenya Strong, her cousin. Amburgey took the lead in the questioning, Williams inserting his own questions when it appeared that "Carl had lost her," but the questioners got very little. Nothing, really, to go on. Tawana would "whisper in Kenya's ear," the source said, and then Kenya would answer. The answers were vague, mostly indecisive. Tawana, through her cousin, made only a few specific points, and very few that hadn't already been broadcast in the original Channel 2 report by Mary Murphy: the abduction by "a white man with a holster and a badge," the six men in the wooded area, the "police officer's jacket."

There was nothing there, the source explained. Nothing to go on. When we got the Newburgh stuff, the things you've reported, there was finally something. . . .

Taibbi and Phillips were more than encouraged.

But on March 13 the Brawley advisers reclaimed the story's epicenter. They'd called a Manhattan press conference to counter criticism from the NAACP, which Sharpton had called the "National Association of Coon People," and to announce a "massive demonstration that will shut Albany down" for April 4, the twentieth anniversary of the assassination of Dr. Martin Luther King, Jr. In his opening assault, Sharpton loaded his biggest guns for Conrad Lynn, the ven-

erable seventy-nine-year-old civil rights attorney who was
serving at the time as chief counsel for the Mid-Hudson Valley NAACP. Lynn had had the temerity to publicly label the
Brawley lawyers' handling of the case a scandal. Lynn, who
first began setting legal precedents in the famous Scottsboro
Boys Case, had filed a formal complaint with Child Protection Services officials stating that Tawana was suffering
"emotional and educational neglect" and had received "in-
sufficient psychological and medical care."

Sharpton accused this hero of the black liberation struggle
of "accepting $7,000 in bribe money" to assist in a cover-up
of the Brawley case. The pencils flew, the cameras churned:
tomorrow's story was virtually written.

But then Alton Maddox took over and all but hollered, Stop
the presses! In answer to a reporter's question, he said that,
yes, Stephen Pagones was "one of Tawana's attackers."

6

"Why're you tryin' . . . to knock holes in our story?"

THEY'D NAMED A NAME, FINALLY. After weeks of threats, weeks of insisting they could name the "six crackers" who'd abducted, raped, and beaten Tawana Brawley, they'd called a press conference on a slow Sunday and had named one: a young assistant district attorney from a prominent Hudson Valley family. Taibbi and Phillips both had the day off, yet they knew as did every other reporter that they'd have no choice but to report the story. True, *Newsday* had run a story the day before stating that Brawley Task Force investigators had been "tracing the activities" of Pagones, among others, and that Pagones was "one of several names that have surfaced as potential subjects of the Brawley grand jury." The Channel 2 reporters wondered aloud whether naming Pagones was simply another example of the advisers taking their cue from press reports; no, they concluded. Impossible! You don't publicly accuse someone of rape, of gang rape and unspeakable racial degradation, unless you have some credible, independent evidence. Especially if you're a lawyer, with a license to protect. And yet . . .

They studied the field tape from the press conference; there was something about Maddox's accusation that seemed unrehearsed, accidental. A voice from off camera, a print reporter, had been pressing the lawyer to get specific; Maddox and Mason had been taking turns making new charges about the "officially sanctioned conspiracy to obstruct and subvert justice in the case of Tawana Brawley," but now Maddox, fencing awkwardly with the reporter over the advisers' charge that D.A. Bill Grady *and* one of his assistants, Stephen Pagones, should be arrested, found himself in a corner.

"Are you saying Stephen Pagones was one of the gang who assaulted Tawana Brawley?" the reporter shouted.

"Stephen Pagones was involved in the case," Maddox said, his voice subdued, unsteady. "He was one of the attackers."

"Lawman Accused" read the headline in the *Daily News*; the *Post* shouted, "DA's Aide in Tawana Rape Gang: Lawyers." The *Times*, more restrained, headed its account "A Dutchess Prosecutor Vows Brawley Case Slander Suit," concentrating in its copy on the suit Pagones's lawyer, Gerald Hayes, had announced he would immediately begin preparing. Even though every print and broadcast account pointed out that the advisers had refused to substantiate the allegation against Pagones, it was clear from the coverage that every reporter had reached the same conclusion Channel 2's team had reached. The allegation had to be reported in detail, both on the reasonable assumption that there had to be something to it and out of concern that if there was something to it and the charge was given short shrift or none at all, later accusations of a racist media predisposition would carry great weight. Thus the advisers seized back the front page and the top of every newscast, and were quoted in their demand that "Governor Cuomo make an immediate arrest of Steve Pagones and William Grady," because Pagones was one of the attackers and Grady "had tried to whitewash his assistant's involvement."

Taibbi tried in his own script to extract the core of the advisers' bombshell allegation.

"There is no middle ground. Tawana Brawley's representatives either played their hole card yesterday or they exposed themselves to potentially devastating counterattack. . . ." His conclusion, after a standard account of the allegation and the denials and challenges from all quarters: "Have the events of the past two days gotten investigators any closer to solving the Tawana Brawley mystery? The answer is 'no.' Have they kept the pot stirring in what is now less an assault case than an all-out racial imbroglio? From all corners today, the answer is an emphatic 'yes.' "

THE BRAWLEY CASE was on fire again, the feeding frenzy among the press escalating to unprecedented heights. A day didn't pass without an inflammatory new "charge" from the Brawley camp, an expression of editorial outrage in one paper or another, or a dramatic "revelation" by some news outlet. The national press—the *Los Angeles Times*, the *Washington Post*, *Time*, *Newsweek*, the *New Republic*—got back on the case. Veterans in the New York news business shook their heads; there'd never been anything like it. Certainly there was a long history of incidents or crimes or historical events that for a day or a few days consumed attention. And there were running stories—trials ranging from the Alice Crimmins child murders case in the sixties to the Howard Beach race killing and Joel Steinberg child murder trial in the eighties, and garish crimes ranging from the Son of Sam shootings in the seventies to the Tylenol murders in the eighties—that saw reporters from every news organization assigned like outriders for the duration. But in the latter part of the eighties, on a story infused with racial paranoia whose central premise wasn't even established in fact, the permanent members of the Brawley press tripped over each other, scrambled, scratched, and clawed to come up with something, anything, each and every day. It was astounding.

In the week after the Brawley advisers publicly accused Stephen Pagones, a range of improbable "lead stories" made someone's front page or the top of one newscast or another:

—an "exclusive" interview in which C. Vernon Mason asserted that Tawana's attackers discussed killing her, but that "one of the assailants persuaded the group against it." Mason said that instead "they devised a scheme to leave her to die" near the family's former apartment. Mason, who had earlier joined his fellow advisers in vigorously slamming the Ku Klux Klan as an "active" cult in the region that had "perpetrated the attack" on Tawana Brawley, now said that the "real attackers" had merely left false clues on Tawana's body—the letters KKK—to "divert attention" from themselves.

—a story asserting that "Tawana was getting her life back together" in Monticello, accompanied by a photo of an attractive, smiling Tawana Brawley in a hands-on-hips come-hither model's pose. The scuttlebutt in the press corps was that a high school classmate of Tawana's had been paid to snap the picture and hand it over.

—still another "exclusive" interview with Glenda Brawley, who said once again that she supported the strategies of the family advisers, adding, cautiously, "I'm not saying Tawana has named Pagones. That's up to the lawyers."

—a gossip column item that private investigator Galen Kelly, who'd had a hand in the Atlanta child murders investigation, had concluded after his own review of the case that Tawana Brawley was neither kidnapped nor raped.

—a rash of "exclusive" interviews with special prosecutor Bob Abrams in which he asserted, again and again, that there were no suspects in the case.

—mass coverage of a preposterous demonstration on March

20, the first day of spring. Sharpton had led a band of sixty protesters to Poughkeepsie, booming to the cameras and microphones, "We're here to shut the grand jury down, even if it's over our dead and arrested bodies." There were as many cops and twice as many counterdemonstrators on hand, local townspeople shouting, "Go home!," "Let her talk!," or "Tell the truth!" but Sharpton held the cameras' attention. The demonstration petered out after a couple of goofy, contrived incidents that resulted in the arrest of two of Sharpton's regulars. Trying to hold the stage, Sharpton shouted that he and a dozen stragglers would "spend the night, sleeping on the ground," if that's what it took to keep the grand jury from meeting. He then carefully reclined on a patch of dry grass and whistled up at the sky—for all of fifteen seconds. Just long enough so the cameras could get their shots. He and his remaining demonstrators then went home. The grand jury wasn't even in session.

And on March 24 there was a performance by the Brawley advisers that was shocking even for them. Summoning the press to the Metropolitan Baptist Church in Harlem (but not allowing them inside—the press conference took place outdoors), the three men guiding the fortunes of Tawana Brawley rained down a series of half-truths and slanderous lies for nearly an hour. The grand jury was meeting in Poughkeepsie's "old slave quarters—just a historical note," Maddox said—even though the Armory was in fact built in 1891, more than sixty years after the abolition of slavery in New York State. Tawana's schoolbooks, which had been discovered the week before in a classroom at Ketchum High School, had, according to Sharpton, been "placed there by the law-enforcement people responsible for her rape, so they wouldn't be caught with the evidence . . . and the white media accommodated them by puttin' it on the newsreel." Stephen Pagones, Mason asserted, "just happened to take four days off from work, from November 24 to November 28, we got the records on that."

And then Alton Maddox stood before the clustered micro-phones. "Now there is a new trick, an effort to engage us in propaganda, an effort to whitewash us." His voice rose. "It's an effort to make us believe that Steve Pagones is something other than a sexual pervert. That Harry Crist is something other than a sexual pervert. To make us believe that even Robert Abrams is something other than a sexual pervert. Robert Abrams . . . you are no longer going to masturbate lookin' at Tawana Brawley's picture. You are no longer going to go into the men's room with your perverted mind and rape our daughters. That is coming to an end."

Amazingly, a small handful of news organizations saw fit to quote one or more of the wild allegations; one respected radio network, National Public Radio, ran Maddox's mastur-bation quote nationwide as part of an update report on the Brawley case.

As ALWAYS, THERE WERE important stories done in that pe-riod, but they were buried by the avalanche of garish head-lines emanating from the Brawley camp or turned into new headlines shaped by the Brawley team's spin. The *Daily News* picked up the story from WKIP Radio about the similar and false story of abduction and rape told by a school chum of Tawana's and not only advanced the story—in the updated version, the two friends might have met and talked only days before Tawana's disappearance—but positioned it in the well from which all of the press drew daily.

The *New York Post* hit home with a revelation quickly obscured by the flood of more "dramatic" headline material; a pair of boots and jeans found in the old Brawley apartment, the *Post* reported, had actually been stolen from a next-door neighbor's apartment sometime just before Thanksgiving during the week of Tawana's disappearance. And the "cot-ton" found in Tawana's nose and one ear was actually ma-terial cut from the lining of the stolen boots.

NBC News won for itself the first announced boycott by the Brawley team when the network (and then local station WNBC) broadcast the original photograph of Tawana taken at St. Francis Hospital in Poughkeepsie, along with provocative details from the investigative files assembled in the beginning by the state police. The photograph showed the teenager naked from the waist up, eyes closed, electrodes and probes attached to her torso, with the faint letters "KKK" visible across her belly. The records broadcast by NBC demonstrated graphically how limited was Tawana's response when questioned in the hospital by police officer Thomas Young. When asked who had assaulted her, Tawana took a pen and scrawled the words "white cop." When asked if she'd been raped, she wrote, "a lot." Did any of the men address any of the others by name? Tawana spoke the only word she ever spoke in the first attempt to elicit her story in a face-to-face interview: ". . . son." That was it. Ralph King, the records said, told investigators initially "it might of been some roofers" he'd had a run-in with who were responsible for the attack on Tawana. NBC's risky blockbuster directly countered the months-long assertion by the Brawley advisers that Tawana had "named her assailants," given "full descriptions," and "told her whole story."

And the second-day stories on the NBC revelations were dominated by the reactions of the advisers.

"I can never in the history of the media," Mason said, "remember a law-enforcement body releasing a photograph of the unclothed body of a victim in a sexual attack to the media. It is a moral disgrace and an outrage. . . . Mario Cuomo, you've displayed the unclothed body of Tawana Brawley to the nation. She's seen it, and she cried."

Said Maddox, "We will be in Dutchess County, in large numbers, to deal not only with the question of the grand jury, but to deal with the secret nature of how you are carrying out this investigation. You have always operated in secret. You have always been a 'Night Rider.' But your horse is no longer riding."

Working the edges of a story that had surged back toward its central figures, Taibbi and Phillips missed each of those beats. A Task Force source had told them something about the boots but they hadn't picked up on the significance of the revelation, and they'd tried unsuccessfully to obtain a tape of the call made to WKIP by the mother of Tawana's friend. WKIP reporter and news director Kim Dillon was working hard at advancing the story herself, and while she let the Channel 2 reporters listen to the tape she refused to release it. "I'd like to punch Glenda Brawley in the face," the mother said on the tape. "She's not helping Tawana. Tawana's just doing the same thing my daughter did." The child's mother screamed hysterically through her locked door each time Taibbi and Phillips approached her, without cameras, in an attempt to establish contact.

NBC's scoop came out of the blue, a clean beat, and the two WCBS reporters found themselves being nudged by management and questioned by colleagues as they pursued their own way through the maze. They'd staked out Abrams and, after having researched the bar association's canons of ethics, pressed the attorney general in a careful but aggressive interview on the possible sanctions Maddox and Mason might face if their accusations against Pagones and others turned out to be unfounded and knowingly false. They learned and reported that Trayon Kirby, the friend who drove Tawana to Newburgh on the morning of the day she disappeared, had run afoul of the law again, this time on a gun charge in Poughkeepsie, and that the Brawley Task Force had embargoed word of the arrest in their continuing but ultimately unsuccessful attempt to squeeze something useful out of Kirby.

But as March drew to a close, the story swirling above them in a dozen persistent and confusing orbits, they'd been unable to get back to Newburgh for an extended stay or to make headway on the fringe. So on March 24, out of frustration as much as anything else, they agreed Taibbi would attend the scheduled press conference by the advisers at the Hyatt Hotel at Grand Central Station. It was the first press conference Taibbi had attended since the fiasco three weeks earlier in the basement of the Bronx Supreme Court building.

Right from the beginning, there was an air of unreality that exceeded anything Taibbi had imagined from reading the clips each day and monitoring the broadcast coverage, an anger and a tone of challenge deeper and more desperate than he'd seen himself the last time he'd been in the same room with the advisers. Maddox began by asserting that the advisers had obtained proof that Harry Crist hadn't committed suicide at all; that instead he'd been murdered by the others in the gang of white rapists when they feared he was weakening and about to blow the whistle. Maddox went on and on, in his halting, attacking style, adding almost cavalierly that state trooper Scott Patterson was also a member of the "gang." The pens flew on the page, the cameras and tape recorders ingested it all.

And then Sharpton, summoning all the dramatis in his persona, waved a photograph high in the air and, as the cameras zoomed to focus on the picture, described it as "proof positive" that Jack Ryan, the assistant special prosecutor handling the bulk of the investigation in Poughkeepsie, had "kicked, beaten, and stomped an innocent, helpless old blind man" during the futile demonstration the week before aimed at shutting down the grand jury. "I got criticized for comparin' Abrams to Hitler, and that's not even what I said," Sharpton intoned. "But I'm sayin' here that Jack Ryan is a Gestapo Wildman. I saw him kick Mr. Coolidge Miller, I was a witness. What could be lower than kickin' and whippin' a helpless old blind man. . . ?" Sharpton read from a photocopy of a chapter in state law handed him by Maddox, explaining that as a witness to the "beating" he was simply prepared to do his duty. A crudely typewritten "complaint" by Maddox calling for the arrest of Jack Ryan was distributed to the reporters in attendance, and as they perused this curiously worded document, Sharpton resumed his performance. "We are calling for the immediate arrest of Jack Ryan for the assault and beating of Coolidge Miller. If Mr. Ryan is not arrested by next Friday, we will go to Poughkeepsie and I will personally exercise my right to make a citizen's arrest of Mr. Ryan, either at the grand jury or at his home, whichever he prefers, and we'll march him down the street in handcuffs like it was done to so many of our people."

The photograph, copies of which were passed around among the reporters (and published by one New York daily), was a still shot taken off a television monitor and showed Ryan, his torso tilted down at a slight angle, standing over the prone figure of a man presumed to be Coolidge Miller. Ryan's hands were extended in a tentative gesture, the purpose of which was unclear from the fuzzy photograph. There were other figures, including two state troopers, in the frame. Taibbi took a long look at the picture and then went to the back of the conference room to pace and smoke a cigarette. Surprised at how little patience he had for the antics of the Brawley team and dismayed at the certainty that some in the room would file stories on the wild, almost hallucinatory charges they'd been listening to, he returned to his seat only when the question session started and waited for an opening.

"Mr. Sharpton . . . Mr. Sharpton!"

"You don't have to shout, Mr. Taibbi. You know, whether you believe it or not, I actually respect you—"

"Doesn't matter to me whether you do or not," Taibbi shot back, refusing to be patronized. "But we've listened to more allegations, a suicide that's now a murder, another cop who's a rapist, a beating by a prosecutor, and a couple of speeches and nonanswers to questions. I'd like you to answer this question: There have been reports, we broadcast one out of Newburgh, that whatever happened to Tawana Brawley might not have been done by a group of whites in Wappingers Falls. What if, for example, the assault was by black men?" Sharpton had conceded that very possibility after the first Taibbi/Phillips report from Newburgh in an interview with a CBS network correspondent—an interview never broadcast.

But now Sharpton paused, taken aback by a question that had nothing to do with the subject of the day's performance.

"Well . . . well, then," he began uncertainly. "Then it wouldn't be racial. But then," he added, recovering, "maybe it's Martians, 'cause there's been UFOs sighted up there, and maybe we ought to have a Martian grand jury. . . ."

BACK AT BROADCAST CENTER, Taibbi and Phillips reviewed the tapes of the press conference and then discussed the event with Sagan. They all agreed they would not run a story for that evening's news. Phillips remembered that someone matching Coolidge Miller's description had caused a disturbance during the Howard Beach trial; three quick phone calls confirmed it. Taibbi called his contacts at other television stations and a source at the Task Force. By nightfall he and Phillips were reviewing—frame by frame, in stop action and slow motion—three commercially broadcast versions of the "incident" plus the surveillance tape provided by their Task Force source. There was no question: not only hadn't Jack Ryan "kicked, beaten, and stomped" Coolidge Miller; he hadn't even touched him. In fact, they concluded, playing the tapes again and again, it was clear that in the eight seconds Ryan appeared on the steps of the Armory his only motion toward Miller—who had instigated the whole incident by roughly shoving a state trooper on the way into an auto insurance hearing—was to attempt to break the elderly man's fall. But he never did touch him; aides quickly summoned Ryan back inside.

"Whaddya think?" Taibbi asked his partner. "Doesn't have

a damn thing to do with what happened to Tawana Brawley, but we've got the tape. . . ."

Phillips nodded. "We ought to call Sagan now, but let's do the story."

THE STORY THAT PROVED the advisers had lied once again ran on March 29, and for the second time the Channel 2 reporting team locked horns with the Brawley advisers. Phillips's editing was sharp and unmistakably graphic; Taibbi's script, after reviewing the advisers' original accusation, burrowed for home.

> TAIBBI NARRATION:
> . . . But the tapes of the incident which we've examined tell an entirely different story.
>
> A lone state trooper is walking through the small gathering.
>
> Here is Coolidge Miller . . . who was involved in a similar fracas with court officers during the Howard Beach trial.
>
> Sharpton and others shout at the trooper . . . and as the trooper tries to walk free of the group, Miller crowds him and then shoves him . . . hard. The trooper turns and grabs Miller.
>
> During the ensuing shoving match, John Ryan, the man in the white shirt, emerges from the Armory and, as Miller slips to the ground, makes a gesture as though to break the man's fall. John Ryan neither whips, nor beats, nor kicks Coolidge Miller. It's not even certain from this tape that he even touched him. Within eight seconds, Ryan returns inside the Armory.
>
> So the Brawley team yesterday either lied outright, or manufactured an incident for their own purposes.
>
> Maddox said, perhaps accurately, that they really can't afford to lie, or be wrong. . . .

MADDOX: *We should be allowed to make a boo boo, but we can't make one, because everybody is waiting for us to make a boo boo.*

TAIBBI NARRATION:
But maybe Al Sharpton, unwittingly, had the real explanation. He is, after all, the self-appointed spokesman. If the facts or the context differ from his version, he said, it doesn't matter as long as the "basic story" holds up: the "basic stories," one can only assume, ranging from John Ryan's alleged "gestapo tactics" last week . . . to the alleged four-day abduction, rape, and sodomy and maiming of Tawana Brawley last November by six white men, one a cop and one, Sharpton and Maddox have charged, a named assistant district attorney. . . .

They ended the piece with Sharpton's preposterous but telling comment about the Martian grand jury, and waited for the phones to ring. They didn't have to wait more than a few seconds—the time it took for the calls to be routed from the main switchboard downstairs up to the newsroom. One call came from Sharpton himself, who demanded a meeting with general manager Roger Colloff and news director Paul Sagan.

Colloff was out of town and in his stead station manager Gene Lothery hosted the meeting. Lothery, soon to become programming vice president for the CBS Stations Division, was one of the highest-ranking blacks at any of the three major networks, and according to Sagan, he didn't buy any of Sharpton's bluster.

"Do you really believe the video shows that nothing happened?" Sharpton kept asking, even after Lothery and Sagan had played the Taibbi/Phillips piece several times. Lothery looked Sharpton square in the eye each time: "Yes. That's what the video shows," he repeated time and again.

Sharpton began the meeting by insisting ". . . you gotta stop this Taibbi, he's biased, his stories are biased, we may have to picket the station." But Lothery and Sagan insisted that yanking Taibbi and Phillips from the story wasn't even discussable. Anything else?

Sharpton "did a one-eighty," according to Sagan. "It was clear that he thought for the first time he was losing control of the story, and that he needed to find a way to get us back on his agenda. He'd only issued veiled threats at the beginning of the meeting; in the end, his approach was basically to say, 'Look, we have to work together, this is important.' We agreed; it was important." The meeting ended.

APRIL FOOL'S DAY was the last time during the Tawana Brawley story that anybody laughed openly, publicly, and on camera. It was also the day that the story slipped perceptibly into one of the absurd corners of the modern news-gathering process occupied uniquely by local television.

It wasn't the machinery that was at fault. In fact, the machinery, as always in the modern age, was a small if unremarked miracle. Channel 2's small miracle, for example, was the work of the station's operations supervisor, Jim Fleischmann.

Fleischmann, a pilot, had on orders from Sagan done an air and ground survey of the Poughkeepsie–Wappingers Falls area back in December. His charts told him that Mount Beacon, in Fishkill, was at about 1,500 feet in elevation, his best chance at a straight microwave shot to Manhattan. A records search led him to the owner of the existing "antenna patch" atop Mount Beacon, radio station WBNR. He negotiated a lease deal—$300 a month for space on the main antenna—and in Poughkeepsie talked the custodian of the County Office Building into letting him set up a semipermanent transmitter link on the roof. If he could transmit from the rooftop in Poughkeepsie to a repeater on Mount Beacon, he reasoned, he'd have line of sight for a microwave shot from the mountaintop to Manhattan's receive towers on Empire and World Trade. All the others would have to lease or deploy their own satellite—or KU—truck, at an operational cost of tens of thousands of dollars a month, if they wanted to get out live from Poughkeepsie. If his Rube Goldberg jury-rig worked, Channel 2 could simply send any of its live mini-vans and broadcast live for the cost of a regular crew.

All he had to do was get to the mountaintop.

"No new toys," Fleischmann explained. "I had to use what was available from the discard pile—some old goldenrods, a little receiver the size of a ghetto blaster. Our transmitting antenna the first time out was going to be a four-foot dish on a tripod on the ground that I'd have to switch on and pan manually; I knew I was going to put the receive antenna in a crow's nest on the tower, facing in all four directions. That way the mountain could be accessible for such a great distance around that we'd literally open up a whole new coverage area, which was what Sagan wanted. The Brawley case was just the excuse to do it, and it made sense."

Fleischmann hit it off with WBNR's chief engineer, Dave Rozak, who time after time made the four-wheel-drive hike up the mountain and, after Fleischmann had installed whatever equipment he'd brought up, would come and pick him up.

"It wasn't much more than a cowpath," Fleischmann said. "A terrible road. We'd slam down, skidding all the way, streams and ravines flowing over the damn road. A lot of places it was a sheet of ice, at a forty-five-degree angle no less, and we'd bounce off the boulders as we came down. Your heart was in your throat."

The jury-rig, the old "toys," didn't always work. Temperature inversions (excessive heat), fog, sleet, snow, the radio frequency disturbances from all the paging services and other broadcast operations—radio and television—all tended to degrade Fleischmann's signal. It got so he had to turn on his

mountain manually and lock the signal in himself each time
Channel 2 wanted to broadcast live or feed tape, since the
automated power-switching devices he'd installed failed repeatedly. Back in New York, they called it Voodoo Mountain. But it was Fleischmann's baby, and when it worked,
primitive as the system was, it was as clean as a live shot
from Central Park, ten blocks from the station.

"If you're a techie," Fleischmann said, "you're convinced
that with a little bit of fiddling here and there, getting out of
anyplace with a broadcast-quality signal can be reduced to a
piece of copper wire. Bink, bink. Nothing more than a piece
of copper wire."

APRIL 1 BEGAN EARLY for the Brawley press corps, and seriously enough in intent. Coolidge Miller was in one courtroom, having been charged with assault against a state trooper
and disorderly conduct stemming from the "incident" on the
Armory steps. Tawana's friend Trayon Kirby was due in another courtroom to answer gun possession charges, and his
proceeding would be recorded by news cameras, a first in
Dutchess County since the state's new cameras-in-the-courtroom statute had gone into effect.

And of course Al Sharpton, shaking off the impact of the
Channel 2 report and a *New York Post* editorial on February
25 lauding television's success in "exposing Sharpton as a
reckless fraud without a following" after having created him
in the first place, was in Poughkeepsie to make his "citizen's
arrest" of Jack Ryan. In a way, his brazen arrival in the city
was an undeniable message that Sharpton and the Brawley
family lawyers were prepared to stay with the play until the
bitter end. The *Post* editorial had been brutal: "Ryan, of course,
assaulted nobody. The television news footage demonstrates
this beyond a shadow of a doubt. . . . The trio's charges [are]
additional examples of their desperate need to divert attention from the actual case. These are people who will say lit-

erally anything. To them, Tawana Brawley is a tool—a brush with which to paint the New York criminal justice system as racist. . . . Whatever really happened to Miss Brawley last November, it wasn't what she said had happened. . . . Sharpton, Maddox and Mason have now slandered Ryan just as they slandered Asst. Dutchess County District Attorney Stephen Pagones. . . . Ryan and Pagones should sue for slander. They'd win. . . . It's past time for the state Bar Association to begin disciplinary proceedings against Mason and Maddox."

But that was just the editorial page. Everybody still had a news hole to fill, and Sharpton and the Brawley story promised a way to fill it.

So the press corps was on hand, a hundred strong. Two New York television stations had booked KU trucks, half-million- to three-quarters-of-a-million-dollar rigs that could transmit directly to a chosen satellite. Channel 2, with Fleischmann on Voodoo Mountain and his support troops on the roof of the County Office Building in Poughkeepsie, was also prepared to broadcast live at any moment. With the KU trucks and live-shot mini-vans parked up and down Market Street, scores of state troopers and sheriff's department deputies standing guard at every entrance to every official building, and the mob of reporters and cameramen shuttling between two courtrooms and surging like schooling minnows at every movement by Al Sharpton, sedate Poughkeepsie—home of Vassar College and one-time way station for FDR on his way to Hyde Park—awoke to a Friday unlike any in its past.

Phillips started out on the Trayon Kirby hearing, which ended quickly enough for her to be able to join Taibbi at the tail end of the Coolidge Miller proceeding. She ducked into the outer lobby of Poughkeepsie City Court in time to hear her partner questioning Miller. The elderly man was shaking his head, repeating that, no, he didn't actually remember being kicked, by Ryan or anybody else. Then Sharpton and Maddox emerged from the courtroom, and Phillips raced outside to make certain her two camera crews were in position and fired up.

Sharpton, though, headed straight for Taibbi instead of leaving the courthouse. Phillips stood on the edge of a cement planter and peered over the heads of the rest of the reporters and cameramen as the two men gestured angrily toward each other.

"Mr. Miller just told me even he doesn't remember being kicked, and obviously the tapes show he wasn't," Taibbi was saying loudly.

"Well, you got your tapes, we got ours," Sharpton said angrily, bellying close to the reporter. "I was a witness, I'm gonna make my arrest."

"You'll never get near him, you know it. It's just a damn media show!"

"Yuh, we'll see."

"Mr. Sharpton, I've gotta ask you—"

"Ask nothin'!" Sharpton cut him off. "Y'all ask yuh damn questions. Why're you tryin' all the time to knock holes in our story?"

Now Taibbi pressed close to Sharpton. " 'Cause there *are* holes! You know there are!"

Sharpton spun around, caught the eye of an aide, Derek "Sunshine" Jeter, and motioned with his head that it was time to go. But he turned to Taibbi and had the last word.

"Far as we can tell, Taibbi, there's only two significant holes in the story Tawana told us. Only two!" He thrust two thick fingers in the air and strutted out to meet his press.

The rest of the day was an exercise in dramatic invention, and bankrupt invention at that. Sharpton and Maddox were turned away at the entrance to D.A. Bill Grady's office, but stayed long enough so the cameras and microphones could record an abbreviated version of the Four Hundred Years of Oppression. Then, swinging a pair of handcuffs, Sharpton, Pied

Piper to the scribblers and lensmen on one of the fourth estate's less glorious days, led a comic procession down Market
Street.

It was high noon when the procession reached the front of
the County Office Building, where Taibbi was standing, microphone in hand, ready to begin his live shot. Yanking the
cables for his mike and earpiece to see how much play he
had, he stepped into the line of march and shouted to Sharpton. The minister and the reporter, who a half hour before
had been screaming at each other in earnest, now played out
a silly charade for the live New York audience gathered around
approximately 560,000 television sets. Taibbi asked Sharpton
to show the handcuffs, and the minister-cum-vigilante, happy
to oblige, swung them menacingly close to the camera and
then leaned into the lens to issue his sternest warnings to
Ryan, Grady, Abrams, Cuomo, and anybody else who came
to his fertile mind. Taibbi, on camera now, smiled in embarrassment, but amusement too; the man's audacious, he
thought. Give him that.

Phillips picked up the procession as it approached the Armory, and bodied in among the other reporters to shove still
another microphone in front of Sharpton. Office workers on
lunch hour scattered to the opposite side of Market Street; a
few hooted, many laughed out loud. Other locals, who stayed
in their offices, peered down from their windows in disbelief.
Sharpton surveyed the cordon of unsmiling uniforms massed
at the Armory entrance and thought better of a direct approach. Instead, he sauntered around the corner to a side door,
waiting patiently for the press mob to catch up with him,
and began pounding soundlessly on the locked heavy metal
door. Looking up toward a window that was hundreds of yards
away from the office normally occupied by Jack Ryan and
the Brawley Task Force, he bellowed again and again, shaking his handcuffs above his head. "Ry-yun! Ry-yun! Ry-yun,
come out here! Ry-yun!"

The assembled reporters roared in laughter. Phillips, scanning the scene, saw that even Alton Maddox was laughing. She'd never seen him laugh before, and never would again.

Unknown to the press corps outside, Jack Ryan was doubled over in hysterics behind the locked door. A source said later that for hours after his intended arrest, Ryan stalked the corridors of the Armory with a toothbrush and a tube of toothpaste sticking out of his back pocket, "just in case" Sharpton cuffed him and dragged him to the pokey, he explained, exploding in laughter each time he came to the punchline.

Taibbi had wrapped his noon live shot long before the scene at the Armory played out. He watched as Nick Fischer and Doug Volpe, his live crew, began the process of breaking down their equipment. Volpe, a young veteran, dismantled the cellular phone link to Control Room 46; Fischer, senior man, had been in on the birthing of the videotape/satellite era in television and had truly seen it all. Poughkeepsie on April 1 was just another live shot, his expression said. The reporter watched him coil his cables carefully, then looked to the roof of the County Office Building. Seven floors up, another experienced technician, Wayne McGuire, was reeling in the video cable that led from the camera on the street to his rooftop goldenrod transmitter, which in turn aimed the pictures from the street to Jim Fleischman's mountain, which finally, in its subinstant's trip of seventy-five miles, carried its cargo to Empire and by cable to Broadcast Center and out again, cables and microwaves alive in synaptic fury, to more than half a million HUTs—homes using television—and in Control Room 46 a dozen highly specialized technicians made sure the work of half as many producers and writers and twice as many researchers and editors and cameramen in the field carried the idiocy of Al Sharpton's charade accurately, faithfully, dramatically, into all those HUTs, a piece of copper wire if ever there was one.

The power had been seized by the Process, Taibbi knew; and live shots and satellites had changed the Process—and thereby television and the news itself—unalterably. The reporter looked across Market Street, at the head of Main Mall. A friend and colleague, just a thesis short of his doctorate in literature, shifted his weight from foot to foot while his station's KU truck, the three-quarters-of-a-million-dollar machine, attached the piece of copper wire by gripping the ground on metal feet and extending it to the Clarke Belt, 26,500 miles high, reaching to the heavens for its very own satellite, the designated transponder reserved for the day yawing in hunger, the even more specialized technician inside the KU twisting his dials and assuring *his* control room that, yes, they were holding spacecraft, and the near-doctor of literature could begin talking about Al Sharpton and showing pictures of Sharpton's shenanigans anytime New York pleased.

The old elements of news gathering were obsolete, superfluous, anachronistic, on Market Street, and Market Street was everywhere; when New York pleased, which was often and anytime, there wasn't time for the reporter in the field to do his research, learn over time, stride into the field to find his story's angles and subtleties and sidebars, *craft* the story. Now the process, piece of copper wire in place, said those tasks had to be performed simultaneously or skipped altogether, the time for judgment and planning compressed to minutes and seconds, the individual and his particular mind's eye replaced by teams of technicians and the eyelet in the sky through which the piece of copper wire was laced, so delicately and wonderfully, again and again and again. The promo writers in New York had just as good a chance of seeing their best notions turned instantly into television as the most seasoned, thoughtful *news* people; they all sat at the same switch. The process was magic and it wasn't; men had invented it, around a core of black box mysticism, and made it work better and better and better. Taibbi loved it casually but loathed it specifically, and knew too that while he could own the process for minutes at a time there was always the risk he'd give in to it, offer his mind as its chattel, fail unal-

terably to make his minutes matter. It had happened before;
it had happened this noon. He'd been a silly talking head and
a willing player in a farce. He could not bear in that instant
to look south down Market Street, where the minister with
the pompadour held fast to his end of the piece of copper
wire while the people who owned it, or should have owned
it, left it in his hands. The reporter looked up at the roof
again. Who knows what he expected to see, but Wayne
McGuire was gone, probably headed for lunch. His minutes
were over, wasted.

IN THE SCRIPT for his six o'clock piece, Taibbi, just another
participant in the day's ludicrous events, wrote derisively and
belatedly of the "street theater of the absurd" along Poughkeepsie's Market Street on April Fool's Day. Sagan, reviewing the script in New York, told him to strike the reference.
    Write it straight, he said.

7

"Perry! Talk to this here black girl!"

WHEN AL SHARPTON stuck out his chin and peered into one camera lens after another to announce the intended "citizen's arrest" of Jack Ryan, one man in the television audience nearly jumped out of his chair. And when the minister without a congregation (save the assembled press) added one of his typical personal flourishes— "I'm gonna drag that little punk off the steps of the Armory," Sharpton said of Ryan— the man watching the office television set raced for the phone, punched the extension for his press aide, and dictated a statement for the media that was stronger than anything he'd said in his sixty days on the job.

"If Reverend Sharpton, Mr. Maddox, or Mr. Mason lay so much as a finger on the body or person of John Ryan," Bob

Abrams dictated to aide Timothy Gilles, "they are on notice that they do so at their civil and criminal peril."

The forty-nine-year-old attorney general was entering the third month of the most vexing and dangerous assignment of his public life. Since January 26, the day Gov. Mario Cuomo had named him special prosecutor in the Brawley case, Abrams had walked a tightrope with no safety net below, knowing that if he slipped his political future in what he called the "post-Cuomo era" would crash with him.

According to a highly placed source in Abrams's office, there was "never any question" that the soft-spoken, bald, and bespectacled attorney general would take on the Brawley case. A few days before the January 26 announcement, John Poklemba, the Cuomo aide and state director of criminal justice who would "run point" for the governor throughout the case, called Jack Ryan and Assistant Attorney General Scott Greathead to inform them that in all likelihood Abrams would get the call. It was not lost on the two men that Cuomo's relationship with Abrams was "cold, at best," and that the governor never asked his attorney general—the state's lawyer, after all—for advice or counsel; even in the Howard Beach case, Cuomo had appointed Charles Hynes as special prosecutor without consultation even though that designation was required by law to come from the office of the attorney general. "The AG hated the way the governor treated him," the source said. "For example, Abrams always wanted to be referred to as Bob, but the governor always called him Bobby, just to get his goat." And a highly placed federal source let it be known to some reporters that when U.S. Attorney Rudolph Giuliani phoned Cuomo early on to offer not only the services of the FBI crime lab and his staff of investigators but also his own involvement if necessary, the governor is said to have replied, "No . . . that's all right. I'm gonna let Bobby handle it."

But Abrams, a career public servant from the Bronx who believed correctly that the passage to his political destiny would be fueled by his demonstrated competence rather than

a dramatic public persona and ceremonial grandstanding—
he declined to be referred to as General, the traditional salutation embraced by his predecessors—did not question the
advice of his senior staff. Ryan, who'd prosecuted homicide
cases out of the Queens district attorney's office, was eager
to take on the Brawley investigation. Greathead, senior assistant and head of the Criminal Prosecutions Bureau, saw the
assignment as a natural extension of his own aims for the
office. At the time, the attorney general's office carried an
enormous caseload—more than 30,000 cases a year—but the
vast majority were white-collar cases in the areas of tax
evasion, consumer rips, insurance fraud, and environmental
violations. Civil cases, no sex appeal. Occasionally the office
went after political corruption cases that generated a few
headlines; but Greathead and Ryan told Poklemba to inform
Cuomo the office was ready and willing to take on Brawley.
They contacted Dennison Young, senior assistant to Giuliani, and had the case papers from the preliminary federal civil
rights investigation messengered over. Poklemba sent down
a copy of Judge Judith Hillery's detailed letter to the governor
explaining why Bill Grady and David Sall had resigned from
the case.

"They didn't know what it would turn into, but they knew
it would be a case that would tax their investigative skills,"
a source in Abrams's office said. "The thing is, given Cuomo's aloof relationship with Bob, this was the kind of case
that normally would have gone elsewhere. Abrams was going
to take it, period. The office had never gone after anything
like this; back to the days of Abrams's predecessor, Louie
Lefkowitz, there was never a comparable case—allegations
that a girl was abducted and raped, with the racial thing
thrown in, and the incredible public outcry."

From the beginning, Bob Abrams handled the Brawley case
with circumspection and caution, befitting his nature. "An
example," the source explained. "We assumed at the outset
that the Brawley advisers were simply looking out for their
client, that they were just naturally and understandably sus-

picious of anybody in law enforcement. There was a con-
scious decision to refrain from qualifying our characterizations
of the case—no 'alleged' rape or 'claimed' assault. Bob went
out before the cameras and called it a 'terrible assault,' a
'shocking and appalling crime.' There was a clear intent to
not antagonize the advisers, even though we knew Bob would
come under attack because, it was true, he'd never actually
tried a criminal case. Some columnists picked up on that part,
and the advisers went to town on it, but we expected it. In
the beginning, it wasn't clear at all that the case was a bag
of shit, so to speak. It was a case, there were leads, there was
work to be done; everybody was eager to get started."

Abrams started by putting together a staff that made it clear
the investigation of Tawana Brawley was the highest priority
in his office. His field investigators included twelve of his
most experienced people, and the eight members of his prosecuting team represented a wealth of legal talent surprising
even to the senior staff who put the team together.

"It was amazing when we started looking at the people we
had, even outside the Criminal Prosecutions Bureau," Greathead would observe later. "There was so much talent that
was just right for this case. There was a woman in a small
part of the office that handles unemployment compensation
cases, Heather Williams, whom I'd hired a few months earlier. When I checked her résumé, I noticed she'd spent two
and a half years prosecuting civil rights cases for the Justice
Department!"

So Heather Williams, a black woman who graduated from
Harvard Law School in 1981, became one of the first members of the prosecution team. Serving under Jack Ryan, she
was joined by others with appropriate skills from Abrams's
vast staff of nearly 500 attorneys, including Stephen Quigley
and John Morabito, former homicide prosecutors; and Charles
Sanders, Suzanne Lynn, and Sanford Cohen, all young veterans of public interest and civil liberties law.

Still, no one in Abrams's office was under the illusion that
a top-flight team and the on-site involvement of the state's

highest law-enforcement officer would automatically placate the Brawley advisers. No one was surprised in the least when Alton Maddox took to the airwaves on black radio station WLIB, within hours of Abrams's appointment, and said, "We are not satisfied at all. We know nothing of Mr. Ryan, and he has no track record in civil rights. That would indicate to us that the governor is skeptical that a crime has been committed. It is obvious that the governor has a vendetta against us. We will not allow the governor or the attorney general to continue to inflict emotional trauma on Tawana Brawley. There will be no cooperation." Maddox and Mason repeated their position that the logical choice of special prosecutor was Charles Hynes, who'd won convictions against three white youths in the Howard Beach case. (As was pointed out by *Newsday* columnist Dennis Duggan, Maddox, Mason, and Sharpton had branded Hynes a racist and vigorously opposed him before mainstream black leaders prevailed and successfully urged Hynes's appointment.)

What *was* surprising, on the morning of January 26, was that Cuomo himself called WLIB, asked to be put on the air, and engaged the Brawley lawyers in an emotional colloquy that lasted fully twenty minutes. "You have a role to play here," the governor pleaded with them. "You have the confidence of the family. You can help to see that justice is done, even though I can't make you do it."

Maddox and Mason, emboldened by the unexpected demonstration of their own importance—the governor of the state had called to talk to them—became even more intransigent. Cuomo "didn't understand" the case, they asserted, and was "incapable of appointing a good-faith prosecutor."

"I implore you," Cuomo said time and again. "Go to the Brawleys. Tell them that the governor wants to help and I will help you in every way I can. The trail is getting colder. Without cooperation, I'm afraid that we're not going to be able to do it."

Give us another special prosecutor, the lawyers countered.

The governor, his gambit an apparent failure, called a halt

to the conversation. "Mr. Abrams is the chief legal officer of this state," he said finally. "He has three times been elected by strong majorities. He is extremely well-equipped for this task, and has all the resources he needs. There will be no other appointment."

CUOMO'S FIRMNESS, COUPLED with his willingness to make the dramatic gesture, seemed to bear fruit two weeks later. For a few hours the standoff between New York State and the Brawley family advisers dissolved. There they were, leading every station's newscast on February 11; Maddox, Mason, Sharpton, and Gov. Mario Cuomo taking turns at the microphone, describing the results of a three-and-a-half-hour meeting that was extraordinary in that it had occurred at all.

"On behalf of the Brawley family," Maddox said, "I want to extend my sincere thanks to the governor for the efforts he made today to get this investigation rolling. Tawana is not physically or psychologically ready to talk yet, but she will certainly at the appropriate time . . . be a witness."

"This is a case that needed to receive the necessary resources," Mason added. "The governor has made his appointment, and has assured us that Mr. Abrams will be involved in the grand jury process."

Cuomo, looking vaguely uncomfortable, began his statement by suggesting that nothing had really changed in the state's position: "Mr. Abrams has been working fifteen hours a day on this matter since I appointed him, and will continue to do so." He then reiterated his oft-stated position that bias-related crimes against anyone—black, gay, Italian—would be aggressively investigated. Sharpton, edging close so he could stand directly over the governor's left shoulder, peered up at the ceiling of the capitol lobby. "But today's development by Mr. Maddox and Mr. Mason," Cuomo concluded, "their willingness to cooperate, takes us a giant step closer in this matter. I assume from this point forward the prosecution will move swiftly, expeditiously, and successfully."

Sharpton actually shouldered the governor away then and grabbed the gooseneck microphone. "We have put aside whatever long-term commitments we have, so that we can deal with the Tawana Brawley case. We needed to break the stalemate, and we have done that. Today is a day of *engage*, not outrage."

The engagement, though, barely outlasted the next morning's headlines. The advisers took turns suggesting to the reporters who were always just a phone call away that they were "going to have to talk to Abrams and deal with a few issues" before committing Tawana to cooperate.

Sure enough, a week after the press conference with Cuomo in the state capitol, the advisers stood alone at the podium in Abrams's New York City press room and announced that the deal was off, the impasse back in place. Two days of talks totaling more than thirteen and a half hours had "proved to us," said Alton Maddox, "that Abrams is aligning himself with the culprits." Mason charged that the trio had learned Bob Abrams had been "destroying" the records of the tips pouring into the special hotline set up by the Brawley Task Force. Sharpton vowed that if the governor refused to replace Abrams, "We're gonna announce a day of civil disobedience like you've never seen before; we're gonna shut down the state capital."

When the advisers were finished Abrams reclaimed his own press room, and an aide replaced the seal of the attorney general on the podium. "At least we were able to remove it before the Brawley bunch started their press conference," a source said bitterly. "I thought it was awfully generous of Bob to let them use the room in the first place. . . . I mean, it was obvious from the first hour of the first day's talks that it wasn't going anywhere. We'd given up hope they were ever going to come around.

"I mean, it was ridiculous," the source continued. "They had an agenda of conditions that were just unacceptable. They wanted Abrams to agree in advance he was going to examine all the key witnesses, that the U.S. Attorney and the FBI would

not be involved, that Abrams would make opening and closing statements—the kind of things that simply couldn't be
agreed to before you knew there were going to be any defendants, or how many defendants, or one trial or five trials.
You didn't know whether the defendants or witnesses were
going to be the kind of people where the jury would be neg-
atively impressed if the attorney general himself came in and
put the full force of the state on top of their heads. Things
like that can backfire, and we didn't feel those were the kind
of commitments we ought to be making lightly; there was a
problem, too, in the principle of making commitments just
to get a victim to cooperate. That's the kind of thing a defense lawyer can really go to town on, making deals of that
type. We were willing to say, and said it frequently, that 'Bob
will be personally involved in all phases of the investigation.'
But that wasn't going to do it. They kept repeating their major 'conditions,' and then they added four or five more. We
figured, why agree to even one ridiculous condition when it
was obvious we were going to have problems with the rest
of them? The second day, we caucused, finally, and said, 'Let's
cut it short; let them do what they're going to do. They'll do
it anyway. And that was that. . . .'"

Abrams had Timothy Gilles take the unusual step of dis-
tributing a detailed memo to the "Reporters Covering the
Tawana Brawley Case." The memo rebutted the claims by
Maddox and Mason that Abrams had violated a "confiden-
tiality agreement" by discussing the "conditions" deemed to
be unacceptable; Gilles, Abrams's director of policy and
communications, attached several newspaper clippings to the
memo, clips of stories in which Maddox specifically had discussed those same "conditions" prior to even meeting with
the attorney general, just in case there were any reporters
who failed to get the point.

They got the point. Tawana wasn't going to talk, and the
man running the investigation wanted it to be known that it
wasn't for lack of effort and good faith on his part.

Two days after the headlines shouted, "Talks Collapse,"

"Tawana Agreement Cancelled," "Brawley Lawyers Halt Aid in Inquiry," the trio showed up at Abrams's New York City press room one more time, unannounced, to attack the attorney general. They'd daybooked a press conference with every news organization in town without bothering to ask permission to use the room; but Abrams shrugged when told the trio was in the lobby and said, Why not?

"No point in making a fuss over it," a source explained. "These were just unusual people; they would do things you would just never expect ordinary people to do."

So Bob Abrams and the Brawley Task Force went to work knowing, and informing the special grand jury, that in all likelihood Tawana Brawley would never tell her story under oath. The early analysis of the available physical evidence relating to the teenager's medical condition and the scene where she'd been discovered tended in each instance to prove the negative: Tawana Brawley had been neither assaulted nor raped. The hospital rape kit test, analyzed by the FBI crime lab in Washington, D.C., showed no evidence of sexual contact.

The potentially explosive witnesses in the early stage— including the mailman who saw the "troop car" filled with white men and the youth who said he saw Tawana "dumped from a car"—retracted their stories or conceded they were false to begin with. Though two of the three men named as "suspects in the attack" by the Brawley advisers refused to be interviewed (Harry Crist had earlier committed suicide), Task Force investigators confirmed that Steve Pagones, state trooper Scott Patterson, and Crist had lived documentably routine lives involving work, family, and friends during Tawana Brawley's disappearance and could in no way have been involved in her abduction, let alone a four-day orgy of rape and violence.

"I mean, there was just nothing there," the source in Abrams's office explained. "Everybody was somewhere. There was nothing that would give you any type of a lead, in terms of the story attributed to Tawana and the few statements she did make. Then you'd hear these rumors, people coming in with wild and fantastic stories. Some guy says he saw her getting put in a car by a couple of Hispanic drug dealers who then drove her to an old abandoned house. And you go out to the house and it's nothing like the guy said it was. Everything was always sort of evaporating into smoke and dust. It was discouraging, early on, in terms of identifying any crime, any perpetrators. It was all going one way; we started really wondering what happened. What had *really* happened . . .''

THE MORE THE EVIDENCE suggested Tawana's story could not be supported, the wilder, it seemed, were the allegations from the Brawley advisers. Abrams kept his cool and his counsel; despite the ever-hovering and voracious press corps, and the ceaseless attacks by the advisers on his character and competence, the taciturn and almost painfully formal father of two managed to avoid having a single inflammatory quote attributed to him.

That is, until he heard Al Sharpton boast about the coming arrest of Jack Ryan. And then a strange thing happened. Abrams's challenge to Sharpton and the lawyers, coupled with the farce in Poughkeepsie on April Fool's Day and an equally pathetic showing in Albany when Sharpton and a tiny band of true believers failed to shut down anything at all, caused public opinion to surge in one of the wild shifts that had come to characterize the case. Abrams was suddenly "winning," winning in the columns and political cartoons on the Op Ed pages, winning too in the minds of many in the regular Brawley press. Even the black press.

Jesse Walker of the *Amsterdam News*, the black weekly which to that point had voiced unqualified support for both Tawana's story and the strategies of her advisers, was as tough as anybody.

The Tawana Brawley sexual assault case fizzled this past week to a state of negatives, most orchestrated by the Rev. Al Sharpton.

Tawana was still not cooperating with the state investigation of her charges of assault by six white men, on the advice of her lawyers, C. Vernon Mason and Alton Maddox.

The Rev. Sharpton, the girl's advisor, had threatened to make a citizen's arrest in Poughkeepsie last Friday of John Ryan, the assistant special prosecutor in the case.

He didn't.

Rev. Sharpton had threatened to close down three state agencies in Albany on Monday, predicting that some 1,500 to 2,000 would be on hand to protest the way Gov. Cuomo and the state have been handling the Brawley case.

He didn't.

He also promised a sit-in at the state agencies on the anniversary of the killing of Dr. Martin Luther King, Jr.

He didn't.

What did happen was that Sharpton and 13 others were arrested in Albany outside state buildings after spending the afternoon marching around the Capitol, banging on gates at the Executive Mansion, tugging on locked doors at state office buildings and trying to block traffic. They were accused of marching without a permit. Included among those arrested was folk singer Pete Seeger.

The *Daily News* commissioned a poll, which showed that a nearly unbelievable 90 percent of whites *and* blacks who were familiar with the Brawley case believed she should testify. Cuomo and Abrams received surprisingly strong biracial support for their handling of the case.

It seemed for days on end that the Brawley team was on the run, that they'd overplayed their hand, that their always limited constituency had shrunk to a hard-core troupe whose influence and impact were all but invisible. The four-person team of FBI agents assigned to the federal investigation filed its first two "21-day Reports" and made it clear there was no evidence of any civil rights violations against Tawana Brawley. Legal experts began urging some members of Abrams's team of prosecutors to get the boss thinking about wrapping it up quickly.

Then, on April 7, Brawley Task Force investigator William West was arrested for selling three ounces of cocaine to an undercover cop in Brooklyn, and the Brawley advisers were revived. It didn't matter that West had been on sick leave almost from the beginning of the investigation. The thirty-nine-year-old West, Sharpton chortled, was "the main investigator on the case, the black [Abrams] danced in front of us and that he expected Tawana to talk to." The Brooklyn minister claimed Abrams had told him personally that if and when Tawana decided to cooperate, it would be West who conducted the interview.

"We never had any reason to suspect they were dope sellers," Sharpton told his suddenly reassembled press entourage. "Dopes? Yes. But never dope sellers."

TAIBBI AND PHILLIPS were back in Poughkeepsie the morning the news broke of the arrest of William West. They'd gotten together after spending two days pursuing different leads in three counties. Their stories from Newburgh and their recent exposure of the advisers in the Jack Ryan "Gestapo Wildman" episode had put them on the media map in the Hudson Valley and, by phone and in letters, the tips had been pouring in. There were two themes: Tawana's disappearance was in some fundamental way connected to her relationships with the people and activities of Newburgh's Crack Alley; and, since none of the evidence gathered so far supported Tawana's story of abduction and rape, someone close to her, the tipsters urged, had to know the truth or at least a piece of the truth.

Taibbi had gone to Newburgh, played a round of golf with Deputy Police Chief Bill Bloom and two of Bloom's detectives, bar-hopped that night in some of Newburgh's unseemliest joints, and spoke to a half-dozen young hookers who worked the tree-lined strip outside the crumbling Washington Hotel (many tipsters maintained that Tawana had "worked parties" as a prostitute, claims many reporters heard and ran down and eventually found to be baseless). Arriving late in Poughkeepsie, he repeated the routine of bars and lowlife. For his troubles, he came away with the names (or, more precisely, street names) of a couple of Newburgh youths who'd supposedly spent some time with Tawana Brawley during her disappearance; and, from a self-described enemy of Ralph King who ducked into a booth in Poughkeepsie's Imperial Bar when told the lone white guy in the room was a reporter from New York, he heard a recitation of King's alleged drug-buying habits. "Small time, small stuff, mostly reefer," the man explained. "But when this Tawana case got big, one day he came in with a few thou, and was looking to buy weight." The reporter also made stops in two Poughkeepsie bars reputed to be the hot spots for whites looking to score cocaine; Hermano L., he recalled, had talked about some white guys from "the other side of the river" who'd initiated a drug deal that had gone sour, with Tawana Brawley caught in the cross fire. Waiting in each instance for someone to recognize him and initiate a conversation, Taibbi asked quietly whether any of the so-called suspects named by the Brawley advisers were regular or even sometime customers. The answer, each time he posed the question, was an unqualified "no."

Phillips had traveled with cameraman Don Janney, by now the third member of Channel 2's permanent Brawley case team, and "made the rounds" of Tawana's relatives and friends. Janney, meticulous about his equipment and insistent that its use be maximized, made certain that every time

Phillips stepped out of the car to approach a possible interview subject she was already wearing a live and hidden microphone, and, if she was entering a house or a building and would therefore be out of his line of sight, that she also carried a portable radio—the "brick," he called it—so she could summon him immediately if need be.

The pair worked Monticello first, since Tawana had moved back into the home of her uncle and father-figure, Matt Strong. Janney backed his car into the lee of a hanging willow tree as Phillips approached the house, took a few deep breaths, and checked once more to make certain her (hidden) mike was on. It was. Just then a yellow compact car pulled into the driveway and a tall, serious-looking man stepped out. It was Strong, she knew.

"Don't worry," she sang in her friendliest voice. "I'm just another one of those pain-in-the-ass media people, coming to ask you stupid questions that you won't answer anyway. . . ."

Strong said nothing, tugged at the brim of his baseball-style cap. But he wasn't hurrying away from her.

"Spring," Phillips tried, advancing slowly, unthreateningly. "Turning into a gorgeous spring day. Hey . . . did you see the homer Darryl Strawberry hit last night? Jeez!"

The Mets star had launched a rocket that grazed the roof in Montreal's stadium and bounced crazily into the bleachers, leaving everybody speechless and causing the umpires and Strawberry himself to wonder whether it was a home run or a double or some hybrid hit that needed a new rule to measure its worth. It was the beginning of the new baseball season; anybody who was a fan at all had heard about Darryl's dinger, had read about it, had probably seen it at least on tape replay.

Strong had seen it, and the cop and the reporter talked a little baseball. Then they talked families, Phillips's two sons and Strong's daughter, Kenya, who was in Spain at the moment and who was dreaming, realistically, of Harvard. Then they talked about Tawana.

"She hasn't volunteered anything to me," Strong said, "and I haven't asked her what happened."

Phillips thought that was odd. Strong looked very much the father-figure; caring, understanding, his pain at the unresolved episode involving the teenager he raised obvious to anyone who studied his face. Tawana, it had been reported, even referred to him as Dad.

"I told Juanita," Strong said suddenly, bitterly, referring to his ex-wife. "I told her not to call the news, but she said I felt that way only because I was a cop and all cops stick together." He dropped his head, shaking it from side to side. "But I warned her because I *am* a cop, and I know about these things. The press . . ." His voice trailed off.

"How's she doing now, Tawana?" Phillips asked, really wanting to know. "How's she coping with all this?"

Strong smiled the smallest smile, leaned toward the reporter. "She's doing remarkably well," he said. "Children have a way of putting things behind them."

They stood in the light of a crisp spring day, the morning frost gone beneath the bright sun, and chatted some more. Phillips had what she wanted, and played the scene out. She took Strong's home number, wrote down her number for him, mentioned that she had a cameraman in the car standing by in case he wanted to be interviewed.

He shook his head. Good man, stand-up guy, Phillips thought. Solid.

"No," Matt Strong said. "I really have nothing to say."

But he did, and he'd said it, and the hidden microphone had picked it up. It was perfectly legal, Phillips knew. And she felt perfectly awful.

PHILLIPS AND JANNEY HIT the road and made a half-dozen other stops. Glenda Brawley, unexpectedly, invited the reporter into her home and, while cartoons blared on the TV set, spent nearly three hours saying a great deal that amounted to very little. Her voice was so soft, her demeanor childlike, Phillips thought. "Al?" Glenda said in answer to a question about Sharpton. "Oh, it's just his job to keep the story in the news."

Phillips stood to leave and asked a final question. "How far will you let this go . . . If you feel that the strategy being used doesn't work, how will you know when to pull out?"

"I'll know," Glenda answered, in her little girl's voice.

Phillips's last words were spoken under her breath. "I sure hope so."

PHILLIPS AND JANNEY STOPPED at the apartments of Trayon Kirby and Steve Pagones—Phillips had been insisting for weeks that she and Taibbi invest some effort beyond phone calls to sources to make certain Pagones had nothing to hide— and when no one was home at either address they completed the tour, heading north toward Poughkeepsie, stopping in to see Wappingers Falls Police Chief Bill McCord and, lastly, Mike Heinrich at the State Armory, who was always good for guidance about the movements of the grand jurors and the Task Force.

The next morning, early, around a room service breakfast, the two reporters and Janney screened the tape shot the day before and talked about what they had. A little of this, a little of that, they agreed; nothing earth-shattering, but some fresh leads. They'd learned that a bank robbery in Wappingers Falls had ended with the dramatic capture of the suspect when he was chased down by helicopters, local and state cops, and residents who'd joined in to help out. Big stuff in a small town, but such was the pervasive impact of the Brawley case that the robbery and capture earned precisely two measly paragraphs on an inside page of the local paper.

Taibbi wanted to go back to Newburgh, to chase down the names he'd learned in his night of bar-hopping. Phillips thought Pagones and Kirby were worth another drive-by and wanted to follow up quickly on the apparent rapport she'd developed with Glenda Brawley. But when she called the desk in New York to check in and learned about the arrest of William West, she knew their plans for the day would have to wait.

"Chris Borgen will cover Abrams in New York," Phillips explained when she hung up. "Sharpton's supposed to be coming up here, for a one-thirty presser at the Armory. I'll cover, if you want to keep making calls. They can send another crew up, you can do the bit about the bank robbery down in Wappingers Falls, and we'll fold it all together for some kind of piece at six."

IT SOON BECAME one of the typically chaotic days of the Tawana Brawley story. A second tape crew and a live mini-van were dispatched from New York, Jim Fleischmann raced up-country to turn on his mountain, Taibbi holed up in his hotel room to make calls and patch together a script, and Phillips and Janney headed out to Market Street and the Armory to await the arrival of Sharpton and the show.

The press was already out in force, standing in loose formation and gossiping about the latest turn in the story. Sharpton arrived late as usual, pulling up in the cream Caddy with Perry McKinnon at the wheel. When he unfolded his bulk from the passenger seat Phillips took note of the wide smile on the minister's face, a smile that stayed put until the moment he stood at the microphones and began his diatribe about William West. "That's his patented catbird grin," Phillips thought, reminding herself to pass the phrase along to Taibbi so he could include it in his script.

Sharpton concluded with a curious statement. "People have tried to discredit Tawana with allusions that she hangs out on Crack Alley. Maybe if she did they would have gotten more in front of the grand jury because she probably would have run into this investigator there; he might have been making a delivery."

When the press conference broke up, Phillips shouldered her way through the crowd of reporters and photographers and fell into step with Sharpton. She wanted to know more

about the minister's allusion to Crack Alley, wanted to press
him again on Steve Pagones. For weeks she and Taibbi had
tried to arrange some kind of meeting with any or all of the
advisers. Three times they'd made appointments, twice for
breakfast in Manhattan and once, in Poughkeepsie, for lunch.
Each time they'd been stood up. Their pitch had been consistent with their view of the Brawley story and all the stories
they'd worked on together: "Give us something to work with,"
they said. "Anything. If you think we're good reporters, and
you've said so even when you felt we were hurting you, give
us the smallest bit of evidence on any aspect of the story and
we'll run it down. That's what we do. . . ." Sure, Sharpton
had said, or had had McKinnon say to them; we'll meet.

"Reverend Sharpton," Phillips called, "talk to me about
Pagones. What have you got on him that would make you
all accuse him as one of the suspects? I mean Taibbi and I
are looking . . ."

Sharpton stopped walking, turning to examine Phillips for
a moment. He looked directly into her eyes. Months before,
in the last days of Howard Beach, he'd tried to work his charm
on the producer sent in to cover the final verdicts in that
charged case, offering at one point to "put her in touch with
friends" who could get her a mink coat, cheap. She'd re-
buffed him politely then; now, as one-half of the reporting
team that was giving him and the other advisers so much
grief, she was asking for his help. He turned away from her
as he resumed walking, searching the faces in his entourage
until he found the one he wanted.

"Perry!" he shouted. "Talk to this here black girl!" Yanking McKinnon by the elbow, he guided him to a position
alongside Phillips. Then the minister walked away from them,
stepping into the Poughkeepsie Diner.

"Here's a number," McKinnon said, handing Phillips a
matchbook, which he opened with the thumb of his right
hand. "Guy came up to us in the diner the other day . . ."
He lowered his voice to a whisper. "Says they've got Steve

Pagones on tape, talking about drugs or something, I think. You call him, tell him you got the number from me."

"Who else did you give the number to?" Phillips asked.

"Nobody," McKinnon answered. "I don't trust nobody but you."

"He tell you anything else?"

"Nope. That's it."

Phillips's brain was working overtime as she ran back to the Wyndham Hotel. Pagones? Drugs? A tape recording? She literally bumped into Janney in the lobby; the cameraman had been back at the hotel for several minutes.

"Janney! Find Taibbi and tell him to meet me in my room. Tell him I've got to make a phone call. It could be important."

"What've you got, Anna?" Skeptical in the first weeks of his collaboration with Taibbi and Phillips, Janney had become familiar with their routines and had come to appreciate their methodology. They were always awash in records and documents they pulled in from every source imaginable; they were constantly on the phone, so much so that he'd angled to take permanent custody of one of the station's portable cellular phones. Working with these two, he found, meant long hours of waiting in the car while they knocked on doors or softened a source, the drudgery interspersed with frantic bursts of activity—often in charged or unusual circumstances. They'd made him a full partner, sharing what they knew, consulting him on strategy and, on occasion, following his lead. Janney, thirty-nine, was a Brooklyn native who worried about his weight and his thinning blond hair and was fastidious to a degree even he agreed was neurotic. The son of well-known character actor Leon Janney, he was fussy and opinionated and inclined to speak his mind no matter whom he offended. He didn't like a lot of people and didn't much like Phillips and Taibbi either, at first. But if they weren't the slickest pair he'd ever worked with—"you guys have a bit of the Keystone Kops in you, bumping into each other and tripping over your own feet," he often observed—he came to like them tremendously, to be protective of them, to trust them. "What now, Anna?" he asked.

"I don't know yet," Phillips shouted back to him, as the elevator door closed slowly. "But get Mike."

Anna Phillips also didn't know that she and Mike Taibbi were about to embark on a wild two-week departure from the main story, a departure that taught them much about the politics and idiosyncrasies of life in the Mid-Hudson Valley, and that convinced them, too, that Stephen Pagones had nothing to do either with drugs or with what happened to Tawana Brawley.

BY THE TIME JANNEY found Taibbi, who wasn't in his room when he first knocked, the reporter had already spent a couple of hours on the phone. His last call, and the one that had sent him roaming aimlessly through the hotel, waiting for Phillips to return, had been to Pagones himself. In answer to a question about why, nearly a month after the initial accusation, the assistant prosecutor hadn't initiated a single step in his threatened slander suit against the advisers, Pagones had said a curious thing.

"Mike, I'm just not sure I want to go through the discovery process," he explained, his voice friendly enough but a bit unsteady. "Just to give them more things to make up stories about."

Taibbi pressed him; he knew the law, too, he explained, and wondered aloud what there was in Steve Pagones's recent past—work records, his performance on certain cases, his associations, finances, whatever—that would provide fodder for the advisers if in answer to a lawsuit those subjects were properly and comprehensively explored.

"I'm not going any further," Pagones said. "You can call [Gerald Hayes, his lawyer]. I've gotta go."

Taibbi didn't mention the conversation to Phillips until she finished explaining her own telephone adventures. The number on the matchbook Perry McKinnon had given her was that of "a guy named Mike," she explained. "He's all hocus-pocus. Won't talk until he's checked us out, so I wait and he's called the desk to see if we really work for Channel 2. He's hesitant still, suspicious; then when I tell him I can't get to him right away, I mean I can't find you but I don't tell him that, I've gotta come up with something. I gave him the bit about how I had some gastric distress and was really having a problem, and he bought it, I guess. Even made a joke about how I wouldn't be having any problems if I'd eaten in his restaurant, it's called the Al Di La or something. When I just called him back he gave me directions. He and his partner, a guy named Fred, are at the Dutchess County Airport, they've got the restaurant there. I'm glad you showed. I told the desk the live crew will feed the Sharpton bitc and that Borgen can do the William West story out of the city, and we can put another piece together for tomorrow with the stuff we've come up with the past few days; but I explained we ran into something and we gotta roll. Ready?"

"Three minutes, see you in the lobby. Oh, quickly: I talked to Pagones." When he relayed Pagones's comment on his fear of the discovery process, Phillips gave a low whistle.

"Jeez, what's he afraid of?" Her mind's eye, like Taibbi's, saw the story on the matchbook cover. "Okay, c'mon. Let's see what these two have to say, and what's on the tape."

On the way to Janney's car they ran into Sharpton again. He was wrapping things for the afternoon, he explained, and was headed for Wappingers Falls to meet Maddox and visit with Glenda and Juanita Brawley, to bring them up-to-date on the case.

"Dinner, how 'bout it?" Taibbi said, as the rotund minister squeezed himself into the passenger seat of his Caddy.

"Yeah, okay. Maybe the Red Lobster, on Route 9. Talk to Perry."

Within earshot of Sharpton, who had the window down, Taibbi and Phillips let Perry have it. They'd been stood up three times, they whined, without even the courtesy of a phone call to cancel. This was the last chance; if your boss

doesn't show, we'll know he's full of shit. Tell him not to
fuck us.

"He won't, he won't," McKinnon protested. "The Red
Lobster?"

"Yeah," Phillips answered. "Eight o'clock. We've got
something to do till then."

McKinnon walked the few steps to Sharpton's side of the
car and bent low, talking to his boss. He stood and looked
back at the two reporters.

"Eight's good," he said firmly. "We'll see you then. No
bullshit."

PHILLIPS AND TAIBBI PULLED into the parking lot of the
Dutchess County Airport, a small airfield built on a rise off
New Hackensack Road in Wappinger, got out of the car, and
walked to the west side of the terminal building, where they
saw the sign for the Al Di La. In a few minutes the door
facing the lot opened a few inches, and then all the way. A
smallish man in brown frame glasses summoned them with
a curled index finger, examined their credentials, and stepped
outside to scan the lot quickly before hustling them inside a
lightless room and securing the two locks on the door with
keys pulled from his belt loop key ring. He led them to a
large circular table covered by a soiled red tablecloth. A second man came into the room from a door that led to a working kitchen; they could hear the rattle of pots and pans and
the shouted exchanges between cooks and waitresses. As the
reporters' eyes adjusted to what light there was, they could
see they were in a large function room, set up perhaps as a
ballroom, which from the looks of things hadn't been used
in a long time; there was a grimy small stage and the light
that struggled through the drawn curtains revealed some dust-
covered speakers and other equipment on the far wall. The
second man, heavyset in a formless sweatsuit and with dour,
suspicious eyes, studied them intently as he settled noisily
into a chair.

"Fred, they got ID?" he asked Fred Spampinato. Taibbi and Phillips handed over their credentials, and Mike Napilatano took what seemed like minutes studying them, flipping them several times with his right hand. Beyond spelling out his and Spampinato's names on request, he said nothing.

"Sharpton's guy, Perry, gave us your number," Taibbi said finally. The atmosphere in the place was foreboding, airless. "Said you guys had a tape on Pagones, something about drugs—"

"They don't know you," Napilatano cut in. "At Channel 2. I called them. They said they don't know you."

"What?" Taibbi was taken aback. Certainly, if they'd dialed the correct number for the assignment desk, anyone there would have verified his identity automatically. "I don't get it; did you call the right number?" He wrote the number down, pulling the page from his notebook and handing it to Napilatano, who handed it to Spampinato, who then left the room.

Napilatano snorted a contemptuous laugh, rolling his eyes in a gesture that seemed to say, These people must think we're idiots. The reporters would soon be seeing that gesture in their sleep. Without addressing the question of Pagones or the tapes, Napilatano launched into a fifteen-minute interrogation that convinced them he was the most paranoid person on the planet. Finally, as if to prove the point, he turned to Phillips, who was attempting to deflect his suspicion that they had walked in wearing "wires," and gradually lifted his left arm, which to that point had been pressed to his side. He let a fillet knife slip from the sleeve of his sweatshirt and settle in the palm of his hand. He held the knife up and turned it several times before placing it conspicuously on the table in front of Phillips.

"I want you to know we gotta protect ourselves," Napilatano said ominously. "That's all we're doin'. Now. What are you gonna do if we talk to you, and if we play you the tapes?"

Phillips, apparently unflustered, launched into what had become their standard pitch with sources who were still potential sources.

"Well, like we said, everything is off the record for now. We make that agreement. If what you have is of interest to us, there'll come a time when we ask you to go on the record, and we talk then about how you can do that. Do you want to do an on-camera interview? Do you want to do it full-face, or in silhouette, or with some other technique to protect your identity? Or all of it off-camera but we can use the tapes? Do we have to distort the tapes if there are voices and individuals who need to be protected? There's a hundred questions to address then, when we're all agreed there's gonna be a story. But for now, we just want to know what you've got, and it's all off the record—"

"How do we know that?" Napilatano cut in. "Why should we trust you?"

Taibbi, the spark now lit at the end of his short fuse, pulled his chair back angrily and stood up. "Anna, fuck it. If these guys can't even make a damn phone call and check us out, they've gotta be full of shit. C'mon, it's a waste of time. . . ." Taibbi played the game with a limit on raises; he was calling Napilatano. Phillips knew the ploy, and gently urged her partner to sit down, give it a few more minutes. Napilatano looked from one reporter to the other, momentarily confused.

At that moment Spampinato returned, and nodded at Napilatano. "It's them. They check out," he said.

"The tapes," Taibbi said, leaning over his chair back; he had declined to sit down again. "Let's have a listen."

"Okay," Napilatano said. "But first you gotta hear the story."

IT TOOK TWO HOURS to hear the story, which had nothing to do with "Pagones and drugs." Instead, it was a serpentine tale involving dozens of characters whose sole purpose, it seemed in the telling, was to frustrate the attempts of Mike Napilatano and Fred Spampinato, two self-proclaimed innocents who moved north from Westchester, to make an honest living. First they'd tried the construction business, specifically a subcontracting company they formed to install synthetic stuccolike exterior surface covering for homes and businesses. The Mafia ran them out of that business, they said, adding that they had tapes to prove local mobsters had corrupted the local organized labor force and gained control of much of the construction business in the Hudson Valley.

Their second venture together was the Al Di La Restaurant. This time it was government—local government in conjunction with the State Liquor Authority—that had laid them low, preventing them from winning a crucial liquor license and all but guaranteeing their failure. Steve Pagones, they said, was the assistant district attorney whose questionable handling of their case sealed their doom. It seemed a liquor authority inspector named Victor Daley had shown up at the restaurant unannounced one night, just at closing time, had "trespassed" on the property by vaulting a locked gate, and had then instigated an "incident" after which Napilatano and Daley, in that order, filed cross-complaints for harassment. Pushing, shoving, name-calling, that sort of thing. Not even a misdemeanor, but a simple violation. For reasons he never understood, Napilatano explained, Pagones had become involved in the case and unilaterally decided to recommend dismissal of the original complaint against Daley, but had let stand Daley's cross-complaint. The judge in the case, from Wappingers Falls, had eventually disposed of the matter by ruling that Daley's complaint against Napilatano should be ACD'd—Adjourned in Contemplation of Dismissal. In practical terms, it amounted to something akin to probation; if Napilatano stayed out of trouble, the complaint would be dismissed altogether after six months. The ACD, however, along with a one-sided description of the "incident," became one of only two reasons cited by the State Liquor Authority—the other was dissatisfaction with the financing of the venture—for its denial of a liquor license for the Al Di La. To complicate matters, which Napilatano seemed fond of doing, the Daley "incident" and the ACD followed warnings allegedly delivered in person by the same mobster who'd supposedly run the two men out of the construction business.

"The guy said to me, 'You'll never get a license,' " Napilatano said, convincingly. "He said he wanted me to put his father behind the register—my register!—and that if I didn't play along he'd own the restaurant, *with* a license, in two months. I guess he meant business."

It was a byzantine narrative, but Taibbi and Phillips were interested primarily in the role played by Stephen Pagones. Finally, Mike Napilatano played his tapes.

The first tape was a fascinating hour-long conversation between Napilatano and Frankie D.,* a kind of middleman between subcontractors in the construction business (like Napilatano and Spampinato) and P.T.,* a minor player in the Genovese crime family who'd moved north and become the Yorktown Heights power who "called all the shots." Frankie D. explained in convincing language that P.T. was his own "Gee"—wise-guy parlance for "godfather"—and how "everything that gets done here goes through him. We got the whole county locked. We did it in Westchester and we brought it up here." Frankie D. explained how several union locals were controlled, how he and P.T. could manipulate job site costs by adding on phantom workers with phony social security numbers and by demanding kickbacks, how double billing and the theft and resale of construction materials were employed to victimize certain developers—and certain subcontractors who declined to go along with the program. It was good stuff. Specific. Names, even phone numbers.

"You gonna play in this league, you gotta play by the rules," Frankie D. warned. "You could make a lotta money, but you gotta know sometimes you pay the price, too. Like a shot in the head, or fifteen–twenty years. But you could make lots of money."

"We left the construction business," Napilatano said. "Figured, try the restaurant. Then, this shit."

After the "incident" with Victor Daley, Napilatano was

frustrated by the way the case was progressing or, rather, not progressing, and was eventually steered toward a lawyer named Lou Viglotti. Viglotti was the village counsel for Wappingers Falls. Pagones was the assistant prosecutor assigned to Wappinger Town Court. When Napilatano learned he'd been ACD'd, he started taping his and Spampinato's phone calls to Pagones.

"How can you just decide to dismiss his [Daley's] complaint against Michael, and give Michael the ACD," Spampinato demanded in one conversation, "when you only hear Daley's side and don't talk to me or any of our five witnesses?"

Pagones, sounding annoyed and cocky on the phone, answered Spampinato in a way that caused the reporters to ask to hear it again. And again. They later agreed that the moment they first heard Pagones's answer they each wondered if the Napilatano case was what had him so worried about the discovery process that he'd delayed initiation of his slander suit against Sharpton, Maddox, and Mason.

"C'mon," the young prosecutor bullied. "I know what happened. I did an investigation. Your guy booted him in the ass! Your friend kicked him in the ass, period!"

"You call it an investigation when you only hear one side?" Spampinato pressed, his voice unsteady. "So you just decide—"

"Yeah. That's it. Look, I gotta go. There's sirens downstairs, something's going on. . . ."

TAIBBI AND PHILLIPS DIDN'T know what kind of story they were hearing in the darkened ballroom near a tiny airfield, but there was plenty of material worth checking. Napilatano, truly at the end of his rope, took them to his cluttered bunker of an upstairs office and, fishing beneath the half-filled glasses and overflowing ashtrays, found a summary of his troubles that he'd prepared a few weeks before when the noose started getting tighter, plus a copy of the State Liquor Authority decision denying a license for the Al Di La. "One day," he said, "we opened the restaurant with fifteen dollars in the register. I met with P.T. in his Cadillac another time and threw one of the tapes I'd made on the seat—it was a copy, of course. I was trying to bluff him into calling off his dogs, but there's people watching this place alla time. We ain't gonna survive."

"Well, here's what we do and how we do it," Taibbi said, finding a seat on the edge of a soiled cot. "We'll get the case papers, all of them. Read the judge's disposition, talk to Viglotti, and eventually Pagones. We'll run checks on all the names you gave us, from P.T. to Frankie D. and up and down from there. We'll find out why an assistant district attorney even gets involved in a violations case, if there's precedent for it, and how and why he can dispo the case without a full hearing on the evidence and witness statements. We'll run a check on Victor Daley, see if we can find out why he was sent down to drop in on you. Learn something about the liquor authority—we've got sources who've been poking around there. And," he said with added emphasis, looking from Napilatano to Spampinato and back, "we'll run checks on you guys. Michael, you say you're a former cop? If you weren't, if you lied to us, if you guys have felony records or any kind of a sheet you haven't told us about, we'll be outta here so fast all you'll see is exhaust. We're not here to take on your case . . ." He looked to his partner, who picked up the cue.

"That's what you have lawyers for," Phillips added. "But if there's mob stuff in the construction part of it, and if there's anything questionable in the business with the liquor license, that's of interest to us. We'll check it out."

Napilatano nodded glumly. Spampinato looked vaguely confused. They seemed like two stumblers who'd made a habit of authoring their own bad luck; but in almost four hours they'd made a convincing case that, in this instance, they'd run into something besides a little bad luck. Fric 'n' Frac, the reporters would later dub them. Maybe Fric 'n' Frac had a helluva story. They seemed convinced they'd done the right thing by agreeing to talk. There were handshakes, phone numbers were exchanged. Taibbi explained his standard communications code that would allow Fric (Napilatano) to know it was Taibbi or Phillips calling without either having to leave a name.

"I use Mike Foley," Taibbi explained. "Been using the name fifteen years. You hear from Mike Foley, you know one of us is calling."

Frac (Spampinato) closed the door quickly when the two reporters left through the side door of the ballroom. They could hear him fumbling with his keys, hear the locks snap into place.

Taibbi and Phillips briefed Janney as concisely as they could during the short ride to the Red Lobster. It was almost eight, and they didn't want to be even a minute late for dinner with Sharpton, McKinnon, and maybe Alton Maddox as a bonus. Sharpton had always promised Maddox would join them when they finally got together.

But it turned out they had a lot more time to talk about Fric 'n' Frac, a full hour in the lobby of the Red Lobster and then the rest of the night. Sharpton never showed. He didn't call the hotel to cancel the appointment either.

8

"Let's see . . . who was she dancing with?"

FOR THE NEXT TWO WEEKS Taibbi, Phillips, and Janney pursued a tangled case that at its edges involved some Brawley story fringe players and even one central figure, Steve Pagones, who were connected in some way to the frenzied Brawley affair. The reporters ran their name checks and learned quickly, from a seasoned organized crime investigator in New York City, that P.T. was who Mike Napilatano said he was, a Genovese crime family worker with several gaming convictions who'd moved north to Yorktown Heights and set up shop. P.T.'s alleged associates, with names like Fuzzy and Rocco and Tony Cigars, were known to the investigator. Napilatano was in fact a former cop; his record was clean. Taibbi and Phillips learned in meetings with Organized Crime Strike Force sources that the mob had moved north, had increased its influence in the construction business among others, and was focusing much of its Hudson Valley interest on the prospective transition of Stewart Air Force Base into a full-fledged, full-service commercial airport. There were already allegations, and one videotaped cash bribe, the reporters were told, supporting the notion that corruptible public officials were being "lined up" for the big push.

If the taped conversation with Frankie D. passed muster with the lawyers from Black Rock, CBS corporate headquarters, it would be the centerpiece of an original and, they thought, significant report on the spreading influence of organized crime in the Hudson Valley. True, it was not a story they would have pursued if they had not been working the Tawana Brawley case, but that was all right. The story's the boss, and all that.

The second part of the Fric 'n' Frac story, the part involving Stephen Pagones's alleged role in the failure of the Al Di La Restaurant to obtain a liquor license, was a different matter altogether. Fric 'n' Frac themselves were the sole link between the two stories, and the reporters (with a little help from Black Rock's lawyers and news director Paul Sagan) were alert to the danger of running the two stories back to back—in series format.

"If Pagones was innocent in the Brawley case," CBS lawyer Rick Altabef explained later of the grueling legal review he imposed on the two reporters, "we didn't want to imply the possibility of his guilt because of the way we described his role in the Fric 'n' Frac stories. Jonathan Sternberg, who reviewed virtually all the Brawley stories with Altabef, felt the same way. Here's this guy, Pagones, who's sort of walking down the street when a safe falls on his head; it was extremely important to us to come out of the Fric 'n' Frac stories in such a way that no one could later accuse CBS of having had a hand in pushing the safe off the roof." But the question of how to play the stories could wait; there was still a lot of work to be done.

Daley, the State Liquor Authority inspector, had disappeared into the ether. He no longer lived at the address given for his court appearance, and no one at the SLA could help the reporters locate him. The deputy commissioner whose signature appeared on the official denial of the Al Di La liquor license dared them to challenge the decision and refused to discuss it; he then hung up abruptly. The decision itself, according to a lawyer from a blue-chip Manhattan law firm who'd worked for the SLA, was "unusual, to say the least. I don't remember the liquor authority ever coming down this hard on an applicant for such a ridiculous and insignificant 'incident,' especially in light of the way the case was disposed of."

The reporters barreled their way through the records and dockets of Wappinger Town Court, reciting their rights of access under the N.Y. Public Officers Law Sec. 87—otherwise known as the Freedom of Information Law—each time a clerk balked at handing over a document. While they were at it, they had Black Rock lawyer R. Bryan Hatchett write F.O.I.L. letters to police officials in Wappingers Falls and Newburgh demanding the records not yet ordered sealed on a dozen figures and incidents from the Brawley case. When Wappingers Falls village attorney Lou Viglotti refused, as they expected he would, to turn over the records generated by Trayon Kirby's arrests and the two "loud arguments" in the Brawley household that required police responses, the reporters had their opening. Viglotti, of course, was also the lawyer who "handled" the case for Fric, Mike Napilatano. Taibbi went in to see Viglotti alone, knowing that since the records were not ordered sealed by the Brawley Task Force they *had* to be relinquished. Viglotti, a dashing young lawyer who dressed impeccably, spoke with precision and flair, and was a former Dutchess County assistant district attorney, knew within minutes that the impatient reporter sitting across his desk was not going to take a simple "no" for an answer. He relented after a halfhearted argument, and as the tension in the office dissipated, Taibbi turned the conversation to the subject of Stephen Pagones.

"Yeah, it's a damn shame," Viglotti said. "He's really been hurt by this Brawley thing, and of course he had nothing to do with it. I played golf with him last week in Florida; he says it's dominating his life. Of course it is. And he's getting married in a couple of months. . . ."

So, Taibbi mused aloud in the car to Phillips and Janney: Here's the lawyer who's gonna handle Fric's case, and he's a golfing buddy of the guy who recommends the ACD. Well, whaddya know . . .

They knew at least that it was time to talk to Stephen Pagones, however they had to arrange it. The assistant prosecutor was undoubtedly aware that the Channel 2 reporters were poking around, hard, on the case he'd handled involving Mike Napilatano. No chance for a formal appointment, they reasoned. They tried dawn stakeouts, Taibbi and Phillips wearing hidden mikes and Janney in the car, camera at his side, ready to move.

Finally, after a few days of frustration, they knew it was time for the direct approach. The story had reached the endgame, which in Taibbi's Boston days meant approaching the key players in the correct chronology, cameras ready to roll, and putting all the cards on the table in an interview setting. If the endgame was played out swiftly enough, in the proper sequence of moves, the key players wouldn't have time to consult each other, cover their tracks, or adjust their stories. In Taibbi and Phillips's "Good Cop–Bad Cop," which had sprung a Puerto Rican youth from jail in two tight reports, the process had worked to perfection: the prosecutor and the police superintendent alternately contradicted and blamed each other in their endgame interviews when confronted with the documentary evidence, leaving them with no choice but to find a way to get the kid out of jail.

This time the sequence started with the judge in the case. Taibbi and Phillips showed up at Wappinger Town Court and, impressing the judge's clerk with the importance of their inquiry, were themselves surprised when the judge called a recess in the morning session and was suddenly standing next to his desk, answering questions, Janney's camera rolling. Yes, the judge conceded, it was a bit unusual to accept the recommendation of the prosecutor, in this case Mr. Pagones, without any kind of substantive hearing on the matter.

"But if there wasn't any appearance or any evidence or witnesses heard," he added, "it could still be done that way, and nobody's absolute rights have been violated. . . ."

Lou Viglotti was reluctant, but he too sat for Janney's camera, conceding in his endgame interview that he'd spoken to a liquor authority contact who'd assured him, incorrectly as it turned out, that Mike Napilatano's appeal of his liquor license denial would not be ruled on until the Victor Daley "incident" was resolved.

"He indicated the appeal decision would be withheld," Viglotti said of his contact, "but evidently the decision was made before we all went to court."

They tried P.T. and from his lawyer received a firm "no comment." Frankie D., the voice on the tape, was nowhere to be found. The Channel 2 team drove to Poughkeepsie.

Stephen Pagones was to be the last interview in the sequence. The reporters knew the precise location of Pagones's office and had instructed Janney to sit in the one lobby chair that would give him and his camera a clear shot if the correct door happened to open. It did; Janney got his shot of Pagones, who stood motionless at his desk before noticing the camera lens pointed his way. In the meantime Taibbi and Phillips explained the purpose of their visit to First Assistant District Attorney William O'Neill (Bill Grady had the day off).

"It's up to Steve," O'Neill said, unhappily. "And if he even agrees to an interview, I'm sitting in on it."

Pagones, as the reporters suspected would be the case, had been alerted and fully briefed on the story they were pursuing.

"Let me call my lawyer first," he said nervously.

"C'mon, Mr. Pagones," Taibbi interrupted. "He's gonna say no; if I'm your lawyer, *I'm* gonna say no. This isn't about

Tawana Brawley, it's about the Napilatano case, period. We're gonna do the story anyway, you know that. They've got tapes of their conversations with you, you know that too, and we're gonna use them. We've got all the records on the case. If we're seeing any part of it wrong, explain it to us. We're not gonna ask you a single question about the Brawley case, and it's in no way the subject of our report. You know that."

Pagones, short and heavily athletic from years of weight lifting, stood still as a stone, though his jaw muscles were working nervously and his thick brows twitched toward each other in concentration.

"All right," he finally said. "But no camera. I'm not gonna budge on that one."

THEY USED THE CONFERENCE ROOM, O'Neill sitting at the far end of the table and Phillips placing her tape recorder directly in front of Pagones, explaining that she and Taibbi would use the audio in whatever report they prepared. Pagones agreed with the reporters' basic understanding of the facts in the case, and on the question of why he even got involved in so trivial a matter and handled it the way he did, he offered a surprising explanation.

"Look," he said. "I'm the prosecutor assigned to that court. I get a call one time from someone at the liquor authority— an attorney, I think—yeah, it was an attorney. And that's why I get involved in the case. I mean, I don't care about the liquor authority, or about whether these two guys get a liquor license. Geez! I did it according to the law!"

Pagones said he hadn't been assigned the case by anyone in the D.A.'s office and hadn't consulted with either O'Neill or Grady about it. Taibbi asked if it was at all unusual to have taken on the case simply because he got a call "from some SLA lawyer." Pagones asked Phillips to turn off the tape recorder. She did.

"Jesus, Mike, I'm scared to death of this. I mean, it's gonna look bad. . . ."

Steve Pagones looked like he was scared to death. In a way Taibbi liked him in the moment, saw him as vulnerable and sympathetic. And, in the moment, the reporter was convinced that the young prosecutor sitting across the conference table from him had not been "one of the attackers" of Tawana Brawley, as the Brawley bunch had charged, if indeed there had been any attackers at all. By his own admission Pagones had taken on the Napilatano case in a way that was unusual at best. The tapes of his conversations with Napilatano and Spampinato described what he would later admit was hardly a comprehensive investigation: none of Napilatano's witnesses had in fact been interviewed or called to testify. Sitting across the table from Taibbi, kneading his fingers nervously, he looked like someone who hadn't done his job very well and now was uncomfortable, facing the music. But that's all he looked like, and sounded like: if he'd been guilty of anything else, in the Napilatano case or elsewhere, he wouldn't have been sitting for an interview at all, the only formal sit-down interview he gave in the eight months of the Brawley affair following the public accusation against him.

"The thing is, Mr. Pagones," Taibbi explained, his voice almost gentle and a clear departure from his interrogator's tone, "it *does* look bad. That's why we pursued the story. But if you're insisting you did it according to the law, and you're convincing when you say that you believe that was the case, then we think it's important that you be allowed to say that. Maybe these two guys just ran into a streak of extravagantly bad luck, and you just had an unwitting role in it. But the bottom line is, they're fucked."

Pagones stared straight into Taibbi's eyes. Phillips turned the recorder back on.

THEY WERE DONE, except for one thing. Fric 'n' Frac, whose paranoia only deepened despite the reporters' constant assurances that they were making progress on the story, still refused to hand over the tapes. They wanted another meeting arranged with the federal investigators they'd talked to and then lost confidence in weeks before, prior to giving the matchbook to Perry McKinnon. Taibbi and Phillips said they'd talked to the investigators and to a half-dozen other federal sources, but that arranging meetings wasn't part of their role as journalists. Napilatano especially saw demons and scoundrels in every corner; he needed some kind of sign, he said, that he wouldn't be endangering himself or his family by going public. He adopted Taibbi's own Mike Foley pseudonym, and every day there were at least a few calls and often a panicked message from Mike Foley left for either Taibbi or Phillips. Fric 'n' Frac required a lot of babysitting.

The reporters also were receiving daily calls from either Al Sharpton or Perry McKinnon. They wanted to know what had happened since McKinnon had handed Phillips the matchbook. All Phillips would say was that they were working on the story.

"Well, is it gonna help us or hurt us?" Sharpton pressed in one call, days before the first story aired. Phillips thought hard. She and Taibbi had discussed it at length with Sagan and the lawyers; there was no question the advisers would go to town with their story, and almost certainly distort it for their own maximum benefit. Can't be helped, Sagan had said. "We can't *not* do a story that we believe is a story just because Sharpton and the lawyers will make hay with it. It's not like we're doing them a valentine. It's a story."

The story's the boss.

"All I'm gonna say," Phillips answered Sharpton, "is that it's not a story that's going to hurt you."

That wasn't good enough, she and Taibbi knew. They heard through the grapevine, and from Fric 'n' Frac themselves, that other reporters—including some of the heavyweights from the *Times* team—had been led to the story. Sharpton was putting the word out that a revelation was about to break linking Steve Pagones to organized crime. It was wrong, it was not an inference that could be fairly drawn from what

Taibbi and Phillips had learned and corroborated; but the
pressure was on. It was time to get the story on the air. The
tapes. Had to get the damn tapes.

When they visited the Al Di La for the last time, Mike
Napilatano was sitting at his liquorless bar, a sad-sack figure
in the same soiled sweatsuit, sipping a Coke and glaring at
the reporters he'd been talking to for two weeks.

"I'm not giving you the tapes," he said to Taibbi. "I just
don't trust you."

Taibbi's wick was lit again, and he tore into Napilatano,
listing the steps—and risks—he and Phillips had taken that
had brought them to the point, finally, when they had a story
worthy of broadcast. *If* they had the tapes.

"You're late," Napilatano cut in. "You said you'd be here
an hour ago."

"We were in Carmel, shooting the office where you and
Frankie D. had the conversation you taped," Taibbi explained.

"Yeah? What color's the building?" Still with the tests!

"Yellow," Phillips answered quickly, drawing on her un-
canny memory for detail and hoping to defuse what was
shaping up to be a major-league explosion. "Fifty-gallon drums
around the yard, in the small entryway. Sign out front at the
head of the long drive. Curved road."

"Wrong," Napilatano snapped. "It's not yellow."

Taibbi stomped out of the bar and went downstairs to the
airport lobby. Phillips led Napilatano down to Janney's car,
explaining that her cameraman could hook his camera to a
small monitor and replay the tape they'd shot. Naturally, the
hookup didn't work at first, and Napilatano harrumphed and
stalked away. Frac, however, stayed behind until Janney had
his jury-rig working, drawing power off the car's cigarette
lighter, and when Spampinato was satisfied the reporters had
been telling the truth—the building was closer to cream than
yellow—he walked back into the restaurant to tell Fric. Phillips followed. Janney followed Phillips. When they got into
the hallway leading to the familiar darkened ballroom they

could hear a spirited argument under way ahead of them. Jesus, Phillips thought; Taibbi's gonna slug him. Her partner was shouting, "No one questions my honesty, you sonofabitch. You fucking string us along for weeks, we work our asses off and come up with what we believe is a legitimate story, and now you're gonna pussy out behind some bullshit about how you don't trust us!"

"Yeah, well, I *don't!*" Fric shouted back. "You're probably wearin' a wire right now!"

Phillips walked a little faster. She heard some sort of commotion ahead, the sound of coins snapping against the linoleum floor.

And when she got into the ballroom her partner was naked down to his undershorts, his jeans and sweater and leather jacket flung in a haphazard heap on the floor around him. His arms spread out, he was looming over the shocked figure of Mike Napilatano.

"You find the fucking bug, and I'll kiss your ass in Macy's window. Otherwise, asshole, give me the fucking tapes!"

Everything stopped. Phillips's first reaction was, Oh, my God, I hope I don't have to take off my clothes, too!

And then Mike Napilatano laughed, a small laugh at first but then a full throaty one. "Not too funny," he said incongruously, "and you're not much of an actor. But here," he said, reaching behind him to three cassette boxes atop one of the dusty speakers. "Grab your clothes. Pick up your money. Here's the tapes."

THE FRIC 'N' FRAC PIECES, dubbed "Just Business" for public consumption, were lawyered heavily but retained most of what the reporters had learned in their two-week foray away from the Brawley story. On April 27, Taibbi's lead-in for the two reports read:

This is a story about two ordinary men who tried a couple of times to go into business in Dutchess County and

*both times, they say, someone knocked them down. In
the first instance, they say, that "someone" was organized crime; in the second, the legal system in Dutchess County itself. Now this is not a story about
leg-breaking or arson on the one hand or payoffs or the
big fix on the other. In fact, what happened to the two
men is subtle as an odor. But we're interested—and
federal investigators are interested—for an unusual
reason. Early on in their troubles, the two men began
secretly taping their conversations and meetings with
the people they feel did them in.*

They were solid stories. A federal prosecutor friend of
Taibbi's called to say they had done a good job of not over-
playing their hand because of the proximity to the Brawley
case and the Pagones involvement. The taped conversation
central to the organized crime piece, the prosecutor said, was
as reliable a narrative of how the mob works as any tape he'd
heard that wasn't the result of a court-ordered wiretap. Press
references to the "Just Business" stories described them as
"inconclusive": probably, Taibbi and Phillips reasoned, because they didn't "prove" the premise as described by the
giddy Brawley advisers. At a press conference on the steps of
New York's City Hall and in the inevitable broadcast later
on WLIB, Maddox, Mason, and Sharpton went overboard in
their praise of the very reporters they'd eviscerated only weeks
before when their prior stories had drawn blood. Now, these
"prominent" reporters from Channel 2 had "taken the assignment" from the advisers and "proven" that Pagones and
of course Attorney General Robert Abrams and Governor
Mario Cuomo—and the entire Federal Bureau of Investigation—were being run by the Mafia. It was manna from heaven
for the Brawley advisers: Maddox, on WLIB, totally misrepresented the "Just Business" stories and, with another two
hours of free and unchallenged airtime, let loose a few more
wild charges. "There's been a lot of other young black women
who've suffered the same fate as Tawana, kidnapping and gang

rape, since it happened to her," the lawyer asserted. "And we know of a man who had 'KKK' burned into his skin with a branding iron, up there. But I won't go into any of that now. . . ." After the second "Just Business" story ran, McKinnon called Phillips and said, "Get ready. Have a crew standing by this weekend. Tawana's gonna tell her story to you and Taibbi."

"Sure," Paul Sagan said sardonically when his reporters relayed the message. "Sure she is." But he asked them to stay in phone reach anyway, and assured them a crew would be available to roll, just in case.

Sagan's secretary buzzed them. There was a call for Taibbi; the caller said it was important. Taibbi picked up the receiver.

"Nice going." It was the voice of a federal source close to the Brawley investigation who'd been helpful whenever Taibbi or Phillips had reached out to him, but who to this point had never called to offer unsolicited assistance. "But if I were you and Anna," the source continued, "I'd get back to Newburgh in a hurry. The *Times* is there. They haven't got it yet, but they're close to running a story that witnesses are now claiming to have seen Tawana there during her disappearance."

TAWANA BRAWLEY DID NOT, of course, tell her story to Phillips and Taibbi that weekend. In fact, the Brawley advisers had used the Channel 2 "Just Business" stories as a pretext to cut off negotiations with all the other reporters and news organizations before whom they'd dangled a Tawana interview, and there'd been a great deal of "dangling" going on around town.

Having failed in their attempts to nudge Abrams off the case or to make a convincing argument in the court of public opinion that the drug arrest of Task Force investigator William West had rendered the state probe impotent, the Brawley advisers tried a different tack. On April 8, Sharpton had announced that if U.S. Attorney Rudolph Giuliani convened a special federal grand jury, Tawana would tell her story under oath. No matter that one of the "conditions" the advisers had listed in their initial meeting with Abrams was that neither Giuliani nor the FBI would have any role in the investigation. Glenda Brawley was allowed to tell selected reporters who retained a rapport with the family that she and Tawana would certainly cooperate with an impartial federal special prosecutor. Giuliani didn't bite, but he did permit the Assistant U.S. Attorney overseeing the federal Brawley investigation, Fred Lawrence, to meet with Sharpton and the lawyers. Predictably, the advisers misrepresented their talks with Lawrence and other staff attorneys, telling reporters about promises never made and conversations that never took place, and the "talks" went nowhere.

On April 19 Sharpton announced that if Giuliani wouldn't take on the case Tawana would "tell her story through one or more news organizations in the next ten days. She will take her case to the public and I can promise you that there will then be an outrage."

The race was on. Media critic Edwin Diamond of *New York* magazine would write later that the "selling of Tawana Brawley" occasioned a spirited bidding war, albeit a war in which money was not the currency dangled as the form of persuasion. If the Brawley advisers were serious about "letting Tawana talk"—and the cynics, who were plentiful, doubted they ever were serious—what they really wanted was the most sympathetic setting and the most agreeable interviewer. The advisers were suddenly more welcome than ever before in the corridors of media power.

Television reporter Geraldo Rivera was convinced for a time that he'd snagged the interview, that Tawana Brawley would appear on the set of his daily talk show and give him an hour-long national scoop. All he got, though, was the advisers. The show went on, accomplishing nothing, all heat and no light. The ratings were high.

ABC network's "20/20" was supposedly in the running for

a while, with Barbara Walters, according to one account, to be the interviewer. NBC News had taken itself out of the game because it had broadcast the nude hospital photograph of Tawana. WCBS had been out of it because of the earlier Taibbi/Phillips stories, though the "Just Business" reports supposedly put them back in the hunt to the degree that Perry McKinnon called and said, "Get ready . . . this weekend . . ."

But perhaps the most intriguing discussions about a possible Tawana Brawley interview took place between the advisers and the famous CBS newsmagazine "60 Minutes." There were six separate discussions, correspondent Mike Wallace taking part in several of them. One of the "60 Minutes" negotiators later explained that they'd hammered out conditions in painstaking detail that finally set the stage for the big interview.

"We weren't allowed to ask Tawana about the rapes, about the actual sexual assaults," the negotiator later explained, "though we knew enough not to do that anyway. Sharpton and at least one of the lawyers would be in the room. Tawana would be sitting with Mike, of course, doing the interview; but we agreed Sharpton could sit behind Wallace, so he could give her a bunch of hand signals. In the meetings, we agreed to a lot of things—including that we'd interview the advisers as well. We really thought we had it ironed out."

They didn't have anything ironed out. No one did. And when the "Just Business" reports aired, Alton Maddox found the convenient device by which to call off all the "negotiations" for what would have been a bombshell: Tawana Brawley's story, in her own words.

"At this point, given the revelations about the Mafia involvement in this case," the lawyer said, "we're not worried about Tawana talking. We're worried about Tawana living. There will not be any interview."

———

ON THE WEEKEND THAT TAWANA BRAWLEY did not tell her story to Anna Phillips and Mike Taibbi, the reporters hit the phones on the Newburgh angle. They learned that Task Force investigators had closely questioned Newburgh detectives—specifically those on the narcotics beat—and had closeted themselves with the records, or "jackets," of some of Crack Alley's more active entrepreneurs.

"They receipted some of the jackets on the names they wanted," a police source told Taibbi. "It's a short list—four or five names. They don't talk to us about where they're going with it, but these are the names they believe know something about Brawley or have already said they know something." The source dictated the names to Taibbi, with addresses, DOB's, and nicknames thrown in.

The reporters needed more. After the original tip following their Fric 'n' Frac stories urging them to get back to Newburgh, they'd sat with Sagan and roughed out a plan of action. If their medium were print, a few paragraphs of hard copy might have done it: "Channel 2 has learned that drug dealers in Newburgh have told investigators they saw Tawana Brawley during parts of her four-day disappearance. . . ."

"I guess you'll be heading north again," Sagan said. "Just tell us what you need. And keep your heads down." He knew they were careful; but he also knew that in the past few weeks a shotgun and a knife had been brandished at close range, for their benefit.

The reporters already had a leg up on the story, of course. Their night forays and frequent day trips to Newburgh had left them with a list of names and a general flow chart for Crack Alley's drug merchants. Law-enforcement contacts a phone call away could run checks on anybody they got close to. And they had some sketchy but authentic information in their back pockets that could serve as a wedge, if need be; the *implication* of dangerous knowledge, like the implication of strength or influence, was as useful as the real thing if employed judiciously.

Phillips and Janney went after Hermano L., the drug dealer/
snitch and "friend" of Todd Buxton who'd first told the reporters about Tawana's possible entanglement, during her
disappearance, in the business and personalities of Crack Alley. A trip to Hermano's home proved fruitless. The neighborhood was a Hispanic Appalachia, with ramshackle cottages
and heavily locked chain-link fences surrounding each post-
age stamp of property. Some of Hermano's neighbors claimed
they'd lived in their homes for five years or more, yet didn't
know the name of their street. Janney and Phillips finally got
to Hermano when his brother told them he "was in some
hospital in Poughkeepsie. I don't know what for, but I think
it's bad." Two calls from a roadside pay phone found him at
Vassar Hospital.

"Here's the drill, Don," Phillips explained. "No camera,
no brick, no nothing. If he's bad off, with tubes and everything, we just go away. If he's got visitors, I'll feel it out and
you stay in the hallway. If he's alone and not that bad off,
we'll just go in, casual, and see what he's got to say. If it's
anything interesting, I'll scramble for permission to do a
camera interview. Got that?"

The receptionist at the information desk never looked up
from her novel when Brawley and Janney asked for directions
to Hermano L.'s room. She blindly tapped a couple of keys
on the computer to her right, threw the screen a quick side-
ways glance, and announced a room on the fifth floor, second
bank of elevators down the hall, thank you. They couldn't
find the room; where it was supposed to be there was a heavy
metal door with a small window, bars showing behind the
glass, and a button to the right instructing "Ring Bell to Enter." Phillips rang the bell, explained to the nurse's aide that
she was visiting a friend, and they were allowed entry. She
and Janney scanned the room quickly, listened to its special
sounds. Phillips saw her man, he saw her. Hermano was a
patient in the hospital's psychiatric ward! Shifty-eyed, rat-
faced, and terrified despite heavy medication, the crack gone
from his system and replaced by a void from the other

side, he told Phillips he'd heard nothing new about Tawana Brawley.

"Got my own problems now," he said in Spanish, struggling to string the words together. "Police brought me here Friday night, thought I was going to kill myself. I didn't really want to commit suicide, though. Just kept saying I was going to jump off the bridge. I just wanted the cops to put me someplace that wasn't jail, because I got to do something about this drug problem I have. But you want to hear about Buxton, or some dealers?"

Phillips didn't, really; it had been weeks since they'd talked, and she wanted now to hear more about Tawana Brawley. But she listened anyway as he launched into his most recent contacts with one major crack dealer.

"He wants me to make drug runs for him. Says he'll pay me five thousand dollars for each run, going down to 139th Street in New York. You wanna know who else makes the runs for him? Who the supplier is in the city?"

Phillips wasn't interested in the careers of Newburgh's drug dealers, but she wrote it all down. Hermano was rocking back and forth on his hospital cot, banging rhythmically against the wall. A sadness coursed through Phillips, a chill of recognition of the horrors she'd seen first-hand in her Harlem childhood, when heroin (smack, duji) was the poison of choice, and even in some of the not-so-far reaches of her own family. She wanted to touch his shoulder, a mother's touch, but she didn't. She cast a glance down the ward and saw a nurse staring at her, questioning. "We'll talk again," she said softly. But he seemed not to hear; he was still rocking, eyes darting or shuddering closed against the vision of some interior terror.

THE REPORTERS NEEDED MORE help, too, and they wanted it before they returned to Newburgh. Their police sources in Newburgh had given them the names (and the business cards with handwritten private numbers) of the Task Force investigators who'd made themselves at home in the headquarters detective squadroom. Either Taibbi or Phillips had earlier tried every name and number, but the company line—no comment—had held firm against their best efforts and conversational gamesmanship. But now they'd had some solid scores and an earned reputation for neither expecting nor seeking handouts. One name in particular, they'd been told, had laughed and cheered out loud in the Task Force war room when their "Gestapo Wildman" story was aired, exposing the advisers.

"Charles L.,"* Taibbi mused, snapping the investigator's business card against the palm of his left hand. "Let's try him—maybe you try him this time, Anna. He chilled me the only time I got him on the phone."

Phillips called the official number first; not here, a voice answered, hanging up abruptly. Then she tried the second number on the business card, the one written in longhand. A male voice answered on the second ring. It was Charles L.

"Hi," Phillips said in her pleasantest voice. "I'm Anna Phillips, from Channel 2 News. I'm Mike Taibbi's producer, you know, we've been working on the Brawley story?" She knew he knew all of that, and waited for a hint of camaraderie or recognition. No dice.

"Uh huh."

Pause.

"Listen, Mr. L., I'm not looking for you to give anything up, I just want to confirm something."

She heard him clear his throat. Here it comes, she thought: he's gonna give me the last word on the subject.

"I'm not at liberty to discuss the Brawley case, but I can refer you to a name in the attorney general's office—"

"No, no . . . listen," Phillips interrupted. "I just want to confirm the fact that the investigation is now centered in Newburgh, that's all. We already know that—"

"I'm sorry . . ."

"Okay, okay, okay," Phillips rattled, thinking she'd lost him. "How 'bout this. If I'm right, that you—that the Task

Force is making progress in Newburgh, that that's where the focus is now, just say 'hot potato.' You know? 'Hot potato, cold potato?' " Phillips couldn't believe what she heard herself saying, couldn't believe she was resorting to a long-forgotten childhood game. But he laughed, and before his laugh died away the reporter cut in again.

"I know you think I'm crazy, but I really need to know from you that you're concentrating on Newburgh, that Tawana was—"

"I'm sorry," he said, "but I just can't discuss it." There was an upward inflection, though, and a thoughtful short pause before Charles L. said his last words: "Can't discuss it . . . hot potato."

Phillips hung up, disappointed at first but then quickly elated. Hot potato! He'd said it! Taibbi, hovering and pacing, looked at his partner's notes and listened carefully to her reconstruction of the conversation.

"It's not dispositive," he said. Damn lawyer's phrase. "But it's the starter's gun. Let's call Janney. It's gonna be an early call and a long damn day in Newburgh."

NEWBURGH HAD BEEN A garment town. Levi Strauss and Sweet-Orr had factories there and had employed hundreds of people, mostly women, and there were diamond shops and dozens of factory outlets. The men worked at the Du Pont plant or over at Stewart Air Force Base. By the fifties, an old-timer told the reporters, the little river town where they made blue jeans and pocketbooks was no longer rural.

"The numbers was the first thing, back as far as fifty-four," the old man said. "Then the prostitutes set up shop along the river, they came down from Poughkeepsie. The cathouses sprung up, one of 'em's now a funeral home, and there were madams who ran the whole thing, Big Nell and Treetop, Little Dolly and Ma Ruthie. You could find them at the Clam Bar or the Zanzibar, which of course were owned by the guys who ran the rackets. But Big Nell, who mostly worked the Eureka Bar, where the Eureka Shipyards used to be before those new condominiums went up, she was as tough as any of the godfathers. One night a guy stiffed Big Nell, and she tore the door off his car."

Then, in the early sixties, the traffic in drugs moved north. First it came by train, stopping in Monroe—"reefer" in the early shipments but heroin soon enough. In the seventies, the factories struggled as foreign competitors undersold them; Newburgh's manufacturers saw their work force heading away to more genteel pursuits, and recruited cheaper labor, blacks first and then Hispanics, and still Newburgh's fortunes declined. In the eighties, in an improbably beautiful setting, Newburgh's east end was fetid with decay, a true urban ghetto; in 1987, in a city whose total population couldn't have filled Yankee Stadium, there were fifty-four serious shooting incidents, some ending in the deaths of innocent bystanders and most in the several streets of Crack Alley; and there were scores of armed assaults, sidewalk muggings, and other explosions of violence tied to the drug trade.

TAIBBI, PHILLIPS, AND JANNEY hit Newburgh at first light on the morning of May 2, 1988. Their first stop, the first name on their list of locals who reportedly had seen Tawana Brawley during those four days in November, was Anthony "Prune" Burden. Prune wasn't home; his mother, gathering her faded blue dress around her as she stood in the doorway of her meager basement apartment and ignoring the red comb dangling loosely from her hair, told the reporters she didn't know anything but that a lot of people thought she ought to. She showed them a collection of soiled business cards left by investigators and one other reporter. Phillips asked to use the bathroom—her favorite stalling ploy—and the old lady kept talking.

"I can't tell you where Prune is," she said forlornly, eyes empty except for the sadness. "I lost him. Lost him to the streets. I'm resigned to that. He's gone."

The Channel 2 team pulled away. Janney parked the car on Broadway, a good six blocks from Crack Alley. They'd work on foot, an open book; it seemed the best plan to plow straight ahead.

They were a magnet or a repellent, drawing the curious bystanders to them or sending the players diving for cover. Taibbi and Phillips split up, working Lander Street first, heading straight for each pod of dealers and reciting from their list of the players they wanted to talk to: Prune Burden, Hester Davis (Randy "D-Day" Davis's wife), and two minors, all of whom had admitted to some level of knowledge, according to the reporters' Task Force sources, of Tawana Brawley's whereabouts between November 24 and 28. Janney shot liberally, concentrating on the Davis house, where sources had told the reporters a party had taken place the day after Thanksgiving, a party Tawana Brawley supposedly attended. The Davis house was the only one on Crack Alley with a backyard swimming pool; D-Day had done very well for himself before the law caught up with him.

One of the innocents told the reporters Hester Davis drove "a small red car. She's around and about today, she'll be back. Just wait."

They didn't have to wait long. When a small red Datsun screamed up Lander the innocent who'd hung around the reporters, laughing and commiserating, aimed a pointed finger and said, "That's it! That's her!"

Taibbi took off, looking back over his shoulder and gesturing wildly for his colleagues to follow. What a sight, Phillips thought, prancing as hard as her heels would allow but still moving faster than Janney with all his gear—her partner, the aging athlete racing against the years in his dress shoes and his linen suit, hacking up the poisons of twenty-plus years of smoking.

At Broadway the Datsun turned left, parked diagonally, and Taibbi rounded the corner in time to see a black woman walking briskly from the car toward a jewelry store entrance twenty feet away. He stopped at the door, lungs bursting, and saw the woman inside talking to a salesman. As Phillips got to the corner, he screamed, "She's in the store!" But Phillips saw something Taibbi had missed. Hester Davis was still sitting in the red car, behind the steering wheel; her passenger was the woman in the store. Phillips and Davis exchanged glances; then, the smiles of coconspirators. Both knew that Taibbi had missed his quarry, that the "they all look alike" syndrome had kicked in.

"Taibbi! She's in the car!"

And now the car backed out jerkily and was taking off, burning rubber. Janney finally caught up, threw his keys to Taibbi, and they piled in their car—which luckily, it turned out, had been parked on Broadway—and took off in pursuit of the little red car, then cresting the hill and heading west on Broadway. Running a light, the Channel 2 car bounced over the same hill. Taibbi hollered, "There it is!" and the chase was on. Only the red car they followed down a half-dozen side streets—probably terrifying the driver, who saw the big beige Ford in his rear-view mirror, a car with all the antennas that advertised, This Is an Unmarked Police Vehicle and You Are in Big Trouble—was the wrong little red car. They'd lost her.

Perspiring, cussing, they found their way back to Crack Alley, parking conspicuously at the corner of South and Liberty. And just like that, looking west toward the base of Lander Street, Phillips saw Hester Davis, animated in a bright red top and gesturing to a group of listeners.

"It's her!" Phillips said, flipping away her shoulder belt.

"No . . . you sure?" Taibbi asked, wiping a puddle of sweat from his neck.

"Dammit, Taibbi . . . fuck it." Phillips jumped out of the car and, waving expansively and shouting in the sing-song of the street, called to Hester Davis.

"Hes-tah! Yo, Hes-tah!"

Hester Davis turned to face the voice calling to her in familiar cadence and, waving automatically, gave herself away and unwittingly invited the very conversation she'd just worked extremely hard to avoid. Taibbi and Janney, the cameraman grabbing his lens, followed Phillips.

Davis denied everything, denied the rumors that either she or her husband, D-Day, knew Tawana Brawley or had even suggested to investigators that they did. Yes, there was a party, she conceded; there were several, in fact. One for D-Day, who'd beaten one of the beefs against him, and another for her cousin, and a few more to boot. It was the holiday week-end, wasn't it?

"So who would know?" Taibbi asked, posing the question loudly enough so that those in the small crowd that had gathered around the impromptu interview could not have missed the point. "Who would know whether Tawana was at any of those parties?"

Davis rubbed her chin. "My cousin," she answered. "My cousin Prune."

"Where is he? He's not home, we checked," the reporter pressed.

Davis exhaled, impatient, wanting to end this bullshit of an interview.

"He don't live at home. He's with his girlfriend, Leenie. Up the street." She pointed lamely up Lander Street and turned to face her friends. The interview was over.

It took only minutes, on foot again, to find out where ex-actly on Lander Street Prune Burden's girlfriend lived. Janney pulled the car around, parked, and the reporters got in. Sev-eral men lounged on the stoop outside the house. Taibbi studied the scene, thinking. "Yours," he said to his partner. "Charm the guys, and if our boy isn't home have a little girl talk with Leenie." He'd never sent Phillips in alone to a po-tentially risky situation, but she was full of fire this morn-ing, all her street smarts aimed at her task. A "black warrior," her husband, Lionel, had called her once. She was ready. "You're on a roll, Anna. We'll watch and listen every second you're gone."

"Take the brick," Janney instructed sternly, handing her a

portable radio. She switched it on, turned the volume to its lowest position, and stuffed it in her oversized pocketbook. She spent all of two sentences and ten seconds cutting through the men on the stoop. She was upstairs for twenty minutes, Taibbi and Janney fretting in the car, each taking turns stopping the other from calling on the radio or making some kind of move, or just assuring each other that Anna was a big girl, tough enough, could take care of herself.

When she emerged from the house she nodded a smile to the men on the stoop and sauntered deliberately back to the car.

"Mr. Prune's gonna talk to us in twenty minutes," she said evenly. "She's gonna go and get him for us." Then she smiled, and cackled her punchline laugh. "She was there!" Phillips hissed. "Leenie told me Prune's been saying it all along. Tawana was at his party. No question? I asked her. That's what he said, she tells me. Tawana was there!"

Twenty minutes later, after coffee and hot dogs and a call to the office, Taibbi and Janney were parked on Lander Street again, Phillips upstairs with Leenie, when there was a sharp rap on the rear passenger side window, behind the reporter's ear.

"You lookin' for me?"

It was Prune Burden. There was gold on all his fingers save his thumbs. He was short, stocky, street-hard, but almost sweet-looking, too. He looked sharp.

"Yeah," Taibbi said, cop's voice, rolling down his window and then thinking better of it and stepping outside. He was nearly a foot taller than Prune and made sure to stand up straight instead of falling into his normal slouch. "My partner, Anna Phillips, is upstairs, with Leenie—"

"Whaddya want with me?"

"Just talk, Prune. C'mon. I'm a TV guy, I'm sure Leenie told you. I'm sure she told you what we're here for. That's Don Janney, our cameraman," he said, pointing. Prune Burden snorted in hostility, but followed Taibbi, who was already walking toward the house. Janney had snatched his gear in a hurry, but stayed outside when Taibbi shot him a subtle shake of the head.

Upstairs in Leenie's second-floor apartment, Prune said nervously, "Yeah, there was a party for me. My birthday's the twenty-seventh."

"Was Tawana at the party?" Phillips cut in. "Don't bullshit me."

"She coulda been there, but I don't know . . ." Prune was nervous, unsure of his ground. Then, looking from Leenie to Taibbi and Phillips, he changed his tune. "But then again, I was in the hospital, you could check it out, and I didn't get out till the twenty-eighth, and they had the party for me that night—"

"What hospital?" Taibbi asked.

"Saint Luke."

"What time were you discharged?"

Prune scratched his temple. " 'Bout late, in the afternoon. You can check it out."

"We will. But you say 'she coulda been there'?"

Prune was shaking his head, eyes flitting about. From off to the side, ten feet away and leaning against the kitchen door frame, Leenie shouted at him, bending toward him for emphasis.

"Tell the truth, Prune! You been telling me she was there, tell the truth! Get it over with! I tole 'em!" She had a little boy a year old, who was roaming around the apartment, chatting up a storm to the television, which remained on, to the imagined friends in his still innocent world; smart as a whip, Phillips had discerned in her earlier visit. How long, she'd wondered then; how long until this bright baby boy is no longer challenged by his environment, but is instead subsumed by it.

Prune stood up, walked to Leenie, faced her in anger.

"Why'd you tell 'em *that* for!" He pulled her by the hand into the kitchen, closing the door behind them. There were hoarsely whispered exchanges until Leenie, voice a plaintive pleading, seemed nearly to be sobbing. "Prune, you can tell the truth. Just tell them! I'm sick of this shit!"

But Prune came out and sat down again in the chair facing the reporters and shook his head, more firmly this time. If he had it, he wasn't giving it up. He wouldn't break.

"I got outta the hospital the twenty-eighth, they had my party after she was found, that juke down Lander. The twenty-eighth. You can check."

The Channel 2 team left the building and waited outside, dispirited and vaguely angry. Clearly, their man had told his girlfriend Tawana Brawley had been at his party. Less clear was whether he'd been telling the truth; they'd failed to get it out of him. Prune Burden appeared on the stoop in a minute or two and sat down. Janney shot fully a minute of tape of the young man, smiling now, spinning the gold on several of the fingers of his left hand. A young boy, thirteen or fourteen at most, strutted by and waved happily to Prune with his left hand. In his right hand, conspicuously, was a roll of bills as thick as an apple. Must have been hard to hold, Taibbi thought, with that bar of gold stiff as brass knuckles stretching across the fingers of that same right hand.

They tried St. Luke's Hospital. Yes, they confirmed, Anthony "Prune" Burden had been a patient in the last week of November. But the on-duty administrator refused to confirm what the reporters would learn only later. Prune had been released the twenty-seventh; the party in his honor that had followed his discharge by a few hours took place the night *before* Tawana Brawley was discovered in Wappingers Falls.

Back on Lander the reporters looked for the juke joint where Burden's party had been held. By now their presence on the street was a certified event, and not one that was uniformly welcome. The manager of a variety store, a heavyset youngish woman, bristled in hostility when Taibbi asked politely where the juke joint was, denying she knew anything about any juke joint and cussing at this white man in his city suit. She fired Phillips a nasty look, but before she could get another word out, Phillips took off on her.

"Fuck you, bitch! I can find a damn juke joint!" She walked across the street, peered into a few windows, and called back to her colleagues.

"Taibbi, here it is. Janney, c'mere, shoot this shit and fuck that bitch. This is the juke. Gimme wide shots, then through the window gimme the pool table, the juke box, the chairs and stuff."

Janney fired away. The dealers watched the scene from a small distance, muttering. Taibbi stood with the woman from the variety, explaining that his partner had a very bad temper. Privately, he enjoyed the joke; always before, with Anna, it was the other way around.

THEY FOUND THE THIRD NAME on their list, a minor with no adult felony record who they felt they could not quote, and his simple off-camera answer before disappearing into his corner of the Crack Alley maze was yes, Tawana had been to at least one of the parties.

Name number four, one of the youth's confederates told the reporters, hung on the other side of Broadway, the Hispanic section. Worked in front of a variety. Here's the address.

He wasn't there. But a group of black youths was there. It was midday now, the sun hot. The reporters engaged them in their usual banter, their serious questions about Tawana Brawley mixed but not hidden in the street jive familiar to both of them.

"You got a cigarette?" Phillips asked a tall teenager who was smoking a filtered brand. She hated Taibbi's Camels, though she smoked enough of them when the pressure was on. The youth asked Phillips if Newports were okay; when she said yes, he pulled a couple of bills from his pocket and went into the variety, emerging with a fresh pack. Phillips took one, accepted a light, and gave the pack back.

The Pavillion Apartments in Wappingers Falls, where sixteen-year-old Tawana Brawley was found on November 28, 1987.
(PHOTO BY MICHAEL HEARD)

Flyer that appeared in The Black American.

Tawana Needs You!

Tawana Brawley

This child has been abused.

She was raped and sodomized.

Her mother has been ordered arrested by Gov. Cuomo because she wouldn't allow them to whitewash the crime against her daughter.

Her father was fired from his job and the family was threatened with eviction.

The Brawley family needs your support.

Tawana has expressed her gratitude for all that you have done and she will be eternally thankful for your continued support.

Please send a check to Tawana Brawley, care of The Black American, 545 8th Avenue, NYC, NY 10018.

William Grady, the Dutchess County prosecutor who was the first to handle the Brawley case.
(PHOTO BY MICHAEL HEARD)

Jan. 29—Assistant Attorney General John M. Ryan, in the attorney general's office after being selected to personally handle the Tawana Brawley case.
(AP/WIDE WORLD PHOTOS)

David Sall, who was special prosecutor on the Brawley case for twenty-four hours.
(PHOTO BY MICHAEL HEARD)

Feb. 10 — Bill Cosby (center) sits with the Reverend Al Sharpton (right) during a New York news conference at which the comedian announced that he and Essence magazine publisher Ed Lewis were offering a reward of $25,000 for information leading to the arrest and conviction of those responsible for the sexual assault on Tawana Brawley. (AP/WIDE WORLD PHOTOS)

Feb. 15 — Boxing promoter Don King (left) and boxer Mike Tyson hold a letter from Tawana Brawley in which she thanks them for their support. Tyson and King announced plans for the formation of a foundation to benefit children who are victims of violence. (AP/WIDE WORLD PHOTOS)

May 5 — The Brawley advisers — Alton Maddox, C. Vernon Mason, and the Reverend Al Sharpton — fielding questions on "Geraldo," the television show hosted by Geraldo Rivera. (AP/WIDE WORLD PHOTOS)

March 24 — Coolidge Miller (center) and state trooper R. Cardona confront each other on the steps of the Armory in Poughkeepsie, where the Brawley grand jury met. The Reverend Al Sharpton (left) accused John Ryan, an aide to Attorney General Robert Abrams, of shoving Miller during a rally for Tawana Brawley. (AP/WIDE WORLD PHOTOS)

June 15 — The Reverend Al Sharpton (right) and talk show host Phil Donahue (standing) discuss the Tawana Brawley case on the "Donahue" show. Also shown are Alton Maddox, Jr., and Glenda Brawley, Tawana's mother.　(AP/WIDE WORLD PHOTOS)

June 9 — Glenda Brawley, Alton Maddox, and the Reverend Al Sharpton at a press conference in the Ebenezer Baptist Church, Queens, N.Y.
(AP/WIDE WORLD PHOTOS)

May 5 — The Reverend Al Sharpton (left) at a New York press conference, charging that Channel 2 reporter Mike Taibbi bribed two Wappingers Falls teenagers to say that Tawana Brawley was at a party during her disappearance. She claimed she was being held by kidnappers during that time. Joining Sharpton are (from left) Alton Maddox, Jr., Gregory Flemming, Sr., and C. Vernon Mason.
(AP/WIDE WORLD PHOTOS)

June 15 — Mike Taibbi looks on as Anna Phillips takes a call from a tipster moments after the reporters aired their Perry McKinnon story.
(PHOTO BY DIANE BIRNE)

News director Paul Sagan, Anna Phillips, and Mike Taibbi reviewing a script before broadcast.
(PHOTO BY LAWSON LITTLE)

July 6 — The Reverend Al
Sharpton (center) with sup-
porters, protesting CBS's
coverage of the Tawana
Brawley case.
(AP/WIDE WORLD PHOTOS)

Channel 2 cameraman Don
Janney shooting over the
heads of demonstrators at a
press conference called by
the Reverend Al Sharpton.
(PHOTO BY MICHAEL HEARD)

Dutchess County Assistant District
Attorney Stephen Pagones holds a
press conference in Fishkill, N.Y, to
announce his lawsuit against the
Brawley family advisers for defamation of character.
(PHOTO BY MICHAEL HEARD)

July 17 — Minister Louis Farrakhan (center), flanked by the Reverend Al Sharpton and Tawana Brawley, at a rally in an Atlanta church. The Brawley family and their advisers were in Atlanta during the Democratic National Convention, hoping to bring national attention to their cause.　(AP/WIDE WORLD PHOTOS)

Oct. 6 — Mike Taibbi interviewing Attorney General Robert Abrams after he delivered the Brawley grand jury report.
(PHOTO BY MICHAEL HEARD)

Oct. 6 — State Supreme Court Justice Angelo J. Ingrassia reads his statement about the Tawana Brawley case. The report concluded that she apparently concocted her story of abduction and rape.
(AP/WIDE WORLD PHOTOS)

"We're not interested in any jive shit," Taibbi said. The kids were laughing. "You say you know people've been saying she was here? Who? Any of you guys? This is important." It sounded stupid coming out, but dammit, Taibbi thought, it *was* important. Janney was taping the exchange; Taibbi had on his hidden mike. The tall youth shook his head; naw, we don't know, he said. But ask him, he knows! He pointed toward a dark two-door car, an eleven-year-old number of the muscle-car species, which was idling half a block away, its driver casually watching the scene. The car pulled up to the group. Taibbi walked around to the driver's window and leaned in.

"Your friends say you know," he said, trying for a voice of authority. "You know that Tawana Brawley was in Newburgh during her disappearance, at some party?"

The driver spun his head, peered directly at Janney and Janney's camera.

"Don!" Taibbi called. "Kill it. Lemme talk to the kid, give it a rest for a bit." Janney dropped the camera from his shoulder but left it running; he was still recording audio.

"So?" Taibbi asked, leaning so close to the youth he could hear his breathing. "You see her?"

The driver smiled. One of his friends jumped into the passenger seat behind him. There were long minutes of bullshit talk that excluded Taibbi; the reporter finally asked the youth in the passenger seat to leave the car. When the driver faced him, there was still, despite his laughter of only seconds before, a depth of nervousness behind his eyes.

"Let's see . . . a party?" he said. His words were tinged in a Hispanic accent. "Let's see . . . who was she dancing with? I'm tryin' to remember . . . Okay, was it E-Z? Maybe Chico? Yeah, Chico."

Chico! Taibbi had heard the name Chico linked to Tawana at least twice in his nighttime saloon forays, most recently with a couple of locals at a bar called Pop's Paradise.

"Okay," he said calmly, rapping the edge of the window, standing and stretching and calling to Janney and Phillips with a flip of his eyes before leaning down again. "We wanna talk to you. We got time. You wanna stop the car and talk? Or do you wanna go somewhere else?"

9

"I would call it paying for
a story. . . ."

THE DRIVER OF THE MUSCLE CAR never told the reporters his
name. But they'd heard his friends address him by his given
name, and its diminutive, and at one pause over the next two
hours Phillips got a call into a police source, ran his plates,
and scribbled down his address and his mother's full
name.

The tall youth who'd pointed out the car was named
Gregory Flemming. On the spur of the moment Taibbi told
the driver, the kid with the story, that if they ended up doing
a report they'd refer to him only as G.

G tried hard to get someone else to tell the story, leading
them to several stops in Newburgh and introducing them to
other youths who, he said, knew at least as much as he did.

At one stop, a school, a group of teenaged girls gathered

around the reporters and talked nonstop for twenty minutes about Tawana Brawley. Several had known Tawana for years, since her Aunt Juanita lived in Newburgh and she herself had been spending more and more time in town. One teenager, a girlfriend of Prune Burden's before Leenie came on the scene, told Phillips flat out that Tawana was at Prune's party though she hadn't seen her personally in the few minutes she'd been there. She added that there were at least two other parties that same night and that there were "other kids around" who could confirm Tawana's presence in Newburgh during her disappearance. She balked at a camera interview, but gave Phillips her home number and offered to ask around on the reporter's behalf.

Just then a contingent of school officials headed toward the group and a Newburgh Police Department radio car rounded the corner and pulled to a stop, two officers emerging from the cruiser. Taibbi and Phillips knew their curbside interview was about to end, even though they had been careful to stay across the street from the school and had instructed Janney to stay in the car and await their signal before pulling out the camera. Taibbi had a quick word with the two cops, dropping the names of his department contacts. The cops explained they had no choice; they'd been called by school security, reporters had become a nuisance, etc. Taibbi headed for G's car.

"C'mon. This has been helpful, but you're the guy who says he saw her, at a specific time and place. I want to hear more of your story."

"Not here, man," the youth said. "I don't wanna—"

"Okay. No problem. Let's get out of town. Anna and I know this pizza joint, out by the Thruway entrance . . ."

The school officials had arrived and, while mollified somewhat by Phillips's explanation of the line of inquiry the reporters had been pursuing and impressed that she'd kept her cameraman in the car, they still insisted that with school just having let out, the certain commotion their presence would cause was simply not acceptable. Phillips looked toward Taibbi, who nodded back at her.

"All right, let's go," he said to G. "Follow us."

"No, I know where that is, that pizza place. There's a Burger King there too. . . ."

"Yeah. You want to go to Burger King instead?"

G called to his two friends who'd trailed along, and who now piled happily into his car.

THERE WERE ONLY a handful of customers at the Burger King; surprisingly, though, none of the otherwise unoccupied employees took much note of the odd group, including one man with a large camera, that filed in and headed for the tables in the rear. Phillips took Flemming and G's other friend to a separate table, about twenty feet from the booth where Taibbi and G sat facing each other. Janney chatted with Phillips a moment, found when they pooled their money that they had exactly $6 between them, and told the two kids they could get one cheeseburger apiece. As the youths strolled back to the table with the cheeseburgers Phillips and Janney had paid for and the Cokes they'd gotten on their own, Janney slid quietly into another booth, which placed him diagonally behind G and facing Taibbi. He would await his signal; Taibbi had told him and Phillips he wanted to work G alone, that he was convinced he was ready to talk. Of all the Newburgh youths who'd told them they "knew" Tawana had been in town during her disappearance, G was the only one who'd told them he'd seen her *and* talked to her.

G was nervous, jumpy. Without his friends at his side it was just this intense bearded man and him.

"What do you want me to do, man?"

"I want you to tell your story," Taibbi answered, trying to sound friendly and sympathetic and not too eager, and struggling for the pitch that had gotten him to stories in the hard corners of the urban beat since his earliest days in newspapering. "Just what you know. Not what you heard on the street, not what you *think* happened. What you know. What you saw and heard. If you talked to her, what did you say? What did she say? Only what you remember."

"You payin' me for this?"

Taibbi shook his head emphatically, automatically. Old reflex; he'd given the speech a hundred times.

"We don't pay. You talk to us, on camera or any other way, it's because you choose to talk to us, you wanna tell your story for whatever reason."

G shook his head, disgusted. "Man, I been drivin' you around all afternoon, introduced you to these other kids, I got no gas in the car—"

"No, I appreciate that," Taibbi cut in. "Believe me. And I know if you've been sitting on what you know that finally talking about it publicly, 'cause that's what it is when you say it on TV, that it can cause you a lot of grief. But we don't pay. That's the rule. You talk to us because you choose to talk."

The kid thought hard; Taibbi could almost hear him thinking. Phillips, at her table, had the two youths busy filling out Burger King job application forms (they'd talked about needing jobs) and was peering past them toward her partner, wondering how it was going. Janney gripped his camera handle, ready to raise it to firing position.

"How you do it?" G asked finally. "I mean, they gonna see me . . . ?"

"That's not a problem," the reporter answered quickly. He knew the kid was ready to go. "Don can move you to a window and shoot you against the sunlight outside so you'd be in silhouette. Or he can stay where he is, you can pull on one of your friends' hat and jacket, and only your friends will recognize you. I'm not saying no one else will figure it out; there's Muzak playing, but even if we distort your voice people are gonna make you and it'll get out it was you. You're gonna have investigators who wanna talk to you, other reporters if they can get to you even though we're not gonna name you. But hey . . ." He smiled as warmly as he could. "It's not like you're fingering anyone for a crime, you're not ratting anybody out. All you're saying is you saw a girl at a party and talked to her. You know, you've been around us all day, other people say they know she was there, too. Some others have told investigators the same thing, we've confirmed that, we'll report that. But you'll be saying something that's important. Because you think it's important."

G said very little while he donned his friend's hat and denim jacket and allowed Janney to clip on the mike. And then, his back to the camera, he told his story. He'd seen Tawana at a party, he said, one of several the Friday night after Thanksgiving. She was with "a guy named Chico, a drug dealer," but at one point he, G, found himself face to face with the pretty teenager.

"She asked me for a ride," he said.

"And what did you say?" Taibbi asked.

"I told her 'no.' "

WHEN IT WAS OVER and his own tension fell away, G resumed his refrain about being out of gas, and how he'd taken the crew around all day and he hadn't gotten a cheeseburger or even a glass of water. Taibbi listened distractedly to the youth's lament; he knew exactly what he had in the can and wanted to get out of the place fast before G changed his mind. Phillips was nodding vigorously, saying, "Let's go!" Janney had gathered up his gear and was poised to leave. Then Taibbi studied G, who was talking a mile a minute. Young kid, doesn't really know how much shit's going to come down on him. He thought of all the other whistleblowers he'd known and persuaded to go public, how he'd tried to protect them but knew in all cases (and always told them) there was no guarantee. How some of them had crumbled under the pressure that followed their public revelations. The downside could be far down indeed, the reporter knew. He'd seen it. The way the Brawley case had been going, G could be in for a rough ride. His life would change.

The youth was still yapping about his empty gas tank. Taibbi reached into his pocket and pulled out the single bill that was there, a $10 bill. Hell, he thought, he'd spent thousands of dollars over the years coaxing sources over company-paid lunches or sending them home in company-paid cabs. All reporters did. And this kid had already done his interview, for nothing, and was going to pay for it big-time in ways he surely didn't understand despite the warnings.

"Here's what I've got," he said to the teenager, addressing him by the diminutive of his given name. "Buy yourself some gas."

PAUL SAGAN LISTENED to the two-minute interview with G twice, debriefed his reporters carefully on the rest of what they'd come up with in Newburgh, and retreated to his office to call general manager Roger Colloff. When he reentered the editing room where Taibbi and Phillips were still screening tapes, he was ecstatic. His news department, under his early stewardship, had broken the story that first day in November. Now, if Newburgh's witnesses were telling the truth to investigators and to his reporters, Channel 2 would own the story outright.

"They're either lying or they're not," Sagan said. "If they're not, well, that's it. I talked to Roger; this isn't even a story that's gonna need much lawyering. Investigators have heard the stories; you guys have heard the stories. We can report it. We're not a court of law; we have different rules of evidence.

"Geez," he added, watching Janney's shots of Crack Alley. "I didn't even know there was a place like this up there. Who knew that?"

"We can run it at five tomorrow," Taibbi said, as deep in

as he ever got on a story and barely hearing his boss. "I'm gonna go up again with Janney tomorrow morning, early. Visit the kid again, we know where he lives, and try for one more confirmation with Anna's 'hot potato' source, Charles L. We hear he's gonna be at the FBI field office up at Stewart, nine sharp."

"And I can start getting the piece together early," Phillips said, thinking ahead to her own role. "I'm gonna have graphics build a calendar effect, peeling away the key days of the story leading up to this point and then wiping clean to all this new stuff."

For long minutes, everybody in the small editing suite watched the tape whiz by, listening to the audio and to their own thoughts. Fric 'n' Frac had been a Channel 2 exclusive only because no other reporters had a way in or had found a way to follow it that made sense in terms of the Brawley story. Their earlier hits proving the advisers had lied did not prove and were not intended to prove that *Tawana* had lied. Now the story had hit a lull again; the week before the Fric 'n' Frac stories, the FBI had officially pulled out. The official explanation was they'd turned up no evidence of a civil rights violation against Tawana Brawley. For three days running, something of a record in the recent history of the case, there'd been nothing in the papers about it. Taibbi had heard from a Brawley investigator that evidence summaries compiled by Task Force assistant prosecutor Stephen Quigley had been making the rounds, and that the summaries showed at least circumstantially that no crime had been committed against Tawana Brawley. The same source suggested that the grand jury had been near the end of the substantive part of its task, "was thinking of wrapping things up" with no definitive answers, when the Newburgh tales started getting hot. Taibbi and Phillips had gotten to Prune Burden and to other potential witnesses the Task Force had not been able to find. Now Channel 2 was about to report that investigators had something more than circumstantial evidence that cast doubt on

Tawana Brawley's story, and the station, a news organization, was going to add to the evidence. That "something more" was a bombshell.

"Call me in the morning," Sagan said to Taibbi. "Early and often."

G's CAR WAS PARKED in front of his house.

"I'm not thinking of an interview," Taibbi told Janney. "I just want to talk to him one more time. Maybe see his family. A few minutes."

The youth's mother, a pleasant and attractive Puerto Rican woman, invited the reporter inside right away. She was running late for work. No, she said, surprised, her son hadn't told her about his interview with Taibbi. But then, he didn't tell her much anymore. Hung around on the other side of Broadway. She worried about him constantly. The crime and the drugs on the other side of Broadway, the Crack Alley side, had taught her to fear blacks and, worse, to feel at times as though she hated them. She thought Sharpton and the Brawley lawyers were hatemongers themselves, the worst kind of racists, she insisted. Taibbi described the interview, explained its importance. Did she believe G could lie about something so important? She shook her head.

"I don't know. He's a problem to me now. Let me wake him."

She called down to the basement and in a few minutes G stepped into the kitchen, shocked to see Mike Taibbi sitting casually with his mother, smoking a cigarette and drinking a cup of coffee. He rubbed the sleep from his eyes, his brow furrowing in concern.

"I didn't want to wake you," Taibbi said. "But I've gotta know. Did you lie to me at all yesterday? I told your mother about the interview."

G shook his head vigorously, clucked the saliva from his mouth, and almost shouted, "No!" He and his mother exchanged unhappy, angry words in Spanish and he fled down to his basement bedroom.

His mother looked at Taibbi, shook her head slowly in a gesture of resignation, and limply raised her two hands.

"I don't know," she said sadly. "He gives me so much trouble."

TAIBBI AND JANNEY KNEW the layout at Stewart Air Force Base from the Fric 'n' Frac story on organized crime, knew too that the FBI field office was in the middle of the maze. They did a single drive-by and parked thirty feet from the building, around a sharp curve in the access road and out of the line of sight from any of the office windows. Taibbi tapped the key pad on the car's cellular phone.

"Charles, please?"

Charles L. picked up the phone.

"Hi, it's Mike Taibbi. I'm not asking for anything, I'm gonna tell you something. Well, then I'll ask for something."

The investigator said nothing.

"Anna Phillips and I are going on the air tonight with a story that at least four individuals from Crack Alley have told you and other investigators from the Task Force that Tawana Brawley was in Newburgh during her disappearance." He quickly listed the names of the people they'd interviewed the day before, including Hester Davis and Prune Burden, and added that two other youths—minors, so they wouldn't be named—had told them they knew Tawana had been there.

"One of them says so on camera," the reporter said carefully. "He says he saw her at a party, she asked him for a ride and he said no. Says he saw her with a drug dealer who we think we're gonna name."

There was a long pause on the line. Finally, Charles said, "And?"

"Well. I'm up here now; in fact, I'm pretty close to

you. . . ." Janney stifled a laugh beside him. "I wonder if we could get together for a few minutes, totally off the record, not for attribution—I know all the rules. There's a place we could have breakfast, maybe even just a cup of coffee—"

"No. Can't do that. Won't do that."

"All right, all right. I expected that," Taibbi said. "I guess I just want to hear you say that we're not off base. We don't want to be wrong in this; we can't be wrong."

There was another infernal pause.

"Well? I mean, are we wrong if we report what I'm saying we're gonna report?"

Charles exhaled. "You wouldn't be wrong," he began deliberately. "It wouldn't be incorrect to report that the Task Force is looking into the same matters you are, in the same areas. If you're saying people are telling these stories, that would not be wrong. I've got to go now."

He hung up before Taibbi had a chance to say thanks.

TAIBBI AND JANNEY HAD ONE more stop. The reporter had typed out a rough script on the dawn drive up, and now needed to do his piece to camera—a stand-up bridge. They went to the heart of Crack Alley. City drug detectives were making a bust, as it turned out, an ideal backdrop for the stand-up.

"A month ago," Taibbi began, staring hard into Janney's lens, "Al Sharpton told me there were only 'two significant holes' in Tawana Brawley's story. Two significant holes. Well, if the stories being told here on Crack Alley are true, then one of those two significant holes may well be that Tawana Brawley did not spend four days in captivity, being raped and maimed and sodomized—that instead she spent part of the time here, by her own choice, with a hard and dangerous crowd of her own choosing. If the stories being told are true, there is only one possible conclusion that can be drawn: Tawana Brawley lied."

TAIBBI REACHED SAGAN AND PHILLIPS on the cellular phone and told them he was headed in. Sagan said the lawyers were standing by and asked him to narrate the parts of his script that he'd completed. When the reporter was done Sagan then read to him the several versions of the on-air promotions he was planning to begin airing within the hour. Even the mildest version had Taibbi grimacing sixty miles away.

Today on Channel 2 News, the Truth about Tawana Brawley. Channel 2 news correspondent Mike Taibbi with an exclusive interview with a witness who reveals where Brawley was and what she was doing when she claimed to be abducted and raped last November. This exclusive Channel 2 news account reveals the truth behind the disturbing and explosive story that stumped investigators and rocked a community. Learn the truth about Tawana Brawley from correspondent Mike Taibbi today, and only on Channel 2 News.

Taibbi had understood from his earliest days in television that if he was going to flourish it wasn't going to be because of his telegenic looks and on-camera charisma; he was merely adequate as an on-air presence. No, it would be his reporting that made him a living; and if management was going to justify the expense and bother of supporting his type of reporting, they were going to have to adorn it and prop it up with promotion.

"Yeah, I guess," Taibbi said uncomfortably, when Sagan pressed him for his views on the copy.

"I know you hate this stuff," Sagan said. "But this is important, too. What's the point of all the work you and Anna have been doing, if nobody sees it? Besides, if these kids aren't lying, any of them, then your story *is* the Truth."

"Yeah, yeah," Taibbi said. "Let it rip, Paul. I'll be in in an hour."

The first "Truth" promo ran just before the noon newscast, and it did its job. In the lobby of the Wyndham Hotel

in Poughkeepsie more than a dozen people were in line waiting to check out. Most of them were reporters, four of them
the entire Brawley team from one New York City daily. Their
bags were packed, lap-top computers in their cases; they'd
heard the same stories Taibbi and Phillips had heard, that
the grand jury was all but done, the case winding down to an
inconclusive end. No point in living up there anymore, their
editors had agreed. C'mon home, we'll wrap it up from the
city.

And then the hotel switchboard operator buzzed the front
desk, asking for one of the newspapermen. He listened for a
few seconds, cussed sharply, and turned to face the others on
the cashier line.

"Upstairs, unpack," he announced bitterly. They were just
minutes from a clean getaway, but someone on the editors'
desk back home had heard the Channel 2 promo for Taibbi's
report and had phoned the Wyndham, ordering his reporters
to stay put and keep their eyes on the tube. The line at the
cashier's station dissolved quickly. The cashier/receptionist,
a pert girl named Holly Arnold, went to lunch early.

NO BRAWLEY STORY TO DATE generated anything near the reaction of the Taibbi/Phillips "Truth" piece on May 3, 1988.
Phillips and editor Tom Lo Presti combined Don Janney's
video with some state-of-the-art graphics effects to create six
minutes of packed and fast-paced television. But even though
the reporters had assembled their narrative carefully, concentrating in the first four minutes on their confirmation that
four other youths had told them and investigators that Tawana Brawley had been seen in Newburgh during her disappearance, it was the interview with G that was riveting,
followed by Taibbi's on-camera suggestion, the first such
public suggestion supported by in-the-field reporting, that
"Tawana Brawley lied." The reporters had identified the Chico
of G's account as Jason "Chico" Colon, a jailed sixteen-year-
old drug dealer who'd been busted with a Thermos full of

crack vials, a couple of automatic weapons, and driving a new Saab Turbo. Lawyers Rick Altabef and Jonathan Sternberg watched the piece several times, Sagan and Colloff crowding into the editing suite as well. No problems, all agreed.

When Taibbi returned to the newsroom after tagging his piece in the studio, he and Phillips shared a quick embrace. But they shook their heads at the applause pouring from some of their colleagues.

"No, man," Taibbi said to planning editor Paul Fleuranges, turning the latter's high-five into a more subdued handclasp. "We didn't prove anything. I mean, we believe she was there— too many people saying it for it not to be true. But right now they're just stories, nothing in front of the grand jury, nothing corroborated. We've pushed the story forward, that's it." Fleuranges nodded, agreed generally with the reporter's assessment, but said no one else would see it that way.

He was mostly right. The *New York Post* and the *Daily News* would play it front page; "Tawana Partying—Witness," read one headline. And the story led every radio newscast for hours. But the editors at the *New York Times* and at *Newsday* were more cautious: they knew what Taibbi and Phillips knew, that the Channel 2 story was an incremental advance in the story, albeit an important and potentially devastating blow to the Brawley team. But ultimately, only corroboration of *any* of the witness's stories would make it a bombshell to justify the promotion, presentation, and electric passage through the rest of the machinery of the New York press. The *Times* ran a cautious account of the Channel 2 story, on an inside page. *Newsday* chose to wait.

Sure enough, ten minutes before eleven, in which the "Truth" story would again be the lead, executive editor Dean Daniels reached Taibbi at home and said G had called the newsroom to "recant" his story. Daniels, worried and with the minutes ticking away toward the newscast, gave Taibbi a number where G said he could be reached.

"All right, Dean. I'll call him right away, and get back to you."

"Jesus, what do you think he'll say?" Daniels had suggested earlier on that Taibbi hang around, tired as he was, to monitor any developments and appear on set again if necessary. Now his worst nightmare was coming true.

"I don't know, Dean. You know he's got to have caught a ration of shit already. I'll call you right back."

G was a wreck on the phone.

"I told you it would be hard," Taibbi said. "But you told me you didn't lie to me. Tell me what you're saying now."

There were voices in the background; G was not at his own home.

"My friends," the teenager began. "They been getting a lot of pressure in the neighborhood. It's not true—"

"What's not true—don't bullshit me now," Taibbi said angrily. His son, Matt, was listening, in distress, a few feet away. "Tell me what's not true."

"The story I told you," G said. "It's not true. I'm recanting it."

"You're saying now you didn't see Tawana Brawley? Didn't talk to her?"

"No. That's right. It's just stuff I heard, about the party and about Chico. I don't know her."

"How do I know," the reporter hammered, "that you're telling the truth now and were lying then? How do I know that?"

G cupped the phone and talked to someone standing beside him. "I'm telling the truth now, man. It's just stuff I heard."

Taibbi called Daniels back and narrated a disclaimer to be read as an anchor follow at the conclusion of his piece.

"Just say that G called the newsroom to recant his story," Taibbi suggested, mind spinning, "saying that his friends have, quote, 'been getting a lot of pressure in the neighborhood,' unquote, and that he's now saying the story he told us was based only on what he'd heard, not on what he knew directly."

"Christ," Phillips said when Taibbi reached her at home. "Whaddya think, Mike?"

"Hell, I don't know, Anna. I mean, you were with me all along—these are the kind of people you run into on Crack Alley. We had confirmation from our state and federal sources on the central claim in the piece—that these people have been saying that they saw Tawana. G was the bonus, for us, only one of three people who told us they knew Tawana was there; but he was the guy on camera and he said he actually talked to her, and if he recants I guess that's all anybody'll remember. But I'm sure we ran into the same problems investigators and other reporters encountered. Finding these guys is one thing, getting them to talk is step two, and getting their stories to stand up—fuck it. We're not prosecutors. . . ."

"Well," Phillips said, worry in her voice. "Get some sleep. I guess we'll go at it in the morning."

SAGAN WASN'T HAPPY TO HEAR that G had recanted, but he wasn't all that surprised, either, especially in light of the teenager's "pressure in the neighborhood" comment.

"I still have no problem with the story," he told his reporters early the next morning. "We'll just say he recanted and say why, and stick by the rest of the story. You know we'll have a response from the advisers today."

That they knew. Reached by phone by print reporters the night before, Sharpton had said he and the lawyers were "rolling on the floor laughing" at the Channel 2 report. "Funnier than 'The Cosby Show,'" Sharpton said, promising a "full response" the next day.

First, though, Sharpton was due in the Brooklyn courtroom of Criminal Court Judge Albert D. Koch along with seventeen other defendants who'd taken part in a December 1987 Day of Outrage disruption at several subway stations. The courtroom dissolved into a chaotic shouting match led by Sharpton and attorney Alton Maddox and ended with bench warrants issued for all the defendants when Sharpton marched them out of the courtroom. Taibbi has gone to Brooklyn to try and get Sharpton's response to his "Truth" report in person, but the minister ignored him and his supporters threatened the reporter and cussed him angrily. But Don Janney, staking out the front of the courthouse, did catch up to Sharpton.

"What'd you think of Taibbi's report?" Janney asked.

Sharpton, who recognized the cameraman, paused long enough to utter a single sentence.

"You'll see this afternoon," he said. "I'm gonna destroy Taibbi."

IT WAS RAINING GENTLY when Janney swung his car in front of the lobby at 524 West 57th Street to pick up his two worried colleagues. He relayed Sharpton's warning and pushed into the traffic heading downtown. The Brawley advisers had booked the Ambassador Room at the Marriott Marquis Hotel on Broadway. The Channel 2 story was all over the radio and the wires, even with G's recantation, and the station had received scores of congratulatory calls, but none of it mattered to the three people in Janney's car. They said little. Traffic was a bitch.

The Ambassador Room was packed, as they knew it would be, the usual press throng augmented by out-of-town reporters and network teams, even correspondent Meredith Vieira and producer June Cross of the CBS newsmagazine "West 57th" and their crew. Taibbi and Phillips took seats in one of the back rows, facing the podium.

Janney set up his camera but was there only to shoot cutaways, extraneous shots, because the station had sent an additional crew to cover the press conference live and pipe it into the newsroom. Suddenly, Janney and every other cameraman pulled their cameras from their carefully selected positions and rushed outside the room. Sharpton, Mason, Maddox, the Reverend Timothy Mitchell of Ebenezer Baptist Church in Queens, and an unidentified and clearly uncomfortable black man had reached the top of the escalator and had headed not for the Ambassador Room but for . . . the bathroom! The cameramen and still photographers trained their lenses on the door, expecting the group to emerge any second. But minutes went by; five, ten, now fifteen minutes. Taibbi sidled up to Jerry Nachman, his former news director at Channel 4 and now a columnist for the *New York Post*, and, as always, Nachman had an answer that made sense.

"I think there might be detectives on the floor ready to pinch Sharpton and Maddox," Nachman explained. "Word is, when Judge Koch issued those bench warrants this morning in Brooklyn, he wanted 'em executed."

Phillips heard the same explanation from a radio reporter, and phoned the assignment desk to confirm it. When she got back to Taibbi and Nachman, the cameras were still gathered around the bathroom door.

"Will ya look at this," Nachman said, a savvy New Yorker drinking in the scene. Crowds of tourists, hotel guests, and who knows who else had gathered behind the cameramen and photographers and were straining on their own to see what luminary would emerge from the men's room.

"Probably think it's some movie star." Nachman laughed. "They're in from Denver or someplace and they think this happens all the time." Then, to Taibbi, "Any idea who the guy is they've got with them?"

"Not G's father, that's for sure," Taibbi answered. He mentioned that G and his family were Puerto Rican, but did not add the bitter comments he'd heard from G's mother about blacks in general and Sharpton and the lawyers in particular.

The group had been in the bathroom for twenty minutes when finally, slowly at first but then with a flourish, the door swung open and Sharpton and the lawyers and the rest of their party began the procession to the Ambassador Room. Two men in trenchcoats who were certainly plainclothes detectives watched, but kept their hands in their pockets and didn't make a move. Taibbi and Phillips lingered in the back while the cameramen settled again into position. Phillips saw Perry McKinnon, Sharpton's aide, over by a table where some coffee and soft drinks were arrayed, and asked him what was likely to happen.

McKinnon shook his head. He looked extremely anxious and unhappy. "I got to talk to you. Later. Where's Mike?"

Phillips pointed to the chairs she and Taibbi had reserved. Her partner had taken a seat. McKinnon shouldered his way between the cameramen and tapped Taibbi on the shoulder.

"Hey. Mike. I gotta talk to you, but not now. All right?"

"Yeah, sure, Perry," the reporter answered, distracted. "Whenever."

Sharpton began, introducing everybody on the podium except the mystery guest. "We'll introduce him later," he said, all portent.

"We are here," he intoned, "to respond and make certain calls on the attorney general on two stories—one that appeared in today's *Daily News* and one that appeared last night on WCBS-TV." The *News* had run a significant story alleging that Tawana Brawley had run away from home at least twice prior to her November disappearance, and that each time witnesses had seen her mother, Glenda, treat her roughly when she came to retrieve her daughter. "That's a nice sonnet in how a girl grows up in Wappingers Falls and other areas in which she lived," Sharpton said, "and how her mother cared about her enough to discipline her. Now, Mr. C. Vernon Mason will talk about the other story."

Mason was a little confused, tripping over the name and identity of the mystery guest, leaving the impression that the guest, Gregory Flemming—the father of the tall youth Taibbi and Phillips had not interviewed—was actually the father of G. The Channel 2 reporters looked at each other, unsure of what to expect; they'd already reported that G had recanted his story.

"We're here to expose the fact that these kids in that story were knowingly manipulated by sinister reporters who without any corroboration or evidence sought to discredit Tawana Brawley," Mason said. "We will handle this legally with the Federal Communications Commission, but it's a very simple matter here. We have witnesses again that can discredit [that story] and we can establish that the party didn't happen." Phillips looked around the room, trying to gauge the response to what had been said so far. All the reporters were scribbling away, but from what she could tell, they all had on their "wait and see" faces.

Maddox took over.

"Today I took the liberty of writing a letter to the grand jury foreman of the Supreme Court of New York State, County of Dutchess," he said formally. "The letter was written in response to the WCBS-TV broadcast which was seen on TV yesterday. I'm asking the grand jury to subpoena the reporter and his producer as well as those persons who appeared in their broadcast. The reason is because this television station and this grand jury are out for the same end: to establish that Tawana was engaged in a hoax." Taibbi and Phillips looked at each other; nothing yet, their expressions agreed. Maddox continued.

"I charge that Robert Abrams has used Channel 2 as an agent to carry out his devious machinations. And that Channel 2, the whore that it is, has prostituted itself and sold itself out to the whim of a prosecutor and to the governor, who has shown the nation why he should not run for president. . . ."

Maddox lapsed into a condensed version of the Four Hundred Years of Oppression. Everybody in the room, Taibbi and Phillips included, wanted to hear from Mr. Flemming. After a few more minutes of Maddox's declamation, they got their chance.

"Um, my son . . ." Flemming began nervously. "They came in and they were laughing and joking about it. They couldn't understand what was happening and what kind of position they'd been put into by the reporter who asked them what they knew about Tawana Brawley. So then they took them to the Burger King and there was some amount of money that was supposed to have changed hands, I'm not sure . . ."

Several reporters in the room shouted, "How much?"

"Um, the maximum amount I heard was a hundred dollars, the least amount was ten dollars. But the thing is," Flemming continued, "to the kids this was just a 'get-over,' you know? Like it was a joke."

The reporters were screaming questions and Flemming stepped away from the microphones, distressed and unhappy to be there despite Mason's pounding him on the back. Taibbi raised his hand to shout his own question, but he didn't have a chance. Phillips couldn't believe what she'd just heard: this man, whose son they'd never even interviewed, was claiming that she and Mike had bribed the kids to get the interview with G! She looked at Taibbi, who shrugged in his own confusion. He was sweating profusely, the collar of his shirt already damp with a spreading stain.

One reporter, a big-league shouter, managed to have his question heard: "Are you G's father?"

"No," Flemming said emphatically, shaking his head. "But they—the kids—they did not appreciate him being taken advantage of by this reporter, they didn't understand the ramifications . . ."

Sharpton touched Flemming on the shoulder and stepped up to the microphones.

"I'm gonna tell you," he stormed, "that the story that Channel 2 bought by wining and dining these kids—if you can call Big Macs [sic] and sodas wining and dining 'em— was a lie, and if they had taken them to the Red Lobster they would have gotten a bigger lie. Maybe they could have poured some white juice on their faces and said they were the six white men who raped Tawana!"

It went on and on. The advisers took turns denouncing Channel 2, pounding away at the bribery theme, describing in vague but monumental terms the lawsuit and the FCC complaint they were preparing against WCBS and Taibbi and Phillips, claiming they'd spoon-fed the reporters their "Just

Business" stories on Fric 'n' Frac, and regrouping between salvos with spot references to the Four Hundred Years of Oppression.

Paul Sagan, watching the feed in his office with some of his managers, shook his head as the press conference was winding up. They're not denying the story, he thought to himself; they haven't said anything about the fact that investigators have gotten these same stories on the record about Tawana being in Newburgh. It's just another staged show, another event aimed at turning attention away from the facts. They've got nothing. We're all right!

But the news director was also worried about Taibbi and Phillips, more worried than he'd ever been. He was certain they hadn't paid for G's interview, but the question had never come up in any of the discussions about the story leading up to broadcast and he knew that, now, his reporters and the bribery allegation would become the story. He wanted to know the facts himself and wanted to make certain Taibbi wouldn't get into a shouting match with the advisers or even with any other reporters.

He stepped out into his newsroom; there was tension and worry on every single face.

"Noreen," he called to Noreen Lark, an assignment editor. "Get down to the Marriott. Tell Taibbi and Phillips to just say 'no comment' when the questions start coming at them. Fast, okay?"

But the questions had already started flying. The minute the press conference ended and the advisers and Gregory Flemming exited the room, the cameras, dozens of them, had turned to Taibbi and Phillips. The two reporters got to their feet, suddenly facing the crush, the feeding frenzy, the gang bang familiar to every news subject unlucky enough to find himself in close quarters with the inquisitors from the fourth estate. They had friends in the room, they'd won respect throughout their Brawley coverage and for their stories before that, but it didn't matter.

"Did you pay 'em, Mike?" asked a television reporter from

a competing station, microphone extended. "C'mon. You know I've got to ask you."

"How much!" another reporter shouted.

"Was it a hundred?"

"For each kid?"

Taibbi loosened his tie, the sweat oozing through his collar and down his back. He couldn't believe it. He wanted to scream, They're full of shit, you all know they're full of shit. They've pulled it on all of you, all throughout this thing, and you're buying it now! Instead, he looked at the face closest to him, the television colleague, and, aware but just barely aware that he was now on someone else's camera, growled an answer.

"We didn't pay anybody for any story or any interview. I'll explain exactly how everything went in my report tonight. Beyond that I'm not saying anything."

Phillips kept her poise, said nothing, started pulling Taibbi in the direction of the door. She was mortified, angry, and felt more isolated and threatened than she'd ever felt; but she was bearing up. Lark came up to them then, whispered Sagan's instructions, and the two reporters began the longest and strangest walk either had ever known. As Al Sharpton and his entourage had been sandwiched by the cameras, lights, and questions when they'd arrived an hour before, now they were being similarly "escorted," and it was weird, disconcerting, mildly terrifying, and had them out of balance. Phillips saw Janney at the head of the pack, walking backwards in front of her.

"Don! Janney!" she called. "What are you *doing?*"

Janney shook his head, kept shooting. He was a newsman. His partners were the news.

Back at the station, in Sagan's office, Taibbi reprised the entire episode with G, only this time including the detail about the $10 he'd given him after the interview, a detail so insignificant he hadn't even thought of it as an issue until it was raised in the news conference. Colloff was there, listening carefully. Sagan scribbled notes; he'd already been called for comment by a number of news organizations and hadn't returned any of the calls yet.

"That's no problem," he said, when Taibbi had finished his explanation. "There's no violation of Standards and Practices; we pay transportation costs in a lot of instances. But maybe," he added, sympathetically, "you should have just taken the kid's car to a gas station and bought him some gas with the station credit card, and kept the receipt." He knew in his own mind how the scene must have played out, though; knew that getting away quick with the interview in the can was the most important thing on his reporter's mind.

"All right. Just do the story, report their allegations. Write an on-camera tag explaining exactly how everything happened. I'll have a statement to that effect for the rest of the press."

Taibbi, still shaken, wrote the body of the piece quickly, explaining in his narration who Gregory Flemming was and allowing Mason to state the case for the advisers: "I would call it bribery. I would call it paying for a story. . . ." Phillips got to work putting the piece together, leaving the editing room now and then to see how her partner was doing writing his tag.

It was a struggle, hateful work, Taibbi thought, to have to defend himself before millions of people (his station's own viewers and everyone else who'd heard the bribery charges through one news organization or another). As he went through draft after draft he thought of Steve Pagones, Jack Ryan, Cuomo and Abrams, state trooper Scott Patterson, and the family of Harry Crist. He might as well have stood wrongly accused himself of being one of Tawana Brawley's rapists, so serious was the charge that he'd bribed a witness to fabricate a story. The calls for him were pouring in, calls from fellow reporters asking for his comment; he took none of them. Finally, he was done. His only worry was that the "explanation" in the tag of his piece was overlong, nearly a minute, and in his shaky state he was worried about getting through it without a slip and with the inflection and intensity he wanted to convey. Somehow, he got through it.

"It is appropriate," he would say, "to discuss our role in this story since it was a central issue in today's press conference." He described the interview setting, the discussions leading up to the actual on-camera interview with G, the fact that G agreed to talk and did so only after a clear explanation that he was to receive no payment, his recognition *after* the interview that G *had* spent hours leading the Channel 2 crew around Newburgh and introducing other local youths who spoke about the Brawley story. "I reached into my pocket and gave him a ten-dollar bill and said, 'Here, buy yourself some gas.' We did not, and do not, pay for stories."

No other news organization quoted Taibbi's assertion that G had given his interview with the clear understanding that he was not to be paid. Press accounts said simply that Taibbi had admitted paying $10 for "gas," the quotation marks added, and the lead stories in radio and other television accounts and in the papers the next day included that "admission" and Taibbi's "denial" that he'd bribed a witness with cheeseburgers and cash. Some of the stories suggested or said outright that Gregory Flemming, the mystery guest, was G's father.

The Brawley advisers had done it again, deflecting press attention—through rhetoric, lies, and misrepresentation—to a nonissue away from the central facts of the case of what had happened to a fifteen-year-old girl long months ago. And they didn't stop with their press conference bombshell, as Taibbi learned the next morning when he started returning the calls from his press colleagues.

"I've got to tell you," said Howard Manley, the *Newsday* reporter who'd been a friend, "Vernon Mason called me up and said he has confirmation—proof—that you and Anna have been going all over Newburgh offering cash bribes to anyone who could tell a story discrediting Tawana Brawley. He's been calling other reporters, too."

"So what do you want?" Taibbi answered, exasperated. "My response? On the record or off?"

"Well . . . I don't know, Mike. How do you want to do it?"

"Are you doing a story? Because if you are it's not 'balance' because you run their allegations and my statement that it's bullshit."

"I don't know, Mike," Manley said. "I haven't even talked to my editors about it. I just thought I'd call you. . . ."

Taibbi told him the story, blow by blow. "On the record or off," he said. Manley never even drafted a story or ran the idea past his editors. Within a month he would leave *Newsday* to join the reporting staff of a national magazine.

With other reporters Taibbi was less patient.

"You know me, you know my work!" he shouted to one radio reporter he'd known for years. "You think I'm stupid enough to go around paying for interviews? No, I'm not gonna do a fucking interview for you—you oughta know better than that!"

Phillips, eavesdropping on Taibbi's angry conversations, grabbed him by the shoulders at one point between calls and implored him to just stop talking.

"Mike, you don't have to do this. They had their say, we had ours. Let's just keep working the story; that's what we always said, that when the shit starts flying you just work the damn story!"

Taibbi nodded, leaning back in his chair, and had closed his eyes in exhaustion when his phone rang again. It was Bill Tatum, editor of the *Amsterdam News*. Tatum had called the station months before, the night the Taibbi/Phillips "Good Cop–Bad Cop" report had aired, and told station management that hiring Mike Taibbi away from Channel 4 was a "brilliant move. He's the best reporter in the city, he cares about minority issues." Now he had a different view; Taibbi launched into his "explanation" once again, and his partner walked away, shaking her head.

"Mike, I don't believe you and Anna bribed anybody,"

Tatum said. "I just think you've been misled on this story."

"It's not just us," Taibbi countered, "it's the investigators from the Task Force, too. And it's not just G, it's four or five other people as well. Maybe more. And I gotta tell you, Bill. I've known you a long time, we have friends in common; I've respected you and appreciated what you've said and written about me in the past. But you're buying the advisers' line on this story, hook, line, and sinker. Except for a piece here and there that almost questions their strategies, you're giving them a pass. You get up there, or send your reporters, and you tell me what you find, and then I'll listen when you tell me Anna and I have been 'misled.' "

"Mike, you know I don't have the staff to send up there—"

"Then don't report the damn story, Bill. Or report it straight, instead of only one way. You've got an important role to play in the black community and you're ill-serving that community if you stand behind the bullshit these guys are putting out without questioning them."

"Mike," Tatum said, "I've known these men a long time. They're good men, the lawyers especially. But if they're wrong in this, if I learn in the end they made irresponsible accusations they knew to be untrue against innocent people, then *I will destroy them.*"

Tatum, a fixture in the community who'd made an unsuccessful bid to buy the *New York Post* from Rupert Murdoch, said it several times in several ways, and more dramatically each time. If the advisers to Tawana Brawley had abused the truth in the ways many in the press believed they'd abused the truth, then he, Wilbur Tatum, the publisher of the city's most influential black newspaper, would "destroy them, absolutely." But, he said, he believed at the moment that Mike Taibbi, a reporter whose integrity and skills he said he still trusted, by the way, had been misled on the Brawley story.

"Did you ever consider, Mike," Tatum said after another

fruitless exchange over the facts in the case, "that someone might have been working roots on Tawana?"

"What?" It had come out of nowhere; Taibbi fought for concentration. "I'm not sure what you're saying, Bill."

"Well, then get Anna, she'll know about voodoo. . . ."

Taibbi put Tatum on hold and shook his head. Phillips was approaching his desk anyway.

"Here," he said, standing up and handing her the receiver. "It's Bill Tatum."

Phillips had found that the pressure of having to defend herself in the black community of which she'd so long been a part was wearing, exhausting, emotionally draining. Each time she participated in a story that challenged the Brawley account she'd hear about it—from black colleagues at the station, some of whom questioned her harshly (one even said he could no longer work with her), and from black journalists in the tristate area with whom she'd shared professional and business relationships for years. She was the object, suddenly, of the kind of criticism and conjecture that had met the "negative portrayal" of black life in America in plays like *For Colored Girls*, books like *The Color Purple*, and movies like *School Daze*. She, Phillips, was saying what she said, reporting what she reported, for the white media!

"Don't let those kids in Newburgh pull your leg," Bill Tatum told her on the phone. "Have you even considered that someone might really have given Tawana something?"

The *Poughkeepsie Journal* had quoted "relatives" of Tawana as saying that Tawana had been forced to drink a "milky white liquid" that had destroyed her memory of what had happened to her.

"You know about voodoo," Tatum continued.

Phillips dismissed Tatum's theory politely, but a week later would be surprised and disturbed to read his "editorial" in the *Amsterdam News*.

"This then presents a dilemma of overwhelming proportions," Tatum wrote. "Something happened to Miss Brawley.

Given the evidence, tainted as it might be, nothing happened. But one does not work oneself up to such a state of trauma without cause! Could it be, as some have observed, the 'working of roots, or voodoo!' That explanation is as good as any that we have heard so far."

TAIBBI AND PHILLIPS BEGAN their recovery from the bribery charges on Friday, May 6, two days after the Ambassador Room press conference. It turned out that even before their "Truth" report had aired on the Eleven, Jason "Chico" Colon was standing in a cell block corridor at the Orange County Jail in Goshen and telling investigators that, yes, he *had* seen Tawana Brawley at a post-Thanksgiving party, and that his story could be corroborated. *Newsday* ran the Chico Colon story that morning, and Taibbi and Janney raced north to put Colon's attorneys on tape and on the air.

"Let's be clear," Taibbi said to William Greher, one of the lawyers, "that Chico Colon has a vested interest in telling this story now, given that he's in jail awaiting trial on very serious charges."

"That's correct, no question," Greher answered on camera. "I'd be a fool to counsel him any differently. This is a quid pro quo, and I've told that already to Jack Ryan. My client would want some kind of guarantee regarding the disposition of his case if he were to come forward and testify under oath before the Brawley grand jury."

Greher added that in two separate prison interviews Colon had let it be known that he'd actually seen Tawana twice in the four days of her disappearance, that he'd met her through her former boyfriend, Todd Buxton, and that "several" witnesses could back up his claim.

"I've known the family a long time, I've represented his mother," Greher said. "I have no reason not to believe him now."

The Greher interview and the emergence of Chico Colon as a potential witness, a direct result of the "Truth" piece, helped a little, but only a little. That night Taibbi and Phillips headed home to their families, forsaking their usual end-of-the-day war-gaming session. They really didn't know where to go next. They knew they needed time for their wounds to heal.

The phone rang early in Taibbi's apartment the next morning. It was a friend, Tony S.,* a federal source who had nothing to do with the Brawley case but had been an important confirming contact on some of the reporter's previous scoops.

"Those . . . bastards," the source said, his voice a hoarse whisper. "God, Mike, they'll stop at nothing. I feel so bad for you, I know what you must be going through."

"Yeah, thanks, Tony," Taibbi answered. He'd slept fitfully; his stomach was jumping. "I mean it, thanks for the call."

"I mean, Jesus! It's just so much fucking shit. And the way the rest of the press just picks it up, runs with it. I've seen it so many times before, but this is—I don't know. It's unbelievable."

Taibbi sat at the foot of his bed, cupping his eyes with one hand and pressing the receiver to his ear with the other. His wife, Beverly, had awakened with the ringing of the phone and moved down to the end of the bed to sit by him, rubbing his back.

"Thanks," Taibbi said finally, searching for a voice of confidence but failing to find it. "Just . . . thanks."

"I just wanted to call," Tony said. "To, you know, commiserate. They'll get theirs, I know that. You know that too, though you're probably not thinking about that now. But . . . to commiserate, you know?"

"I know. I know, Tony. Thanks a lot. You don't know how much I appreciate the call."

It was a lousy Saturday.

And then, in the half hour after 6:00 A.M. Sunday morning, Taibbi, Phillips, Paul Sagan, and Roger Colloff all picked up their copies of the *New York Times*; they scanned the front page and grabbed for their phones immediately, each trying to call the others.

The page-one headline read, "In Brawley Inquiry, a Turn to Drug-Infested Streets." The seven-man *Times* reporting team had published its own version of the Taibbi/Phillips "Truth" piece, repeating the assertion that at least four witnesses had told investigators that they saw Tawana Brawley at a party when she was supposed to have been in captivity. The *Times* reporters added several additional witnesses they'd dug up on their own, and recounted their own brushes with violence in the seamy world of Crack Alley. It was familiar, supportive, confirming, comprehensive, and cautious. It was, after all, the *New York Times*.

After Taibbi had talked to his partner, agreeing they would race to the station to build a follow-up report based on the *Times* findings, he grabbed his paper and read through the report again, and when he was done he held the paper to his face and kissed the front page, more passionately than he'd kissed Beverly in weeks.

10

"Come on, Rule Three, dammit!"

THE CHURCH HAD BEEN the soul and center of New York's black community for as long as there had been a community that was so identified. It had provided leadership and leaders, and rhetoric eloquent and passionate enough to effectively frame the issues and agenda of a people in authentic need. Anna Phillips had known it first-hand, growing up in Harlem. Though raised a Catholic in a church-going family, she went with her family to many events and services at Harlem's powerhouse church, the Abyssinian Baptist Church, whenever Adam Clayton Powell, Jr., or another local light had sought its podium. "Harlem is the center of American black culture," her father had told her from her youth. "Don't ever lose sight of that." She knew too that while in the Brawley case Al Sharpton and lawyers Mason and Maddox employed one strategy through the press to reach one audience—the audience that was empowered and now intimidated, mostly white but partly black, disbelieving of the tale but believing enough that such tales had been and could again be true to suppress their questions and their own building rage—it was to the black church, in the black church, that the Brawley advisers made their purest pitch. In the black church, the Four Hundred Years of Oppression stood for more than the inevitable hunk of each news conference when the cameras shut down and the reporters distracted themselves with worries about deadlines and leads; it was autobiography, unvarnished and unassailably the truth, central to the discussion of any other issue.

As scholar Eric Lincoln had written in 1973 in the foreword to Gayraud S. Wilmore's *Black Religion and Black Radicalism*, "The Black man's religion was the organizing principle around which his life was structured. His church was his school, his forum, his political arena, his social club, his art gallery, his conservatory of music. It was lyceum and gymnasium as well as sanctum sanctorum. . . . It was the peculiar sustaining force which gave him the strength to endure when endurance gave no promise, and the courage to be creative in the face of his own dehumanization."

Taibbi had seen and heard the power of the black church, first-hand, only once in the months of the Tawana Brawley case. It was a midweek evening at Brooklyn's Bethany Baptist Church, in mid-March, the story in a lull and the exposure of the advisers still to come in the Jack Ryan "Gestapo Wildman" farce, and Taibbi had driven to Bedford-Stuyvesant from his Manhattan apartment just to listen, to look for the core of fire that made its way to the streets, to the airwaves of radio station WLIB, to the letters he'd begun to receive.

They were all there: Sharpton, Maddox, Mason, Juanita Brawley, Glenda Brawley and Ralph King, their toddler, Tyice, and a packed church. It seemed to Taibbi, roaming the balcony and ignoring the hostile stares of the congregants, that it wasn't the lawyers or the details of the Brawley story that moved the people in this place of refuge; it was the recitation of their hurt, the repetition of their expectations, the reminders of their unfinished history that dragged them to their feet time and again, the wail of anguish or defiant joy rising from them, feeding on itself. It was Sharpton who moved them, the Wonder Boy preacher with no congregation save the Congregation of the Blessed Moment, and he was no less than brilliant.

"All y'all have to do," he shouted from the lectern, his inflections raw and blacker than he'd ever allow in a press conference, "is to look around this church at all the different colors we all are, and y'all know who's been doin' the rapin'." Old theme: Taibbi had heard versions of it before, on WLIB and in the edited versions of the Four Hundred Years of Oppression the "white press" had been made to endure in press conference after press conference. But now Sharpton added verse after verse, in rhythmic passion astonishing in its force, and the Congregation of the Blessed Moment swayed and nodded, shouted in agreement, became infused with an energy and humanness unknown or unexperienced in the mundane workaday world of the empowered, the entitled; the white world.

Now, on the morning of Mother's Day, 1988, Anna Phillips and Mike Taibbi screened the tapes of the Brawley advisers' appearance the day before at Bethany Baptist Church, tapes that had been shot but not used for reasons that soon became obvious, and they knew that they themselves were now part of the litany. Sharpton's homily was about "Bad Mike" and his "litany of lies."

"Mike Taibbi," he shouted, "on Wednesday night we gave you the benefit of the doubt that maybe you were just conning us, but after Friday night, with your story of this drug dealer Jason Colon, we see that it is a vendetta, a racist, in-

sidious vendetta by a berserk reporter trying to make a liar
out of a little girl.

"We are calling on Channel 2 to fire Mike Taibbi . . ."
The crowd roared and stood to applaud. ". . . and we're not
making no open-ended request. If by Tuesday Channel 2 News
refuses to stop this man from using the public airwaves to
cover a political position against Tawana Brawley we will
call for a boycott of Channel 2 in the city of New York. And
let me tell you," he shouted above the cheers, "when we talk
boycott we're not them sissies in the other organizations, we're
not talking about sending out no press releases. We're sayin'
if you choose to go ahead with this vendetta, we will lay in
and sit in, in your studios, your hallways. We will close off
your advertisers, we will picket your studios, we will agitate
until no self-respecting person watches Channel 2 in the city
of New York!"

Maddox spoke.

"The days of responsible Negro leadership are over. We're
not interested in Negro leadership and not interested in even
looking like Negroes. We are starting a black army. We are a
people that have been raped and abused and we are not going
to act in a civilized manner. That is sick. Somebody said,
'Maddox, you came up to Poughkeepsie with hate in your
eyes, hate in your heart, hate in your mind,' and that's right!
That's right! What would I look like, going up to Poughkeepsie with love in my heart. . . ."

It was Mason's turn. The applause, on the tape, was tre-
mendous.

"Mike Taibbi," he said. "Let me expose the man right now
before I get diverted. Mike Taibbi, I did an investigation on
you, and what I found out from your former colleagues at
Channel 4 is that you are of Italian and Hawaiian descent.
But more importantly, that your whole forte while you were
at Channel 4 and your whole forte now is to try to discredit
anything in the African community. Mike Taibbi, it was not
bad judgment, it was not by happenstance. Mike Taibbi, you

went up there with all of that racial animosity; and you're not alone, you're not unique, you're not the only racist. . . ."

Mason wasn't finished; there was still his latest fiction to get through. He asserted that G had called him after talking to his mother, "a black woman . . . who scolded her son for letting this classless man into their home," and said, " 'Taibbi was going around the neighborhood offering money to everybody.' " Mason reminded his audience that G's father had already told the world about the bribery in the Wednesday press conference. ("Jesus," Taibbi said nearly under his breath, unbelieving, "lie after lie after lie . . .")

"And Mike Taibbi," Mason concluded. "You don't think we have our sources? We know that you sat at the breakfast table with this black woman and she told you her son didn't even know this little girl, and asked you not to run your story. But no, you'd already spoken to Dan Rather of the network news and offered him the story, 'cause you were gonna make your career off of Tawana Brawley. . . ."

Taibbi could listen no longer. He'd been told when he arrived in the newsroom that another station, one of the city's independent stations, had fashioned a complete report from the same material he'd just screened and run it the night before. There'd been no call to Channel 2 for comment or response from either management or Taibbi himself. He'd phoned the station, enraged, and left two messages for the news director, a man he knew personally, but neither call had been returned. Geraldo Rivera had done another show, jumping up and down when he lost control of the broadcast, which effectively gave the Brawley gang another hour of unsupervised and (effectively) unchallenged national airtime.

"Come on, Moon," Phillips said gently. Her husband, Lionel, had once remarked jokingly that Taibbi "had a perfectly round face, just like Moon Mullins, the comic strip character," and she'd taken to calling her partner Moon in their private moments. "Come on, let's just get the piece together.

We can forget about this stuff, not even use it. There's no need to."

Their follow-up story based on the comprehensive *Times* report on the witnesses from Crack Alley who claimed to have seen Tawana Brawley during her disappearance made the two reporters feel better. A lot better. They screened it several times when Phillips and editor Tom Lo Presti had finished putting it together; it was heavy on graphics inserts with direct quotes from the *Times* account. They were riding the Gray Lady for all she was worth.

"If the *Times* had learned something counter to what you guys had learned," Sagan told them after reviewing Taibbi's script for the piece, "then the *Times* would have said so. When Roger called me this morning after reading their story, all he could say was, 'Terrific, terrific!' "

General manager Roger Colloff would later agree to meet for the second and last time with a representative of the Brawley team, despite Taibbi's disbelieving response: "How can you meet with these bastards! Why the fuck are you gonna see 'em?" "Because we'd meet with anyone who had what we believed was a legitimate grievance with our coverage," Colloff had answered. "Don't worry. We'll hear them out; we're obligated to do that."

"They sent [Rev.] Timothy Mitchell," Sagan would explain later. "He said he was the representative. We met in Roger's office. Gene Lothery was there as well. Mitchell gave us the long speech—Tawana was his daughter, the daughter of all black men, how would we feel if she was our daughter. . . . Mitchell said he didn't believe that CBS was racist, only that there was some 'misguided reporting.' He even said, 'Hey, I'm not asking that you fire Mike Taibbi. I'm just demanding that he be taken off the story.'

"At that point [station manager Gene] Lothery said, 'One thing we make clear: we are not negotiating. Mike Taibbi and Anna Phillips are not coming off the story. You can discuss the story, but not that issue. Taking them off the story is not discussible.' Roger made the same point, emphatically. It was clear soon enough that [Mitchell] hadn't even seen most of our stories. We had to point out that Gregory Flemming [Sr.] wasn't even the father of G. Mitchell seemed to be reading from a list of points prepared for him by someone else. He kept referring to his notes; he was really uncomfortable. He referred to Anna only vaguely, like an afterthought; he thought you were the 'big white guy,' that she'd do what she had to do because that was her job. It was your stories that were scaring them. They believed Anna by herself would not have had the impact. . . .

"I tried to debate the facts with Mitchell; he seemed like a reasonable man. We went through our standards, talked about the stories, talked about Newburgh, about the *Times* story that followed ours. But he turned it into a discussion about racism, not about the facts of the story."

But on that Sunday, while Taibbi had makeup applied and prepared to go into the studio for the early broadcast, Phillips sat alone in the darkened editing room and let her mind roam, deep into the maze of her own history, emotions, perceptions. Her thoughts fell to Mason's comments on the tape of the day before, the inevitable comments exalting the virtues of "black women, and the black daughters who are the daughters of all of us." Once, driving alone with Taibbi during one of their camera-less forays north, they'd gotten into an edgy discussion about their personal lives and struggles. It was odd; they almost never argued, their perceptions and views so closely aligned that a friendship, something to endure, had begun and would surely flourish. But now Taibbi, at least half Polynesian but in total a racial admixture of uncertain lineage, was talking about his own struggle to emerge from a troubled New York childhood, about his need, eventually realized, to develop a coarse shell to arm him for the battles in which, more and more frequently, he seemed to be engaged. And Phillips—friend, colleague, partner—had snapped.

"You don't know, Taibbi, you just don't know. When you're black, you're black every day of your life, and every day of your life is a battle, and your life is a war. . . ." She'd surprised herself by her own flash of anger. The rest of the ride had been quiet.

Black women, she thought. I wonder how the black women of slavery would feel about the Brawley incident, about what's being done with the Brawley incident. The rapes, countless rapes, they had to withstand, silently, helplessly. Absent the right to refuse, resist, or protest, much less accuse, they bore their burdens and their bastard children in a world of unspeakable degradation. What would they do, what would they say, were they sitting in Bethany Baptist Church listening to Sharpton and Mason talk of their "greatness," their agony, their suffering? If only they could speak out now, Phillips thought. If only . . .

IT WAS POURING AGAIN, damn incessant rain, on May 11, when Phillips, Taibbi, and Janney returned to Poughkeepsie. A week after the "Truth" piece, only days after the conclusion of its terrible fallout, they were simply back on the story. Lyle Harris, a reporter on the team from the *Daily News*, had scooped the press corps with a detailed account of the renewed activities of the grand jury. Harris had come up with the names of a number of Tawana's friends, from Wappingers Falls and from Newburgh, who were now being summoned to Room 10 in the Armory, where the grand jury met. Among those called were four potentially key witnesses: three of Tawana's girlfriends from the Pavillion Apartments and an eighteen-year-old from Wappingers Falls named Darryl Rodriguez, who identified himself as "Tawana's boyfriend" and who investigators believed was holding back direct knowledge he had about Tawana's whereabouts during her disappearance. The case was alive again.

Taibbi went directly into the Poughkeepsie Diner, where a half-dozen reporters were sipping coffee out of the rain, to discuss the recent turns in the story and to gauge his changed relationships with some reporters whose opinions and knowledge he valued. Things seemed to be all right, just all right. Phillips, less interested than her partner in reprising Newburgh and its fallout, climbed into the rain gear Janney handed her and walked toward Harris, who'd become a friend and who was drifting glumly, alone, beneath a huge umbrella. Harris paced, Phillips paced with him. The Brawley story, they agreed, was toughest in some ways on the black reporters covering it, especially those who, like the two of them, were keenly aware of their heritage and had in their professional lives sought consciously to honor it. Each time a black reporter learned something that cast doubt on the story and then reported it, that reporter risked being labeled an Uncle Tom (or an Aunt Tomasina, Mason's phrase); and the distance between the reporter and his or her still silent black friends grew larger and larger.

"I don't know," Harris lamented in the rain, "whether this is the best story I've ever been on, or the worst." Phillips didn't answer right away, and Harris, pacing still, finally answered his own question.

"I guess it's the worst."

The witnesses, Tawana's friends, began arriving at the courthouse, cameras suddenly appearing to greet them, and the early hours of the morning wore on. Taibbi and Phillips were about to leave when Richard Pienciak, Harris's colleague and the head of the *Daily News* team, approached Phillips. The *News* had run an "exclusive" interview with jailed Newburgh drug dealer Randy "D-Day" Davis, in which Davis asserted that while "he had plenty of parties," he had videotapes of each of them that would prove Tawana never attended any of them. Pienciak hadn't seen any of the videotapes (and neither had investigators), but he muttered something under his breath about Channel 2's coverage of the case, and when Phillips said she didn't quite hear him he made it clearer.

"You know," he said, shaking his head, "journalism isn't

a multiple choice test, about who you decide you're going to believe."

Phillips, who'd spent days after the Newburgh report keeping her partner's temper in check, exploded in anger herself.

"Well, where the hell do you come off, Pienciak. I suppose running an interview with Randy Davis and talking about tapes you never saw just about *proves* Tawana was never in Newburgh! What is it, one set of rules for you and another for us?" She turned and walked angrily to Janney's car, slamming the door when she got in; it was exactly the kind of exchange her nature and personality dictated couldn't happen. But it had.

Still, it didn't take long for Phillips and Taibbi to learn that their rough days after Newburgh had had a positive effect as well. In fact, it was extraordinary: while they were being hammered in New York City, while other reporters were sniping at them, the story itself was opening up to them. From the people who knew their work or knew them personally to total strangers who were only among the millions following the case, there was a sentiment expressed in letters and phone calls—especially in the phone calls that were suddenly being returned—that they'd taken an unfair hit. Their off-the-record conversations with investigative sources were more substantive, providing them with leads they assumed would have been denied them routinely when they were fishing with the rest of the pack. The witnesses they knew had appeared before the grand jury opened their doors now, invited them in for conversation and coffee, and, if the reporters asked, often agreed readily to silhouette or even full-face interviews. Most of what they learned as they backtracked through the case had been reported before, but Taibbi and Phillips felt they were regaining their footing while building up their taped record.

There were even people with good reason to view them with something other than affection who softened that view after their public battering over the false bribery charges. Lou

Viglotti, for example, the Fishkill attorney whom Taibbi had maneuvered into an awkward on-camera role in the Fric 'n' Frac story, first reacted to the bribery charges by sending him a bitter note: "Dear Mike," the salutation went. "On a recent news broadcast, I learned that you paid G $10 for gas. Enclosed please find $5 as payment for the gas you caused me." When Taibbi unfolded the note, five single-dollar bills fluttered to his desk. But a week later, in Poughkeepsie, he ran into Viglotti outside Alex's Restaurant and the lawyer shook his head, offered a rueful smile, and greeted the reporter with the warmth of new kinship.

"Unbelievable," Viglotti said.

"Yeah, well. I guess this whole case is just so full of shit that anybody who touches it gets at least a little dirty."

They went to Catskill that day and, after waiting two hours, managed to speak to heavyweight champion Mike Tyson. The champ, who'd given Tawana his $35,000 Rolex watch in addition to setting up a $100,000 fund for her along with boxing promotor Don King, hadn't said a word about the case since he'd made those gestures in February. Taibbi instructed Janney carefully as Tyson's buff-yellow Rolls-Royce Corniche pulled to a stop: leave the camera out of sight until and unless he agrees to an interview. You don't piss off the champ.

"I don't know," Tyson said, his voice small and suspicious as he considered the careful questions Taibbi and Phillips posed. "Maybe I got taken advantage of. . . ." A longtime member of Tyson's entourage, a still photographer, had told Taibbi the same thing moments before in the gym over Catskill's police station, where trainer Kevin Rooney was waiting for his famous fighter. "On the way to Japan, for the Tubbs fight," the photographer said, "he kept saying it. That he'd been a chump, that he wished he hadn't gotten involved." Taibbi wanted Tyson to say it on camera—if the heavyweight champion of the world disavowed the case and the handling of the case by the Brawley advisers, if he personally urged Tawana to get it over with, it would be a significant statement. But Robin Givens, still Tyson's wife at the time, pulled up with tennis pro Lori McNeil and called a halt to the tentative sidewalk interview.

"All he's gotta be thinking about now," Givens said, "is the Spinks fight next month. He's gotta start training. Sorry." She led Tyson into the gym, locking the door behind them.

Taibbi and Phillips had other business in Catskill. The one-time sister-in-law of Tawana's uncle Matt Strong was incarcerated in the Green County Jail, charged, ironically, with an abduction and kidnapping in Newburgh. But in a jail-cell interview with Phillips, the drug-addicted woman said that while her Newburgh dealer specialized in luring young black girls into prostitution and crossed paths frequently with Todd Buxton and Randy "D-Day" Davis, she'd never heard him talk about Tawana Brawley and didn't know the girl herself.

The days of mid-May went by, filled with hits and misses and plenty of reasons to keep going. There were people who wanted to talk to them now, people close to the case or close to the Brawleys, and the reporters just hadn't been able to get to them yet. Yet the repetitive routine of the work, arising each day and meeting with Janney to go over the list of the day's tasks, was again nourishing, invigorating.

One morning, leaving early under a cloudless sky that promised a gorgeous day, they poked north slowly on the scenic Taconic Parkway, instead of the prosaic Thruway, just for the pleasure of it. Just above Ossining, Taibbi yelled to Janney to stop the car, right away! Back it up, back it up! Janney did, confused, and Taibbi, having grabbed the doubled plastic bags that earlier had carried the team's morning fruit and coffee, sprinted across the traffic-free parkway to the southbound lane. A minute later he skipped back to the car, a little-boy grin of glee on his face and a monster of some sort clawing its way through the plastic bags.

"Always had this thing about turtles, always stop for them and take them off the highways," he said, pulling open the

back door. Phillips, in the backseat, recoiled in horror. The
object of her partner's affection and sympathy was a snapping turtle with a shell a foot or more in diameter. Its claws
had ripped clear through the plastic bags, and though Taibbi
held it by its tail, it didn't seem he could hold on to the
thrashing beast too much longer. The turtle's head, fat as a
fist, flew out like a berserk piston, giant jaws attacking the
air wildly.

"What are you gonna do with that thing, Taibbi! Where
the fuck do you think you're gonna put it?"

"Backseat, of course; no room up front with Don and me."
Taibbi laughed. "There's a swamp a little farther north; we
can just let it free there!" He hefted his enraged package in
Phillips's direction.

"Oh shit, holy shit!" Janney moaned. He'd broken his rules
by even allowing his partners to bring coffee and snacks into
his car, and now this idiot was swinging a slimy, muddy,
pissed-off, and probably about-to-piss giant fucking turtle! But
Taibbi knew the joke had gone far enough when the lethal
piston came close to scoring a hunk of human thigh—his
own—and he walked down the rise in the highway embank-
ment and let the creature go.

There were days like that, some laughs amid the muck of
the Brawley story. Once it was a roadside picnic by a pretty
lake after an impromptu stop at an Italian deli. Janney talked
about his friends, his new girlfriend, his love of ballet. Taibbi
and Phillips talked about their families, the spouses and children they missed so badly.

There were dinners on the good days, days when they'd
made progress, dinners accompanied by selections from the
wine list by Janney, who knew how to select from a wine
list. On the bad days, after they'd been skunked when another promising lead turned to dust, the rides home or back
to the hotel were silent. One bad day, without Janney this
time, Phillips and Taibbi drove south, depressed, and passed
a meadow by one of the Thruway tolls where in the after-

noons a large family of deer always gathered to feed in the fading light. But this time they weren't feeding; they were huddled, some with their heads bobbing in distress. Taibbi pulled the car over and the reporters walked to the fence to have a closer look. It was a wake, the family gathered around the fallen carcass of a big buck, ten points at least.

Tawana Brawley, the case and the story, would soon be in its third season of a New York year, and they, and the investigators, they knew, were still to a large degree spinning their wheels, following wisps of smoke and hints of a terrible truth, while a trio in the city agitated toward a violent or at least hateful resolution.

THEY KNEW FROM their Task Force sources that Jack Ryan and Bob Abrams were being urged by their understaff to "think about taking the steps needed to begin winding things up," and that a subpoena for someone in Tawana's family, if not for Tawana herself, might be the final step leading to the conclusion of the case. But that step was "a couple of weeks away at least," one source told Taibbi. Another lull. Taibbi knew it wouldn't last, but Beverly had booked and canceled and rebooked a getaway to Mexico, one of those *Times* travel section specials, and now he said yes. For four days he sat with Beverly on a Yucatán beach, reading novels, meeting people who knew only vaguely about the Tawana Brawley case and who certainly were not eager to discuss it.

ANNA PHILLIPS WAS HARDLY IDLE while her partner was sunning himself in Mexico. By the time he returned she'd compiled an inch-thick file on a subject they'd both wanted to explore for some time: the presence and history of the Ku Klux Klan in the Hudson Valley. Not much to it that had a current application, she'd concluded after reviewing the material and making a few phone calls; not in a dozen years anyway. There'd been a lynching or two in the forties, cross burnings in the fifties and sixties by Klan groups made up mostly of prison guards, and a last gasp of public agitating in the mid-seventies. The history was fascinating, though. A 1924 Klan rally and cross burning in Poughkeepsie's Dutchess County Fairgrounds attracted a turnaway crowd of more than 3,000 people. There were reportedly attempts by Klan factions in the thirties to murder several prominent blacks, including the great actor Paul Robeson when he traveled north for a performance, and in one widely reported incident members of "Klan No. 237 visited a Negro church, entering in hooded robes, and sang 'Onward Christian Soldiers.' Upon leaving, they tossed a $50 'donation' to the pastor." In the last recruiting drive in the seventies, the "Invisible Empire" tried without measurable success to build new Klaverns in Newburgh, Pine Bush, Poughkeepsie, and Wallkill.

Phillips tentatively booked interviews with three sources who had direct knowledge of Klan activities and prepared a detailed summary of her findings for her partner. On Taibbi's first day back he located two old Klansmen who still lived in Ellenburg; they were bored on the phone, boring, knew almost nothing about the Brawley case. Ancient history, they said of their own lives. Now they just wanted their lives to last a little longer without "dredging up all that old stuff," as one pathetic old Grand Dragon put it. "No. There's nothing left."

But Phillips had also pursued another line of inquiry she and her partner had been putting off: finding Tawana Brawley. Since the "Rev. Al Grabs Tawana" story in the beginning of March, reporters weren't sure where the teenager was living, though it had to be in Monticello since she was attending Monticello High School. Phillips, ever the maternal figure, had a notion bordering on fantasy that if ever she could sit with Tawana, alone, the burdens weighing down on this poor child would soon have the words pouring from her.

Phillips had been to Monticello twice before without Taibbi, once with Janney to visit Matt Strong and once with camera-man Nick Fischer to look for Tawana as the school day ended at Monticello High. She thought she'd been careful then, but she'd not been careful enough. The principal, Bob Harding, had spotted her and Fischer parked in the school lot and had sternly asked them to leave. Now, driving up again with Taibbi and Janney, she was aware that two other reporters had been arrested for trespassing on school property; one of them, a young reporter, had tried to pass as a student and now faced a formal court hearing. Harding was serious. Taibbi reviewed the rules with his two colleagues.

"Everything by the book this trip," he said, drifting into what Phillips called his Journalism 101 mode. "We approach everything straight ahead, Harding and Matt Strong espe-cially. If we find out where Tawana's living we stake her out but that's all we do. Just remember Rule Three."

Rule Three had often been the centerpiece of Taibbi's Jour-nalism 101 conversations with Phillips. Something that just evolved early in his career as a television reporter, he ex-plained, and then was refined in his Boston years when so many of his stories exposed him to the possibility of lawsuits and counterattack. Rules One and Two were simple, ob-vious: you don't take freebies, from anybody, for anything; and you don't do outside work for corporations—voiceovers for stereo manufacturers and deodorant commercials, that sort of thing. But Rule Three was the bitch:

"You just make believe," Taibbi had explained, "that from the moment you begin work on a story everything you do, everything you say, all your conversations with sources—in person and on the phone—the way you handle yourself in the street, the way you deal with your colleagues and bosses, you make believe it's all being recorded, audio *and* video, and that if the tape's ever played back for a jury or the gen-eral public you won't be exposed as having done anything illegal, unethical, or even embarrassing."

It was impossible to live by Rule Three without slipping—

handing G the $10 for gas after his interview was a damaging
violation; stripping for Fric to get the tapes would have made
for an embarrassing video, to say the least; and many source
conversations straddled the line by definition alone—but you
had to try, Taibbi had lectured. And in its easy applications,
the ones that should be obvious, the rule had to be law. Thus
Taibbi and Phillips never went after the twenty-three Dutchess County residents who sat on the Brawley grand jury though
they knew who some of them were, and in their conversations with official sources they never questioned specifically
what evidence and witness statements were being considered
by the grand jury, didn't use lies or other unacceptable verbal
ruses in their fencing with sources. They tried not to misrepresent themselves, and if they were profane or cajoling when
they worked Crack Alley's mean streets, well, so what? How
else to get a useful conversation going, especially the type of
conversation they needed to get going? Yes, they wore hidden mikes when approaching some people, and they occasionally aired bits from those "interviews." But it was legal,
and a hard story is like a hard contest in any venue: you take
what the defense gives you. Within the rules; within Rule
Three.

"So let's just play it straight," Taibbi said when they hit
Monticello. "There's some sympathy for us out there, we've
seen it; let's ride it as long as we can."

Bob Harding was impressed and slightly amused by their
approach. Taibbi and Phillips had marched directly to the
principal's office, asked politely for a few minutes of his time,
explained in some detail what they knew and still sought to
learn, posed no obvious questions about "Tawana's mood"
or about "how the other kids were treating her," and wondered if, when it was convenient, he cared to join them for
lunch or dinner.

"Sure," he said genially. "Tomorrow night? I've got a Ro-
tary meeting right after school. I can see you about eight? A
drink at least."

And then Bob Harding talked for a half hour, explaining how he'd hand-delivered the grand jury's letter of "invitation" to Tawana Brawley should she decide that, finally, it was time to tell her story. He didn't give away much else, but he liked the reporters and they liked him.

They drove to Main Street, stopping in at a Playland game parlor where teenagers, including Tawana, were known to hang out. The place was nearly empty at that hour. "Later, at night," the proprietor said. "You'll have better luck then."

They stopped by Matt Strong's house, but it was Strong's ex-wife, Juanita, who opened the door. Phillips sagged in relief. It had taken all of her strength and will just to get out of the car, so unnerved was she at the prospect of facing Strong again after having aired a small bit from her surreptitiously recorded interview with him. He'd not returned any of her calls since then, and she'd edged away from Taibbi when they approached the house and let him knock on the door and face whoever answered.

"I'm Juanita!" Juanita Brawley pronounced immediately upon seeing the enemy. A comb was jutting from one side of her hair, and there was fury in her eyes.

"Yes, I know," Taibbi said. "Is Matthew home?"

"I'm Tawana's aunt," she answered. "*I* raised her." She paused only slightly. "And Tawana wants your job, she wants you fired!"

It went on like that, Taibbi and Juanita Brawley talking at each other and getting nowhere. Phillips was mortified. The scene was surreal, she thought; here was Juanita, who called the Channel 2 newsroom that long-ago November Sunday morning, puffed up and reveling in her attachment to her now-famous niece's case. And here were Phillips and Taibbi, standing on Juanita's ex-husband's stoop imploring her to speak for the record, for their camera, about a case now notorious for the fact that the alleged victim *refused* to speak! And the whole purpose of their trip to Monticello anyway was to get fresh videotape of the silent teenager; the fantasy of the interview with Tawana, Phillips knew in the moment, was exactly that, fantasy, and suddenly she was ashamed of herself, ashamed of what the case and their role in it had come to. You didn't have to invent racism or go hunting for it, she knew. It was everywhere. What the hell were she and Taibbi doing talking to this ridiculous woman? She was buried in her depressing thoughts, not helping her partner at all. When she failed to pick up on one of the usual cues, he knew the scene had played. Juanita slammed the door.

PHILLIPS HAD BOOKED them into the Nevele, one of the famous Borscht Belt resorts. Her colleagues were aghast as they drove slowly up the winding drive leading to the hotel's towers and cottages, senior citizens moving slowly about the grounds, some in wheelchairs, a few straining under the weight of golf bags. "The only people close to our age are the help," Taibbi observed sarcastically. But then they all laughed, as though on cue. What the hell; when would any of them have gotten a chance to sample a real Catskills resort?

It was dark and raining again when they returned to the Playland parlor, and, as the proprietor had promised, the place was alive. Janney stayed in the car, camera at the ready, as Phillips and Taibbi wasted a few bucks in change playing Skeeball badly. But the reporters had also been scanning the room, and they followed quickly when a black youth about Tawana's age left the parlor alone.

Yes, said William R.* He knew Tawana, was in several classes with her at Monticello High. Janney's camera, from a distance, was rolling. The hidden mikes were working just fine.

William seemed intelligent, pleasant, happy to stand in the steady rain and talk.

"What do I think?" he said. "I think she lied. I think she's caught in a lie. I think she doesn't know how to get out of it."

Phillips asked if he knew where Tawana was living these days. Sure, he said, no problem. He gave the precise address, described the color of the house, and his directions were right on the money.

They did a single drive-by, just to get the lay of the land. Dead-end street, a tough surveillance. Lots of cars, plenty of windows for the curious to peer out of. Oh well, what the hell. It's what we're here for, they all agreed. Tomorrow, when school lets out. They'd booked a few other appointments for the early part of the day.

When they returned to the house the next afternoon at 2:30 they saw quickly they weren't the only inquisitors who'd found out where Tawana was living. A reporter and a photographer from the *Poughkeepsie Journal* were sitting in their car, right in front of the house. The reporter had seen Tawana the day before, but without a camera. She and her photog had the same thing in mind as the Channel 2 team. By nightfall, though, everyone knew it was futile. The grapevine on the street had done its work. Tawana never showed. They met Bob Harding for drinks, as arranged, Janney sitting a few seats away as though he were in no way connected to his two reporters. Harding, it turned out, had his own "watcher" sitting a few seats away from him; it was Monticello's police chief, Walter Ramsay. Everybody enjoyed a laugh when the bit of mutual gamesmanship was exposed, and the ensuing conversation was enjoyable. But not much help. The Channel 2 team headed back to the hotel to regroup. There was still work to be done.

Phillips had developed a migraine. The tension. The damn situation. Her Matt Strong "problem." It had gotten to her. They checked into the Concord Hotel this time, and Phillips begged off when Taibbi knocked on her room door and asked her to join him for a few late-night home visits. First on the list was the Strong home, again.

"Can't do it, Mike. Just can't." He looked at her, more than a little concerned; she'd never spit the bit, given in to fatigue, not once. She was all but swooning, clutching the door frame for support.

"Okay, Anna. No problem. Maybe it'll work out if it's just me and him. Get a good night's sleep; we're gonna pick up the surveillance at six in the morning."

Strong let Taibbi in, took his barking dog, Midnight, out and tied the dog to its leash, and then talked for two hours. He'd been following the press coverage of the case closely and, given his own suspicions, believed Taibbi's efforts had been tough but fair.

"I told Juanita long ago," he said bitterly. " 'Cooperate, so it doesn't blow up.' But she didn't, and it *did* blow up. It blew up to all of this." He waved his hands disgustedly. "I'm exhausted by it.

"Tawana has never told me what happened. I don't know for a fact that she's really told the lawyers, either. That's what Juanita's said. But I guess it's the lawyers who'll decide." He shook his head. "I can't just tell Tawana, 'Go talk, get it over with.' She just wouldn't do it."

Taibbi reviewed the facts of the case as he knew them, relaying some specific statements made by witnesses at the Pavillion Apartments he and Phillips had interviewed in the past several days, especially the statements suggesting Tawana was in her old apartment during her disappearance and had climbed into the garbage bag in which she'd been found. Did Strong think, knowing Tawana and having raised her, and as the adult who knew her best, that she could have made the story up? Or at least key parts of it?

Strong sighed, his pain evident.

"It could be a lie," he said softly. "The evidence just doesn't add up. I'm a cop, I look for evidence." He spoke angrily of Sharpton and the lawyers, said their handling of the case, especially if it turned out to be a hoax, "would really hurt the cause of black justice. No question."

No, he wouldn't say any of it on camera. And yes, he was still furious at Anna Phillips, still included her in the group of "journalists who'd snap pictures through the windows" or pose as students to get to Tawana.

"I'd have done the same thing Anna did," Taibbi said. "I've done it, worn a hidden mike and then used part of the recorded conversation. Neither of us likes to do it, and frankly she's devastated that you feel the way you do about her, but it's legal and sometimes it's the only way. You're a cop, Matt. It's just a technique."

Strong scowled in disagreement. "Well, I still won't talk to her. You didn't do it to me, she did. I trusted her. I liked her."

Strong's daughter, Kenya, came in then and, seeing the television reporter sitting with her father at the kitchen table, glared at him, demanding recognition. A beautiful girl whose eyes conveyed a subtle and probing intelligence, she seemed about to say something, and Taibbi waited; then she turned away suddenly and left, skipping upstairs to her room. But when the reporter was about to leave, Kenya materialized at the back door and confronted him.

"I'm not saying anything about Tawana, or about the case, not that I know anything," she said quietly. Her father was still in the kitchen. "But *you* people did this." She shook her head sadly and looked Taibbi, a white man more than twice her age, square in the eye. "'It never would have come to this, if it wasn't for your profession." He wanted to protest, to explain, to separate his and Anna's role from the performance of others in the "profession" he never regarded as much more than a craft. But Kenya Strong's eyes bored directly into his, and her eyes were on fire, waiting, just waiting, for him to come up with an excuse or a cop-out. "You're right, Kenya," he said finally, softly. "I'm sorry that you are right, but you are."

While Taibbi was at the Strong home, Phillips was sleeping fitfully. She'd taken a long hot bath and then crawled into bed, pulling the covers up over her head in an attempt to drown out the racket of her inner distress. She didn't know why it was bothering her so much, this thing about Matt Strong. And the story itself . . . she hated it, she really hated it.

EVEN AT 6:15 A.M., when the Channel 2 team pulled to a stop in a lot across the main road at the head of Tawana's street, it was apparent they'd been spotted. They sat and waited anyway, Taibbi in the driver's seat and Janney, camera hot, beside him. Phillips sat dispiritedly in the rear. The kids gathered, waiting for their school buses. Phillips dragged herself to the task and went out to talk to them, asking which bus Tawana took.

"Coupla minutes," she told her colleagues when she got back in the car. They waited.

When the bus pulled to a stop it obscured their view of Tawana's house, and not knowing whether the teenager had sprinted from the house to jump on, Taibbi threw the car into gear and took off in pursuit. Five minutes, ten minutes passed, the bus making several stops to pick up more students. Finally it approached the school—a middle school, the wrong school! Taibbi wheeled the car through a screeching U-turn and returned to Tawana's house, just in time. There she was, running for an idling taxicab.

"Whooo-eee!" Phillips yelped, as the cab pulled away and Taibbi hit the gas. "'We got her, we got her!'" It was the first time she'd laid eyes on the subject of the story that had dominated her life, overwhelmed her life, for nearly four months. Her awful night seemed far away, the interviews in the rain and the tedium of the stakeouts were suddenly noble things, worth it. She laughed and screamed then, and Janney, shooting, hooted along with her. Taibbi, driving hard, shouted at them. "Rule Three, guys. Come on, Rule Three, *dammit!*"

They were headed toward the high school, slowed in town by the morning traffic and the interruptions of the traffic lights. Taibbi maneuvered the car alongside Tawana's cab; Janney made a tripod of his chest and elbows and steadied his shot. Tawana looked toward the lens and quickly looked away, suppressing a small smile. Then she looked at the camera again with hooded eyes, almost posing, a pensive, complicated expression on her face. It was that look that finished the job Taibbi's Rule Three admonition had begun, Phillips thought. What are we doing, she asked herself, chasing a kid who has to take a taxi to school to avoid our camera, to avoid people like us? This is journalism? We've interviewed her friends and relatives, sometimes with hidden mikes and Janney's camera out of sight, and we'll put it on the air. She suddenly understood Taibbi's Rule Three as never before. What would a story about us doing this story look like, sound like? she asked herself. Later, cutting the piece with editor Christine Twomey, she wiped the audio from the tape shot during the chase, the shouts of glee and triumph she and Janney had let loose. And, as she and Twomey fiddled with the video, slo-mo-ing it and freezing Tawana's haunting expression, her heart went out to the girl.

"Poor girl, poor child," she called softly to the screen, to the image of Tawana Brawley racing to school with no one but a bored cab driver to share her distress. "Where's your mama when you need her, child?" Phillips was saddest for Tawana then, felt her own ever-present mother's sympathy most acutely. She shuddered, fought back tears.

And then she cut the hell out of the piece.

IT WAS AN ODD SMORGASBORD of a piece, something of an update, and, with most of the shots taken in the rain and with Tawana's frozen Mona Lisa at the end, Taibbi and Phillips, as was their habit, assigned their private story slug: the "Moody and Ethereal" piece, the story of how the pressure was building on a sixteen-year-old girl: pressure from friends and family, either interviewed on camera or quoted in paraphrase; pressure from the confluence of specific events in the case, including Chico Colon's promised testimony and the new direction of the Brawley grand jury, as confirmed by sources. Now, Taibbi wrote, the grand jury was "focused on proving the Brawley story is false, as represented by her advisers." The reporters' backtracking at the Pavillion Apartments, where Tawana had been discovered, had earned them interviews with key witnesses: the woman who saw Tawana "climb into the bag, pull it up to her chin, hop twice, and then lie down"; the two neighbors who helped her to the ambulance and saw her respond twice to commands or ministrations, clearly not unconscious; the man who saw a black teenager matching Tawana's description "skulk" around the rear of the Pavillion Apartments at 7:30 Thanksgiving morning.

Taibbi had blown one potentially important interview— with the parents of one of Tawana's closest friends. An intermediary had set up the meeting, and the parents, furious at Tawana and not quite sure of their own daughter's truthfulness, wanted to go on camera and demand that Tawana talk, now, because it was her friends and her friends' families who were taking all the heat. The parents' anger was genuine, impressive; they even offered to try and round up two other couples whose daughters had been close friends of Tawana's and who had been brought before the grand jury. Everybody on camera, they'd suggested. Taibbi thought it was a good idea but a risky one, for all the parents. "You'll become targets of the advisers," he warned, launching into his standard whistleblower speech. "Why don't you think about it, talk it over with everyone else. I'll call you later tonight. If you're all still willing, we are, too." Phillips, itchy and barely restrained, couldn't believe her partner wasn't going to pull the trigger. Janney, waiting in the car, was only a summons on the brick away. But Taibbi wouldn't do it. When he called later, the answer, of course, was that everybody'd thought it over and Taibbi was right. Too risky. No interviews.

Still, the "Moody and Ethereal" report was highly effective. The witness interviews were compelling and specific,

the admonitions of friends and relatives emotionally powerful. At the end of the piece, Taibbi made his point.

*A broader question lies beyond the problems still to be
resolved by one sixteen-year-old girl. One after the other,
the friends and relatives of Tawana Brawley brought up
the "cry wolf" syndrome. They wondered aloud whether
the next black victim will be taken seriously . . . or
quickly enough. And they wondered whether black defendants or complainants in cases with racial overtones
will get a fair hearing. A defense lawyer in Poughkeepsie told us he fears the latter scenario might have already kicked in—he described one troubling case in
some detail—and he said he feared it could be the start
of a pattern.*

*But the pressure now is squarely on a young girl in
the middle of the storm that bears her name. It is six
months—two full seasons later—and she takes a taxi
to school past a cop guarding the drive. And friends and
relatives and supporters are saying, to each other and,
this week, to us, "This isn't normal. This isn't right.
This has to end."*

It didn't take the Brawley advisers long to respond. Glenda
Brawley had been served with a subpoena to testify before
the grand jury on May 24. She'd told a reporter, "This is just
a piece of paper. I can throw it in the trash." In case anybody
missed her point, Sharpton called a press conference and, with
the cameras rolling, tore up a copy of the subpoena and slowly,
dramatically, dropped the strips of paper to the ground. When
one television station's crew showed up late, Sharpton simply held up another photocopy of the subpoena and performed his routine a second time.

On May 24, Glenda Brawley sat in the studio of radio station WLIB instead of Room 10 at the Armory in Poughkeepsie. "We can't get justice," she said again and again in her

child's voice. "Tawana's doing pretty good now. She's not gonna let this incident hold her back. But she needs someone she can put her faith and confidence in, and listen to her story, in order to be fair. We want justice, someone that's willing to go to bat and support us. . . ."

But Maddox, Mason, and Sharpton dominated the two-hour show, the cameras recording it all through the studio's glass front, and they were wild. William West, the Task Force investigator who'd been busted for selling drugs, was "connected to Noriega," Mason asserted. Sharpton talked about all the "suspects." State trooper Scott Patterson was getting away with it "because his Daddy is number two in the state police," the minister asserted. Steve Pagones "was exposed trading liquor licenses for the mob, but his Daddy's a judge." Even Tommy Masch, the Paino's mechanic, had "left the county" to avoid arrest, Sharpton said, adding that he'd learned that "all the suspects would meet at Cracker Corner, that was their spot, where they'd talk about blacks and plan all their schemes."

Maddox took off on Cuomo and Abrams, charging that the governor and the attorney general of the state "are saying, 'Our sons will rape you, and you better not say anything about it.' " The lawyer said, "Cuomo told us when he met with us, 'You gonna make these white folks mad, you gonna get these people angry.' "

And then Mason tore away at the media, and at Channel 2 in particular. "The media has been hounding this family, to the point where Mike Taibbi goes and sleeps with Juanita Brawley's dog, Midnight, in the garage, all night, overnight, so he could do this number that he did chasing Tawana to school, talking about how unnatural it was that she was going to school in a cab. She went to school in a cab to avoid his perverted self. Anybody who goes out and sleeps with a dog to get a story—and the station that stands behind his perverted self—they're standing behind a whole lotta mess. . . ."

It was happening again. *What* garage? There *is* none, Taibbi thought, listening to the feed. What the fuck are they talking about! He dialed WLIB and asked to speak to news director David Lampell.

"Isn't there *some* ethic of fairness with the facts that applies to talk shows, even on LIB?" he demanded to know. "I mean, shouldn't some of this horseshit be challenged, and not just the stuff about me?"

Lampell answered that his station played by the same rules employed by every other talk show. "Phil Donahue and Oprah Winfrey included. If you want to come on the show, be our guest."

The calls started coming in to Taibbi, some from other reporters. They said Mason had phoned them, or Juanita had called them, to tell them about Taibbi's sojourn with Midnight.

"I can't fucking believe this!" Taibbi hollered to one reporter from one of the city's four major dailies. "You buy this? You're actually asking me to comment on this; to *deny* it? Go ahead. Write your fucking story!"

No one wrote the story. But it got out there anyway.

11

"Is it the defense . . . that black people cannot receive justice?"

WHAT TELEVISION DID, as the eighties edged to a close, was to embrace the "Big Event" so automatically, with such routine technical mastery, that anything less than seamless excellence would have shocked the viewers in Teaneck and Roslyn Heights, Chelsea and Westchester, in the same way those first "live shots" shattered the norm way back in the "primitive" early seventies. Then, in the early 1970s, when pictures from the scene were produced by "newsfilm cinematographers" whose issue had to come to life in slow and bulky processors, then to be shaped by film editors with racks and view finders and hand-twirled cranks, the idea of impromptu live coverage was fantasy for all but stop-the-presses events and was for the most part unthinkable for local television stations. When Delta Flight 88 went down on Logan

Airport's Runway 4-Right in 1975, killing all its passengers, only one Boston television station, WCVB-TV was able to finally project live pictures from the scene, and then only because the station's morning gab show had generated enough revenue and ratings to pay for a huge Winnebago, specially outfitted, for "remote shoots." It took the Winnebago seven hours to travel twenty-two miles and deploy the then-cumbersome technology and raise a live picture, by which time most of the dramatic pictures were history.

The murder of Lee Harvey Oswald in November 1963 was the American viewer's first experience as instant witness to a major breaking story; but then, way back then, network television's available machinery was churned to the max because a president had been assassinated, and the stations handed over their air because there was, simply, no other arguably acceptable choice. It was electronic news gathering (ENG) and portable studios called mini-vans or live trucks, in the late seventies, and the competition in the Clarke Belt, 26,500 miles above the earth, among the owners of more and more satellites, that changed the game forever at both the local and the national levels. By the late eighties, the viewers—Joe and Josephine Six-Pack, as they were dubbed in city after city—had a right to a different view. If they heard there was an earthquake in Armenia, a plane down in Scotland, a coup in Manila, a sudden-death playoff in the Masters at Augusta—or a fire in the Elizabeth tank farms or a hostage stand-off in the Bronx—they expected to be able to punch on the tube and see it now.

June 6, 1988, was surely going to be one of those days in New York when Joe and Josephine Six-Pack, not to mention everybody with a vested interest in the Tawana Brawley case, would turn to the tube. Local television and the Brawley advisers, after all, had held each other in relentless embrace for half a year, feeding each other and sometimes trying to destroy each other, circling, plotting, feinting, and tossing howitzers, stroking shamelessly at times and then retreating when each gesture of courtship failed, but inevitably re-engaging. It was endless, exhausting; but the proposition that fueled the hideous tarantella—the prospect of proving once and for all that the criminal justice system was as racist as the advisers claimed or that a trio of cynically ambitious self-promoters had done irreparable damage to as important a cause as there was in American life—was irresistible. When Glenda Brawley, after defying her subpoena to testify before the grand jury, was ordered to explain to State Supreme Court Justice Angelo Ingrassia on June 6 exactly why she had ignored the lawful order of that same criminal justice system, a genuine "moment of truth" was assured. Their rhetoric didn't matter: Vernon Mason reacted to the subpoena by saying it was proof that "Mario Cuomo is as big a racist as Lester Maddox . . . and Bob Abrams as big a racist as Bull Connor. They're the 'KKK' of the eighties." But the subpoena was a subpoena, the contempt hearing before Judge Ingrassia a lawful and unavoidable step in the process. Glenda Brawley, along with her lawyers and Al Sharpton, had been saying all along that "it would be better to go to jail than to cooperate with a cover-up." On June 6, the mother of Tawana Brawley would be brought to court knowing that if she failed to explain her absence before the grand jury she faced a thirty-day jail sentence for contempt and a $250 fine. The *New York Times* called it "the most significant legal development in the tangled case," and it was.

It was also a development about which no one in the Brawley Task Force had any illusions. May had been a tough month, many of the key witnesses in what had become the process of disproving Tawana Brawley's story either changing their own stories, refusing to come clean, or being exposed as liars themselves. Trayon Kirby, who'd driven Tawana to Newburgh that fateful November day, had claimed at one point that he'd "spoken to Tawana several times" during her disappearance. He also handed over twenty-two letters or notes Tawana had written to him—several of which included graphic and revealing descriptions of her sexual adventures—and the promise of his useful testimony won him lenient treatment on gun, drug, and stolen-car charges. Then he failed two polygraph tests, finally admitting that his story about having talked to Tawana during the four days was fiction.

A dozen Newburgh witnesses, Chico Colon among them, offered believable accounts that placed Tawana in that city on several occasions when she was supposedly in captivity. But some, like Hester Davis, simply recanted when it came time to tell their stories under oath, and others, like Colon, offered up the names of corroborating witnesses who then declined to offer corroboration. The most promising story-teller from Crack Alley was a fifteen-year-old who had no felony record and no outstanding beefs—meaning he had no known motive for telling the story—who said he saw Tawana after a party that Friday night. She was "out on South Street, and got into a small green car, a Datsun, I think. Another black girl was driving, and they took off." The youth's corroborating witness was a drug dealer supposedly involved with Tawana in some way who had fled to Florida. Russell Crawford of the Task Force and FBI agent Hilda Kogut, who continued to "monitor" the case after the Bureau formally pulled out, tracked the dealer down in Florida and came home empty-handed. No way, the dealer insisted. Didn't see her.

The grand jury had already been presented with most of the evidence in the case. Most of the physical evidence had been tested and retested by the forensic experts at the FBI Crime Lab in Washington, D.C.

The Task Force, at Jack Ryan's direction, had taken every available step short of issuing the subpoena to Glenda Brawley. Contrary to the advisers' repeated claims that Ryan had "never offered to show Tawana mug shots of the suspects" or explore ways of eliciting the teenager's cooperation other than sworn in-person testimony, Ryan had in fact sent a letter to Alton Maddox, dated May 13, a final informal appeal that made just such an offer:

Dear Mr. Maddox:
    It is our understanding [that] your client Ms. Glenda

Brawley has stated there are circumstances under which she would be willing to allow her daughter to meet with our investigators.

We are interested in exploring with Glenda Brawley the circumstances under which Tawana Brawley's co-operation could be obtained and justice insured. We do not, however, feel it would be ethically appropriate for us to contact a person represented by counsel directly. . . .

Maddox ignored the letter. Sending out the subpoena was the only step left.

"Abrams kept asking us," an investigative source later explained, " 'When is this going to be over?' In April, I kept saying 'by the end of May, for sure.' Then, when the subpoena went out, I said it would end in June. 'We're not gonna go through the summer with this,' I told Bob. 'It's not worth it.' "

Ryan and the Task Force still had the job of convincing Pagones and Patterson, whose innocence was already corroborated by evidence and other witness interviews, to come in and testify, without immunity, so a grand jury report could be framed in the context of wrongly accused public officials seeking to clear their names. Abrams, Ryan, and rest of the inner circle met and decided to throw down the gauntlet, "to end this thing."

"We polled our people, and nobody really had any illusions that she'd come in," the same source recalled later. "But we'd never know if we didn't try. And there was a sense too that if we took the formal step of subpoenaing her, she couldn't get up when the investigation was over and say, 'I would have come in if they'd asked—but they didn't.' Look. The decision to subpoena her made sense. She was there, she's the mother, she'd claimed at one point she went into the old apartment the day Tawana was found to look for her, and she'd gone to Newburgh later to tell police her daughter was there. Yeah, we knew when she defied the subpoena that June 6 was going to be a circus. . . ."

Everybody knew that, no one more than the people in the broadcast news organizations who had ridden the story from the beginning, and as the big day approached, the jockeying for ringside seats picked up in earnest. Who would hold down positions in Judge Ingrassia's modest courtroom? Who would track the Brawley team members? And who would stick to Market Street, ring number one, if the *New York Post* had it right three days before the big event? "Tawana's Mom to Get 'Black Army' Escort," read the *Post* headline. Leading the army, the newspaper said, would be Black Muslim leader Louis Farrakhan, who had visited with the family during the week. And, just to keep interest at a peak, Al Sharpton told the *Post* that Tawana herself would probably be in court on June 6. "Most children want to be in court to say good-bye to their mothers before they go to jail," Sharpton said.

Abrams sent letters to Mason and Maddox "inviting" them to make their accusations about Tawana's attackers and provide their evidence under oath, or else, Abrams said, "I will assume you have no such evidence."

The lawyers responded by firing off thirty subpoenas of their own, to Cuomo, Abrams, Grady, Sall, Pagones, Patterson, and a weird assortment of journalists, public officials, and other race-crime principals who had nothing whatsoever to offer in a hearing whose limited purpose was to determine whether Glenda Brawley had had a reason to ignore a lawful order of a lawful grand jury.

"We will be prepared to tell what we know and Tawana is prepared to tell what she knows," Sharpton said, "if the witnesses we subpoenaed are examined and cross-examined. If not . . . well, if you missed the Selma-Montgomery march, don't miss Monday."

It would be a day for the ages in sedate Poughkeepsie.

———

FOR MIKE TAIBBI AND ANNA PHILLIPS, however, Monday promised only to be the ultimate contrivance in a never-ending farce orchestrated by the Brawley advisers. Both now believed that Tawana Brawley's tale of abduction and rape was fundamentally false even though they were prepared to believe, still, that "something" had happened to the girl. Encouraged by what they'd learned in their research for their "Moody and Ethereal" report and fueled by fresh leads after it was broadcast, they had staked out new initiatives.

Phillips had started tracking down the rumors—which were plentiful and were now being passed to the reporters by people who identified themselves and claimed to have direct knowledge—that Glenda Brawley had been depositing large sums of money, donations from the sympathetic, into her credit union account at IBM and that she was planning to leave the area soon. One of Glenda's co-workers, from Pine Plains, said reluctantly that she might at some point be willing to say on camera what she told Phillips on the phone.

"I trained Glenda when she first came in, and I still consider her a friend," the woman said. "And she must still consider me a friend, because she still talks to me. The last I knew, she had an RFT [request for transfer] approved. She wanted to go to Charlotte, North Carolina, but the IBM facility there only has Sales, and she was an assembler. So Manassas or Raleigh were the only places approved. She said her grandfather owned property down there he'd sell to her for a dollar.

"One day," the woman continued, "Glenda came in and started talking about the case. She said, 'They're all watching me.' She told me Tawana's 'thing' was drug-involved. About the money from donations? I don't know. There's a lot of stories going around."

Phillips said she'd keep in touch.

Taibbi, meanwhile, believed that if the end was near, it was time to nail things down, and that meant making direct approaches to the people with the answers. He called a federal official he knew was intimately familiar with the entire record of the case and arranged a dinner. East Side restaurant, rear dining room.

"There are only two scenarios not contradicted by the evidence in hand," the official said over coffee, after reviewing that same evidence. "Either Tawana Brawley did it to herself, or she did it with the help of a friend."

A sensitively placed state official was even more specific at lunch two days later. Taibbi had deliberately not reached out to him up to that point because their prior contact on another important story had almost gotten each of them in a jam.

"I was wondering when you'd call," the official said, anxious but clearly in agreement that the time had come. He described a litany of complaints concerning the performance of lawyers Maddox and Mason, complaints that would be formally submitted to the appropriate disciplinary committees when the case was concluded. "It's just a suggestion, but you ought to do the same thing, on the stuff they've said about you. The bribery stuff, I'm talking about. We checked it out." He smiled. "But that's your decision. We've got our submission pretty much prepared."

What about the status of the grand jury investigation? Taibbi asked.

"We're essentially done now. Hopefully in the next few days, or just after Glenda's contempt hearing, we'll get Pagones to come in, and frame the report in the context of a request by a public official to clear his name of unfounded charges. We think he'll go for it even though he's still balking, and if he does Patterson might follow. The report could then say: Tawana Brawley was certainly not abducted on November 24, not held captive for four days, not raped, sodomized, or assaulted repeatedly by a gang of men, white or otherwise. Pagones, Crist, and Patterson had nothing to do with her; their alibis are solid and corroborated. Tawana Brawley may have spent time in Newburgh, may have attended one or more parties there, and certainly had numerous contacts and friends there with unsavory or criminal backgrounds. Tawana Brawley also spent time in the old family apartment, at the Pavillion Apartments. She was seen there Thanksgiving morning, we believe, and in the hour before she was discovered. She had reason to concoct a wild story to escape the probable severe discipline of her mother and Ralph King. She may have had knowledge of a story similar to the one she told, a story told by [a girl] we believe was known to Tawana Brawley. The details of her appearance and condition on the day she was discovered could have been self-inflicted. All the materials needed to produce that condition—*all* of them—were available to her on the scene, inside and outside the apartment, according to the forensic evidence. The writing on her torso was done gently enough so as not to leave a mark beneath the lettering. No, there is no smoking gun to absolutely prove *nothing* happened to Tawana Brawley. But the circumstantial case is overwhelming, and it all goes one way. The episode as related by her lawyers and adviser did not occur. Period."

Taibbi and Phillips huddled with Paul Sagan behind closed doors to discuss the startling information disclosed by the two officials, even as newly appointed assistant news director Steve Paulus conducted another planning session for June 6 in his next-door office.

"Un-be-liev-able," Sagan kept repeating. Taibbi kept pacing and peering out the window as he went over each detail again and again. "Mike, there's no way either of these guys will go on the record? Of course not," Sagan said, answering his own question. "Of course not."

Though Phillips, Taibbi, and Sagan had seen their doubts grow inexorably, they'd all been troubled by the same nagging doubt that had done so much to silence the potential critics of the Brawley advisers. How could she possibly have done it to herself? Who would do that, who could do that? Something had to have happened. . . .

Now, if the two officials had told it straight, and both were known as honest and judicious men, the three people in Sagan's office knew the answer. It was preposterous, maddening, especially in light of the campaign aimed at their reporting efforts. Every Wednesday at 5:00 sharp—you could set your watch by it—Sharpton's band of hard-core followers showed up at the entrance to the Broadcast Center's West Fifty-seventh Street lobby. A special police detail arrived early to set up the traditional blue barriers to contain the pickets, who chanted—"Mike Taibbi, have you heard, this is not Johannesburg" or "Abraham Lincoln slept on a log, Mike Taibbi slept with a dog"—and taunted the on-air personalities they recognized and any black employee they spotted. Taibbi and Phillips, on Wednesday afternoons when they were in the city, entered and exited the building by the back door.

But the picketing was just a gesture, a disruption of the normal commerce on Fifty-seventh Street between Tenth and Eleventh avenues, aimed solely at a couple of reporters. No one at the Broadcast Center seemed to take offense despite the weekly imposition of threats and unpleasantness. In fact, Sagan and his two beleaguered reporters were complimented constantly by people in the building they would normally never have heard from, executives and network types, prop managers and soap opera performers, maintenance men and security guards. The Wednesday picketing was seen as something of a badge of honor to many in a building whose occupants had suffered in prestige in recent years: there had been massive personnel cutbacks, and internal squabbles and conflicts had been exposed, publicly and embarrassingly.

The real shame, and the danger, lay in the genuine possibility that the posturing and pot-stirring by the Brawley advisers might set off an unwarranted explosion of racial violence, starting on June 6, and that innocent people, children too, would be led into battle over the wrong case.

Anna Phillips's younger son, Eric, was one of those children. She'd enrolled him in a New Jersey school noted for its attention to black issues. Eric's teacher was planning on bringing her class to Poughkeepsie, to take part in the Market Street demonstrations. Eric, inquisitive by nature, wanted to participate. Phillips, who never failed to share the details of the Brawley story with both Eric and her older son, Lionel, had to have a hard talk with her younger son: "Eric, if I thought this would end up being a learning experience, I'd allow you to go, but as it is now, I can only predict that the whole day will end badly." She did not have to say "no." He made his own decision not to attend.

THE SMALL CITY of Poughkeepsie had been a way station along the Underground Railroad and a center of abolitionist activity in the years leading up to the Civil War. But despite that history, and even though slavery had been abolished in New York State by Gov. Daniel Tompkins in 1817, the residual effects of a race-based caste system, in Poughkeepsie no less than in other American cities, never disappeared completely. On June 6, 1988, in the minds of the hundreds of outsiders flocking to the modest city or already arrived, there had to be one common thought: this would be a day, a checkpoint of sorts, to measure the progress from those long-ago days of slavery and separation, or to concede that not much of a distance had been traveled after all.

The security was intense and was laid on early, hundreds of state troopers, sheriff's deputies, and city police officers guarding key buildings—the Armory, the courthouse—or holding down posts on rooftops and other overlooks and at strategic points along Market Street. The Brawley advisers had announced that Minister Louis Farrakhan and his bow-tied "security force" would "escort" the family to the courthouse, and promised that "busloads of demonstrators" would also journey north from New York City. Judge Ingrassia had allowed cameras to be set up in his 100-seat courtroom, the largest in the building, in advance of the certain argument from attorneys Mason and Maddox that they should be expelled, and the reporters drew lots for the forty seats allotted for the press. Those subpoenaed by the Brawley lawyers—or their lawyers or representatives—were guaranteed seats or informed they would be summoned if it came to that. That left fewer than fifty spaces, to be filled on a "first come–first served" basis, the judge explained.

Everyone waited, and the sun rose over Market Street, its heat relentless. It had been decided in the last of the planning sessions in Steve Paulus's office that Chris Borgen would cover the courtroom hearing, Taibbi would cover the street scene and pursue whatever angles developed there, and Phillips would stay at the Broadcast Center, coordinating the editing of whatever pieces her two reporters came up with. Five cameramen and a live crew rolled north well before dawn, Jim Fleischmann four-wheeled it to the top of his mountain and switched it on. Black Rock lawyers Douglas Jacobs and Susanna Lowy were dispatched to argue for Channel 2 in the likely event that Borgen's and the crew's presence in the courtroom became a point of contention by Alton Maddox and Vernon Mason. They drove up with Steve Paulus, who would run the show on the scene. Planning editor Paul Fleuranges had typed a three-word admonition at the bottom of the set-up sheet distributed to all hands: "Expect the worst."

In Poughkeepsie, many who had been part of the case simply expected . . . something. Justice Judith Hillery, who five months before had allowed William Grady and then David Sall to resign as prosecutors, kept appearing on the sidewalk outside the courthouse, pocket camera in hand. Grady himself and Sall and Sheriff Fred Skoralick crisscrossed Market Street, killing time making small talk in Alex's Restaurant and then heading back to the courthouse, only to reemerge as the morning wore on. Mason and Maddox were due in court for a 10:30 A.M. hearing on the cameras-in-the-courtroom issue. By noon the only lawyers who had appeared were Robert Abrams, Jack Ryan, and Scott Greathead. The minutes ticked away.

Then a police order went out over bullhorns, detouring all traffic from Market Street. The show was about to begin.

The buses were allowed to park on the east side of Market Street, and from them emerged several hundred people, the vast majority brought up from New York City. Shortly after the buses emptied, a caravan of cars pulled slowly up the street. The lead car, a Lincoln surrounded by a circle of Farrakhan's bow-tied minions, stopped just north of Milt's Cigar Store, on the west side of Market. Sharpton emerged in his favorite pale blue suit, clutching the hand of a heavyset woman in a purple silk blouse and a sparkling white linen suit. Glenda Brawley, tinted contacts giving her eyes of blue beneath a freshly assembled coiffure, had never looked better. Juanita and Ralph King stood to Glenda's left, Farrakhan and one of his beefier security guards to Sharpton's right, and, after Mason and Maddox joined them, and several dozen in their selected entourage took up positions to the rear, they walked slowly, ceremoniously, to the front door of 10 Market Street, the Dutchess County Courthouse.

The curious, and the professionally curious wearing press identification, pushed in to get a close look from behind the police barricades, cameras held high to record the day's initial confrontation. When Deputy Sheriff J. J. Thompson explained patiently that the lawyers, Sharpton, and Glenda Brawley could certainly be admitted but there wasn't room in the courtroom for the entire entourage, the first angry words were exchanged. At one point Maddox and Farrakhan, arms linked, were allowed to enter the glass front doors, Ralph King agitating just outside; but they emerged after only a few minutes and, with Sharpton beside them, led everyone back to the cars. Reporters and cameramen raced to follow, Taibbi among them, and when Sharpton and the lawyers suddenly peeled off and sprinted across Market Street, Taibbi and cameraman Jim Duggan stayed right with them. The three advisers went into the lobby of the Barclays Bank, one of Farrakhan's bow-tied guards positioning himself outside the door, arms folded, discouraging any further pursuit. Taibbi reached behind him and tried to open the door; Sharpton shouted, "Get the fuck away from me, Taibbi," and the "guard" shouldered the door closed.

"I'm security," the guard said.

"You work for the bank?" Taibbi asked in a voice of challenge. "If you don't work for the bank I've got just as much right as anyone else to go in there."

Steve Paulus had caught up to the scene, and he urged his reporter firmly to back away.

"It's not worth it," Paulus said. "Listen . . .."

Sure enough, demonstrators had formed in several places, some by the Lincoln to which Glenda Brawley had returned, and some thirty yards south on Market. Both groups were shouting derisive slogans aimed at "Mad Dog Mike," and a few from each group had broken off and now followed the reporter, making barking sounds and hollering references to "Mike and Midnight." Taibbi, at Paulus's suggestion, retreated to the back of the courthouse to monitor the feed from the hearing.

MADDOX, THE "LEAD ATTORNEY" for Glenda Brawley, had gone up to the courtroom after his impromptu caucus. He first tested the extraordinary patience of Supreme Court Justice Angelo Ingrassia by demanding that Ingrassia step down from the case and from his role as supervising judge of the Brawley grand jury because "possibly Your Honor and the governor of this state had engaged in some ex-parte conversations . . . coming out of this subpoena."

"Let's clear the record right here," Ingrassia said in a firm, low-key voice. "This Court will state unequivocally for the record that in all his sixty-five years he has never spoken to the governor, never spoken to any member of this governor's staff, has never met the governor, doesn't know the governor, and is, quite frankly, of the opposite political persuasion of the governor. So whatever information you have is erroneous."

Maddox attacked the formation of the Brawley grand jury, misstated its racial composition, alleged incorrectly that the names of the panelists were disclosed in open court and that the subsequent work of the panel was "not done in secret." The lawyer then said he "would be offering evidence in the course of the hearing" that Abrams had orchestrated leaks to the media, including the release of the hospital photographs of Tawana Brawley and early police reports, "in an effort to defame the Brawley family."

That evidence might not be pertinent or relevant to this proceeding, the judge suggested. What about due process? Maddox countered. Isn't Glenda Brawley entitled to a fair, complete, and comprehensive hearing?

"She absolutely is," Ingrassia answered, "and what she's entitled to [in this proceeding] are basically three things: Was there a lawful mandate of the Court, one. Two, was she served with that lawful mandate. And three, did she willfully violate it. Those are the issues before this Court, is that not correct?"

"No," Maddox answered. "It is not." When the lawyer said nearly under his breath that he "suspected as much . . ." Ingrassia pressed him.

"What was that? You 'suspected . . . '? Are you making any implications?"

"As I was speaking before I was interrupted," Maddox said testily, "I would hope that all matters pertaining to this case be aired publicly. . . . I can find no better place than here for us to lay out the entire story."

But the story that Maddox and C. Vernon Mason proceeded to lay out was not the story of what had happened to Tawana Brawley. Instead it was the story of "trusted Bob Abrams . . . who can ensure that the outcome [here] will be predictable and that the injustices that have been heaped on persons of African descent in the state will continue." It was the story of a vicious media conspiracy orchestrated by Abrams and Cuomo, a conspiracy that guaranteed that Tawana's rapists—and Maddox and Mason named names again, in open court and as officers of that court—would go free.

Maddox implored Ingrassia to "give greater definition . . . to due process" because of the existence of that conspiracy. "Because of that," he said, "I ask you to search your heart, mind, and soul because four hundred years of oppression is riding on this case and we have reached a point when the African nation in this country, and particularly those Africans in New York, are thoroughly disgusted with the way that justice is administered and they are thoroughly disgusted with black victims of racial crimes being told by a grand jury that they are hallucinating and that what happened to them amounts to a hoax. I hope that from this day forward that we can wipe clean those four hundred years of injustices and begin to proceed into the twenty-first century like intelligent and civilized men and women."

Ingrassia, apparently moved, leaned forward to address Maddox, inviting the attorney to be seated while he framed his answer.

"Let me say this," the judge began. ". . . those present in this room who know me know that I have never had to look for words. . . . This is a very unpleasant task at best to preside over a matter such as this. Believe me, it's not pleasant.

"The last part of your statement about four hundred years of oppression is moving and there is a great deal of truth in it, a lot of right in it. . . . But there is no way under the sun that I can avoid my duty and recuse myself from a difficult or unpleasant task just because I am asked to or just because I feel I would rather do that than do my job.

"So, that application [that I step down] is denied."

The next "application" to be argued involved the presence of cameras and reporters in the courtroom. Maddox hammered away again at the release "by the attorney general" of the hospital photographs, and when Ingrassia pressed him again on whether he had any evidence to submit to support that charge there was another sharp exchange.

"Judge, you know," Maddox said, "to say that you have no such evidence before you . . . would suggest that you have to be blind or just simply oblivious."

"No, Mr. Maddox," Ingrassia countered above the murmurs in his courtroom. "What that means is that this Court can only deal with relevant, valid evidence that's admissible under the rules of evidence. You know that, and I know that. So let's not play games."

Mason spoke for the first time, adding confusion to an already confusing presentation.

"Your Honor, I think, most respectfully, that the point that you have concluded with is really missing the point, which is this: One of the things . . . is that we have presented evidence to grand jurors, including cooperation in this particular case, over a period of years. It has never really mattered."

Mason attacked Abrams's chief press spokesman, Timothy Gilles, for leaking grand jury testimony "almost on a daily basis." He referred to the drug arrest of Task Force investigator William West as proof that "we're talking about all kinds of Noriegas" in the Brawley case. He suggested that the federal government, in the person of "the great white knight, Mr. Giuliani, never dealt with police brutality, never dealt with race crimes." The local district attorney, William Grady, "had identifications, had evidence," Mason charged, "that Pagones, Crist, and Patterson were perpetrators in this case," but instead of making arrests, "he walks into Glenda's house and says, we have no suspects because they were the wrong color. They were the wrong people, they were too elitist." Glenda Brawley, Mason asserted, simply had no one to turn to for justice. And, he said, finally turning to the question at issue, the presence of reporters in the courtroom, let alone cameras, would only add to Glenda's trauma.

Mason attacked several reporters by name, including Channel 4's venerable Gabe Pressman, "who is a friend of Governor Cuomo." And then he took off on "a reporter with Channel 2 whose name is Mike Taibbi." Channel 2's lawyers, Jacobs and Lowy, leaned forward to listen.

"Here you had a man," Mason said, "who came up in the Newburgh area, paid, bribed witnesses to fabricate a story on Tawana Brawley . . . some guy named G, whose father immediately contacted us.

"More importantly than that, we found out that there was

several hundred dollars which this reporter paid for this fabricated story. . . .

"This reporter, so racist, desperate in his lack of journalistic integrity, even went to the point of sleeping with a dog in the garage of Juanita Brawley the night before he was coming out with a camera to chase—"

"With a what?" Ingrassia said, startled. "I didn't hear that."

"With a dog named Midnight," Mason answered. "That's the dog's name, Your Honor."

"Male or female?" the judge asked, not quite suppressing a smile.

"You will have to ask that," Mason said, not smiling at all. "That may be a very good question for Mr. Taibbi."

It went on like that for twenty minutes, with additional detailed attacks against the *New York Post* and other named reporters. In the end Ingrassia ruled that no issues of fact had been raised by the two lawyers and that the reporters, and the cameras, would stay.

As THE HEARING DRONED ON, the scene on Market Street settled into a kind of tense vigil. It was a workday, and nearly every window was filled with one or more pairs of eyes peering down in wonder and curiosity. The demonstrators held their places; Glenda Brawley sat in the Lincoln with Ralph King, eating Chinese food; the assembled journalists for the most part guarded their positions jealously, though some broke away to grab a quick snack. At one point Taibbi and Paulus strolled into a lunchroom, but when the reporter looked around he saw at least five of his confidential sources seated at various tables and, declining to make eye contact with any of them, told Paulus he'd decided he wasn't hungry after all. Returning to Market Street and sweating under the hot sun, Taibbi saw a half-dozen demonstrators, most of them older women, head for a bench in the shaded lee of the County Office Building. They took seats, squeezing close, fanning themselves. As Taibbi walked toward them several noticed his approach; he thought they smiled.

"Hi," he said in his most genial voice. They didn't answer. They weren't smiling after all. One of them muttered to the others, "That's that Taibbi."

"Listen," the reporter continued. "All that barking and stuff; you people can't possibly believe that I really slept with a dog—"

"Yes! I do believe it!" one of the women hissed immediately, the others picking up the refrain. There was anger in their eyes, hatred too. They turned their backs on him and he moved away, shaken as much by the words of a few old ladies as by anything that had been said to him or done to him in his months on the Brawley story. As he crossed Market he looked down the street in the direction of a fresh sound: it was the children brought up to join the demonstrations, probably Eric's class among them, taunting him and waving placards in his direction. There were barking noises too, coming from the mouths of children. He rejoined Paulus and shook his head; he was hating the day.

Glenda Brawley, who shortly after three in the afternoon unexpectedly took off in the Lincoln, was not having a good day either, as it turned out. Her lawyers spent the rest of the session in Judge Ingrassia's courtroom declining to argue a single fact in her defense against a certain finding of contempt. At one point Maddox had a court officer bring "papers" to the bench, but suggested the judge would be "wasting his time" reading them.

"I know you may have a dental appointment or something tonight," Maddox said. "I don't want to delay that. Let's not waste each other's time. I have an idea how you are going to be deciding."

Judge Ingrassia refused to take the bait, as he in fact refused to take it throughout what was surely the most trying session over which he'd presided in his decades on the bench. He literally begged Maddox and Mason to present the "issues of fact" that the lawyers insisted would prove their client was improperly served and therefore could not be held in contempt. The judge offered a continuation, a delay, but Maddox, looking several times as though he was simply going to bolt the courtroom, said of the judge's offers, "I don't think it's necessary, I really don't. I don't think it's going to do any good here."

Robert Abrams, Jack Ryan, and Scott Greathead had been sitting in silence for more than two hours; they'd not argued a single motion because no motions had in fact been "argued." They wanted at the very least to have Glenda Brawley brought into the courtroom so she could face the judge directly and understand the consequences of her lawyers' tactics—understand that she would go to jail. Finally, at a point when Ingrassia's exasperation seemed about to boil over, the judge turned instead to address a question to Jack Ryan, asking him what the government's claim was as to the issues.

"Your Honor," Ryan said, rising to speak for the first time. "At this time we would agree with the Court's assessment that the purpose of this hearing is for the People to go forward and prove that a grand jury subpoena was served—that is, received by Glenda Brawley—and that she did not appear before the grand jury on the date and time called for."

Maddox stood and spoke again.

"Judge, I want to say one thing and then I think we can terminate this. I want to say this based on my own personal opinion, my own personal beliefs. I do not believe that Glenda Brawley has a snowball's chance in hell of getting justice in New York. My own—"

"Even if you are correct, Mr. Maddox," Ingrassia said, "even if you are correct—"

"May I finish?"

Ingrassia continued speaking. "That still doesn't give her the right to defy the lawful mandate of this Court, does it?"

"No," Maddox said, "[it] gives her the right if she's not in fact a citizen of this country, she's not given the protections of citizenship; it gives her the right not to fool herself as to whether a government exists for her."

Maddox argued no issues of fact, saying that "the only thing these televised proceedings are doing is satisfying the bizarre appetites of racists at their six o'clock dinner this evening. . . . If raping Tawana and kidnapping Tawana is not enough," he continued, "then Glenda Brawley will submit her body to further punishment so that white America can get some added satisfaction."

Ingrassia asked Maddox to have his client brought to the courtroom "so that she would know what she faces," but the lawyer said he didn't know where she was.

"You're tying my hands," Ingrassia said, clearly frustrated.

"I rest on my papers," Maddox said. "With the understanding that this is an exercise in futility . . . your conclusion is predictable." In the background, not quite under his breath, Mason muttered, as he had all afternoon, "Tell him, tell him. This is outrageous. That's right, tell him."

The judge tried one last time to turn the hearing into a hearing, suggesting that he could think of many valid, legal excuses to explain one's failure to appear before a grand jury and urging Maddox to argue at least one of them. No point, Maddox countered. "Your toleration level is apparently low."

"I don't think it is," Ingrassia said. "If my toleration level were low, Mr. Maddox, it would have exploded a long time ago."

Maddox continued to bait the judge: "I have been in Ku Klux Klan dens and they were pretty cool for a while—"

"They *what?*" Ingrassia was genuinely shocked.

"They were cool for a long time. I know about toleration levels. But in any event . . ."

Ingrassia waved his hands. "I don't think you are comparing me to—"

"I am not making the comparison," Maddox said, eyes burning.

Ingrassia closed his eyes, brought a hand to his forehead,

and managed somehow to bring the discussion around to the point at issue, the hearing that could result in a jail sentence for a woman not even in the courtroom. He engaged Maddox one last time.

"You're sure you don't want to bring your client up here?"

"Judge, my client already knew the outcome of this. . . . She has no confidence in the judicial system here, black people in this state have no confidence—that's no surprise to the judiciary."

"Let me ask—"

"I am pretty sure," Maddox steamrolled, "that Mr. Abrams would ask for his thirty days maximum allowable by law. If you reach that right now we can all leave."

"Mr. Maddox, is it your defense—"

"I have no defense."

"Is it the defense in this case that black people cannot receive justice?"

"Yes," Maddox said. "Absolutely."

Jack Ryan rose to be heard: "The People would ask that the respondent appear in court before the Court renders its decision."

But Glenda Brawley was long gone. Ingrassia said the Court "had no other alternative" but to certify that Glenda Brawley "is in criminal contempt . . . in violation of Section 750A, Subdivision 3 of the Judiciary Law, and is sentenced and committed to the county jail for a period of thirty days, and fined the sum of $250 for her contempt." Maddox wheeled and left the courtroom before Ingrassia even finished announcing his ruling. Mason stayed at the defense table, muttering, over and over, "How could they do this to us?"

Robert Abrams rose and spoke the only words he was called upon to speak in the entirety of the hearing. "The grand jury is prepared to have Glenda Brawley appear before it on Wednesday of this week," he said, suggesting to Judge Ingrassia that Ms. Brawley could purge herself of her contempt and avoid jail if she appeared by that day.

The courtroom cleared quickly. The only occasion on which

the case of Tawana Brawley was discussed in a court of law had ended chaotically, its central figures not Tawana Brawley, not Glenda Brawley, but two lawyers who'd argued anything but law for the better part of a Poughkeepsie afternoon.

STEVE PAULUS BROUGHT Attorney General Bob Abrams to the roof of the County Office Building for a live interview with Taibbi and Chris Borgen. Against the lovely last light bouncing off the hills of the Hudson Valley, Abrams was mournful, angry.

"It's time to think about winding this investigation down," he said. The behavior of Glenda Brawley's lawyers was "reprehensible and irresponsible. They failed utterly to offer a defense." He mentioned again that he would urge that execution of Glenda Brawley's arrest and incarceration be held off for two days, to give her a chance to change her mind and testify before the grand jury. He left the roof, accompanied by a single aide. Taibbi and Borgen filed several reports; Taibbi's comprehensive report at six was uninspired, though it included carefully paraphrased references to what he and Phillips had learned about Glenda Brawley's plans to move out of state and about the probable conclusions of the grand jury.

"DAMN!" SAID ANNA PHILLIPS, watching the Six in one of the two editing rooms she'd been shuttling between all day, putting her reporters' pieces together. "*Say* something, Abrams!" She'd found the whole day incredibly depressing, sitting mesmerized for long stretches as she screened the field tapes piped in via Jim Fleischmann's mountain. Though she'd learned to expect anything from the Brawley team, she didn't expect a *movie,* and that's what seemed to be coming from Poughkeepsie: a movie complete with cheering and surging crowds in conflict or celebration, people scaling light poles and squeezing onto benches to get a better look, faces in every window (Look at that! Look at that!); the pushing and shoving and angry words that built tension, the quick urgent movements and sudden developments (the sprint to the bank by Sharpton and the lawyers with a few reporters in the chase, her partner included), then the roadblock of Farrakhan's security guard. Phillips closely studied the shots of the protesters, especially the children; very few of the chants she could make out were about Tawana Brawley, and many of their signs made it plain. Mike Taibbi was the enemy of the moment.

Phillips, in New York City, hated the movie, knew how Taibbi must have been feeling seventy-five miles to the north. She knew they wouldn't, but part of her secretly hoped that Maddox and Mason, in the courtroom scenes she was monitoring, would come up with something, *anything*, something hidden and startling to prove that the cynics (herself and Taibbi included) were wrong about Tawana and Tawana's story, so the children outside would have a reason to be there, a justification for their heartfelt taunts and pubescent anger. But the tape from the courtroom came to an end, the lawyers' performance to an end, the movie to the saddest end possible. Abrams, whose interview with Taibbi and Borgen was broadcast live, was merely epilogue, afterthought; and in the man's reticence, his unwillingness to just *say it*, Phillips thought, he was going to let the evil bastards get away with it—evil bastards! She'd actually thought those words of black men she'd only months before admired for what she knew of them, and of their role in Howard Beach.

Phillips called home; no one answered. She went back to her desk, in the Annex, where there were no television monitors on, and sat for a while in the blessed silence.

ON MARKET STREET, the Six broadcast over, Taibbi drifted aimlessly for long minutes, watching the demonstrators get back in their buses and then joining the remaining press contingent at the entrance to the courthouse. Suddenly, a group of a dozen or so men hopped off the lead bus, having recognized him, and rushed him, shouting that they were "going to take care of Mad Dog Mike." Taibbi stood his ground and shook his head stubbornly, out of confusion more than determination; the cameras were on him again. There were plenty of cops around and one of them, sensing the possibility of just the kind of incident that had luckily been avoided throughout the long hot day, pulled Taibbi to the open back door of a nearby cruiser and bent his head beneath the roof post, shoving him into the backseat, as though he were a suspect resisting arrest. The cruiser screamed around the block, the two deputies in the front seat explaining as they drove that it was for the reporter's own good, they were just trying to protect him. They deposited him back by the mini-vans that had been recording the pool video from the courtroom, and wished him luck.

TAIBBI DROVE BACK to Manhattan with Don Janney, profoundly depressed by the day's events. No, he agreed later when he sat with Phillips and Sagan in the news director's office; there'd been no surprises, really.

"But if Abrams says it's time to wind it down, and there's no 'smoking gun' proving Tawana's story is false . . ." Sagan thought aloud.

"Then that's it," Phillips said. "The advisers win, they remain heroes. They can cry cover-up and be believed, Glenda's a martyr, and Tawana never has to talk."

They sat in the office in silence for a few moments, not knowing where to go next. Certainly the drama would continue over Glenda Brawley's persistent defiance and her disappearance that afternoon; without question, the lawyers and Sharpton would turn the drama into melodrama. Nonstories, really, they all knew, that could nonetheless turn into real violence, and, in that way alone, real stories.

"We'll see in the morning," Sagan said finally, wearily. He'd reminded his reporters many times that the best outcome was for the story to just go away—the best outcome for everyone but the public. "Just keep working at it, guys. There'll be plenty to do." What, exactly, he didn't know.

His reporters checked their late mail. There were a few more hate letters, mixed among the messages of encouragement and thanks, and two letters for Taibbi that contained crude death threats. One of those letters, from a correspondent who would send three similar "messages," included a swatch of toilet tissue crusted with excrement.

By the time Taibbi got home it was too late for the goodbye dinner he'd wanted to make for his son, Matt, who was finishing the last exams after his freshman year at New York University and was preparing to leave for a summer of work on Cuttyhunk Island in Buzzards Bay prior to transferring to another college in upstate New York. Taibbi had gone to Balducci's the Sunday previous and purchased the makings for Matt's favorite meal, veal cutlets and Dad's own recipe for fettuccine, a crisp Chinese apple-pear for dessert. The ingredients were still in the fridge, though, and Taibbi, Beverly (known as "B" in the household), and Matt ordered Chinese delivery and ate quietly, somberly, at 10:30 at night. The story had gotten to them all.

And when Matt called the newsroom the next day to tell Taibbi he was packed and ready for his four o'clock train, last exam taken, his old man went into a mild panic. Today? He just hadn't known it was happening so soon; it had just slipped his mind; he wasn't ready. His boy was leaving the nest, and he wasn't ready for it. "Come on up, grab the subway," Taibbi pleaded. "Have lunch with Anna and me. We're working on a follow to yesterday's stuff, but it's easy. Come on. Lunch."

Later, Taibbi drove his son home, picked up the boy's gear, and took him to the Eighth Avenue side of Penn Station. They stood on the sidewalk, father and son; best friends, too.

"Well, Dad." Matt seemed unsure of what to say.

"Cut the shit, son. I'm not going downstairs with you, you know how to take a train, and we're not gonna do a scene."

"I just want to say," Matt began, adjusting the heft of his

several duffels and other assorted gear. "You know, it's been terrific, tell B. I just want . . ."

"Yeah, yeah, yeah. I love you, son. Now get the fuck out of here."

"I love you, too."

They threw their arms around each other, hard. Matt walked toward the station, and though he didn't look back he raised a hand once, knowing his father was watching him all the way.

That night, in the sudden quiet of the apartment, Taibbi decided to cook the good-bye meal anyway and just have it with Beverly. He set out candles, and place settings with linen napkins instead of their usual paper towels, and cooked with a frenzy for an hour. But when Beverly came home and they sat at the table, the dinner steaming hot and so pretty, Taibbi suddenly started crying.

He hadn't shed a tear since childhood. But that night, inconsolable and not knowing why, he cried on and off for hours.

SAGAN WAS RIGHT. There was plenty to do in the days that followed the contempt finding against Glenda Brawley, who had immediately dropped out of sight. A source with direct access to Sharpton called Anna Phillips and, Quasimodo-style, intoned a single word: "Sanc-tu-ary!"

"What?" Phillips asked.

"That's it. Their strategy. I just talked to Sharpton. They're gonna have Glenda seek sanctuary in a church. Don't worry, there'll be an announcement."

That there was. It took place two hours later, on the steps of Queens Criminal Court in Kew Gardens, where Sharpton had been ordered to appear on disorderly conduct charges stemming from an earlier Day of Outrage demonstration.

"Glenda Brawley will be seeking religious asylum," Sharpton announced. "And we will force you, Cuomo and Abrams, to come in and arrest her, and show the world how beastly you are."

Maddox issued the challenge directly. If any effort was made to arrest his client, he said, "they will have to come through me. Please have a bullet designated for me. We will stand tall and we will stand as men, protecting the rights of black women."

The first choice as Glenda Brawley's religious "sanctuary" was the Ebenezer Baptist Church in Queens, whose pastor, the Reverend Timothy Mitchell, had stayed in with Sharpton, however uncomfortably, for all the months of the Brawley case. Mitchell would tell Sharpton a day later that Glenda would have to leave. But that night, Sharpton, introduced as "the Moses of our time," told a cheering crowd of 400 supporters and the cameras and microphones allowed in for a photo opportunity that "we slipped through the dragnet! We'll wait them out the way we've waited for four hundred years. If they come to arrest Glenda, we'll have a Day of Indignation that will make the Day of Outrage look like a cocktail sip. We will close this city down, subways, trains, and bridges, on the day of her arrest. She will not answer the grand jury. She will not testify. She will not answer the judge's call or the attorney general's call." Sharpton finished with his inevitable tag line: "Even your arms, Bob Abrams, are too short to box with God!"

The headlines bawled: "Brawley's Bullies!" The columnists howled. "Sharpton has taken his farce, the latest act in his media vaudeville, into church," scorned Pete Hamill of the *New York Post*. If someone has to go to the slammer, wrote Bob Herbert of the *Daily News*, "Glenda Brawley has three high-profile advisors who more than qualify. No one would weep at their confinement." The sanctuary strategy, intoned the *New York Times* editorial page, "was the behavior of advisors more interested in getting to the top of the news than to the bottom of the case." Jerry Nachman of the *Post*, in the style that caused him later to be singled out for vicious attack by the Brawley advisers, wrote: "Glenda Brawley has allowed herself to be taken hostage by those terrorists of civilized behavior, Maddox, Mason and Sharpton."

Outside the church, by the Main Street entrance, a brace of skinheads tried to provoke a confrontation and, in the deliberate absence of a high-profile police presence that might have heightened the tension, violence was a clear possibility. It was exactly what the advisers wanted.

Sagan wouldn't play. "They're not making news anymore," he announced to his staff at the morning meeting on June 7, after the skinheads had come and gone. "They want to continue to use the media, but we're not going to play into their hands." No round-the-clock vigil, he ordered. Listen to the police radios, run a crew past the scene now and then if you've got a camera in the area. That's it. Mike and Anna will just keep working on whatever they come up with.

For Phillips, that meant pushing ahead on the money angle. There was no shortage of callers and letter writers she needed to get back to, and she and her partner knew that the IRS was already conducting a probe of Sharpton's finances on several levels, one possibly having to do with unreported donations related to the Brawley case. Sharpton, typically, had admitted not filing tax returns for at least three years but insisted that he shouldn't have to pay taxes anyway, since he, like all blacks, did not enjoy the fruits of citizenship.

Taibbi, meanwhile, learned that Abrams, quoted in one morning headline as despairing, "The Probe Is Doomed," had let it be known to the Dutchess County sheriff's department that he'd have no objection if a move was made to arrest Glenda Brawley as soon as possible. Taibbi and Janney raced upcountry and from a Wappingers Falls police source picked up a copy of the "File 5 All Points Bulletin" permitting any police officer in the state to arrest Glenda Brawley on sight. Taibbi knew too that the next day, June 8, Steve Pagones's lawyer, Gerald Hayes, was going to hand-deliver two letters to the Brawley grand jury setting out the "conditions" for his client's cooperation with the panel. Michael Heard, the young desk assistant who'd worked with Taibbi and Phillips on the Brawley story on several occasions and would soon work with them almost full-time, was summoned from the city. Heard

ran a records check on a tip Taibbi had received from a bail
bondsman, and the records he retrieved allowed the reporter
to assert that if Glenda Brawley was sent to the Dutchess
County jail, it wouldn't be her first visit. Her first incarceration, Taibbi reported, followed her conviction "in December of 1979 for the Class D felony of Grand Larceny in the
2nd Degree—for collecting unemployment compensation
while she was working." Heard also ran point on a stakeout
of Stephen Pagones and, with the help of three camera crews,
Taibbi was able to push through the cordon of sheriff's deputies who'd escorted Pagones to lunch at a pizza joint and
get a couple of questions in. Yes, Pagones said cordially; his
suit against the Brawley advisers was very much alive, "but
we're going to wait for the appropriate time, after the grand
jury finishes its work, to file it."

IT WAS FRIDAY, JUNE 10, the long week coming to an end.
Phillips and a friend from the *Daily News* were on the phone
killing time, trading war stories and consoling each other.
Taibbi was talking to the manager of the boatyard where he
and Beverly kept their sloop, *Cariña*. Barbara Nevins, a first-
rate reporter whose cubicle was diagonally across from Taibbi's, stood up and called to him.

"Mike, Anna around? There's a call for her."

Taibbi cupped the phone. He was in the middle of an important discussion about his depth-sounder, which was on
the blink.

"Who's it?"

"Guy named Perry," Nevins said. "Want me to take a
message?"

Taibbi looked across the newsroom to where his partner
was sitting. She was hunched over, deep in conversation with
someone.

"Nah. Switch it here. I'll take it." He told the yard manager he'd call back in a few.

Nevins switched the call.

"Perry? Perry who?" Taibbi said, mildly annoyed. "This is Taibbi."

"Mike. It's Perry! Perry McKinnon."

Taibbi's mind fought to focus. McKinnon, Perry. Sharpton's guy. Where the hell had Perry McKinnon *been!* He was always there, though he was nowhere to be seen in Poughkeepsie. Let's see . . . when was the last time I saw him . . . ?

"Oh, yeah. Perry. Geez, I haven't seen you since, well, I don't know when."

"That's right," McKinnon said. "Since the Newburgh press conference, the bribery bullshit. I told you then, I told Anna, I got to talk to you."

"Well," Taibbi said, trying to put it together. "Go ahead. I'm listening. Talk away."

Perry McKinnon talked for half an hour. Taibbi never did call the boatyard back, and *Carina* went into the water with a balky depth-sounder, again.

12

"I'm not leaving the movement. I'm leaving Al Sharpton . . ."

IT WAS A STRUGGLE every day now, and it was a struggle at which Mike Taibbi was no longer succeeding. Though it went against all his training, all his history, he'd begun to take the Brawley story personally.

Part of the problem was the sheer length of the assignment. A reporter could cover an armed conflict or a slash of terrorist activity, as he had during a stint as a foreign correspondent for ABC News, or a spectacular crime and the trial to follow, as he had many times as a local television reporter. But each of those stories promised downtime, departures from the main story line, and at least they were real events whose characters and characters' motives were clearly defined, whose sidebars mattered, whose outcomes could be predicted with a high degree of accuracy by a competent, properly dispassionate observer, which is all Taibbi ever wanted to be. Even the coverage of a political party and its eventual candidate in a presidential campaign, the conventions as final punctuation, was an assignment, as Taibbi had found twice, that while dreary and enervating was nonetheless a kind of rolling drama whose actors, whose winners and losers, could be tracked and studied and highlighted as though they were athletes in pursuit of a championship, no more than that, the stories about them filled with agate and locker-room quotes.

But the Brawley story had reached the point where it burned him up. In the days after Glenda Brawley's contempt hearing, Taibbi was on the phone whenever he had a spare moment, trying without success to convince the troubled doubters in the black power structure to speak up, speak out, get on the record, get off the dime. He learned that in the week before the April 19 New York Democratic party presidential primary, the word had gone out from the Jesse Jackson camp that under no circumstances was the candidate to be photographed with any of the Brawley advisers; certainly, the protocol went, he would decline to meet with any of them. Back in March, Jackson himself had resisted the overtures of the advisers; after initially asserting that "the case was being handled by competent attorneys, Maddox and Mason, and the community would do well to follow their lead," the candidate had been briefed first by Bill Lynch of Manhattan Borough President David Dinkins's office and then by Gov. Mario Cuomo himself. Three days after his first statement on the case, the Reverend Jesse Jackson addressed the issue for the last time, speaking from the podium of Atlanta's Ebenezer Baptist Church.

"After talking to Governor Cuomo," he said, "I am convinced that everybody is interested in justice taking place in the Brawley case so there will be a constant deterrent by law against any kind of racial violence or rape. To be sure, the governor is concerned, the lawyers are concerned, and I am not going to be involved in it because there is so much local concern and activity . . . [which] I am convinced will bring about justice in that situation."

When Taibbi approached the key people in Jackson's New York organization, Dinkins among them, no one would talk, on or off the record, about the order to keep the Brawley advisers away from the candidate. One high-ranking campaign official all but pleaded: "Please, check me out with your colleagues at CBS; they'll tell you I'm an honest man. But I can't talk about this, I just can't. If you get it, you're going to have to get it from Dinkins." Taibbi knew Dinkins personally and had dealt over the years with a number of people on his staff, and he left six messages. Not one of the calls was returned by a man, the city's ranking black politician, who had always returned Taibbi's calls.

By June 10, the morning of Perry McKinnon's call, at the end of the week that began with Glenda Brawley's contempt hearing and concluded with the woman in religious "sanctuary" and the headlines agreeing that the Brawley probe would surely fail to solve the mystery, Mike Taibbi was convinced, and was angered at the prospect, that there would be no heroes in the case of Tawana Brawley; that the forces of evil, of deliberate untruth, would win.

TAPE LIBRARIAN HOWIE SCHLECHTMAN tapped Anna Phillips on the shoulder and, when she cupped the phone in annoyance at the interruption, pointed across the room. Taibbi, standing and with the phone in his ear as always, was waving her over, more animated than she'd seen him in weeks. By the time she reached her partner's cubicle, he was repeating the instructions for a Monday morning meeting.

"You'll never guess who that was!" he said to Phillips after he'd hung up.

"Mike, I'm in no mood to play guessing games. Just tell me." If it was another tipster with a tale that would send them off on another wild-goose chase, she thought, well, she just wasn't going to bite. She was tired of chasing ghosts, sick of being attacked by the Brawley advisers, sick and tired of explaining her position to every other person whose views differed from what she was reporting. She was distressed more than anything else by the prospect of a stalemate, for she knew instinctively how the advisers would play it out for the black community: a stalemate would confirm Tawana Brawley's story, would place her name indelibly (and illegitimately) on the growing list of blacks denied justice, would propel Sharpton and the lawyers to preposterous new heights of prominence.

Taibbi was grinning, studying his notepad.

"Just tell me," Phillips bristled, her mood so foul she almost turned and walked away. "Who was it, Mike?"

"He asked for you. It was Perry McKinnon."

Phillips arched her eyebrows, curious.

"When was the last time you remember talking to Perry?" Taibbi asked.

Her mind raced backward to the bribery press conference on May 5.

"That's right!" Taibbi bellowed. "May 5! That's when he broke from Sharpton and the lawyers. He was gonna tell us the whole thing was a hoax, that the advisers were making it up as they went along. He's gonna say that now!"

"On camera?" Phillips asked, still not sold. She wasn't willing to trust *anyone* from the Sharpton camp. "Do you believe him? Why should we trust him?"

Phillips's paranoia was hard at work; she sensed a trick, she wanted to proceed cautiously. "Did he give you his home number? Let me call him. I want to be my own judge on whether he's telling the truth now or not."

When she got off the phone ten minutes later the cloud had begun to lift. She sat for a minute at Taibbi's desk, drumming her fingers, thinking hard.

"All right," she said, turning to Taibbi, who was pacing a few feet away. "Let's talk to Sagan."

"You guys believe him?" Sagan asked, once he'd shut the door to his office.

"Maybe," Taibbi answered. "We'll put him through the wringer Monday. We're not running out there now, because who knows? I want him on our turf. We're not gonna walk into a trap, go out to Brooklyn."

"Anna, what do you think?" Sagan asked.

Phillips shook her head, noncommittal. "Don't know. Let's see if he even shows up."

TAIBBI HADN'T MADE IT EASY for Perry McKinnon, picking an obscure Greenwich Village restaurant called Shopsin's General Store for the meeting. Shopsin's was a tiny place known only to the people who knew about it, so to speak; there was no name over the door; it was safe from tourists and casual drop-ins. McKinnon would have to ask people how to get there.

Over the weekend, worried about the locale of his Monday meeting, Taibbi had stopped in to see Judy Joice, who, with her husband, Wes, owned a well-known Greenwich Village saloon called the Lion's Head. He'd asked whether he could use their apartment for a long preinterview if the subject showed up.

"If he shows and he says what he says he's gonna say," Taibbi told Judy Joice, "he could be the key witness in the whole damn case. But I don't know: if it's a setup I don't want to do him in my own apartment, and if he's the real deal I want something a little less antiseptic than a rented hotel room. I want him to feel at home. I won't tell him whose home it is."

Judy said she'd think about it, call Wes, and talk it over. Sunday night she reached Taibbi and said okay.

On Monday morning Phillips only half-expected Perry McKinnon to show up. But he'd been sitting at a table in Shopsin's for ten minutes before she and Taibbi arrived.

"Well, good. Perry," Taibbi said by way of greeting, after

McKinnon had embraced Phillips like an old friend. Now that McKinnon had shown up, the reporter knew his belated instinct was right: Shopsin's, a tiny, chaotically friendly and intimate room, was exactly the wrong place to have met. The owners, Ken and Evie, invariably sidled over to talk whenever Taibbi dropped in. Ken in particular was something of a news junkie; he'd insist on being introduced to the stranger, launch inevitably into a discourse on the Brawley case. "C'mon," Taibbi said, waving Ken off. "Sorry we can't have breakfast here. But we can pick up some stuff, and we've got a place where we can talk with no interruptions."

They stopped at a deli and bought fruit and juices and soda, muffins and pistachio nuts and Hostess Twinkies, a half-dozen cups of coffee. McKinnon took the couch in the Joice apartment, Taibbi and Phillips sat in easy chairs on either side of him. They made small talk for a few minutes; everyone was a little nervous. Then Taibbi called the meeting to order.

"Perry, we're gonna use our tape recorders, just as a way of taking notes. What you say here isn't gonna be used for air, nothing will be attributed to you. But you know too we're gonna ask you when we're done to go on the record, and if you do, your life will change. . . ."

The same old drill, Phillips thought impatiently, testing her recorder and placing it in position on the coffee table. Let's get on with it. She thought back to the beginning of her own involvement in the case, of the hatred she'd felt for the men who had assaulted Tawana Brawley, of the kinship she'd felt with the men she knew from Howard Beach who were now going to bring another pack of animals to justice. Now here she was, almost four months after she'd begun working on the story, and if Perry McKinnon had the truth in him she was going to help reveal, for all the world to see and hear, that the Tawana Brawley story was a hoax, the men by Tawana's side frauds, stinking opportunists, interested not at all in the truth but instead in their own futures. She needed to hear his story more than any story she'd ever pursued. Hurry up, Mike, she thought, as her partner completed his speech. Start talking, Perry. Don't stop till there's nothing left to say.

What McKinnon said, over the next six hours, was extraordinary. In painstaking detail he recounted his experiences first with Al Sharpton and then with Sharpton and the lawyers through the months of the Brawley case. Sharpton, he said, was an out-and-out fraud "who'll use anyone till he uses him up"; but he'd believed in Sharpton in the beginning because he believed in the movement, and Sharpton's brass and bluster seemed to be necessary tools at a time when "working through the system" just didn't seem to be doing the job. McKinnon, who was head of security at Brooklyn's St. Mary's Hospital when he first met Sharpton, remembered everything—how Sharpton had conned McKinnon's boss into signing the lease for the cream Caddy he still drove, how Sharpton, with the help of Don King, had muscled his way into a role as "local promoter" for performances by black rock stars—Lionel Ritchie and Michael Jackson among them—by demanding money and tickets in exchange for a promise to *not* stage disruptive demonstrations. He talked about Sharpton's meetings with underworld figures, about the cash from "fund-raisers" Sharpton shoved into his own pockets; he provided the history and the account numbers of the accounts Sharpton had set up as a way to siphon money from the National Youth Movement—which, McKinnon asserted, wasn't any kind of "movement" to fight drug use, as Sharpton claimed, but just a way to raise money.

And then Perry McKinnon talked about the Brawley case.

"They had nothing," he said of Sharpton and the advisers. "Right from the beginning. They never had any facts, never did any investigation. Sharpton had a room in his [Brooklyn] apartment that was stacked floor to ceiling with newspaper clips; *that's* what they had, whatever the press had, period. I offered to do an investigation—I'm a former cop, a former private investigator—but they weren't interested." An insider who'd attended most of the key meetings in the case, meetings with Tawana and the Brawley family, with Attorney General Bob Abrams, with Don King, Mike Tyson, Bill Cosby, with reporters, McKinnon now recounted tale after tale of manipulation, cunning, deception. "They never had any evidence to back up anything they were saying. When they took off on you guys, on that bribery bullshit, I said, That's it. I knew it was bullshit. I broke away. They were just running their own agenda, on the back of a sixteen-year-old girl they didn't even care about, and didn't believe. Even Sharpton told me, several times, 'I think it's bullshit,' meaning her story."

Phillips pressed McKinnon on his background, emphasizing that she and Taibbi would check every detail. The reporters knew the history of the Brawley case cold, almost to the day; they reviewed every event, each incident, dozens of checkpoints in the case leading up to May 5.

When they were done with the preinterview, the three people in the Joice apartment were exhausted.

"What about other reporters?" McKinnon asked Taibbi finally, breaking the silence. "There's a couple others I've trusted in the past. What should I do about them?"

Taibbi waved the question away, shaking his head. "We don't own you, Perry. I mean, I'd hope you would wait till after we air our interview, but if there are reporters you trust, then reach out to them. There's no more important story in this Brawley thing than what you've just told us. The more people who report it, the better. I mean, eventually . . ."

Taibbi smiled. McKinnon nodded, deep in thought.

"I'll call you tonight with the location for the on-camera interview," Phillips told McKinnon, embracing him again. "It'll be early. It shouldn't take as long as today; we won't ask you to do the whole thing on camera, but most of it; be prepared."

"And bring everything you've got," Taibbi added. "Your military discharge papers, PI's licenses, photographs, records, employment contracts, high school yearbook if you have it, anything you've got. Everything. They're gonna come at you, you know that."

"Oh, I know that," McKinnon said, almost too casually. "I expect that. I'll be there, Mike. It's time."

McKinnon headed for the West Fourth Street subway station after leaving the reporters on Sixth Avenue. Taibbi and Phillips went back to Taibbi's apartment, where he'd parked his truck on the street out front, but they'd taken ten minutes too many with Perry McKinnon.

"Sorry," one of his neighbors said. "I told them you'd be right back, that you lived here. I pointed out the press visor you had showing. But they didn't give a shit. Took 'em a few minutes, but they got in."

Taibbi's truck had been towed.

"Fuck it," he said to Phillips. "I'll take care of it later."

SAGAN WAS STUNNED, looking from Taibbi to Phillips and back again as they tripped over each other recounting Perry McKinnon's story.

"Can we believe him, on all of it?" Sagan asked.

"Well . . . we've got concerns," Phillips answered. One concern had to do with Derek "Sunshine" Jeter, another Sharpton aide, whom McKinnon had described on Friday as ready to jump ship himself. But the front page of Sunday's *Newsday* had carried a photograph of Tawana arriving at Bethany Baptist Church to "visit her exiled mother," and, prominently in the background, there was Sunshine, dressed in his Sunday best, standing beside Al Sharpton.

"But Perry's too good," Phillips added, addressing her own fears. "Yeah, we've been burned by the Brawley camp before, but there's no way Perry was sent in to us by Sharpton. Not off what he said."

"And," Taibbi interjected, "think of how the rest of the press will play it. Every reporter who's covered this damn story knows Perry McKinnon. He made most of the press calls, all the daybook stuff on all the press conferences. He was the buffer and the link to Sharpton. He shows up in so many of the pictures, he's on tape all over the place, we'll have no trouble finding him in our own archives. He's legit, a real insider."

Sagan was still worried. The previous week he'd been startled to learn that Taibbi's conversations on his private phone line were audible—air quality, an editor said—on a phone in an editing room on the other side of the building. The editor, Jeff Morgan, was a friend of Taibbi's and just happened to have been assigned to that room, known as Super One, which was used at times for its limited special-effects capabilities. Morgan had picked up the phone at one point and instead of a dial tone heard Taibbi in a detailed discussion about the status of the investigation with one of his most sensitively placed sources; Morgan was able to repeat several key exchanges almost word for word, and Taibbi was alarmed. A sweep by the phone company discovered that "some lines had been crossed—probably an accident" in the room near Sagan's office where the trunk lines were bundled. And, too, one of Phillips's friends in the building had warned her that Sharpton did in fact have an "inside source" within CBS—a claim Sharpton had made publicly—who was "running information" to the minister about the angles being pursued by Taibbi and Phillips.

"Careful," Sagan warned. "Handle this whole thing in the strictest confidence. Colloff and the lawyers will have to know, of course, but other than that keep it here. Anna, book a hotel room and use your own charge card, no CBS direct billing. And," he added after a pause, "book two crews. Use a two-camera shoot to cover cutaways so there won't be any question of our putting words into McKinnon's mouth. Everything straightforward." The news director kneaded his forehead, deep in his own thoughts. "Why don't you guys leave me alone for a few minutes, start setting things up. I'll call Roger and fill him in on what's happening."

Phillips headed for the planning desk, praying silently that Paul Fleuranges wouldn't notice the obvious omissions in her set-up sheet. Of course, he noticed.

"Anna," Fleuranges said, smiling as always, "what's up here?

You book two cameras? And you left off the location, stupid! Come on back here and fill this thing out right!" She signaled to him to keep his voice down but it was too late; everyone on the assignment desk, ten feet away, was already tuned in. She felt bad about it; she'd worked on the desk herself, and knew the desk, the heart of the newsroom, *had* to know everything.

"I don't know, Paul," she said casually, loud enough to be heard by everyone on the desk. "It's just a possibility, but if it works out it could be okay. Just give me Janney and Jim Duggan. Roll them out of the garage early in separate vehicles, both of them with gear, and tell them to monitor their car phones. At around eight-thirty I'll call each of them if it comes together, and tell them where to meet me. If it happens, I'll probably need them all day long."

As she walked away, looking for Taibbi, she heard the whispers on the desk, and she smiled to herself. If she were still on the desk she'd have been leading the chorus of whispers—What are they up to?—and trying out one scenario after another.

Just then Sagan's secretary called to her.

"Paul's office," she said. "Taibbi's already in there."

Sagan was hanging up his hotline phone, the one that connected him to Roger Colloff's office directly, when Phillips walked in.

"Roger has an idea," Sagan explained. "He thinks we should polygraph McKinnon. Whaddya think?"

Taibbi and Phillips looked at each other, shrugged.

"I'm not bothered by it," Phillips said after a few seconds. "Mike, you know somebody who could do it?"

Taibbi knew a number of polygraph experts in the New York area, and offered to check with some federal contacts to find out who was the best. "I'd feel safer," he agreed, thinking back on the Newburgh tales and their aftermath, "if we had a better idea he was telling the truth."

As it turned out, most of the more frequently used polygraphers were out of state attending a convention; but one federal source suggested Victor Kaufman, a veteran and one of the good ones. Kaufman was willing to take on the job.

At seven the next morning Phillips was inspecting the suite she'd booked at the St. Moritz Hotel on Central Park South. Comfortable sitting room, a couple of couches and easy chairs and a round dining table; a large separate bedroom. Taibbi arrived at eight; at eight-thirty Phillips reached Janney and Duggan. The two cameramen set up their equipment quickly and carefully. At nine sharp Perry McKinnon was in the lobby, dressed in a comfortable cotton open-necked sport shirt; Taibbi took him up to the room.

Everybody went through coffee and danishes while Taibbi and Phillips inspected McKinnon's documents. They'd already run a criminal records check; he was clean. They'd called Reidsville, Georgia, his hometown, and confirmed that he had been on the police force there. He checked out at St. Mary's Hospital. His discharge papers, army commendations for three combat tours in Vietnam, and various licenses seemed authentic. McKinnon settled nervously into an easy chair and faced Taibbi and Phillips, who shared a couch and studied their notes.

"Speed," said Jim Duggan quietly, as he turned on his camera.

"Speed," Janney said. "Anytime, guys."

THE ON-CAMERA INTERVIEW took more than two hours and filled five complete videocassettes. Victor Kaufman arrived just after noon.

"Sure, that's okay," McKinnon said, when Taibbi said he'd forgotten to mention that they wanted him to submit to a lie-detector test.

Kaufman and McKinnon went into the bedroom, and the Channel 2 team watched in fascination as the elderly lie-detection specialist assembled his own rig and attached the sensors to McKinnon's arms and chest.

"I need three questions," Kaufman explained casually, professionally, leading Taibbi, Phillips, and the cameramen back into the sitting room once McKinnon was hooked up. "I'll run a lot of other questions past him, to establish his response levels, but you'll have to decide the three questions that matter, having to do with the issue you're exploring. They have to be answered by a 'yes' or 'no' answer." The reporters thought quickly, reviewing the key allegations McKinnon had made in his marathon interview and then arriving at the most obvious question of all.

"Ask him," Taibbi suggested, "if he lied about anything in his television interview with us. That's one. Then, did Al Sharpton express his own doubts about the Brawley story, two. Three, was Alton Maddox interested in the facts in the case."

Kaufman wrote the questions down carefully.

"Give me two hours, thereabouts," he said. "Maybe a little more. No interruptions." He went into the bedroom and pulled the door closed behind him.

PHILLIPS SCANNED THE SELECTIONS on the hotel's movie timetable. Good luck; *Fatal Attraction,* the sexy Glenn Close/ Michael Douglas thriller, was due to start in a few minutes, and no one but Taibbi had seen it. They sat in the dark with the volume turned low, hooking into the movie—two reporters, two cameramen, all veterans, huddled around a TV while the biggest story any of them had ever worked on was turning to either gold or dust next door.

Glenn Close was in the bathtub, face under water, ready to rise in her final murderous thrust, when the noise of a chair pulling back and the metallic clicks of machinery came from the bedroom. By the time Victor Kaufman opened the door, signaling to the reporters that they could come in, Glenn Close was dead and the credits were rolling.

Janney shot liberally as Perry McKinnon was unhooked from the machine. Kaufman studied his notes, checking off certain highlights, and answered Taibbi's questions as though he'd merely completed another one of the ten thousand tests he'd administered in his long career. Which, from his point of view, is all he had done.

Perry McKinnon's answers to the three key questions were truthful, Victor Kaufman said. As an expert witness, he'd have no trouble testifying to the accuracy of the results he'd obtained.

AT SEVEN THAT NIGHT, Taibbi, Phillips, Sagan, and executive producer Dean Daniels sat in the dark in an editing suite as editor Harry Cannon rolled the tapes of the interview. McKinnon was electric, dramatic without being melodramatic, absolutely persuasive. Sagan and Daniels, young executives whose race up the fast track had kept them inside for most of their careers, were stunned, reduced to periodic expressions of disbelief that the story they'd managed (and that at times had managed them) could be exposed so devastatingly by the rhythmic, pulsating narrative of a single individual.

When the last of the five interview tapes had finished, Cannon nudged the lights on, and still everyone sat in silence.

"Dean," Taibbi said finally. "You could run a hunk of this at eleven. You know, I could sit on the set and say we'll have the rest of it tomorrow." Daniels shook his head slowly, but it was Sagan who answered.

"No. It's not a sil/sot," he said, using the jargon that described a simple voiceover read leading to a bit of sound on tape. "Do it the way you guys want to do it. Whatever it takes. We run Perry McKinnon tomorrow. I'm staying around tonight, until you guys wrap. We'll talk about it when you've got it down."

When Sagan and Daniels left the room, Phillips hauled over her two crates of more than 120 field cassettes. She ran Cannon through a high-speed drill, her memory at work, and located a half-dozen shots of McKinnon. She found him in the crowd at demonstrations in Poughkeepsie, in the line of march in a February Day of Outrage, in a 1982 clip of an incident at St. Mary's, a hero that day; she cued up the tape when Sharpton, on the day of the arrest of Task Force investigator William West, yanked McKinnon to his side to "Talk to this here black girl," Phillips herself, the day she and Taibbi embarked on the Fric 'n' Frac stories. She found the tape of an interview with Tawana Brawley from January 14, a tape she and Taibbi had been led to believe had long since been recycled.

By 11:00 P.M. Phillips and Taibbi knew the McKinnon story cold, knew every picture that was available, had isolated every interview cut that would have to be included.

"How long?" Sagan asked, walking with his two reporters to the CBS hangout at Tenth and Fifty-sixth Street that would forever be known as the Slate, no matter how many times the joint changed hands.

"About twelve minutes," Taibbi said, picking out of the air a number that seemed appropriate. "Maybe a little more, but not much more."

"Whatever it takes. It's worth everything it's worth."

They sat in the Slate a quiet half hour. Phillips ordered white wine spritzers, Sagan Perrier and lime, Taibbi shots of Jack Daniel's with beer chasers.

"Tell me," Sagan asked suddenly, apropos of nothing at all. "How many news directors have you had . . . how many do you think were any good?"

Taibbi tossed down his last shot of the night. Phillips studied her partner carefully: when he was flying high, he could be insufferable.

"Maybe three or four, out of a couple dozen," Taibbi answered finally. "Three or four were real newsmen; the rest were salesmen. But this," he said, speaking of the moment, their moment. "This is reporting. This is the news. This is the damn story."

They raised their glasses, all three of them, and toasted the night, their night, and, finally, a hero named Perry McKinnon.

———

TAIBBI'S PHONE RANG at 6:15 the next morning. Anna Phillips was in a state; her radio alarm had awakened her to the lead story on WCBS Radio, News 88: according to the *Daily News,* an ex-aide to Al Sharpton had said "the Tawana Brawley case was a pack of lies." The ex-aide's name was Perry McKinnon.

"Fuck!" Taibbi shouted. "Fuck, fuck!" He paced, phone in hand, then sat at the foot of his bed; his wife, Beverly, woke up, alarmed.

Phillips, though upset herself, heard herself calming her partner down. "Come on. Let's just do the piece."

"Right. Okay," Taibbi answered finally. "It's no big deal. We've got him in the can, we've got his story like nobody else has it; we'll just do it better. It's a television story. See you in—what?—an hour?"

Sagan called. "I've told radio we've got the story, that you'll give them a few soundbites within the half hour, they can stop crediting the *News.* You ready to roll?"

By the time Taibbi got to the station, WCBS Radio reporter Art Athens was waiting, tape player in hand, and within minutes he had pulled several cuts from the McKinnon interview, which played again and again throughout drive-time and all morning long, twice every hour. Chris Borgen, anchoring WCBS-TV's morning news cut-ins, grabbed several soundbites as well. Traffic from Jersey was tough, and Phillips didn't get to the newsroom until 8:30; she and Taibbi reached Sagan on his car phone.

"Well, guys . . ."

"No problem," Phillips said. "We're gonna cut it for the Noon."

"The whole damn thing," Taibbi added. "No problem."

Phillips collected her crates of archived field cassettes, pulled the McKinnon interview tapes from Sagan's locked cabinet, and booked side-by-side editing suites, Rooms 4 and 5, on the assumption that at least two editors would be needed to assemble the monster piece. She asked for Harry Cannon and a talented young editor named Karen Lindauer; Lindauer cued up a couple of shots Phillips wanted to freeze and highlight, shots of McKinnon next to Sharpton or talking to Phillips herself.

The whole newsroom was buzzing, word of the impending blockbuster reaching everybody from the makeup artists to the most isolated technicians back in Microwave Control. Lisa Sharkey Gleicher, producer of the Noon, was told to put her format together with a twelve-minute hole at the top, at least, but to float everything else until she got a reliable number from Phillips. Managing editor Jean Harper marshaled everyone to the single task: do anything that's needed, anticipate what's needed, to help Taibbi and Phillips get their story on the air. Otherwise, she said, stay out of their way.

Taibbi plopped himself noisily in front of one of the writers' computers and accepted the coffee, cigarettes, and ashtray brought to him by a desk assistant. He logged onto the computer, spread his notes on the desktop beside his keyboard, lit a cigarette, and gulped down half a cup of coffee.

Phillips stopped by his desk on the way to the coord session where she planned to build the special effects the piece would need.

"Okay, Mike . . . you ready? Start writing."

It was 8:55 A.M. Taibbi slugged his story—MC KINNON —and soon was typing furiously.

FORTY MINUTES LATER Taibbi was reading the first half of his script for Phillips and Sagan in the news director's office, pacing all the way, paraphrasing the McKinnon interview segments almost word for word and then describing the ground he planned to cover in the rest of the script.

"Why don't you narrate this now?" Phillips suggested. "I'm done with the effects, I can start cutting this part of it with Karen."

"And Mike," Sagan added. "When you finish the second half of the script just bring it into Harry's room and start cutting it yourself. It may be the only way the thing gets on the air. I'll fax what you've written to the lawyers," he said, as he trailed them out of his office. "And, oh, Mike, take out that 'scam'—here it is," he said, pointing to the word. The reporter had written that McKinnon claimed he "was present at shakedowns and other Sharpton scams."

"Jesus, Paul," Taibbi shouted. "They *are* fucking scams. This guy's been reaming us for months, and now you're gonna worry about using the word *scam*?"

The newsroom fell silent. But Sagan ignored the outburst and simply crossed out the word on Taibbi's copy of the script, replacing it with "capers."

"No 'scams,' " he said quietly, firmly. "Let's go."

Taibbi laid down his narration in a single take while Phillips and Sagan explained to Gleicher and Harper that the story would be cut in two segments, which would then be "married" in a third editing room.

"You want more help, Anna?" Harper asked Phillips. "Someone to run tapes between the two rooms while you and Mike are cutting?" Before Phillips could answer, Carol Marin, a seasoned and accomplished producer in her own right, volunteered for the menial yet critically important task. Phillips explained her labeling system, showed Marin how she'd organized the McKinnon tapes—1 through 5 for the full-face interview tapes and 1b through 5b for the Duggan tapes shot in reverse. She pointed out the other key archive tapes on which both she and Taibbi would rely, and then, Lindauer's fingers flying, Anna Phillips dove to the task.

It took Taibbi little more than twenty minutes to complete the second half of his script, just over an hour's total writing time for the entire piece. Nothing like a little pressure, he thought to himself, pulling the script from the printer. No problem, said the lawyers. Sagan signed off on it.

"Now, how long?" Sagan asked, looking at the Est Air (es-

timated airtime) numbers at the top of Taibbi's script when
he punched it up on his own computer. "Looks like—let's
see—"

"Yeah," Taibbi said. "It's long. About eight minutes plus
for each half, seventeen total. Maybe a little more, but not
much."

Sagan shook his head, whistling softly to himself. He'd have
to rearrange and cluster commercials to run it straight through,
though that wasn't even a hint of a problem for him, and
Colloff had authorized commercial kills for later in the afternoon. But seventeen minutes!

"Didn't you tell me twelve minutes last night?" he said to
his reporter, quickly adding a smile. "I mean, even for Taibbi,
six minutes over is a bit much."

Taibbi smiled, too. "I lied." He bounded through the
newsroom then, looked in on Phillips, who ignored him, and
then took his seat next to Harry Cannon in the editing suite
next door. After Cannon had laid down the first narration
cut, Taibbi looked to his right through the thick smoked glass
that separated the two editing suites. Phillips must have felt
his gaze, for she looked over then, and offered a thumbs-up
and a smile as wide as Manhattan. Taibbi returned the gesture and added a wink, and then caught Carol Marin's eye.
He held up the index finger of his right hand, and then the
same finger twice in succession, the second time with the
thumb and index finger of his left hand curled against it. He
wanted McKinnon tapes 1 and 1b. Marin was in his room,
tapes in hand, in a flash. It was 10:15 in the morning.

The next hour was one of the most extraordinary hours
any of the five people in editing suites 4 and 5 had ever known
in their collective television careers. There were times, all of
them knew and had experienced, when an hour was barely
enough time to put together a complicated two-minute piece
on deadline. But Phillips knew her 120 tapes to the date, subject matter, specific scene, and time code, and she and Taibbi
had the McKinnon interview down thoroughly. And there was
something else, something that propelled each mind to a fe-

ver of impossible efficiency: it was the adrenaline of release, escape from the dungeon of doom and futile rage into which they'd all been thrust by the Tawana Brawley story.

"Everyone. Get the fuck out of my editing room!" Phillips boomed when the latest head, Paul Sagan's as it turned out, ducked in to see if everything was all right. Sagan slipped away quietly, smiling to himself, all but snapping his ever-present suspenders. Truth is, he would explain later, he didn't feel any pressure at all that morning!

And with the door closed again to the racket outside, Phillips and Lindauer resumed the task of creating television at warp speed. Next door, Taibbi and Cannon mirrored their efforts; and Carol Marin was everywhere, in both rooms at once, it seemed, quiet and perfect and on the money, no mistakes, as though she too had lived with the story for months, which, in a way, of course she had.

Taibbi and Phillips, linked forever now, seemed always to look toward each other at precisely the same moment, exchanging smiles, raised thumbs, vigorous nods, clenched fists. It was delirious; it was deliverance. It was . . . fun.

At 11:20 they were done, Sagan instructing editing supervisor Rich Gottfried on how the marriage of the two halves of the Perry McKinnon story would be carried out.

"One shot," Sagan told Gottfried, looking at his watch. "Anna will call the take from part one to part two. Got it?" Gottfried had readied two master tapes, one to serve as a backup. He rolled the masters, rolled part one and, on Phillips's cue, part two. The take was perfect, to the split second. When the marriage ceremony was over, it was barely 11:40. Twenty minutes to spare!

"Great, guys, unbelievable," Sagan pronounced, taking the spare master from Gottfried. But Karen Lindauer was fretting. There'd been a flash frame, a single frame of the wrong picture, left on the wrong side of one of her supersonic edits, a flash no one at home would even notice; but she had.

"I'm fixing it," she announced, grabbing the show master from Gottfried. "There's time, dammit!"

No one argued with her. There *was* time.

At noon straight up, Taibbi and Phillips would later hear from friends in the news business, at least eight New York newsrooms, broadcast and print newsrooms, came to a virtual standstill, and stayed that way for eighteen minutes. In Perry McKinnon, there had finally arrived a hero in the Tawana Brawley case.

TAIBBI NARRATION:

Perry James McKinnon says he comes not from the country, but from behind the country: Georgia's deepest backwoods, at a time when the Klan rode free and it was considered an insult for a black man to look a white man in the eye.

But he got beyond the hostility of outright segregation to serve not one, or two, but three combat tours in Vietnam . . . and won three Bronze Stars, a Good Conduct Medal, several commendations for valor. After the war he began a career in law enforcement in Georgia . . . and then in private investigations and security . . . winning commendations every step along the way, and then taking his career and his beliefs to New York.

(Sound full: super November 26, 1982: sound of cop saying, "One shot was fired.")

TAIBBI NARRATION:

His dependable dedication thrust him into the headlines in November of 1982. The man who fired that shot in a ward at St. John the Episcopal Hospital also had two hand grenades and several handmade bombs taped to his body. The "Hospital Hero" who ". . . Defused the Human Bomb" was Perry James McKinnon.

Perry McKinnon has no criminal record of any kind. We checked. He believed in the movement for black justice . . . and still does. He believed for a time over the past year and a half that the movement needed brassy, outspoken leaders like Al Sharpton. Believed it privately until the Tawana Brawley case.

But he kept his beliefs private until last Friday, when he called me and producer Anna Phillips. There isn't a reporter on this story who doesn't know Perry Mc-Kinnon—he was always there, usually in the background until Sharpton summoned him to transmit a message directly.

(Sound on tape: Sharpton: "Perry! Talk to this here black girl!")

TAIBBI NARRATION:
"Talk to this here black girl!" Sharpton ordered Mc-Kinnon when Anna Phillips sought some information.

Well, McKinnon did talk, to Anna and to me. And what he had to say was clearly not what the reverend had in mind.

TAIBBI: *Did you call us or did we call you?*
PERRY: *No. I called you.*
TAIBBI: *Did you choose to talk to us, or did we somehow entice you to talk to us?*
PERRY: *No. Of my own free will. You did not entice me, and nobody from CBS, nobody . . . I came to you.*
TAIBBI: *Did we offer you any money or have we paid you any money?*
PERRY: *No.*

TAIBBI NARRATION:
McKinnon served as Al Sharpton's right-hand man for most of a year prior to the Brawley case. He says he was with Sharpton when he met with mobsters and other assorted con men . . . was present at shakedowns and other Sharpton capers, and was Sharpton's direct and constant link to the press. But with the Brawley case, he says he all but lived with the man he now calls a "stone swindler, who'll use anybody until he uses him up."

PERRY: *We would be together sometimes eighteen hours a day.*

TAIBBI NARRATION:
It started in early January for Sharpton and Perry . . . and lawyers Alton Maddox and C. Vernon Mason. Dutchess County D.A. William Grady still had the case but was within days of walking. . . .
    Perry talked to Tawana's stepfather, Ralph King.

PERRY: *He told me some white guys had snatched her . . . at the corner, by the gas station, and hit her in the head and took her to a wooded area. And began to rape her, all of them, over and over and over again. And that as far as he knew at the time . . .*
TAIBBI: *Did he say how many men?*
PERRY: *He said "four."*

TAIBBI NARRATION:
And at the Brawley home later that day, he said, Glenda Brawley told him she'd seen evidence in the old family apartment in Wappingers Falls that convinced her . . . and Perry . . . that Tawana spent some time in the apartment when she was supposed to have been in captivity.

TAIBBI: *What did that suggest to you?*
PERRY: *That suggested to me that Tawana was there.*
TAIBBI: *And that Glenda knew it?*
PERRY: *Glenda knew it.*

TAIBBI NARRATION:
The ex-cop and seasoned investigator had his first doubts about the case that day, about the sketchy story the Brawley team had been putting out . . . about six white men, some from law enforcement, repeatedly raping, sodomizing, and maiming Tawana over a four-day period. Driving Alton Maddox back to New York, Perry McKinnon expressed his doubts . . . and warned Maddox.

PERRY: *I said, "Something is wrong with the case, watch it." I said there's no facts, I don't see anything that says that she was raped. This is before we got any medical records. I said, "I don't think there's any evidence for rape, there's something wrong with this. I got a gut feeling that something is wrong with this. I don't think without some more facts, or a lot of facts, that you can prove any rape."*

TAIBBI: *Did you warn Maddox?*

PERRY: *I warned him. I said, "Legally, you're going to be in trouble legally trying to pursue this." He said, "I'm not going to pursue this legally. I'm going to pursue this politically!"*

TAIBBI: *That was his answer?*

PERRY: *He said, "I don't care about no facts."*

TAIBBI: *This is what he says, the first trip up?*

PERRY: *That's right.*

TAIBBI: *What did you think?*

PERRY: *I said . . . I thought it was nuts.*

TAIBBI NARRATION:
McKinnon, the investigator, offered to . . . investigate. Sharpton said, "Good idea."

PERRY: *I said, "Look, you got problems with this situation here. There is no way that you're going to get any groundwork done without an investigator, in that area. Someone from your team is going to have to go up there and do investigative work. You've got to question people, you're going to have to relook at the scene. I would even take her, and as stressful as it may seem, take her and get her to walk through the scene with me again as far as she could remember. 'Cause it's vital."*

TAIBBI: *And his answer was?*

PERRY: *He told me—Sharpton at that time first told me, "I think you're right. I don't want to get caught out here on a limb." Those were his very words.*

TAIBBI NARRATION:
But Maddox, according to McKinnon, said, "Forget about it."

PERRY: He said, "No, I don't think we need no investigation. We don't need no investigation or nothing like that 'cause I know what happened." I said, "How do you know? Who's telling you these things?" He said, "I know, I don't need no investigators. Those crackers done it."

TAIBBI: Did you say, "Listen, I'm trained at this stuff, and if there are perpetrators I can go up there and find them"?

PERRY: That's right!

TAIBBI: Did you make the case . . .

PERRY: Oh yeah, I made the case.

TAIBBI: Tell me what you said.

PERRY: The case was not made at that time to Maddox, but to Sharpton. Because Maddox is difficult. He is bent on the destruction of a system.

TAIBBI NARRATION:
So the die was cast. On January 14 Glenda Brawley told reporter Chris Borgen of the tactic her lawyers devised that today is being repeated. She would go to jail rather than testify before any grand jury—and be the martyr.

GLENDA BRAWLEY, January 14: My lawyers advised me often not to testify. If we have to go to jail then we would have to go to jail.

TAIBBI NARRATION:
At that time Tawana still had not given anybody a detailed narrative account of her alleged ordeal. She told reporter Borgen she wasn't even able to talk to her therapist.

TAWANA BRAWLEY, January 14: It's getting better.

BORGEN: Do you feel that you need help, or do you feel that you're getting help?

TAWANA BRAWLEY: *No, I know I need help. But I don't think I'm getting help that good, not that well. She's not doing a very good job. I shouldn't say she's not doing a very good job because it's partially my fault; I'm not ready to talk.*

TAIBBI NARRATION: *But Sharpton, Maddox, and Mason were beating the drum, leading marches, agitating successfully for a special prosecutor with whom they never intended to cooperate. Perry McKinnon knew he was in a dangerous game.*

PERRY: *This case is not about Tawana. I hope the viewers and the people—whoever sees this segment of it—understands that. I'm telling you, this whole situation is not about Tawana Brawley.*
TAIBBI: *What's it about?*
PERRY: *It's about Mason, Maddox, and Sharpton sort of . . . taking over the town, so to speak.*
TAIBBI: *They told you this?*
PERRY: *Yeah. Their exact words were, "If we beat this, we will be the biggest niggers in New York."*
TAIBBI: *Those were their exact words?*
PERRY: *Yeah, those were their exact words.*
TAIBBI: *Whose exact words?*
PERRY: *Sharpton's.*

(Sound full: marching, demonstration, fade audio)

TAIBBI NARRATION:
They played the press like a child's top, spinning the cameras and microphones this way and that, because, after all, they were supposedly alone with Tawana's explosive story. In fact, what exploded next was the March 13 public accusation that Assistant Dutchess County D.A. Stephen Pagones was one of Tawana's abductors and attackers. Maddox, according to McKinnon, took the other members of the Brawley team by complete surprise.

PERRY: *A lot of things that were said at news conferences were instantaneous, unplanned, out of emotion.*
PHILLIPS: *What was Sharpton's reaction to Alton Maddox when he mentioned Steve Pagones as an alleged
attacker?*
PERRY: *Shock! Because he stared directly at me, 'cause
we had discussed before all these impromptu situations
that no one knew about until the news conferences. . . .*
TAIBBI: *What did Sharpton say to you at that news conference. . . . I mean, now the cat's out of the bag.*
PERRY: *He said, "Did you hear that? Did you hear that?
He said Stephen Pagones!" He said, "I'm going to have
to talk to him, because he keeps saying these things
that I've got to get out, and promote, and live down,
and back up."*
TAIBBI: *Was there ever any evidence, that you heard
discussed, suggesting that Steve Pagones was one of the
attackers?*
PERRY: *In a word? No.*

TAIBBI NARRATION:
*There wasn't evidence for anything at that point, Mc-
Kinnon says. The two lawyers and Sharpton were making it up as they went along. There was no case—only
a media show. McKinnon broke on the day after our
story in early May that residents of Newburgh's Crack
Alley had told investigators . . . and us . . . that Tawana had been in the neighborhood during her disappearance. The Brawley team attacked us, accusing us
of bribery and fraud. But McKinnon believed our story
was true because a week before our story even ran he'd
gone to Newburgh himself and had learned what we'd
learned. And had passed it on to the Brawley advisers.*

PERRY: *When y'all did your report, I found the report
. . . factual. What those kids told you was what was
told to me by a separate bunch of kids. Okay, I don't*

have to be hit in the head by all the bricks of the Empire State Building to say the whole damn neighborhood can't be lying at the same time. One guy told me, "Listen. Tawana was up here. She went to two parties—the day before, the evening before they found her. She was up here, in Newburgh, partying."

TAIBBI NARRATION:
That tore it for Perry McKinnon. He broke from the team. So now he's willing to talk about everything, including the donations that have been pouring in to the Brawley team.

PHILLIPS: *You witnessed some of the money coming in?*
PERRY: *I was a counter, I counted . . .*
PHILLIPS: *What was the biggest take?*
PERRY: *That was about forty-two, forty-three hundred dollars. Right there at Bethany! Because we had an arrangement with the Reverend Jones—he worked out something so that we could have rallies there every Saturday. On several occasions they got as low as fifteen hundred dollars, thirteen hundred dollars. That's about as low as I've seen it.*
TAIBBI: *But forty-three hundred dollars one day?*
PERRY: *And they allegedly gave all of this to the Brawley family. Now, plus, I've seen envelopes of checks and cash coming through the mail from all over the United States.*
TAIBBI: *Big piles of it?*
PERRY: *Piles. Stuffed into big office envelopes. Stuffed in. Mason's had some, Maddox has had some, because people are aware of both lawyers nationally with this case.*
TAIBBI: *Did they continue to solicit money after Sharpton specifically had expressed his own doubts about Tawana's story?*
PERRY: *Yeah.*

TAIBBI: *So they already knew, or suspected, that the story didn't add up, and they continued to solicit money?*
PERRY: *Right.*
TAIBBI: *Did you ever say, "Hey, listen. This could be criminal fraud. I know the statutes"?*
PERRY: *No.*
TAIBBI: *Did you think that in your own mind?*
PERRY: *Yes.*

TAIBBI NARRATION:
He then talked about the roles played by all three of the advisers.

PERRY: *They are frauds from the beginning.*
TAIBBI: *Mason, Maddox, and Sharpton?*
PERRY: *That's right. Not so much Mason. Mason, being in the black community and in the political set, has got to go along with these guys. He's in too deep to pull out now. Mason is a mainstream guy.*
TAIBBI: *But you believed at that point that Maddox and Sharpton had crossed the line where you would not go?*
PERRY: *That's right. I'm not going with a lie. I'm not going with fraud. I'm not going with misleading the people as to the real purpose of having them on marches.*

TAIBBI NARRATION:
And finally, he spoke at length and eloquently about Perry McKinnon's reasons for going public and exposing himself to genuine risk in a very volatile situation.

PERRY: *They're building all the makings . . . of a riot. The weather is hot; there are a lot of young blacks out there who for one reason or another are deprived of the level of life that you and I have. They are easily convinced that these guys are right, because they see the other crowd following.*
TAIBBI: *What do you think happened to Tawana Brawley, off of what you saw from your privileged inside seat?*
PERRY: *What happened to Tawana Brawley? The Ta-*

wana Brawley story may be . . . that there is no Ta-wana Brawley story. The real story is the political agenda of Sharpton, Maddox, and Mason.

Let me say this, and if it's aired, I want Sharpton to understand this. Especially Sharpton, who misunderstood everything every great man tried to teach him. I'm not leaving the movement. I'm leaving Al Sharpton, and his garbage, his rabble-rousing, his bullying, his street mentality. This is the latter part of the twentieth century. I'm not going to lower myself to the street mentality to deal with a crisis. I'm not going to make a crisis, to deal with a crisis.

TAIBBI: *You still think there's work to be done?*

PERRY: *There's work to be done, but administratively, across the table. Everything they say is divisive, and it's not about Tawana Brawley. Never has been, never will be. If they catch anybody, if in fact she was raped, it won't be because of Mason, Sharpton, or Maddox. That's if the incident even took place.*

TAIBBI: *And you don't think it did?*

PERRY: *I have no evidence that it did! I'm a private person, a person who was for Tawana. I was for her, I'm still for her, but as a mature man. As a mature man.*

What am I going to accomplish? The truth. And I don't care, if I'm by myself I'm by myself. Let me tell you something: that's where your manhood starts, with the truth. And everything else is just a building block to make you a bigger man. But a man starts with the truth. It starts with the truth.

TAIBBI NARRATION:

Did Perry McKinnon tell us the truth? We had Victor Kaufman, who has administered over ten thousand polygraph examinations, administer one more. These are the results.

KAUFMAN: *The first relevant question was, "Was Al-*

ton *Maddox interested in the facts of the Brawley
case?"*
TAIBBI: *And his answer was?*
KAUFMAN: *No.*
TAIBBI: *And that answer was truthful?*
KAUFMAN: *Truthful.*
TAIBBI: *Next question?*
KAUFMAN: *Next one, "Did you lie at all today during
your television interview?" Answer, "No."*
TAIBBI: *And that answer was . . . ?*
KAUFMAN: *Truthful. Third, "Did Alfred Sharpton ex-
press doubts about the Brawley case?"*
TAIBBI: *His answer was?*
KAUFMAN: *"Yes." And it came out truthful.*
TAIBBI: *Now has Mr. McKinnon told the truth to us?*
KAUFMAN: *Yes.*
TAIBBI: *Without question?*
KAUFMAN: *Within 90 percent of accuracy.*
TAIBBI: *In terms of your experience as someone who has
conducted ten thousand polygraph examinations, is this
the type of examination and are these the kind of re-
sults that would allow you to be comfortable, testify-
ing, should it ever be brought before a court of law?*
KAUFMAN: *I wouldn't have any problems testifying in a
case like this, on a test like this.*

THIS TIME, when he returned to the newsroom after his on-
set tag, Taibbi acknowledged the applause from his colleagues and threw his head back, pumping a fist toward the
ceiling. He and Phillips met in the middle of it all, all the
cheering, the victory whoops, the screaming phones no one
was willing to answer just yet, a working newsroom of scores
of faces, each face astounded, joyous, at what had just been
accomplished; and the reporter and the producer, partners,
hugged each other for all they were worth, and found those

same partner's eyes that an hour before had been linked in the middle of something quite close to magic, and they didn't say anything, didn't have to, of course, just stood there, holding on to each other, holding on to the moment.

13

"I'm basically a surveillance expert. I bug houses. . . ."

FOR THE FIRST AND ONLY TIME in his New York years, Mike Taibbi, trailed by Don Janney and his camera gear, was ushered without the requisite security checks and searches into the office of the United States Attorney for the Southern District of New York. An hour after the Perry McKinnon story hit the airwaves, Rudolph Giuliani was ready to talk, on the record and on camera.

"Some of the things Mr. McKinnon said were so forthright and detailed," Giuliani said, "that a federal prosecutor would be irresponsible if he didn't follow up on it."

The famed prosecutor, who had convicted the heads of the Mafia's five families and broken new ground in the prosecution of Wall Street's inside traders, whose public image was such that any pronouncement by him carried the weight of his amazing success rate and his unquestioned personal integrity, was now willing to speak at length and in detail about the federal involvement in the Tawana Brawley case and about the performance and behavior of the Brawley advisers.

"They didn't return phone calls, and then they made serious false statements about their dealings with our people," Giuliani said of Sharpton and the lawyers. "They lied outright, yes. They certainly were not acting like people who in good faith wanted to have something investigated."

And if McKinnon's story was true, Taibbi asked, that the advisers continued to solicit and collect money on the basis of a story they knew to be false? There was a range of criminal statutes, mail fraud chief among them, Giuliani answered, that could be at the center of a federal prosecution.

And for the first time, Giuliani publicly discussed the reasons why the FBI quit the case in April.

"The Bureau had come to the conclusion then," he said, "that there had been no rape, no sodomy, no maiming. And not only was there no evidence to support any of those allegations; the facts that were in hand all went the other way: they all tended to prove that the Tawana Brawley story was plainly untrue."

Seventy-five miles away, in the offices of the Brawley Task Force, investigators and staff prosecutors were "absolutely giddy," according to a source, having seen the McKinnon report at noon and then played the tape several times. Said the source, "We kept saying to each other, 'That's a wrap. We can all go home now.' " A subpoena was prepared for Perry McKinnon in New York and served within an hour. He would appear before the grand jury the next day. Robert Abrams released the following statement:

> The statements made today by Perry McKinnon, if true, are astounding and explosive. Mr. McKinnon is quoted as being willing to cooperate with our investigation. If he is, depending upon the quality of the evidence he has to offer us, we'd be prepared to put him before the

Grand Jury and have him tell everything he knows about the Tawana Brawley case.

The statements that have been reported amount to a damning indictment of the motivation and credibility of the Rev. Sharpton, and the attorneys involved in this case, Alton Maddox and Vernon Mason. Perry Mc-Kinnon has participated in the private deliberations of the Brawley advisory team. Indeed, during the two long days of negotiations that I held in this very office with them in February, Sharpton, Mason and Maddox would, all three of them, routinely be joined by Mr. McKinnon for their private, closed-door caucuses. Moreover, at demonstrations in front of the Armory in Poughkeepsie, in the last several months, Mr. McKinnon was observed in close conversations with Brawley family members and advisers.

Clearly, these charges, coming as they do from a high-level intimate of the Brawley advisers, deserve imme-diate and careful attention. If Mr. McKinnon is right, then attorneys Maddox and Mason and Rev. Sharpton have been consciously perpetrating a hoax not only on the black community, but on all the people of the State of New York.

The advisers had a ready-made forum from which to begin their counterattack. At 3:00 P.M. on the afternoon of June 15, a pair of Ruth Tour buses pulled to a stop on the Marcus Garvey Boulevard side of Bethany Baptist Church in Bedford-Stuyvesant. The hundred studio guests for that afternoon's taping of Phil Donahue's program, who'd expected to see a show with the theme "When to Sue Your Doctor," would instead be squeezed into the already jam-packed crowd in Glenda Brawley's "sanctuary." The talk-show host explained that "when the opportunity to interview this woman hiding in this church came up, we grabbed it. Just like anybody else would have."

But by one estimate, Glenda Brawley was "interviewed"

for approximately four minutes of the one-hour national broadcast, the rest of the time taken up by the harangues of Maddox, Sharpton, and Mason, who each expended considerable energy and passion in the task of discrediting Perry McKinnon.

"He's a bald-faced liar and a desperate man," Maddox shouted. "I never discussed any aspect of the case with him."

"They're trying to take this man who drove me around sometimes," Sharpton wailed, "and say he had knowledge of Tawana's story. He never had knowledge, he never talked to Tawana, never heard the story from Glenda. Ya'll can rent a Tom every day to get on TV."

Sharpton ran the show. Despite Donahue's attempts to replicate his signature style of instigating useful dialogue by playing devil's advocate and soliciting challenging questions from callers and members of his live audience, the atmosphere in the church was simply too loaded for that dialogue to take place. Any "challenging" questions—from Donahue or audience members—were shouted down by the Brawley partisans, who were in the overwhelming majority and whose derision and hostility were such that after a while there simply weren't any "challenging" questions posed.

"I think it would be hard to argue that it added anything new to the case," Donahue would later concede to reporters. Sharpton, though, was thrilled.

"I think that the fact that we were able to talk unedited for an hour to the nation and put our points out was of significance because most of the media is biased against us," he said. Sharpton added that the talk-show host told him afterward that "he thinks [the program] got a good response. His ratings will be high, and I think that was his main concern." The ratings were high: the show's 11.8 rating and 30 share (percentage of sets in use) easily wiped out Donahue's competition, the normally dominant Oprah Winfrey show.

But few in the New York press corps were interested in the "unedited" points being put out on the Donahue show by the Brawley team. Instead, in every newsroom, the search was under way in the archives for photos and tapes of one Perry McKinnon, the "hero," the "rebel," the courageous Brawley camp "defector." And, throughout the city and in Albany, reporters didn't have to work very hard at all to obtain official statements of praise for McKinnon and condemnation of the Brawley advisers.

"Just imagine," said Governor Cuomo, "if we'd ended this investigation a week ago, and McKinnon came forward today. Then where would we be? I think it's important we stay with this investigation as long as there's a chance we can get to the truth." Hazel Dukes of the NAACP said, "I'm saddened and angry that we've come to the point where people would use a young woman for their own personal ambitions." Manhattan Borough President David Dinkins suggested publicly, finally, that "if the Brawley story is false, if it turns out to be a total hoax, then it would be harmful generally to the black community."

Reporters assigned to Bethany Baptist Church heard different versions of the first strategy employed by the Brawley advisers and their hard-core followers: McKinnon, the line went, was "just my driver," Sharpton shouted into every available microphone, "and not a very good one at that. He maybe saw Tawana twice." Said Bethany's pastor, the Reverend William Jones, "It's not at all unheard of for whites to buy off blacks at critical junctures in history," a prelude to the advisers' later charge that McKinnon had been paid "hundreds of dollars" by Taibbi and Phillips first for the reporters' Newburgh stories and later for his own interview.

In Channel 2's newsroom that afternoon the phones did not stop ringing. By the time Taibbi returned from his interview with Giuliani he had a stack of more than fifty messages to get through, many of them calls of congratulations from colleagues in other newsrooms in the city or from fellow employees in the Broadcast Center, and Phillips had handled dozens of calls of her own. Other calls came from people offering new tips and leads; one caller, a former employee of Sharpton's National Youth Movement, said she would try and get the reporters together with a number of her former co-workers, whose stories, she promised, would expose Sharpton even more than Perry McKinnon had. A dozen radio talk shows wanted Taibbi and Phillips on the air, *People* magazine wanted interviews; they declined. ABC's "Nightline" asked permission to use the McKinnon story for Ted Koppel's broadcast the next night, with credit, of course. Sagan said fine. McKinnon pieces were prepared for the "CBS Evening News" with Dan Rather and the next day's "CBS Morning News."

Taibbi broke for dinner between the early and late newscasts to join Beverly and meet a childhood friend, Andrea Anastasato. Greek, as she was known to her closest friends, had fled Greenwich Village in the early seventies, seeking and finding a free-form life in Key West, Florida. She worried constantly about her old friends, Taibbi among them, who'd stayed behind, in the mainstream, in the city; and as luck would have it, she returned to town to see him and other old friends on the day the Perry McKinnon story exploded. Sitting in a Lower East Side Japanese restaurant, she fretted aloud over the danger she perceived Taibbi to be in. Though he insisted it was McKinnon who courted and faced the risks, Greek would not be persuaded. Finally, she took a trinket from her charm bracelet, a talisman from her youth, and extracted a promise from Taibbi that he'd carry it with him for the duration of the Tawana Brawley story.

"It's an evil eye," she explained, holding the gold-wrapped gem up to his eyes. "In my culture, it wards off evil spirits. I believe in it, and so should you."

Taibbi had little patience for the occult, or for dreamy speculation about topics ranging from life on other planets to the existence of beneficent spirits. But he studied the gold/blue talisman, and tucked it carefully in his wallet. Beverly said she'd have a chain made, and she did. And, later, he wore it.

THE ORIGINAL SEVENTEEN-MINUTE, TWENTY-SECOND piece ran at noon, five, six, and eleven, augmented by reaction stories, the ratings for each broadcast going through the roof. Several members of the CBS high command, in Los Angeles for the annual CBS affiliates meeting, took early flights east and caught the last broadcast. When Taibbi and Phillips arrived in the newsroom the next morning, planning editor Paul Fleuranges handed them a message he said he'd taken personally, and urged the reporters to return the call immediately.

"This is a joke, right?" Phillips said, studying the message.

"We'll find out soon enough," Taibbi answered, finding two adjacent phones and dialing the four in-house digits.

"This is Mike Taibbi from local," Taibbi said to the secretary who answered the phone. "I'm returning Mr. Tisch's call. My partner, Anna Phillips, is also on the line."

Like so many others who'd seen the Perry McKinnon story, CBS chief executive officer Laurence Tisch wanted to commend McKinnon's bravery and eloquence and compliment the reporters on their work in helping to bring his story to light; and, like those other callers, Tisch wanted to know where the story was going to go from there.

"I don't know, Mr. Tisch," Phillips said. "We've had so many calls, so many new tips and leads on areas we've been working on—like how much money's been donated and where the money is now. . . ."

"And of course, McKinnon's on the way up to the grand jury in Poughkeepsie already," Taibbi added, "and with Giuliani and the Organized Crime Strike Force waiting in the wings, there are any number of stories that could develop just as a result of his testimony and any evidence he brings in."

Tisch asked questions for another ten minutes—the same questions, Phillips thought, smiling, that had been raised by so many other people who were captivated in one way or another by the Brawley story and now wondered about McKinnon's credibility and his ultimate effect on the case.

The reporters worked through the morning, returning calls and leafing through the morning papers, cleared by Sagan the night before to work on follow-ups while Chris Borgen covered McKinnon's grand jury appearance in Poughkeepsie. It was clear from the treatment of the story in each paper that the advisers' original strategy of merely diminishing or dismissing McKinnon's role wasn't going to get the job done. Every paper published pictures from its own archives of McKinnon doing anything but "driving" Sharpton. The *New York Times* front-page picture showed McKinnon on the phone, flanked by Sharpton and Mason, during a break in the February "negotiations" with Bob Abrams. *Newsday* showed McKinnon leading a Kennedy Airport demonstration in place of Al Sharpton, who had earlier been arrested for trying to block a highway entrance. An upstate paper highlighted McKinnon in the background behind Governor Cuomo on the day the governor and the Brawley team announced a "break" in the stalemate over the appointment of Robert Abrams as special prosecutor.

Every local television station ran McKinnon stories; reporter Tim Minton of Channel 7 had even found McKinnon, in Brooklyn, and in a brief sidewalk interview Perry repeated his most damaging allegations.

And *Newsday*'s Ron Howell did some digging on his own, locating movement leaders including Jitu Weusi, vice chairman of the National Black United Front, who blasted the advisers' McKinnon strategy to bits.

McKinnon was a "trusted aide-de-camp" and "confidante," Weusi told Howell. "At one meeting I attended with Sharpton and others, McKinnon was more or less running the place. He sat in on all the sessions. I've known Sharpton for a number of years, and this was one of the more competent guys he's had with him." *Newsday*, as did several other papers, published large segments of the transcript of Channel 2's McKinnon story verbatim. The editorial and Op Ed page treatment of the McKinnon revelations was fairly consistent from paper to paper: in the contest between Perry McKinnon on Channel 2 and Glenda Brawley and the family advisers on the "unedited" Donahue show, McKinnon was the hands-down winner.

"It was clear," wrote Dorothy Rabinowitz of the *New York Post*, "that no new noise issuing from the Brawley troupe was going to compare with McKinnon talking." There was the "unforgettable moment," she said, "in which McKinnon said he was leaving Sharpton and 'his garbage, his street mentality, the bully mentality.' And he wanted, as a 'mature man,' to get at the truth. Now phrases like 'mature man' are not exactly emotional bell-ringers: not in the rhetorical ballpark with high fliers like 'human dignity,' 'justice' and the like. Still, those simple words, in McKinnon's mouth, carried devastating weight—as did the tersely passionate comment which followed: 'That's where your manhood starts—with the *truth*.' "

The phones kept ringing. Phillips took a call at one point from Torre Garcia, a friend from her days in Sales at Black Rock.

"What is it, six years?" Phillips asked. Garcia, she'd learned back then, had attended St. Mary's High School in Jersey City and knew a number of Phillips's nieces. The two women had socialized a bit, shopped for shoes together, that sort of thing.

"Yeah," Garcia said. "It must be six years. I saw you on television yesterday, in that story, and I told my boyfriend, 'I know that girl!' "

They caught up on old times, talked about the Brawley story, talked about getting together again.

"I'm working temporary now," Garcia said, "but I'll be looking for a permanent job soon. I'll be getting married to my fiancé."

Phillips offered to write a letter of recommendation if her old friend needed one. Then she saw Taibbi waving at her frantically. Again. She hung up.

"I don't know," Taibbi said, fingering the single page of notes he'd taken during his last call. "Guy named Tyrone, calling from a subway station phone. I could hear the trains pull in and out, screeching. He says he's pissed at a guy he did a job for—he was just a driver and carted some equipment around—because the guy never paid him. But here's the punchline: he says the guy he worked for was actually doing a job for Sharpton. Bugging the lawyers. Yeah," he said, taking note of Phillips's startled expression. "He says Sharpton hired the guy to bug the others 'in case the whole case falls apart.' He says Sharpton told his guy, 'This whole case is bull, but it's too late now.' "

"Holy shit," Phillips said. "What else did he give you?"

"Not much," Taibbi said, studying the few notes he'd taken. "Wouldn't give me a phone number, wouldn't even give me the name of the guy he worked for, except to say he's known as Sammy and he hangs out on this block in Jersey City. Didn't think Sammy would talk to us."

Phillips took the sheet of notes and studied Taibbi's scrawl. "What do we do?" she asked.

Taibbi shrugged. Sagan was out of town for the day.

"I can call Colloff and the lawyers," Taibbi answered finally. "If it's true, this is the end of it. The story's over. If it's true," he said again.

Roger Colloff said he'd be down in the newsroom in an hour or so. Taibbi picked up the morning papers again, looked for the columns he hadn't read yet, and soon was lost in a provocative piece by *Daily News* columnist Juan Gonzalez headlined "Tawana Tale & the 'Hideous Heart.' "

National issue or national hoax, Gonzalez wrote, the case "has stirred deep anger and bitterness among whites and blacks in this state." No matter that the Brawley advisers might have known all along that Tawana Brawley was not abducted, raped, and covered with dog excrement by six white men. . . . It is enough, Gonzalez wrote, "that there is a pattern of blacks being brutalized or killed by whites and of their killers going free, and of faceless grand juries repeatedly investigating, and then absolving, those killers." The more Mason, Maddox, and Sharpton "are vilified and attacked by the white establishment, the more poor and disaffected blacks rally to their side." Could it be, questioned Gonzalez, "that as Edgar Allan Poe wrote in a classic 19th Century short story, the beating of a 'hideous heart' is driving the judicial system of New York crazy in an effort to prove its innocence? The 'hideous hearts' ticking under the floorboards of this state's legal system are from all those dead black bodies that never got justice, and for whom law enforcement never gave a damn. The deafening clatter is driving New York's legal system crazy, and making its pleas of innocence nearly impossible to hear."

Taibbi read the Gonzalez column again. He thought of the comments made to E. R. Shipp of the *New York Times* by civil rights lawyer William Kunstler—that "the big issue is the fairness of the criminal justice system toward black people . . . not Tawana herself." It doesn't matter, Kunstler said, whether Tawana's story was a hoax. "The thing is on a larger plane now. It's not a legal issue: it's a political issue."

The beating of a "hideous heart" was something, conceptually, that made the passions of the throngs at Bethany Baptist—the Congregation of the Blessed Moment, after all—suddenly understandable. The congregation *wanted* Tawana's story to be true, certainly, but needed to believe only that it could be true, because such things had happened so often, and recently enough. It would take more than Perry McKinnon, Taibbi knew then, to dispel that belief, to quiet the beating of that hideous heart. After the excitement of the day before, the newsroom seemed very quiet.

"YOU GET TO PLAY news director," Taibbi said to Colloff, the two of them closeted in Sagan's office. Channel 2's general manager, who had steadfastly supported his reporters throughout their Brawley coverage, offered an enigmatic smile. A lawyer and a veteran of CBS battles, including the messy aftermath of the network's controversial documentary on General William Westmoreland, Colloff had maintained daily contact with Sagan over the direction the story was taking. In fact, there'd been dozens of weekend calls, calls at night, at the break of dawn. Now, the day after the Perry McKinnon coup, Taibbi was describing a new angle which, if true, would effectively end the anguish of the Tawana Brawley story.

"I don't know, Mike," Colloff began. "Is there any way you and Anna can follow this up? Did this Tyrone give you anything else to work with besides a first name and an address?"

Taibbi shook his head, thinking. "What are the chances," he asked rhetorically, "of our staking this guy out, a guy whose name we don't know and who we couldn't identify if we saw him, and coming away with either an interview or the tapes, or both?" He didn't wait for Colloff's answer. "Nil," he said. "Chances are, even if we find the right guy, we drive him underground and lose any chance anyone might have of bringing the story to light. It's not like we have subpoena power or the ability to get a warrant."

Colloff asked again about the tipster. "Did he *sound* believable?"

Taibbi shrugged. "He said he was pissed and he sounded pissed, but beyond that I can't say." A thought occurred to him then. "Look, Roger. How do we know this guy only called me? How do we know he's not so pissed at Sammy that he's diming him out to everybody he can think of, other reporters or even the feds?"

"And?" Colloff was going to let the reporter make up his own mind.

"Well. Maybe it's worth a call. I'm not gonna blow it. This could be the most important story of all of them."

Taibbi picked up the phone and dialed the direct number for a federal source who'd been tracking the recent developments in the Brawley case and who was directly knowledgeable about Al Sharpton's work the previous fall as a federal informant. Anything about Sharpton bugging the two lawyers? he asked. He described the tip from Tyrone. The source said he'd check to see if his office had received a similar tip. Taibbi didn't ask for a call back, and the source didn't offer one.

"Now what?" Colloff mused aloud, after Taibbi had hung up the phone.

"I really don't know," Taibbi answered. "But if they already had it, I'm sure I'll find out about it. And if there's anything there, they'll find out about it."

"What else have you got going?" Colloff asked.

Taibbi thought for a minute. "The money. The stories going around about Sharpton and Glenda depositing something around a million bucks in her credit union account are bullshit, but we've confirmed that she's cashed some third-party checks in some fairly large amounts—in excess of five grand, and less than ten. That sort of thing. There may be a way to get closer to that story."

Colloff nodded slowly. "And what about McKinnon?"

Taibbi shook his head. McKinnon suddenly, improbably, seemed to be ancient history. "Perry's gonna get hammered," he said. "He's gonna take a beating."

IT STARTED ON THAT NIGHT'S EDITION of "Nightline" with Ted Koppel. Despite the renowned journalist's unparalleled ability to control his own interview setting, Sharpton and Vernon Mason demonstrated their own skill, as they would on every talk show, at "getting their points out" on unedited live broadcasts. They repeated the fictions that "there'd been no rape test, because Tawana had been picked up as homeless," that they'd "seen FBI reports identifying the assailants," that "all the tests proved Tawana wasn't faking." They said, again and again, that the first two prosecutors in the case had "paid off the NAACP lawyers . . . and covered up for the suspects, a state trooper and an assistant district attorney," and that, according to Sharpton, "we have the facts and the evidence to prove [who] did this."

But, said Sharpton, "Mr. Cuomo and Mr. Abrams has done everything but call these people before the grand jury; they've even got an ex-friend of mine and tried to make him my aide, who's a very sick man—his family will expose that in the morning—to try to discredit a story he doesn't even know."

Koppel picked up on the reference to McKinnon, part of whose Channel 2 interview had been included in a recap of the case by reporter Jeff Greenfield at the beginning of the broadcast.

"Now, Mr. Sharpton," Koppel said, "you're saying that tomorrow morning Perry McKinnon's family is going to reveal what?"

"That he has some mental problems, Ted," Sharpton answered. "But I don't want to waste our six and a half minutes on all that—"

"No," Koppel interjected, "I'm not going to waste six and a half minutes."

"Fine," Sharpton snapped. "He has some mental problems. Mr. McKinnon has some history of medical problems in terms of mental disorders—"

Mason cut in. "Perry . . . has mental problems over a period of years. His family has tried to assist him with that. But we're going to go public tomorrow with that, to show that this man, who Bob Abrams has embraced as the key witness in this case, is going to be discredited himself."

Anna Phillips, watching the broadcast at home, phoned Taibbi immediately. Her partner, exhausted, had dozed off, and turned the set on in time to see "Nightline" dissolve into a highly uncharacteristic shouting match, with Sharpton, Mason, and Howard Beach prosecutor Charles Hynes all trying to squeeze in their final points while the host admonished, ". . . now we can all try and talk at once and guarantee that none of us will be heard . . ."

"Get with Janney," Phillips told Taibbi. "I've called Perry. Sharpton and Mason are saying his family is going to expose him in the morning on his mental problems. You're going to have to ask him about his mental stability, ask him what family member they could be talking about."

There was a police detail outside McKinnon's Brooklyn

apartment. McKinnon met Taibbi on the street along with his brother, the Reverend Gregory McKinnon, and his sister-in-law, Marion. McKinnon, nervous and strung out to exhaustion, said on camera that he'd voluntarily sought treatment for stress after the last of his three combat tours in Vietnam and had had no problems since then. His relatives vouched for his integrity and stability.

And the next morning the advisers trotted out a man in his sixties named Alvin McKinnon, who said he was Perry's first cousin. His only specific charge to back up the advisers' claim that the thirty-nine-year-old Perry was a "basket case" after Vietnam was that "Perry talks a good game, but he doesn't follow up."

The Brawley team had just begun. Over the next two days they charged that Perry McKinnon was a bigamist, a forger, a wife beater, a man who "hated blacks," who had raped a white woman, who refused to pay child support, who had joined the Mafia, who "had killed and would kill again," and who had "beaten a child . . . nearly to death." Before each "announcement" the advisers said they would provide "documentation" to support each charge. They provided nothing. At the end of the assault, Alton Maddox offered the most improbable, unlikely condemnation of all. He never spoke to McKinnon, he said, "because frankly, he smells bad. He has a bad odor, and I chose not to be around him or near him." Several papers and television stations quoted Maddox.

Taibbi and Phillips had been compelled to file reports that essentially defended McKinnon and dismantled the advisers' attacks against him.

Then, late Friday afternoon at the end of another long week, Phillips tapped Taibbi on the shoulder and whispered loudly that he should step to the cubicle next door, where Chris Borgen was on the phone. Sharpton had called Borgen, out of the blue. Phillips had snatched the recording device she used at times to tape telephone interviews and had affixed it to Borgen's phone.

It was an odd call; Sharpton was conciliatory, even nervous.

"I'll be honest, I'm not going to lie," Sharpton told Borgen. "I thought that Mike was doing this out of a lot of, whatever. . . . But maybe Mike and Anna went this far because they thought they had somebody that was really inside, 'cause they see him with us all the time."

Sharpton insisted that *he'd* never charged that Taibbi had paid for any stories—that it was Mason who'd made the allegation. "But I'm saying maybe I created a relationship that McKinnon used to mislead Mike into thinking an inside guy was saying this was all a hoax. I'm saying that maybe Mike really thinks his reporting is true."

"I think he does," Borgen said. "I think he believes exactly what he's reporting."

"Yeah, but, but, but, Chris . . ." Sharpton stammered. "If he's dealing with someone who believes what he's saying it's easy to pass a lie-detector test. When McKinnon says, 'I think these guys have a political agenda. I think these guys wouldn't let me go after the facts,' all that's true! But he didn't know what Tawana's story was!"

Sharpton insisted he "absolutely" still believed Tawana's story, but that "in the long run, I may owe Mike Taibbi a big apology. Mike may of just got suckered in by McKinnon. I honestly believed until now that Taibbi just had a hard-on for this case, and for us for some reason, that maybe he thought we were really perpetrating a hoax. But maybe he doesn't have racist motives—and if I find that to be true I'll be man enough to come to him and to Roger Colloff and say I was wrong."

Taibbi and Phillips listened to the tape of the fifteen-minute phone call several times, once with Colloff while huddled in Sagan's office. It was a different Al Sharpton, without question. Something was up. They wondered what had prompted the call.

"Anything on Sammy?" Colloff asked.

"Nothing yet," Taibbi answered.

When the reporters left Sagan's office a few minutes later, a young desk assistant named Linda LaVergne sidled up to them and mentioned casually that a fellow named Sammy had just called for Taibbi, but that she hadn't known the reporter was in the newsroom.

"You what!" Taibbi boomed. "We were right here, I've got a beeper on, I'm *always* reachable! Shit, what did he say!" He pulled LaVergne into Sagan's office, where she reacted to the outburst by dissolving into tears. When she recovered she said Sammy had sounded upset.

"He said he knew that Taibbi was looking for him, and other reporters and investigators, too. That's all," she said, sobbing again. "He said he wanted to talk to Taibbi."

The reporters waited an extra hour before leaving the office. They took LaVergne aside and Taibbi apologized: It wasn't her fault, they explained. Everybody was under enormous pressure. She said she understood.

Sammy didn't call again. Taibbi left specific instructions for everyone on the desk to reach him at his weekend house on Buzzards Bay, should anything happen. Anything at all. He told Phillips to stay in touch, stay close to home, be ready to move. Beverly was waiting in the car on West Fifty-seventh Street. They made the long trip north, Beverly driving.

Taibbi slept poorly that night, and on Saturday night slept barely an hour before snapping his eyes open, awake for good. There was a 3:00 A.M. tide in Buzzards Bay; Beverly had bought him an early birthday present, a new Penn surf-casting rig, and he hadn't tried it out yet. The blues were in, they always were this time in June, and the week before a few striped bass were brought in above the thirty-three-inch limit, keepers. He grabbed his gear, hustled his springer spaniel into his truck, and drove five miles to the peninsula where the fishing was always good on the turn of the tide. He was early, though. After a dozen desultory casts he wedged his rod handle in the crook of a couple of rocks, thinking, listening to his dog slap around in the shallows of the gentle breakers.

Other fishermen arrived and soon enough were beaching snapper blues. Someone caught a small bass, held it up briefly, and released it. There were some curious looks when Taibbi left, empty-handed. The fishing was still good.

When he got home it was barely 5:00 A.M. Still too early to phone Phillips, he thought. He called to his spaniel, and they walked slowly down to the end of the Point, a quarter-mile stroll to the docks where a fishing fleet of some sixty boats tied up. Taibbi and his wife knew all the boats by heart, who skippered which boat, where each lay along the slips. Standing at the docks, first light coming up over the harbor, he noticed with a start that something was wrong. One boat was out of place, a small bay scalloper that was usually moored on the other side of the channel but now was tied up awk-wardly, as though it had put in for emergency repairs, along-side what the locals called the mud dock. Taibbi walked over to the intruding vessel and studied the name on her transom for a long minute before the irony kicked in. The boat was named *Risky Business.*

"*Risky Business,*" Taibbi repeated to himself several times, walking back to his house. At 6:00 A.M. sharp, he dialed Phillips's number in New Jersey. She was awake too, she said: had been awake for an hour or so, lying in bed, eyes open.

"Listen," Taibbi said. "Call Michael Heard. There's the Sharpton call, the call from Sammy. We've gotta try something. Why don't you and Michael go over there this after-noon, a real gentle surveillance? Get out of the car now and then, take a stroll. Give him a chance to see you, or send Michael in to try him. If he really wants to talk to us, if that's what it's about, he'll reach out. I'll take an early train."

"All right," Phillips agreed. "We'll give it a shot."

Phillips sat in bed, pondering the implications of Taibbi's phone call. She'd reminded her partner of the reasons why they'd stayed away from Sammy to that point—that they only had a first name and half an address, that their chances of coming away with anything useful and of not blowing it completely were frighteningly small. Now it would be her play, hers alone, Taibbi a couple of hundred miles away. She called Heard, gave him directions to her house.

"Bring your camera," she instructed. "If we do see him, let's get some stills at least."

They waited until 1:00 P.M. to head for Jersey City, Phillips driving. When they got close to Sammy's address she improvised the plan.

"We'll do one drive-by," she said, "and if there's anybody around we'll park around the block and you make the first approach." Lately, because of her work on the high-profile Brawley case, she'd been as recognizable in some places as Taibbi. Sure enough, there was a group of preteen girls in the middle of the block on Oak Street where she believed Sammy lived. Driving slowly, she copied down the license plates of several cars parked on the street.

A few minutes later, Heard approached the group of girls, asking if anybody knew where Sammy lived. One girl, in a bright yellow outfit, pointed to number 37. Know what kind of car he drives? Heard asked. A light blue one, she answered. Sauntering away slowly, Heard joined Phillips in the car, briefed her on what he'd learned, and they found a good surveillance position in a church parking lot across the street and sat. After an hour, Phillips, impatient, drove to the home of a New Jersey law-enforcement source and informed him that if he was going to stay around the house she might need his help before the day was out. She and Heard drove back to Jersey City, parked again in their surveillance location. They waited, watched. They saw the girl in yellow again, left the car, and approached her. Had Sammy returned? they asked. Yeah, she said, pointing to his light blue car. Phillips studied the car, memorized the license plate. "I'll walk around the block, you make the approach," she instructed Heard. When she came around again, Heard was standing next to a short, stocky man who, hands dug deep into his pockets, seemed nervous, distracted, looking up and down the street. Heard and the stranger were standing on the steps of the house at

37 Oak Street. As she fired off several shots on the still camera, Heard walked back toward her car, the short man suddenly gone from view.

"Let's pull out of here," Heard said, sliding his gaunt frame into the passenger seat. "He's suspicious. I gave him the line about wanting to buy some stereo equipment, but he got jumpy when I called him Sammy. Said nobody called him Sammy except for a few people. He said a lot of people were looking for him, he was in a lot of trouble. Then some lady stuck her head out of the door and started interrogating me, and then she was screaming and yelling and I said, 'Shit, got to go,' and he ran inside."

Phillips drove home after debriefing Heard and calling her cop friend. "We can get him," she told Heard; "forget about the soft surveillance." When she and Heard got home she called Sagan and Taibbi's apartment in New York. No answer either place, just machines. She then submitted willingly to a tough grilling by her husband, a seasoned newsman himself. There's no story, Lionel insisted, without Sammy. She knew she'd have to go back to Jersey City, and soon.

When the phone rang, Phillips expected it to be Taibbi or Sagan. Instead it was her cop friend. The plate she'd asked him to run came back to a Torre Garcia. "Torre Garcia!" Phillips shouted aloud, hanging up the phone without even saying good-bye. So it's *not* just a coincidence that Torre called me a few days ago, after six years! She thought back to their phone conversation, recalled Torre's interest in the Brawley case and in Phillips's coverage of it.

"Let's go," she said to Heard. "We're going back."

But before she could leave her house the phone rang twice more. Sagan said he'd help with crew arrangements, and instructed her to stay in touch no matter how late it went. Then Don Crawford on the weekend assignment desk called to say, "Someone named Samuel McClease called, and says you probably want to talk to him. He says you were by his house today." No, Crawford said, a little unnerved by the urgency in Phillips's string of questions: McClease didn't leave a number. Yeah, Crawford said, if he calls again I'll patch him through to you.

A half hour later, Anna Phillips was standing in her family room, holding the phone, talking to Samuel McClease. Yes, McClease said, Torre Garcia was his fiancée. No, he didn't want to talk about his "situation": Channels 4 and 9 had already been by, but he'd already been served with two federal subpoenas, and . . .

"Look, Samuel," Phillips cut in, "the guy who ratted you out to us obviously ratted you out to a lot of other people, and he told us what your situation is. I just want you to tell us what you told the feds, and what you'll tell the grand jury."

"It's dangerous," McClease whined. "There are people who might want to kill me—"

"Well, I'm gonna talk to you, Samuel," Phillips insisted. "Taibbi's gonna be here in a few minutes, you can wait till then to tell the story, but I'm not taking 'no' for an answer. I don't give a fuck what you say, I'm gonna come to your door, I'm gonna ask for you."

McClease laughed then, nervously. "Torre told me you'd be the most persistent." He paused, his anxious breathing audible on the phone. "All right," he finally said. "I'll meet you."

"Meet me on the corner of Oak and Martin Luther King Boulevard," Phillips instructed. She knew Jersey City. "I'll work out a place we can talk."

Phillips and Michael Heard showed up at the appointed time and place, and McClease was there. Damn, she thought to herself. Where's Taibbi? Nobody'd heard from him yet.

Taibbi was nowhere near to joining her. The brutal heat of the spring and summer of 1988 had been causing all kinds of problems for the bridges along the Amtrak route between Boston and New York, and on the afternoon of June 19 the railroad bridge over the Connecticut River in Old Saybrook was stuck in the up position for fully three hours, its gearing swollen to immobility, Taibbi fretting along with several hundred other passengers who sat and waited, the air-conditioning turned off, while a repair crew lumbered over from New London.

By the time the reporter reached his Manhattan apartment it was nearly 11:00 P.M. and there were twenty-one messages on his answering machine, some from Phillips, several from Paul Sagan, most from the assignment desk repeating that Anna had "connected" and instructing that as soon as he called the office, a spare car or Don Janney, if he hadn't left yet, would be sent down to him. Janney, who had been anxiously waiting for the signal to move, raced down to the Village and, screaming at Taibbi to get in the car, tore through the Holland Tunnel and radared his way to the last location Phillips had phoned in. Bouncing over the battered streets of Jersey City, doubling back and tearing up one-way streets, they finally spotted Phillips on a corner, the thin frame of Michael Heard nearby and another black man, short and stocky, shifting his feet nervously, hands dug deep in his pockets. It was raining lightly, not much more than a mist expelled by the oppressive humidity.

"We'll do the formal introductions later," Phillips said edgily as Taibbi approached her. "Drive with me and Sammy. Michael can ride with Janney, and they can follow us."

McClease led them to the apartment of a friend, a fashion model as it turned out, who was enormously patient with her middle-of-the-night intruders. Janney and Heard sat on a couch in one of the unlit corners of the apartment. Phillips and Taibbi sat facing McClease, who was sweaty, jumpy. He looked mildly terrified.

"Show me the subpoenas," Taibbi said after Phillips had briefed him quickly on the little she'd learned during her long wait. He read through the documents once, surprised at the specific nature of the materials and information McClease was commanded to produce by Assistant U.S. Attorney Federico Virella: ". . . all originals and copies of tape recordings

and other forms of surveillance work performed by agreement with Al Sharpton and the Friends of the National Youth
Movement."

Taibbi walked over to Heard, asking him to copy the information in the subpoenas word for word, and then, kicking
off his shoes and pacing slowly, he nodded to Phillips and
they launched into the most careful and comprehensive version of the whistleblower speech they'd ever given. Phillips
picked up every cue, was *hard* with McClease, making certain he understood the vicious counterattack he would have
to withstand from both the advisers and that segment of the
black community who were still "true believers" in the
Brawley cause and case and who were already riled beyond
imagining by the revelations of Perry McKinnon. McClease
kept nodding, insisting he understood all of that and had
thought of it often in the weeks during which he'd wrestled
with the idea of coming forward.

The reporters studied him, hoping their senses were sharp
enough, despite their exhaustion and the enormous events of
the past weeks, to see clearly, hear the nuances in Mc-
Clease's voice, and assess accurately whether he had it in
him to either tell the truth or take them for an awful ride.
They exchanged glances when their "warning" speech was
over.

"The truth is, Samuel," Taibbi said, "if you're going to tell
your story to the feds, to a grand jury, then you and your
family and anybody you care about are gonna be at risk anyway. Word'll get out, there'll be speculation, *wild* speculation if what's happened up to now in the Brawley story is
any indication. You talk to us on camera, on the record, just
tell the story straight, at least it's out there in your version.
Like McKinnon. I'm not saying it'll minimize the risk, the
dangers; but it won't make things worse. You'll be in the
system, and though I can't say and wouldn't suggest what
the feds will do with you, whether they'll offer immunity,
you'll at least be protected and they'll be sensitive to the
need for protection for Torre and anybody else you name.

Standard practice. McKinnon had a police detail outside his apartment within an hour of our report. You're walking into this with your eyes open, if you intend to honor the subpoena. Talking to us won't hurt, and it could help."

McClease stared hard at his two inquisitors, flew a nervous glance at Janney and the camera in the dark corner of the far end of the room. He looked back at Taibbi, closed his eyes deliberately and opened them again, nodding slowly.

"All right, tell us your story, Sam," Taibbi said. "No camera. Not for the record. Not yet."

McClease was persuasive, even though he didn't have a touch of Perry McKinnon's dignity; in fact, he admitted from the jump that he'd been engaged for years in what could accurately be called criminal activity, and he looked the part. He described the types of "surveillance" jobs he'd taken on, the equipment he'd used, the methods and manning certain jobs required. He said Al Sharpton had hired him in an uptown Manhattan sidewalk meeting on February 3.

" 'What are you gonna do?' " he quoted Sharpton as asking him. "Anything you want me to do," he said he'd answered. Sharpton said he'd be in touch, and twelve days later, contact made, a McClease accomplice, going in as part of Sharpton's ever-shifting entourage, "dropped a wire" in each of three locations: Sharpton's own rented house on St. Mark's Place in Park Slope, Brooklyn, and the home and office of C. Vernon Mason.

"He would set up a certain scenario," McClease said of his "employer." "Sharpton would be the 'bait,' so when they said everything's wrong with the Brawley case it'd be on tape. He told me, 'The game is over. The ball's gonna drop. I got to cover myself. This situation is getting out of hand.' "

McClease said the most damaging statement in the eight hours of taped conversations was a relatively short segment in which one of the lawyers—he didn't know which one— said, "This case is bull. But it's too late for us to get out."

"Look," McClease said. "I knew that this was all a game to them, a political farce. It was all being done for personal

gain only. Tawana wasn't anything to them. It was just 'she.
. . .' They said they knew there was no rape, no kidnapping.
That it was a four-day party—including partying with a police officer. A white police officer." McClease said that in
the sections of the tapes he'd listened to there was never any
discussion among the Brawley advisers of the legal case, "only
which people they would target next, who they'd call a racist, and getting the crowd to follow them."

Sam McClease said Sharpton agreed to pay $11,000 for his
services, which he'd never paid. He said he knew and would
admit that he'd been involved in illegal acts, but that he would
produce the tapes and would testify before a federal grand
jury, as commanded.

He sounded believable enough, the reporters agreed later,
when he said it was "conscience" that moved him to come
forward.

He said Sharpton had called him the previous Friday afternoon, and set up a meeting and picked him up, driving "all
over Manhattan."

"He asked me, 'You gonna fuck me?' " McClease said. "I
said 'no.' "

Friday, the reporters thought simultaneously. The Sharpton call to Borgen.

Phillips motioned to Janney, who set up his camera in
minutes and clicked it on. It was three o'clock in the morning; Phillips, in a casual white summer outfit, and Taibbi,
barefoot and wearing jeans and a faded black cotton shirt,
leaned forward on Janney's command.

McClease took a deep breath and said, "Here goes. This is
it, isn't it?"

"Speed," Janney said softly.

"Mr. McClease," Taibbi began formally. "What do you do
for a living?"

"I'm basically a surveillance expert," McClease said, his
voice barely above a whisper. "I bug houses."

And then he told his whole story again. His story was exactly the same, on camera, the second time around.

"What about the tapes?" Taibbi asked, when the interview was over.

McClease said they were in a "safe" location in Long Branch, New Jersey. An hour down and an hour back, a little time in between to "take care of some things" with his "partner" before retrieving the tapes in question.

"Call him," Taibbi suggested. "Right now."

McClease paused a beat, then went into his friend's bedroom and huddled in the hallway outside with a red telephone, dialed an eleven-digit number, and spoke for several minutes.

"I won't be able to get them until noon tomorrow," he said. "My partner can't meet me till then, and I'm due at the grand jury at ten A.M. What do I do?"

"We will not suggest or ask that you defy a lawful subpoena," Taibbi answered, "but you've been commanded to produce the tapes. I'm sure if you called Virella and told him you couldn't produce them until the afternoon he'd allow a delay; it's the tapes he wants."

"And then," Phillips added, "if there was a way we could meet you and dub at least some of what's on them, we'd want to do that. Without interfering with your responsibility to the U.S. Attorney's office."

McClease nodded numbly, asking only that the reporters agree to forgo broadcasting anything about the story until, say, two in the afternoon, because he had "some things to take care of."

Taibbi raised a hand, anticipating a description of "evidence" from other jobs that McClease and his "partner" intended to dispose of. "We don't want to know about any of that. We're not gonna hear about it. We don't want any knowledge of anything about your criminal activity, just the job you did for Sharpton. But we'll agree to hold off broadcasting anything, not even any promos."

McClease appeared to be stressed to the breaking point. He said he would agree to a polygraph examination if the reporters could work it out.

"I trust you guys," he said finally, not all that convincingly. "But I gotta call Torre. She's bullshit at me for all this—for talking to the feds, and you guys."

From the sound of McClease's half of the conversation, Torre Garcia was indeed furious at him. He pleaded and cajoled, tried a few soothing assurances, to no avail. She'd hung up on him, he explained.

"We want to hear the tapes," Phillips repeated when they dropped him off a half-block down from Garcia's house. They watched him walk to the house and then drove up slowly as he rang the bell and banged forlornly on the door. When they pulled alongside he walked over and said, "She won't let me in. I don't even have the keys to the car."

Phillips offered to put him up in a motel for the night, but he shook his head. Yes, he said, he'd still hold up his end of the bargain the next day, but for the time being he'd just wait Torre out. She'll come around, he said. When the reporters left him, Sam McClease was sitting on the steps, in the now-steady rain, sobbing.

AT FIVE IN THE MORNING Phillips called Paul Sagan and briefed him on what she and Taibbi had. Three hours later the two reporters and Sagan screened the interview with Samuel McClease. Everything seemed to make sense. Sharpton had served a voluntary hitch as a federal informant, and might reasonably be assumed to have developed a knowledge of and perhaps an affection for surveillance techniques. There was his strange call to Chris Borgen on Friday, Torre Garcia's call to Phillips, Sammy's to Taibbi after claiming he'd met with Sharpton. There were the subpoenas from the office of the sharpest prosecutor anyone in the room had ever known. The idea of Sam McClease being a Sharpton plant, a setup designed to entrap the very reporters whose Perry McKinnon story had rocked the Brawley camp, seemed not only far-fetched but beyond Sharpton's capabilities.

"I'd like to have the tapes, or at least something from the tapes," Sagan said.

"So would we," Taibbi answered dully. "Maybe we'll get 'em, maybe not. But for now, what we know is that Mc-Clease is a witness who's sworn out statements twice to federal investigators, who's under a lawful subpoena to appear before a federal grand jury. Presumably none of that would have happened if they thought the guy was a flake or a fake."

Taibbi and Phillips were exhausted, running on adrenaline and nothing else. They'd talked on the drive into town from Phillips's house about how so many of the stories in the history of the Brawley case, literally dozens of stories, were "source" descriptions of "statements" made by witnesses or of "evidence" said to be in someone's hands. Many of those stories had evaporated, or had turned out to be totally baseless; much of the "evidence" had likely never existed and, they knew, had never been obtained by investigators—they recalled the "I want him dead. I want Skoralick" note Tawana had supposedly written, and Randy "D-Day" Davis's videotapes that "proved" Tawana had not been in Newburgh—but the stories had flown under banner headlines nonetheless. Here, the reporters agreed, they weren't depending on a "source" or on a description of his "statement" or "testimony." They had the witness himself.

No, they didn't have the tapes, and they might not get them. But on the drive in, and in the editing room listening to Sam McClease again, they believed his story.

"Crank it up again, guys," Sagan said, when they'd raised neither objections nor any red flags. "Let him tell his story."

At 11:00 A.M. McClease called. He said he'd gotten a delay for his grand jury appearance and was phoning from a roadside pay booth, on the way to Long Branch; he added that he might phone again within an hour or two once he'd retrieved the tapes—except that he was being tailed. Has to be the feds, he said. Taibbi said he'd readied a crew car with high-

speed dubbing equipment, and that if McClease called again
and it was possible to rendezvous, he still wanted badly to
have a portion of the tape for broadcast. McClease, nervous,
said he'd try his best to get another call in.

Sagan drafted a promo, and scheduled it to run in the hour
after two in the afternoon.

Today at Five . . .
*This man reveals that Al Sharpton hired him to bug the
phones of Tawana Brawley lawyers Mason and Maddox.*

McClease: *I bug houses . . .*

*Startling new information in an exclusive interview with
Channel 2:*

McClease: *I was contacted February 3 by Al Sharpton . . .*

*And this insider confirms that Sharpton and Tawana
Brawley's two key lawyers know her story isn't true.*

McClease: *You know, it's all been a game . . .*

Sharpton's alleged double-dealing in the Brawley affair.

An important break.

A Channel 2 News exclusive today at five.

The McClease story was straightforward enough, the reporters thought, a seven-minute narrative spun with minimal adornment and few production gimmicks around the basic
story told by Sam McClease. They didn't say they'd heard
the tapes, but they didn't say they hadn't heard them, either.
The story played at five, at six, and at eleven.

Taibbi, whipped physically but rallying for each broadcast
in a fresh shirt and tie brought in by Michael Heard, tried
hard to "sell" the piece in his on-camera introduction.

TAIBBI, ON CAMERA:
Last Wednesday we presented the story of Perry Mc-Kinnon, Al Sharpton's former right-hand man and a Brawley team insider. McKinnon broke ranks and told us Sharpton and the lawyers had assembled the Tawana Brawley tale of abduction and rape on a "pack of lies."

But Samuel Milton McClease's story, if you can imagine it, is even more devastating. And if it is borne out by the evidence, it will tear the Brawley team apart and render their seven-month story a total sham.

You see, Samuel McClease told us at three o'clock this morning, and is now going to tell a federal grand jury, that he was Al Sharpton's private bugging expert. And that his targets, on Sharpton's orders, were Alton Maddox and C. Vernon Mason.

Leaving the set after the first broadcast, Taibbi thought that he and Phillips had delivered the knockout blow, the story to end the Tawana Brawley fiasco: a story even more important, they'd told each other, than Perry McKinnon's more dramatic *J'accuse* of the week before. But in the newsroom there wasn't any applause this time; some of their colleagues nodded thoughtfully, others actually looked away, concern on their faces. Veteran makeup artist Jack Engel, watching Taibbi scrub off the thick pancake covering the bags under his eyes, was the first to pose the questions Taibbi and Phillips would hear for weeks to come, to their dismay and regret.

"So where the hell are the tapes? You believe this guy?"

14

"The government was in league with 'Mad Dog' Mike . . . and . . . 'Aunt Jemima' Anna . . ."

THEY WERE IN TROUBLE AGAIN. Mike Taibbi and Anna Phillips, who only five days before had broadcast a benchmark story that for the second time had revived the official investigation, who had spent all there was of their energy and skill on a running story that it seemed might go on forever, who thought they were home, bruised but safe, were instead as alone and as deep in the wilderness as they could be.

The first hint had arrived in a phone call ten minutes before the McClease story would run for a second time, at six. It was McClease himself.

"You've killed me," McClease told Taibbi, who'd taken the call at the assignment desk. Everybody on the desk had fallen silent, knowing it was McClease on the line.

"Where the hell are you?" the reporter added. "Where are the tapes?"

"I'm at Torre's house. I don't have the tapes yet."

"You *what!*"

"No. Listen," McClease pleaded. "Please, you've gotta understand. There've been people driving by the house, you know, driving slowly. I got a phone call, from some other guy I did a job for; he says I'm finished."

"Well, why the fuck didn't you just get the damn tapes and get into the system?" Taibbi shouted. "What the hell did Anna and I tell you this morning, why did we waste our breath?"

McClease was gulping air. He sounded as if he was suffocating.

"I gotta go. I'll talk to you later. I'm still gonna get the tapes; there was just a mix-up."

"You gonna be home?" Taibbi asked. "At Torre's?" The last thing Taibbi wanted to do was trek out to Jersey City again and babysit McClease. Yet, if there was still a chance to get the tapes . . .

"Yeah," McClease said. "I'll be at Torre's, I think. I'll call you if—"

"We'll call you if we don't hear from you in a couple hours," Taibbi cut in. "We'll take hotel rooms in the city; we're only fifteen minutes away. Call our desk number, the one we gave you; they can find us anytime. Look," he said, glancing at the wall clock. "I gotta go on the air."

"Okay," McClease said. "Okay, I'll talk to you."

The second hint of impending trouble was another phone call Taibbi took, a few minutes after he got off the air. It was Richard Pienciak of the *Daily News*, the other reporter to whom Perry McKinnon had chosen to talk and an aggressive reporter both feared and respected by the Brawley camp.

"Jesus," Pienciak said. "This came out of left field. Could you put me in touch with this guy, Mike? You think he wants to talk to print?"

It was a preposterous request from one reporter to another. Taibbi simply said no, though Pienciak persisted, and when he cupped the phone to tell Phillips who he was talking to she yelled at him to hang up, don't talk to him! Phillips remembered Pienciak's sidewalk lecture to her in the rain after the Newburgh mess. But her partner held up a hand.

"I can't do that, Richard," he said into the phone. "You know that."

"Well, then I gotta ask you," Pienciak said testily. "Did you hear the tapes or not?"

"Is this a question for the record, or what?" Taibbi asked.

"Yeah. For the record."

"Then I'm not gonna comment. No comment," Taibbi repeated. "I'm not the story. Christ, I'm just a reporter."

"Oh yes, you are the story," Pienciak said. "That's your answer? No comment?"

"That's it," Taibbi said, thinking of his most recent conversation with McClease and realizing suddenly that despite his almost painful fatigue it might be an exceptionally good idea if McClease came up with the tapes. Like right now.

Pienciak called back in a few minutes. He wanted to know if Taibbi had "tipped" Giuliani's office to McClease. Taibbi answered with another "no comment"; shit, he thought, there wasn't a reporter alive who didn't check with official sources now and then to see if an anonymous tipster who'd dropped a dime on someone hadn't in fact dropped several dimes, to other reporters and to the law, but Taibbi couldn't think of a single good reason to discuss that obvious point with Pienciak. He told Phillips and Sagan about the call.

"Well," Sagan suggested, prophetically as it turned out, "it won't be the first time someone who didn't get the story spends his energy attacking the people who did."

The attack would come later. The first item on the agenda of the Brawley press corps was to react to the latest Channel 2 bombshell. Reporters in Albany heard from Governor Cuomo, who earlier in the day had taken a call from Taibbi and agreed he would make himself available for comment after he'd seen the story he described briefly for him.

"I don't know whether this guy is telling the truth or not," Cuomo said after the Six broadcast. "I can't tell for sure who is telling the truth about Tawana Brawley. I'll believe [this one] when it's proven."

Other reporters, including Channel 2's Randall Pinkston, gathered in the hallway outside Alton Maddox's Brooklyn office, kept away from the door by a beefy security guard, while the advisers met to discuss the McClease allegations. Even at a distance reporters could clearly make out some of the shouted exchanges, Sharpton at one point wailing, "I ain't even got keys to Mason's house!"

It was Mason who came out first.

"Don't give me any garbage about somebody making some deal with Al Sharpton!" the attorney roared. "We're living in South Africa." Obviously, Mason shouted, sweating profusely, McClease "works for the government."

He turned and stalked back into Maddox's office, slamming the door. When the three advisers finally emerged, one reporter shouted, "Is it a split?"

Sharpton wrapped an arm around Maddox's shoulder. "Does it look like a split?" he spat.

But outside, on Court Street, Maddox turned away wordlessly from his two colleagues and went his own way.

TAIBBI, PHILLIPS, AND MICHAEL HEARD took rooms at the Essex House Hotel on Central Park South, a few blocks from the Broadcast Center. Dozing fitfully, Phillips heard the phone ring at 10:30 P.M. It was Dean Daniels, executive producer of the Eleven. McClease had called; the desk had given him her phone number at the hotel.

"Let me know," Daniels said. "Soon as you hear from him."

Phillips called Taibbi, who dragged himself from his own deep but troubled sleep and came up to her room. He was almost asleep again, sitting on the floor and leaning against the wall, when McClease called.

"I got a lawyer now," he told Phillips. "He says I'll surrender and turn in the tapes as soon as my status is clarified."

"You mean an immunity deal?" Phillips asked.

"Yeah. Like that," McClease answered. "And I'm not supposed to talk to you guys anymore. I mean, it's nothing personal, I trust you guys—"

"What about the tapes?" she pressed.

"Like I said," McClease explained. "My lawyer . . ."

Phillips shook her head when McClease had hung up. She didn't have to explain a thing to her partner, who pulled himself up from the floor and lit a cigarette despite the fact that another one was still burning in the ashtray on the foot of Phillips's bed. It wasn't working out the way they thought it would, they agreed, keen observers of the obvious.

"Order yourself a nightcap," Taibbi suggested. "I am. We're gonna need a good night's sleep because tomorrow's gonna be a bitch."

Tomorrow began with the Brawley team's predictable counterattack on WLIB. Since Taibbi's was the only room with a radio in it, Phillips and Heard came down, and they all ordered breakfast. The food arrrived just as the Mark Riley show began.

"Whaddya think?" Taibbi asked, noting that Maddox wasn't on the program and scanning the accounts in the morning papers that referred to the shouting match at Maddox's office the night before. "You think Maddox has broken?"

"We'll see," Phillips said, standing to claim her breakfast on the pull-out table.

Mason started with a long harangue whose centerpiece was his "confirmation" that McClease was hired "by Giuliani, [Mayor Edward] Koch, Abrams, and Cuomo" to spy on the advisers by "dropping these bugs." Sharpton interrupted him to assert that he'd confirmed that McClease was a known drug dealer and cocaine addict. Then Mason took off on the

two reporters sitting down to breakfast in an eighth-floor hotel room.

"And we're very, very clear," he shouted, "that the government was in league with 'Mad Dog' Mike Taibbi and his
black sidekick, 'Aunt Jemima' Anna. . . ."

Phillips paused a beat and then convulsed in laughter. At
that very moment she was removing the stainless steel cover
from Michael Heard's plate of pancakes!

They all laughed heartily, not knowing it would be their
last laugh until the saga of Sam McClease faded into
memory.

For the rest of the week the Brawley press corps dug into
McClease's background, tracked his sputtering progress toward
the grand jury, confirmed details of his employment and military history, raised reasonable questions about his reliability
based on that history, and speculated ad nauseam about the
tapes.

For Taibbi and Phillips, though, merely following the story
of Sam McClease was not enough. Pienciak was right; the
Channel 2 reporters had truly become the story. And they'd
become targets as never before of the Brawley advisers and
their core of true believers.

Taibbi received several pointed, believable telephoned death
threats and another foul package in the mail. The Wednesday
demonstration on West Fifty-seventh Street was the largest
and angriest yet; the M-28 crosstown bus was rerouted for
hours, a Ford dealership and the other businesses on the block
shut off from their customers. Phillips's mother, who lived
in the family brownstone in Harlem, was visited by three
strangers who said they'd "heard Anna was interested in selling the building . . ." and wanted to know if there was a
way they could get in touch with her, right away. The elderly woman, who spoke little English and wasn't fully aware
of the risks her daughter had courted in her months on the
Brawley story, gave them Anna's home number. The phone
in the Phillips home rang for days with crank or threatening

calls; Phillips sent her son Eric to live with a relative. The fallout after McClease was different and more ominous than anything she'd ever known, including the fallout from the whistleblower interview she'd helped her partner bring to the public only days before.

"Perry McKinnon," a federal source told Taibbi, "is a triple off the wall in the bottom of the eighth to drive in the go-ahead run. McClease, if he's the real thing, is Bill Mazerowski, the homer in the ninth to win it." But, the source cautioned the day after the McClease story aired, no one anywhere knows whether Sam McClease is the real deal. We don't. You don't.

Taibbi called another federal source, in Brooklyn, a field investigator who'd been directly involved with Sharpton's work as an informant. In fact, the source had a couple of months earlier held out the possibility of delivering some of the Sharpton "tapes" to Taibbi, but Sagan and Phillips had nixed it. Part of the reason had to do with the representation by the source that the tapes were inconclusive.

"We sent him out, what, sixteen times?" the source had said. "And every time he was with someone we were targeting, the wire would suddenly go down, or if he got close to something he'd just talk bullshit. He never turned anybody over."

You run that story, Phillips had reasoned, and Sharpton can come out a hero: the feds squeezed me, he could claim, and, yeah, I agreed to go out for them, but I conned the dumb bastards every time. Never gave 'em anything. And besides, she had insisted, we're not going after the advisers; we're trying to find out what happened to Tawana Brawley. Sagan had agreed. "We don't need it," he concluded. "*Newsday* and the *Voice* already did the story on Sharpton's career as an informant. You've got other things, closer to the Brawley story. Get after those."

But now Sam McClease was in the very air they breathed, the name on the lips of everyone from the Brawley advisers to the reporters who'd concluded after the McKinnon revelations that the advisers were down for the count. Taibbi's Brooklyn source said he wanted to check his files, there was something he remembered that might be useful. Ten minutes later he called back.

"Yeah," the source said. "Here it is. It's September, still Howard Beach, right? Well before Brawley. We're wiring up that fat body again and Sharpton goes into one of his riffs. I mean, he's naked from the waist up, getting wired, and he's running off at the mouth. 'You want me to bring in Mason and Maddox?' he said. 'I can bring you Mason and Maddox!' We weren't interested in Mason and Maddox, but apparently Sharpton was."

It was an uncorroborated source allegation, but Taibbi wanted badly to find a way to use it. He wanted to go for the Sharpton informant tapes, just to use them as context for the contention by his unnamed source that Al Sharpton had offered to target the lawyers long before Sam McClease ever came on the scene.

"Do a standard follow," Sagan instructed. "Maybe some more of the technical stuff, how he said he did it."

So Taibbi and Phillips dug into the McClease interview and fashioned a report that simply added detail to the base allegations in their initial story. "McClease described some of the equipment he uses," Taibbi wrote, "in his claimed career as a bugging expert. Top-of-the-line recorders by TX and Ampex, the bugging gear itself by Marantz and Delta. Carver amplifiers to boost the audio, state-of-the-art sound-activated mikes . . ."

On Thursday, June 23, the *New York Times* reported that McClease had finally agreed to talk in exchange for immunity from prosecution "for illegal break-ins and other possible offenses." McClease's actual surrender to federal authorities took place just before 5:00 that afternoon. Taibbi, on the set at the time preparing to intro another follow-up report, took a call from a federal contact confirming the latest development and, with Paul Sagan of all people acting as his "field producer," raced downtown after his report so that he could assert at six, live from Federal District Court, that "Samuel McClease is finally in the system." The tapes, supposedly, were in the system with him, or at least on the way.

The next day, Friday, at eleven in the morning, a highly placed source in the attorney general's office reached Taibbi and issued an ominous warning.

"Dig harder," he said. "From what I'm hearing from the feds, you could still have a problem. If you know any of McClease's accomplices, or have a line on anything at all that will shore up his story, you better go after it, and right now."

The reporter, who'd thought the day before, again, that he and his partner were home free, again, repeated the conversation to Phillips, Sagan, and Roger Colloff.

Colloff knew as all lawyers knew that it would be improper for Taibbi to make direct inquiries about a matter now formally before a grand jury; but the cryptic warning struck a nerve with him, as it did for everyone in Sagan's office.

"Who can you call?" he asked evenly. "There's got to be someone who can tell us if we've got a problem, and how serious the problem is. . . ."

Taibbi, pacing nervously, looked at Phillips and mentioned a name, the name of the federal contact, a friend, really, who had called "to commiserate" after the bribery allegations by the Brawley team following their Newburgh reports.

"He's not on Brawley," Taibbi thought aloud. "But he's a friend, and he's plugged in enough to get what we need in a hurry."

"Call him," Colloff said softly. "Now."

Taibbi walked to his cubicle, dialed the direct number, and was surprised when his friend, and not a secretary, picked up the phone. After describing the warning from his state source, he said, "I've got to know. You know I've never come for a handout or a one-way favor. But it's my dick that's on the chopping block, and if I've got a problem on McClease I've got to know. . . ."

Sit tight, his friend urged, saying he would make a few calls. A half hour later Taibbi's phone rang.

"The tapes are in. Your dick is safe."

SAGAN AND HIS WIFE, Ann, headed for the Kutztown Fair in Pennsylvania, the annual Amish crafts and quilting fair. Phillips planned to open her doors, as she'd always done before the Brawley mess, to the friends for whom a weekend was never complete without a visit.

Taibbi and Beverly, who'd been putting off their cruise for weeks, contemplated a week or two off and some lazy sailing on their beloved Buzzards Bay. There was a favorable tide at eleven Saturday morning; with luck, they could be moored in their home port by Sunday morning.

But when they got to their boat, ahead of the tide, Taibbi insisted on a short nap and, putting his head down, slept for the next twenty hours.

Phillips was just as tired, but she'd slept fitfully Friday night and called Tom Farkas on the desk as early as she thought he'd be in.

"Oh, Anna," Farkas said. "I was just about to phone you."

"Oh, yeah? What's up?" She hoped it was good news.

"Well, Newsday's running a front-page story . . . okay, the bottom line is that there's 'no smoking gun' in the tapes."

Phillips's heart stuck in her throat. "Who do they attribute it to, what source?" she asked. But she barely heard Farkas's answer. No smoking gun, she thought after she hung up. She slipped out of bed carefully, trying not to disturb her husband, and headed downstairs to the sunroom, thinking: The tapes are in, right? Though she told herself again and again there was nothing to worry about, Lionel's persistent voice kept cutting through: "Anna, did you hear the tapes?" "Anna, you better wait for the tapes!" "Anna, you should have made it clearer in your story that you *didn't* hear the tapes." "Anna, what if there are no tapes? You've worked too hard to fuck up now. You know it was your responsibility to let the viewers know that you didn't hear the tapes!"

Lionel rarely offered advice or counsel, which meant that when he did she took it to heart. He was a fifteen-year veteran of the New York news scene, much respected and admired, and for the first time he had questioned her news judgment, and Taibbi's by extension. Phillips had countered with the standard rationale, Taibbi's rationale and hers too: that the feds wouldn't have gone down the road with McClease if they didn't have good reason to believe his story; that there was no way McClease could have been a Sharpton plant; that the advisers were certainly acting as though they believed a bugging operation had taken place (Mason had even filed a motion for dismissal in a case involving a Long Island client on the grounds that his home and office had been bugged and any client conversations, therefore, were compromised); that there was no percentage, finally, for McClease to simply invent the story and walk into a five-to-ten for perjury and obstruction of justice just to see his mug on the tube.

But even as she'd mounted her defense, Phillips knew instinctively that she was on questionable footing. She'd always viewed the case emotionally, much more so than her partner; still, when Taibbi had been attacked it was she who kept him from gratuitously attacking the advisers, helped keep him on the story of what had happened to Tawana Brawley. In subtle ways they'd moved toward and sometimes through each other's positions. She'd trusted his instincts as a reporter, as someone who had an idea of the game, and she'd learned his rules and followed them, and played them back to him constantly. But the McClease story had bothered her in a way she'd been unable to articulate as it was unfolding. *She'd* become the tough cynic. Lionel's warnings had added to her discomfort.

She called every source she had, knowing that Taibbi was off the screen, somewhere on his boat; she needed to get a sense of what was going on at the U.S. Attorney's office. She found out soon enough.

"Are you sitting down?" Farkas asked when he finally got through to her. "Giuliani just called a press conference. The tapes are blank."

THERE WERE FIVE PAY TELEPHONES on Cuttyhunk Island, and Taibbi had given everyone, Phillips included, a list of the numbers, "just in case," he'd said Friday afternoon, only half seriously, "you've got to reach me. I'll be checking in with Matt there, because we'll probably sail to the island in the first day or two. Matt'll have an idea where we are."

Phillips, that Saturday afternoon, kept trying the numbers. Finally someone answered one of them and agreed to find Matt Taibbi.

"I don't know where they are," Matt said, picking up on the urgency in Phillips's voice. "They could be anywhere between here and Connecticut. But as soon as I hear from them—"

"You've got to hear from them!" Phillips nearly shouted, illogically. She could hear the blood pounding in her ears, a tidal wave of fear roaring through her. "You've got to tell him, he's got to get right back to New York. The worst has happened."

Her phone rang all afternoon and evening. Colloff wanted to know what it meant; Sagan returned early from Pennsylvania and said he'd help prepare a script in Taibbi's absence; weekend producer Lisa Sharkey Gleicher wanted to know how to handle Giuliani's press conference and any follow-up reports. "I don't know," Phillips kept repeating. "I don't have an answer. I guess just report it straight. I'll keep making calls."

She finally reached a federal source at home. That's it, the source explained, sympathetically. The tapes are blank; not even used. Phillips wanted to cry.

When Taibbi finally woke up on his boat, it was Sunday morning. Beverly suggested that he was in no shape for a long sail and that instead they should just drive to their house and give him a day or two to recover his strength. We've got two weeks' vacation, she'd reasoned. He offered no resistance. They off-loaded some perishables, and as soon as they were in the truck, Taibbi fell asleep again. When they got home he headed straight for the bedroom, hardly opening his eyes, and within minutes was gone again.

At three o'clock Sunday afternoon, Beverly shook him awake.

"I've been talking to Anna," she said, as gently as she could. "You've got to get dressed and go back to New York. I waited until the last minute to wake you. There's a four o'clock train from Providence. . . ." He nodded through her recitation of the story, numbly, suggesting as she handed him a cup of tea that it wasn't that bad, he'd reported it straight, it wasn't his problem.

But it was.

"REV. AL & PALS ARE TICKLED PINK," shouted the headline in the Sunday *Daily News*. Slapping high-fives and "doing a victory dance," the *News* reported, Sharpton and Mason led a jubilant rally among their supporters at Bethany Baptist Church.

"We're coming to get our deed papers," Sharpton sang, in reference to the suit he and the lawyers had been saying they intended to file against Channel 2. "We're coming this Wednesday to see what color curtains we want in our new building!"

Richard Pienciak completed the *News* coverage with a pointed and peculiar sidebar aimed directly at Taibbi and Phillips, a "chronology" of events leading up to the discovery that the tapes were blank and to the arrest of McClease on perjury and obstruction of justice charges. Pienciak wrote that federal investigator Carl Bogan and Assistant U.S. Attorney Federico Virella met with McClease "after being tipped to the story by Taibbi." Taibbi knew neither man. Pienciak wrote incorrectly that the McClease story was first aired at noon the following Monday. He wrote that "the Channel Two story was immediately called into question because the tapes were not played on the broadcast and no direct quotes were even offered," and added gratuitously that "Sharpton lashed out at Taibbi, who has been accused in the past of having paid for at least one since-retracted Brawley story," a reference to the Newburgh interview with G.

It was vicious stuff. But curiously, as Taibbi read the *News* on the subway home from Penn Station, he wasn't particularly angered by it. I'm a big boy, he thought. I fucked up, and I deserve the hit. By the time he sat down in his apartment, listening to the calls on his machine from Sagan, Phillips, Colloff, other reporters, friends, and sources, he understood *why* it was such a major fuck-up. On the heels of the Perry McKinnon story, with all its power and consequence, after the months of labor and effort he and his partner had invested in an honest effort to chronicle and advance a story of importance, he'd rushed a piece on the air that *sounded* true, that he believed (and still believed) could be true. He and Phillips had worked hard on it; they'd done it by their book, submitted the story to their protocols and rules, kept alive any possible chance to hear the tapes themselves and, when no one said otherwise in the editing room that Monday morning, had put together a story that reflected their belief in the story Sam McClease had told them. It would have been better to have waited a day, Taibbi knew a week later, to hell with the competitive imperative; or to have written it more cautiously, or to have said point-blank, high in the piece, that he hadn't heard the tapes and therefore couldn't be *certain* they existed . . . but here's the story and here are the unanswered questions about it and here's the context that makes it believable. . . .

The calls on his machine from friends and sources made it plain that a lot of people were just *disappointed* in him. "Shit, I thought you'd *finished* 'em," one friend said.

Taibbi called Phillips. Her line had been busy the several times he'd tried to reach her before leaving Massachusetts.

"Oh, Mike. It's been a terrible weekend," she said.

"Yeah, I know. I'm sorry. I guess we just hit it in the morning."

"You know," Phillips said, repeating a line she'd used often over the past weeks, "they're like Jason," a reference to the *Friday the 13th* movie killer. "They keep coming back. You can cut off their arms and legs, shoot 'em and stab them, lop off their heads, and they keep coming back." She laughed weakly.

"See you in the morning, Anna," Taibbi said gently. He turned on his set to catch the top of the Eleven, and was surprised when Channel 2 had nothing by way of a follow-up on the Sam McClease story.

WITHIN A FEW DAYS Sam McClease was released on bail to the custody of his parents in Newark and ordered to wear a wrist monitor and to check in with federal authorities on a daily basis. He left jail insisting to reporters that he'd been telling the truth, and told Phillips and Taibbi at his parents' house that somebody had switched the tapes, that he wasn't in total control of the situation.

He gave the reporters a copy of a navy commendation he'd received for his work ". . . on the dedicated Electronic Surveillance Measures platform" aboard the USS *Nimitz* while stationed in the Mediterranean. He agreed on a fourth visit from Taibbi and Phillips, to make a final attempt to produce the tapes; after a series of phone calls, a drop-point was arranged in Manhattan, and the next day the reporters—with two cameras in position—waited for eight hours to see if Sam McClease would come through. He didn't; but he claimed that at the precise time his man had shown up at the scene the contact had seen Phillips and an "unidentified man" strolling "suspiciously" on the sidewalk outside the location. It was true, dammit: Phillips was indeed outside the office where the tapes were to be delivered, along with one of the intermediaries who'd set up the rendezvous. They were getting coffee. She thought she'd seen a car drive by, hesitate, and then pull away. She'd walked to the corner in time to see that the car, a lone black male behind the wheel, had come to a stop, double-parked, halfway down the block. The car had then taken off.

"Fuck it, fuck you," Taibbi said to McClease, the last time he and Phillips began their day with a visit to McClease in Newark. "I think you're full of shit. When you've got the tapes, *you* call us." And he'd taken his partner by the elbow and stomped off.

But they didn't walk away from the McClease story, not just yet. They couldn't. The papers kept running updated accounts not only about McClease but about the lawsuit the Brawley advisers were going to file "today," or "tomorrow," or "soon," against Taibbi and Phillips and CBS. The *Amsterdam News* ran a long and confusing two-part interview by publisher Bill Tatum with accused murderer Larry Davis, who had been detained at the Metropolitan Correctional Center for a few days while McClease was there. Davis "confirmed" that Taibbi had paid McClease and that McClease had been employed by Giuliani and Taibbi, the paper reported. It was total bullshit. But it was in print.

So Taibbi and Phillips kept hacking away, trying to learn once and for all who Sam McClease really was, and what he had really done. A source not directly connected to the Brawley investigation would finally explain why the feds had believed in McClease in the beginning, and why and when they came to have their first doubts.

"Carl [Bogan] was playing 'real estate man,' that first day," the source explained. "You know, he's got a briefcase, he's working the street where McClease is staying. When he knocks on the door at McClease's place there's no answer.

"So the next day he's doing it again, the same routine, only when he knocks on McClease's door McClease himself opens it and says, 'Oh. Hi. You were here yesterday!' Bogan's surprised, and McClease explains that he's got this sound-activated video taping system; and the thing is, he does! He shows

Bogan the tape of his visit of the day before. So naturally, when McClease tells him about the Sharpton bugging job, Carl buys it completely."

But the first hint of trouble, the source said, came after McClease was "in the system."

"We had him at the Vista Hotel, and one day we take him over to our audio lab. We've got all this state-of-the-art equipment. John Gardner's our audio guy. McClease is looking at all the stuff, and he's got most of it down. He's very impressive. We leave McClease alone with Gardner, who gets around eventually to asking about the Sharpton bugging job. Later, we get a call from John. He says McClease was all right until he started describing the tape speed he used on a certain piece of equipment. John says he checked and the speed McClease listed didn't meet any industry standard; it couldn't be done, or something like that. We figured then, that's the first crack in the eggshell."

Taibbi learned that McClease had "done all right" on a polygraph test, but that the test wasn't conclusive. But no one ever got to the bottom line on Sam McClease, proving or disproving his original story.

"He's either the real thing, and really was a part of a Sharpton bugging job," another federal source concluded, "or he's the most amazing pathological liar anybody's ever come across."

SOMEHOW, THE BRAWLEY STORY lurched back to the question of what had happened to Tawana Brawley. The *City Sun*, the city's other black weekly (based in Brooklyn), ran a front-page "blockbuster" asserting that "Tawana Was Raped." Based on medical reports but containing several crucial fact errors and misstatements, the article raised legitimate questions about the quality of care and treatment Tawana had received the day she was discovered, and concluded that her rape was "proven" because a document from the Westchester County Medical Center listed her "diagnosis" as "rape." The "document" was not shown or described. In fact, according to an official statement from the office of Bob Abrams, the "document" to which the *City Sun* referred was not a diagnosis or a physician's report but merely a "billing form," whose use of the word "rape" was a shorthand reference to the alleged problem for which the patient had sought treatment.

Meanwhile, Perry McKinnon was still talking, still testifying, Glenda Brawley was still holed up in her "sanctuary" at Bethany Baptist Church, and Stephen Pagones was being guided inexorably toward a decision to testify without immunity before the grand jury.

A Channel 2/*New York Times* poll whose results were made public the last week of June showed that even after the McClease fiasco, only 7 percent of all New York City residents polled believed Tawana Brawley's story. The figure among blacks was only 18 percent. Only 4 percent of all New Yorkers polled had a "favorable impression" of Al Sharpton. The "favorable impression" figures for Maddox and Mason were 6 percent and 7 percent, respectively. But half the blacks polled and more than a quarter of the whites said they believed the judges and courts "showed favoritism" toward one race or the other, and even higher percentages believed the police showed racial favoritism. The conclusion drawn by many respondents was that racism did indeed exist in the criminal justice system, but that the Tawana Brawley case was the wrong case to offer as proof.

ON WEDNESDAY, JULY 13, having regained their footing after the last crazy surge in their coverage of the Tawana Brawley story, Taibbi and Phillips filed an "update report" from Poughkeepsie. The grand jurors were taking a two-week vacation, Taibbi reported, their term likely to be extended so they could hear from Stephen Pagones, consider the final pieces of evidence, and prepare a formal report on their investigation. Drawing on their sources for one last, exhaustive review of the evidence, the reporters asserted the following:

—that there was still no "smoking gun" that absolutely disproves the story told on Tawana's behalf.

—that there are uncorroborated witnesses who have claimed under oath that they saw Tawana during the four days, in Newburgh and elsewhere.

—that there is no evidence—after hundreds of witnesses were interviewed and scores presented to the grand jury—to support a single aspect of the original story of abduction, forced captivity, rape, sodomy, or physical assault.

—that sources believe that at least one key witness, a friend of Tawana's, is still withholding information about Tawana's whereabouts during her disappearance.

—that sources believe that another key witness actually saw Tawana on Thanksgiving morning as he looked out his window, though he could not positively identify her.

—that in all likelihood Tawana saw and spent time with very few people during the four days.

The grand jurors and the members of the Brawley Task Force went on vacation after that Wednesday session. Taibbi and Phillips made plans for their own break, at the end of the week, and would only learn later, from a Task Force source, how close they came in the next two days to playing an integral if unwitting role in one of the potential high dramas of the Tawana Brawley story.

"The governor simply decided that Glenda Brawley was going to be arrested," the source began the story. "She was still holed up in her 'sanctuary' at Bethany—at least we thought she was. There was no way to make sure, no way to clamp on a surveillance. The responsibility for Glenda's arrest was technically with the Dutchess County sheriff's office—they had to execute the warrant. . . ."

Taibbi had learned earlier that week, on Monday, that Assistant Dutchess County Sheriff J. J. Thompson and several aides had traveled to Manhattan for a secret meeting with New York Police Commissioner Benjamin Ward and department chief Robert Johnston, two state police colonels, and two assistant attorneys general. He'd even dispatched a camera crew to try and tape the principals when they left. The subject of the meeting, he'd learned, was how and if Glenda Brawley could be arrested, either while in the church or on the way to the Democratic National Convention, which Sharpton had promised publicly he would disrupt with "massive demonstrations."

"The thing is," the Task Force source later explained, "as far as we were concerned Glenda was one of 280,000 people in New York State for whose arrest there was then an outstanding warrant, and many of the others were for serious violent crimes—rape, murder, armed robbery. This was a woman who defied a subpoena to testify about her daughter, that's it, a minor misdemeanor, and she was hardly a threat to society; the risks of violence and injury were great, we argued, if we tried to force the issue at the wrong time, in the wrong place. But [the governor's aide] John Poklemba called me and said he wanted to 'make sure Bob [Abrams] was aware . . . that he expected Glenda to be arrested.' It was, he said, the 'number one priority' for the state police. The governor was always saying publicly that he 'didn't want to be giving instructions' to the attorney general, but he was constantly writing letters and releasing them to the press, or communicating his instructions to Poklemba or others. This time he made it clear. If you listened to the governor, the continued freedom of Glenda was a blight, a threat to our whole justice system, our rule of law. If you ask me, it was the governor's rhetoric that helped the case assume such huge proportions."

On Saturday, July 16, the governor ordered State Police Superintendent Thomas Constantine to overrule the attorney general's staff and "effect the arrest of Glenda Brawley." The attempt failed miserably. "Constantine was calling us from pay phones on the Thruway," the source said. "He said he'd been contacted by the governor directly. So they covered the airports and the bridges, but forgot to cover the Williamsburg and Brooklyn bridges, and Sharpton and Glenda and the buses made it through the net."

But three days before the bungled attempt, Abrams's people, trying to head off a confrontation through their own initiatives, "sprung" one of Glenda's old boyfriends from prison and sent him in under cover to Bethany Baptist Church, trying to draw her out. "There were cruisers on a half-dozen corners, a chopper in the sky," the source explained. "But they wouldn't let Glenda come out. And then, the next day, you and Anna are out on Long Island, and it was the closest we ever came to arresting Glenda Brawley."

Taibbi and Phillips were on Long Island to begin work on another story, a different story, finally. The day after the Brawley grand jury broke for its two-week vacation, the two reporters scheduled a day of preinterviews with potential sources for a story updating the two-decades-old saga of the Shoreham nuclear power plant. The interview logistics were set up in Hauppauge, Suffolk County, by Alan L.,* a source with connections in journalism and politics, who'd been instrumental in a previous Shoreham report on "60 Minutes." Alan L., it turned out, had also been one of the "intermediaries" in the abortive attempt by "60 Minutes" to snag a Tawana Brawley interview; he knew Sharpton and, remarkably, had maintained a "working relationship" with him. Midway during the preinterview session, Alan L. was reached by beeper and told that Sharpton needed to speak to him, urgently.

"He's desperate for coverage," Alan L. told Taibbi and Phillips after talking to Sharpton. "He says there's a blackout on talking to him, none of the stations and none of the papers care about his going to Atlanta with Glenda and Tawana. So I said to him, 'I'm not coming into the city. You want to talk to me, bring Glenda out here.'"

Alan L. had also returned a call from a contact in Abrams's office, whom he told of the Sharpton entreaty.

"Sharpton told me he'd meet me out here, at the Holiday Inn, Exit 56 on the Expressway. About four or five this afternoon."

Taibbi and Phillips shrugged, only marginally interested. They were happy to be at work at last on another story; in the previous week they'd found the time to read hundreds of pages of documents on the Shoreham controversy, and the sources they were talking to that morning were hinting they could provide hard evidence that the Long Island Lighting Company, LILCO, could be proven guilty of obtaining hundreds of millions in rate increases based on deliberate misrepresentations of the time and money Shoreham would cost. (LILCO would later be found guilty in a Racketeer Influenced Corrupt Practices suit, though the judge in the case threw out the verdict and the Shoreham controversy dragged on.)

On the other hand, the reporters thought, breaking for lunch, they had a Canadian Broadcasting Company film crew along with them. The CBC producer, Martin Byrke, was preparing a documentary to run in Canada and a dozen foreign countries before the American presidential election on the relationship between American politics and the institution of journalism, and Taibbi and Phillips had been chosen to represent local television reporting. Byrke said he'd be more than happy to provide camera coverage.

Following the afternoon interview session on Shoreham, Taibbi and Phillips, with Alan L., Byrke, and the CBC camera crew in tow, set up a standard surveillance in the parking lot of the Holiday Inn, hidden mikes in place for Alan L. and Taibbi. Taibbi and Phillips knew nothing at first of Alan L.'s contact with his source in Abrams's office, but it didn't take them long to spot several unmarked cars ringing the perimeter of the lot, lawmen slouching low in the front seats, and the several choppers swinging low, slowly.

Sharpton didn't show. Ten minutes after the appointed hour Alan L. went inside to find a phone and emerged a few minutes later with the latest improbable but true story in the improbable Tawana Brawley saga.

"A black girl in Kingston was found murdered," he said. "She had 'KKK' scratched on her body. Sharpton was literally out the door, heading out here with Glenda, when he heard about it. But he went to Kingston instead."

Phillips made several calls and confirmed the story of the murder of Anna Kithkart in Kingston, New York. A black man would later plead guilty to the murder, a white drifter would admit "defiling" the corpse. Sharpton was turned away by Kithkart's family; but he'd made the trip north, instead of going to Long Island to meet with Alan L.—and Mike Taibbi and Anna Phillips, a CBC camera crew, and a waiting state police contingent.

"I think the thing on Long Island would have worked," the Task Force source later explained, "if Anna Kithkart hadn't been killed. We tried to keep that under wraps, but it got out. If it hadn't, Sharpton and Glenda would have gone out there, I'm convinced of it. I think Alan's idea was brilliant, I really do."

EPILOGUE

"My name is Tawana Brawley. I'm not a liar, and I'm not crazy. . . ."

ON AUGUST 3, 1988, Mike Taibbi and Anna Phillips broadcast a twelve-minute-thirty-second report on a scandal involving the Metro North Railroad Police Department. It was a story that had fallen into their laps, a scandal of major proportions involving a concerted (and successful) effort by some of the department's uniformed veterans to oust their chief. The centerpiece of the report was a home videotape of seven of those veterans involved in some shocking shenanigans while on tour at Grand Central Station. One of the officers, a sergeant, hammered a confused, homeless black man with racial taunts; he drew members of the general public into embarrassing, sexually tinted skits; he walked a part of his tour stark naked, save for his hat, boots, tie, and gun. Before the report even ran, the head of the railroad, aware of the exposé to come, announced that the seven cops had been fired outright, stripped of their commissions. The story would run worldwide.

It broke on a Wednesday, "picketing day" on West Fifty-seventh Street. Al Sharpton, back from Atlanta, where the local and national press in town for the Democratic National Convention had virtually ignored his staged demonstrations with Glenda and Tawana Brawley, was on the picket line when a squadron of still photographers approached the entrance to the Broadcast Center. With the cameras in sight, Sharpton grabbed a bullhorn and began a chorus of his standard cry: "No Justice! No Peace!" His followers waved their "Mad Dog Mike" and "Aunt Jemima Anna" placards above their heads. But the photographers swept past, into the lobby.

"What're you guys doin'!" Sharpton shouted to the last of the photographers, lowering his bullhorn.

"Gotta get a still shot," the photog answered. "Taibbi and Phillips broke a story about a cop scandal. They've got a cop walking his beat, nude, on camera!"

For Mike Taibbi and Anna Phillips, the Tawana Brawley story was essentially over. They knew as much as any other reporters in the city how the Brawley grand jury report would read; with Shoreham and now the Metro North cop scandal, they had two fresh stories, and were happy to have them. They told Sagan they'd stay current with Brawley, making their maintenance calls, but that the next (and last) story would likely be the release of the grand jury report and a final press conference by Bob Abrams and Jack Ryan.

They were wrong. The next story, five weeks later, was the last of a half-dozen "encyclopedic," astonishingly comprehensive reports by the team from the *New York Times*. Taibbi had been alerted by a source that the *Times* was close to a final blockbuster.

"Do you think," Roger Colloff had asked Taibbi a few days before the *Times* report was published, "you could pierce the veil one more time?"

"I don't know," he answered. "My source tells me they're

going to rely on the same evidence we've used in our previous reports, especially our July 13 update. We know they believe that three people have direct knowledge about Tawana's whereabouts during her disappearance—Deanna Daniels, her friend from the Pavillion Apartments; Darryl Rodriguez, her latest boyfriend; and Todd McGue, the bus driver. Our source tells us that McGue 'had a habit of picking up attractive black girls.' The source says they even sent in an undercover female and McGue made a play. They say no one can even confirm that Tawana got off the bus where and when she says she did—and that she and McGue were 'flirting.' More than just idle talk. But," Taibbi added, "that's all we've got. The *Times* apparently had more. The Quigley reports [evidence summaries by Assistant Attorney General Stephen Quigley]—maybe they've got it in writing. . . ."

They did, apparently. The *Times* had only a few facts that Taibbi and Phillips weren't aware of, but those facts were startling. When Tawana Brawley was discovered in the garbage bag on November 28, 1987, the *Times* reported on September 27, investigators had also found an excrement-encrusted pair of "lady's gloves" in the bag along with her. "Tawana limped sometimes, but not at others," in the weeks after she was discovered. Beneath the headline "Investigators Say She Faked Condition," the *Times* concluded with the following paragraph:

> *Neighbors told the grand jury that in February they overheard Glenda Brawley saying to [Ralph] King: "You shouldn't have took the money [from donations] because after it all comes out, they're going to find out the truth." And another neighbor heard Mrs. Brawley say: "They know we're lying, and they're going to find out and come and get us."*

The next day, at the Quality Inn in Newark, New Jersey, Al Sharpton, C. Vernon Mason, and Alton Maddox commanded the attention of the entire "Brawley press corps" for the last time. They'd promised, again, that this time "Tawana would tell her story." And this time, Tawana—along with the fugitive, her mother, Glenda—showed up.

"Good afternoon," Sharpton began, his voice a grim and nervous shell of its usual bluster. "On yesterday, a leak that constitutes a felony by law was printed in the *New York Times*. It is very strange to us that a paper that assumes such prestige would accommodate a felon to leak grand jury information, and try to use that leak to discredit one that seeks justice. We have come today because we have an opportunity for once to challenge the judicial system."

Sharpton talked about Perry McKinnon, and about Sam McClease "and the blank tapes." He went through a short version of the Four Hundred Years of Oppression. He seized upon the gloves found in the garbage bag along with Tawana Brawley.

"If this grand jury already had a glove found in a bag, already had overwhelming evidence of a hoax, already had friends that would talk against Tawana, what did they need an extension for? Did they need time to put a glove in a bag? A glove that Grady didn't see? That Sall didn't see? A glove that no one knew about until now? It took seven months to put a glove in a bag? You would have to be a fool or a racist or both to believe this leak."

And then, after asserting that the "fight for Tawana Brawley will begin October 8," the day after the extended term of the grand jury was due to expire, he introduced Tawana Brawley. The function room at the Quality Inn was packed with Brawley supporters, who cheered wildly.

Dressed in a white sweatshirt emblazoned with the word "Kamikaze" along its edges, Tawana spoke publicly, extensively, for the only time in the agonizing saga that bore her name.

My name is Tawana Brawley. I'm not a liar, and I'm not crazy. I simply just want justice, and then I want to be left alone. My family and I thought we couldn't get any justice, so we decided not to cooperate. We had no New York Times *to leak to; so we got Alton Maddox, C. Vernon Mason, and the Reverend Al Sharpton to fight for us. They, under extreme pressure, have done so. We have said I will give full testimony to an impartial grand jury . . . impartial grand jury! . . . or to a congressional committee. Why won't they let me? Mr. Abrams, you know the truth and I know it too. Why don't you just step aside and let me speak to people who I know will help me?*

I wish to thank God, for sparing my life. He will see me through. I don't know the future, but I do know Who holds it. He holds my hand, and He let me live. He'll stop the cover-up once and for all. I have not deceived my family, my advisers, and most of all, my people. I trust in God, and He will see me, and my Mom, and my family, through.

What only a handful of people knew that day, not the *New York Times*, not Sharpton and the Brawley bunch, and not Mike Taibbi and Anna Phillips, was that in the last week of August, the last week that testimony was heard by the Brawley grand jury, Jack Ryan had stayed up late at the Wyndham Hotel, drinking and trading speculation with one of the FBI's fiber analysis experts. According to a source who later told the story to Taibbi, Ryan and "almost everybody else on the Task Force" had been going home for nights on end trying to write on their own bodies, believing by that time that there was an overpowering possibility that Tawana had written the racial epithets on her own torso and clothing, had "faked" the condition in which she was discovered.

"There was a period there," the source said, "when everybody was going home and trying it, going home and burning washcloths and T-shirts, and trying to write on themselves. We'd heard before that the writing on Tawana's shirt consisted of 'carbonaceous material.' Burned cotton fiber. Jack Ryan had tried it, too. We were always disappointed that at the hospital nobody had thought to take samples of the writing on her body. The writing on her shirt was still there, and though you could burn a washrag and use the charred bits of it to write on a shirt, nobody could find a way to write on his own body; the stuff just sort of crumbled up. Then one night Jack's wife, Barbara, who was getting tired of the whole thing, took one of Jack's burned washrags and stuck it in some water, making a kind of paste, and it worked! Jack did it on his own body, and it looked just like the writing on Tawana. He called the FBI and they tried it, and it looked just like the photos of Tawana!

"Anyway, it's late at the Wyndham bar, in August. And the FBI's fiber analysis expert, who's gonna testify the next day, says at one point, 'Oh, by the way. That charred cotton fiber stuff? We found some of it under Tawana's fingernails, in the fingernail clippings that were taken at the hospital.' And Jack says, not getting crazy about it, 'Don't you think that's just a *little* important?' And that's how we got the 'smoking gun.' "

When Bob Abrams leaned into the microphones clustered on a table on the gym floor of the Armory on October 6, the day the Brawley grand jury was formally dismissed and its report accepted by Judge Angelo Ingrassia, he talked about the "charred cotton fiber" beneath Tawana Brawley's fingernails and gave the assembled reporters their lead. He and the Task Force and the grand jury had learned only a little about Tawana Brawley's four-day, ninety-hour disappearance. They failed to prove conclusively that she spent time in Newburgh. ("One witness maintained before the grand jury that he, like others, did see Ms. Brawley in Newburgh during this period, [claiming] he'd been previously introduced to her by a boyfriend of hers." But two other individuals—"one to whom Ms. Brawley allegedly spoke and the other who was allegedly present—both testified and denied the incident." There were "inconsistencies" and a "lack of corroboration" in the Newburgh stories, the grand jury concluded.) They failed to come up with a single confirmed witness who'd spent time with her during the four days, and they could account for only a few hours of her disappearance. But the circumstantial forensic and medical evidence proved "beyond a shadow of a doubt," Judge Ingrassia concluded, that Tawana Brawley had fabricated her story of abduction, rape, and defilement. Steve Pagones's alibi was solidly corroborated; field investigations and interviews established that neither Scott Patterson nor Harry Crist had had anything to do with Tawana Brawley.

"We know the facts. We have solved the case," Abrams said. "The allegations that she has made are false. Justice has been done."

Abrams recommended a slate of legislative reforms based on the investigation of the case, among them that harboring a fugitive, even in the case of a misdemeanor (Glenda Brawley's contempt charge), should be a felony offense. He urged a tougher obstruction of justice statute, based on the actions of Sharpton and the Brawley lawyers, and suggested greater latitude in the admissible testimony by medical professionals in cases of rape (or alleged rape) against minors.

The attorney general released a detailed grievance against the Brawley attorneys, Mason and Maddox, based on "knowingly false statements" made against Stephen Pagones, Scott Patterson, and the late Harry Crist, and based also on their actions on behalf of their clients, including advice to defy lawful process, which violated their obligations as officers of the court. Abrams's grievance even included the charge, based on a review by Task Force investigators, that the attorneys had lied when they'd charged Mike Taibbi with bribing witnesses. "By Mr. Mason," the grievance read, "that a WCBS-TV reporter bribed witnesses with several hundred dollars to fabricate a story concerning Ms. Brawley's presence in Newburgh during the time of her disappearance."

Through the fall and winter of 1988–1989, investigations were under way against Al Sharpton by the U.S. Attorneys in Manhattan and Brooklyn and by the Organized Crime Strike

Force. Mason and Maddox were the subjects of probes by the disciplinary committees of the appellate courts in Manhattan and Brooklyn, disbarment a real possibility.

The Brawley advisers simply faded from the airwaves of WLIB and from the news columns of the *Amsterdam News*, whose publisher, Bill Tatum, had vowed back in May to "destroy them" if their wild charges proved to be exactly that—wild, unsubstantiated, and false charges against innocent people. The Wednesday demonstrations outside the CBS Broadcast Center on West Fifty-seventh Street simply ended.

Having lost their audience in New York, the advisers took Tawana Brawley to Chicago, where Minister Louis Farrakhan of the Nation of Islam promised to take her into the Muslim fold and give her a "proud Muslim name" and to exact vengeance on her attackers.

Stephen Pagones called a press conference, his first ever, to announce the institution of his defamation lawsuit against Sharpton, Maddox, Mason, and Tawana Brawley. Sharpton showed up, seeking a confrontation, but was locked out of the press conference and missed Pagones altogether.

Sharpton and Mason, with Maddox as their attorney, filed a motion with State Supreme Court Justice David B. Saxe for "pre-action disclosure" against WCBS-TV, reporter Michael Taibbi, and producer Anna Phillips. In his motion, Maddox repeated every misstatement of fact and outright lie that had punctuated his stewardship of the Tawana Brawley case, adding that "Samuel McClease is a government informant who was assigned to the Tawana Brawley investigation for the odious and obvious purpose of discrediting" the advisers; that "the NAACP was paid off to misrepresent the Brawley family"; that "Robert Abrams entered into an illicit relationship with the news media to humiliate, defame, and discredit Ms. Brawley and her representatives"; that "WCBS-TV [was] mounting a vicious and false campaign to dispute and discredit the evidence that Ms. Brawley had been kidnapped and raped," bribing "young men of African descent in Newburgh" and "employing Sam McClease to invade the privacy

. . . of the petitioners"; that WCBS-TV "placed Perry McKinnon on a local newscast to discredit and defame the representatives of Ms. Brawley"; and that the effect of the foregoing was "to place the petitioners in a false light before the public and destroy their reputations."

Maddox's intent was to force WCBS-TV to maintain and turn over all as-broadcast and nonbroadcast videotape materials, all notes and files maintained by Taibbi and Phillips, and to require Taibbi and Phillips to be deposed prior to and independent of the filing of an actual lawsuit.

CBS attorneys Douglas Jacobs and Susanna Lowy argued that pre-action disclosure is only allowed in rare and special circumstances, not close to being met in the instant case. Justice Saxe agreed.

While the allegations made "are dramatic," Justice Saxe wrote in his opinion, "they fail to satisfy the prerequisites to the relief sought. I fail to see . . . any potentially viable causes of action for which pre-action disclosure is necessary." Nonbroadcast resource materials are protected, the judge ruled, and pre-action depositions of Taibbi and Phillips may not be compelled.

Still, two newspapers reported incorrectly that Taibbi, Phillips, and Channel 2 had been sued, finally.

THE TAWANA BRAWLEY STORY refused to die completely. Taibbi and Phillips filed two additional reports, one involving a cross burning by teenagers behind the James S. Evans Elementary School in Wappingers Falls following several days of racial tension, and another based on a call from Glenda Brawley to Mike Wallace of "60 Minutes," offering her story and Tawana's story if there was money to be made. Wallace declined.

On November 28, 1988, a year to the day after Tawana Brawley was discovered in the trash bag behind her old family apartment in Wappingers Falls, three different news organizations filed three different stories. The *Poughkeepsie*

Journal corrected a prior front-page story that a frequent complainant about racial harassment, a black woman named Elaine Disnuke of Wappingers Falls, had had her front door "defiled with excrement." The village police chief, William McCord, called the paper to say that after Disnuke's original complaint the state police had undertaken a videotape surveillance of her property, and that surveillance "caught" the woman, on tape, smearing the excrement herself. Disnuke was arrested for "falsely reporting a racial incident."

On the same day Tim Minton, a reporter for Channel 7's "Eyewitness News" in New York, reported that Tawana Brawley was prepared to admit that "she did write the racial slurs—including the letters 'KKK'—on her own body," that she did in fact spend time during her four-day disappearance in the old family apartment, but that she was forced to do so "by her kidnappers." Minton's report was constructed around an interview with Al Sharpton, who insisted, "I'm saying she will in fact say she was forced to do many things . . . and that the only ones lying are those that say this changes her story."

Finally, that same day, Michael Cottman of *Newsday* ran a "year later" interview with Tawana herself, who lived now in Virginia Beach. "It bothered me," she said of the grand jury report. "But I was ready for it. People just don't understand, they don't know what happened. Now I know there are two justice systems: one for whites and one for blacks, and that we need to build a bigger and better system. The people who followed the history of this case know the truth. I don't want people to forget about my case. I don't want them to forget what happened to me. . . ."

And every one of those late stories, from the cross burning in Wappingers Falls, to the admission by Al Sharpton that Tawana had "written on herself," to the plea by Tawana Brawley that she not be forgotten, was an exclusive.

A year later, nobody else in the media picked up any of those stories.

She'd never told her own story. No one *knew* her story. But her story was over.

On a late December noon, Perry McKinnon met Anna Phillips and Mike Taibbi for lunch in Manhattan.

"I never told you this," McKinnon said to Taibbi. "But I wanted to tell you, a month before the Newburgh stuff, that it was all bullshit. Remember? It was at the Wyndham. I whispered to you? But you were playing the hard guy. 'Fuck you, you've always been full of shit, you and Sharpton,' and you walked away. I would have told you. I would have told you then. You and Anna. But you blew me off."

Taibbi laughed. Phillips laughed. And then everyone fell silent, a terrible, awkward silence. McKinnon looked away, into the distance; Phillips looked toward Taibbi, who asked the waiter for the check.